CHINA
2000

INTERNATIONAL BUSINESS SERIES

This series of books focuses on today's increasingly important phenomena: international bsiness. Sponsored by the University of Hawaii's Pacific Asian Management Institute (PAMI), one of the key centers in the world for developing international business expertise, the series is devoted to international business, with an emphasis on the Asia-Pacific Region. Books in the series will help faculty, students, and business professionals acquire the knowledge and communication skills necessary for working in an ever-changing, international business environment.

CHINA 2000

Emerging Business Issues

LANE KELLEY / YADONG LUO

Editors

International Business Series

SAGE Publications
International Educational and Professional Publisher
Thousand Oaks London New Delhi

For information:

SAGE Publications, Inc.
2455 Teller Road
Thousand Oaks, California 91320
E-mail: order@sagepub.com

SAGE Publications Ltd.
6 Bonhill Street
London EC2A 4PU
United Kingdom

SAGE Publications India Pvt. Ltd.
M-32 Market
Greater Kailash I
New Delhi 110 048 India

Printed in the United States of America

Library of Congress Cataloging-in-Publication Data

China 2000: Emerging business issues/edited by Lane Kelley and Yadong Luo.
   p. cm. — (International business series)
  Includes bibliographical references and index.
  ISBN 0-7619-1180-4 (cloth: acid-free paper)
  ISBN 0-7619-1181-2 (pbk.: acid-free paper)
   1. China—Commerce. 2. Business enterprises—China. 3. Corporations, Foreign—China. 4. Industrial management—China. I. Kelley, Nelson Lane, 1937- II. Luo, Yadong. III. Series: International business series (Thousand Oaks, Calif.)
  HF3836.5 .C458 1998
  338.8'8851—ddc21
                    98-8901

This book is printed on acid-free paper.

99 00 01 02 03 10 9 8 7 6 5 4 3 2 1
JF

Acquiring Editor:	Marquita Flemming
Editorial Assistant:	Maryann Vail
Production Editor:	Wendy Westgate
Editorial Assistant:	Denise Santoyo
Typesetter/Designer:	Danielle Dillahunt
Cover Designer:	Candice Harman

Contents

An Introduction to Emerging
Business Issues for China 2000

LANE KELLEY
YADONG LUO

> When China awakens, the world will tremble.
> *Napoleon Bonaparte, 1817*

As the turn of the century approaches, China is emerging as an economic giant. The World Bank expects that it will become the world's largest economy early in the next century. In the early nineties, China became the leading exporter to the United States of 11 different product groups. The United States's deficit with China was its second record largest, following only Japan, and predicted to surpass Japan's deficit as it opens its markets.

China's open market reform and rapid economic growth have enticed a tremendous surge in activity and market investment by multinational companies. China is second only to Japan as Asia's largest and fastest growing market for most products. Real growth in gross domestic product (GDP) has averaged 9% per year since 1981 and hit over 10% in the past 5 years. By the year 2000, China's consumer market will be larger than that of the United States or Western Europe.

ix

Who is part of this? All of the big international players but especially those from Hong Kong, Taiwan, Japan, and the United States, with foreign direct investment from Hong Kong totaling approximately 60%. Who is Boeing's biggest customer outside of the United States? China. The growth of China's airline industry is just beginning, with China airports actually numbering less than those in the state of Ohio. China, with more than one fifth of the world population, is growing at an economic rate of 10% to 12% per year with a GNP/per capita at price parity of approximately $2,500. Some forecast that this figure will grow to $7,000 by 2000. This is largely due to the pragmatic economic reform and the unabated opening to the outside world, which are still steadily carrying on today.

In many ways, China is taking steps toward a market economy. Massive migration from the countryside to urban areas, though widely misinterpreted in the Western press as a threat to social stability in the People's Republic of China (PRC), represents the inevitable workings of a market economy. The gap between urban and rural wages in China is higher than in any other country. It is true that the tens of millions of people moving around China looking for employment are a worry to the leadership in Beijing, but this phenomenon indicates that jobs are no longer being allocated as strictly as they were in the past, and should be viewed as a sign that marketization is occurring.

Another sign of increasing marketization is the reduced relevance of "the plan" to actual economic performance. China's economy is actually much more marketized than is recognized by the bureaucrats who continue to churn out plans in Beijing. Looking at the Eighth Five-Year Plan in hindsight makes it clear that there was very little connection between the plan set forth in 1990 and what actually happened. For example, many of the economic targets were fulfilled more rapidly than expected. Within just 3 years, enormous growth in GDP, trade, and foreign direct investment (FDI) had already been achieved. Though the central government retains approval power over large-scale projects in critical industries, the grip over all sectors and levels of the economy as laid out in the Five-Year Plan model has loosened. Table I.1 presents some key indicators of China's economy in 1995.

China's effort to engineer industrial growth has included measures designed gradually to introduce market competition, encourage mergers and acquisitions, and foster the expansion of collective enterprises. As a result of industrial reform, firms have had increasing autonomy over determining how and with whom they will conduct business. From methods of production to decisions about hiring and firing workers, Chinese business organizations are becoming less and less dependent on central authority. Managers have more responsibility for finding

TABLE I.1 China's Economy in 1995

Nominal GDP	$692.6 billion
Real GDP growth	10.2%
Retail price inflation	14.8%
Cost of living index	17.0%
Population	1.198 billion
Per capita GDP	$578
Per capita urban income	$468
Per capita rural income	$190
Official unemployment rate	2.9%
M1 supply growth	16.7%
M2 supply growth	29.5%
Reserve money growth	20.6%
Foreign exchange reserves	
(excluding gold)	$73.5 billion
Exchange rate (4/15/96)	8.532/$1

SOURCE: International Monetary Fund, *China Statistical Yearbook*, and U.S. Bureau of the Census.

productive inputs, determining appropriate production and inventory levels, and locating markets for their products. Bankruptcy and unemployment, unheard of in the past, have also increased in recent years, demonstrating that poor firm performance may result in failure for the firm and unemployment for the firm's managers.

As a result of these changes, Chinese industrial performance has improved considerably, leading to dramatic levels of macro-economic growth. As Table I.2 indicates, the annual increase in industrial value added averaged 11.7% between 1981 and 1990. While the growth rate of this key indicator reached a two-decade low of 3.2% in 1990, it managed to climb to 21.7% just 2 years later. The estimates included in Table I.2 also indicate that between 1981 and 1990, Chinese GDP grew at an average annual rate of 10.4% (8.7% per capita). GDP growth has been above 10% since 1992. The Asian Development Bank estimates that this rapid growth will continue through the end of this decade. The countries of Eastern Europe and the former Soviet Union that are also undergoing economic reform have not grown nearly as rapidly. Growth in Hungary was only 1.8% between 1981 and 1985; and in Poland, GDP growth averaged less than 2% between 1981 and 1989. As Table I.3 indicates, average GDP growth in all developing economies was only 4% during these years, and average GDP growth in all post-socialist economies was negative.

In the course of this economic development, firms in China, including both local Chinese and foreign businesses, are reengineering and restructuring or-

TABLE I.2 Growth Rate of Chinese Economic Indicators (% per annum)

Year	Growth Rate of Added Value in Industry	Growth Rate of GDP	Growth Rate of Per Capita Industry GDP
1981-1990	11.7	10.4	8.7
1990	3.2	3.9	1.6
1991	13.3	9.3	8.1
1992	21.7	14.2	12.7
1993	20.7	13.5	12.0
1994	17.4	11.8	10.3
1995	13.6	10.2	8.9
1996*	8.5	8.0	6.8
1997*	8.9	9.0	9.0

SOURCE: Asian Development Bank (1996); Chinese State Statistical Bureau (1995).
NOTE: * Asian Development Bank estimates.

ganizations in an effort to pursue realistic business or investment strategies and accommodate firms' strengths and weaknesses to the peculiar environment where the industry and market structures are drastically transforming and government policies are frequently changing. When firms operating in China have found an imperative to adapt themselves to the local settings and the competitive needs, scholars in Chinese business and management studies have

TABLE I.3 International Comparison of GDP Growth

	Growth Rate of GDP, 1995 (%)
World	2.6
Industrialized countries	**2.0**
United States	2.1
Canada	2.4
United Kingdom	2.7
Japan	0.5
Developing Countries	**4.0**
Latin American	−0.3
Asia	7.9
China	10.2
Countries in Transition	**−1.8**

SOURCE: Asian Development Bank (1996), China State Statistical Bureau (1995).

TABLE I.4 Comparison Among Kaisha, U.S., and Traditional Chinese Firms

| | *Organizational Forms* | | |
	Kaisha	*U.S.*	*Traditional Chinese Business Organizations*
Motivational source	Security & harmony	Intrinsic & financial	1. Family security
			2. Outgroup: (a) self-development; (b) financial
Capitalization	Keiretsu & financial group	Owner's equity	Family support
Decision making	Ringi-sho group consensus	Participation	Autocratic
Structure	Hierarchical	Multidivisional	Informal
Selection	Nepotism through universities	Merit	Nepotism
Incentives	Longevity	Merit	Both

observed the need to narrow the gap between business studies and business practice.

Indeed, the organizational and managerial system in China is complex in the sense that it not only differs drastically from organizational forms in other economies but also varies fundamentally among organizational forms within China. Table I.4 shows that traditional Chinese business organizations are idiosyncratic with Kaisha or typical U.S. firms in motivational source, capitalization, decision making, organizational structure, selection process, and incentive systems. As shown in Table I.5, each organizational form in China has both advantages and disadvantages, largely influenced by its institutional environment, structural characteristics, and organizational competencies. Managerial differences among these organizational forms are revealed in such areas as budget system, governmental intervention, institutional support, strategic orientation, decision-making autonomy, and strategic flexibility.

This volume aims to fill some gaps in the field by collecting and editing some high-impact chapters on the critical emerging business issues in China written by those who are among leading scholars in the area. These issues were seen by us as, on the one hand, central to a better understanding of doing and managing businesses for the next century in China, and, on the other hand, deficient in the literature that had to be redressed. It is our hope that this volume will provide an in-depth analysis of Chinese business and management at this juncture.

TABLE I.5 Organizational Forms Within China

	Organizational Forms			
	State-Owned	Collectively Owned	Privately Owned	Foreign Venture
Budget system	Soft	Hard	Hard	Hard
Strategic orientation	Defensive	Innovative	Proactive	Analysis
Institutional support	High, from central government	High, from local government	Low	Depends
Governmental intervention	High	Low	Low	Moderate
Structural benefit	Low	High	Moderate	Low for joint venture
Autonomy	Low	High	High	High
Flexibility	Low	High	High	Moderate

The present collection consists of three major parts, namely emerging business issues for Chinese domestic firms (the first four chapters following the Introduction), emerging business issues for foreign firms in China (the following six chapters), and emerging finance, taxation, accounting, and human resource management issues (the last six chapters). In the first part, issues that are examined include strategic orientation, decision making, managerial behavior, firm growth, environmental traits, ownership type, mergers and acquisitions, and the like. These chapters will show that different organizational forms encounter heterogeneous environments, thus necessitating idiosyncratic strategies appropriate for a given organizational form. The second part deals primarily with two important issues, international joint ventures and greater China cooperation. Although the category of wholly foreign owned subsidiaries has been growing in recent years, equity and contractual joint ventures (IJV) remain dominant and accounted for 73.55% of total FDI value in 1994. At the same time, although more than 40 countries or regions from all over the world have directly invested in China, almost three quarters of the total FDI in the country has come from the Chinese community, namely, Hong Kong, Taiwan, Singapore, and Macao. Part 3 addresses four emerging issues that appear to be fundamentally influential on local or foreign firms in China—capital and security markets, foreign exchange reform, new taxation and accounting systems, and emerging human resource management practice. These special issues impact the operation and growth of Chinese firms, whether local or international, in a significant manner.

Specifically, Chapter 1 assesses the configuration between strategic orientation and industrial environment for Chinese township and village enterprises (TVEs), the organizational form that has played an increasingly important role in Chinese economic development and structural reform. Luo, Tan, and Shenkar argue that the complexity, dynamism, and hostility of the industrial environment influence TVE managers' perception of competitive pressure, which in turn affects the firm's strategic orientations, such as innovativeness, proactiveness, risk-taking, and analysis. Based on a survey of TVE managers in Tianjin and Jiangsu, they demonstrate that complexity and dynamism of industrial competition have a systematically positive impact on TVEs' innovativeness, proactiveness, risk-taking, or analysis.

As China is moving away from the rigid, centrally planned economy through a series of market reforms, private enterprises are more free to operate throughout the country. With the relaxation of control, they can now enter into some industries that were restricted in the past. In addition, private businesses have also benefited from a number of government measures. For example, when the government relaxed the price of many "small commodities" (household items), new markets are available for private commodity producers. They took advantage of this opportunity and expanded their scale of operations. In Chapter 2, Lau, Ngo, and Chow review the development and contribution of private businesses to the Chinese economy. The political and market environment are analyzed to picture the current position of private businesses in the national economy. Major characteristics of private businesses and their owners are presented through three survey results conducted in different periods. Managerial implications, in terms of macro environment, competition, resources, management structure and governance, and leadership and human resources are discussed.

Economic transition has given birth to a new diversity in organizational forms and a plurality of property ownership types, and has turned the Chinese economy, previously dominated by state-owned enterprises, into one in which different organizational forms, including state-owned, collectively owned, private, foreign joint ventures, and completely foreign-owned enterprises, coexist and compete. Firms exhibiting different ownership types are subject to different environmental constraints, and vary significantly in their access to resources and their ability to exercise strategic choice. Following the environment-strategy-performance paradigm, one would logically expect that different forms of organizations adopt different strategic postures that are consistent with their respective environments in order to achieve a fit, which is crucial for their survival and success. In Chapter 3, Tan sheds some light on the environment-strategy configurations among different ownership types from a strategic group perspective and using Hrebiniak and Joyce's (1985) model.

Mergers and acquisitions are an integral part of any market economy, enhancing economic efficiency by reallocating and recombining corporate resources for better use. In recent years, mergers and acquisitions have become one of the "hot" business issues in China as they serve as a dominant approach for firms' restructuring and reorganizing on a market basis. In Chapter 4, Peng, Luo, and Sun postulate that mergers and acquisitions will become an increasingly common strategy used by Chinese enterprises, especially state-owned, seeking survival and expansion in the next century. They also illuminate the logic and characteristics of merger and acquisition activities in China using an interdisciplinary approach, drawing on research in management, finance, economics, sociology, and law, as well as China studies. Two well-known cases are used as illustrative examples.

Since the late 1980s, China has been the leading destination country in the world for direct foreign investment. International participation in China's economic development has played an increasingly important role in the country's reform programs. Based on four in-depth case studies and survey data collected from a sample of 90 U.S.-China manufacturing joint ventures, Yan reports in Chapter 5 on several key characteristics of interpartner configurations and relationships in the negotiation and formation stages of joint ventures, including founding negotiations, pre-venture ties between the partners, the means of first contact, the significant differences in partner motivations and strategic objectives, the mix of partner resource contributions, and the structure of management control exercised by the partners over the venture's operation. The rich, longitudinal case data are used to illustrate the dynamic changes in the venture's founding characteristics over time. Yan also identifies and discusses several new trends in international joint ventures in China that may have significant implications for forming and managing strategic alliances in China in the upcoming century.

Complementary to Yan's chapter, Luo argues that the operation and performance of joint ventures in China are also influenced by industry structure. When expanding globally, multinational corporations are likely to achieve higher performance than firms operating domestically, because the former benefit from the industry structure variance between the host and home country by investing those distinct resources that can enhance firms' competitive advantages vis-à-vis rivals in indigenous markets. It is recognized that industry structure imperfections in China constitute a dominant factor that not only makes foreign direct investment preferable to trade or licensing, but also determines the relative attractiveness of the Chinese market over other developing countries. Empirical evidence in Chapter 6 finds that the relationships between industry's profitability, sales growth and asset intensity, and firm performance are similar to those existing in developed market economies. However, the relationships in two areas, structural uncertainty and the number of firms in an industry, diverge according to the context.

The relationship between a multinational corporation's headquarters and its foreign subsidiaries has recently shifted in focus from control to strategic orientation because orientation is an efficient "mid-range" instrument linking global integration and local responsiveness. The global strategy literature asserts that the alignment of an interorganizational network to its uncertain global environment is critical for international expansion. Chapter 7 assesses the environment-strategy configuration and its performance implications for international joint ventures in China. Based on a survey of top IJV managers, Luo and Tan find that managers' perceptions of increased environmental complexity and hostility are positively related to Analyzer (between proactive and defensive) strategy. Proactive and defensive strategies are either negatively or non-significantly linked with contextual uncertainty. Thus, IJVs in China exhibit distinctive Analyzer strategies in an uncertain context. These strategies are significantly associated with perceived environmental complexity, dynamism, and hostility.

It is realized that the ability of Chinese enterprises to satisfy evolving domestic demands and to compete in the global marketplace continues to be severely constrained by a lack of technological sophistication. Technological innovation is now imperative across much of the Chinese economy, but this will be both very costly and very difficult. The magnitude and nature of the required effort have prompted the Chinese authorities to actively seek foreign sources of technology. In Chapter 8, Martinsons and Tseng examine the regulatory environment for transferring technology to China and analyze situational factors that facilitate transfer processes. The discussions contained in this chapter will help potential participants to develop realistic expectations as they seek to benefit from the second stage of the modernization drive in China and provide useful knowledge for those who are managing the technology transfer process.

One of the key business issues shaping the Chinese economy in the new century lies in the handover of Hong Kong to China. In Chapter 9, Chow and Kelley explore different strategies and adaptive processes of some of the large corporations as Hong Kong's laissez-faire economy is unified with perhaps the most dynamic socialist economy in the world. Indeed, the 1997 handover offers both opportunities and challenges. The relationship between Hong Kong and

China will be increasingly interdependent. China's vigorous economic growth contributes to the momentum of Hong Kong's economy. At the same time, China benefits by learning the rules of the game in the international market as Hong Kong companies have long been at the forefront of an adaptable trading center linking the East and West. According to Chow and Kelley, maintaining good relationships and cultivating ties with China's elite have been solid strategies for ensuring Hong Kong's position post-1997.

Foreign direct investment in China originates primarily from two sources: Chinese community investors and Western multinationals. Although more than 40 countries from all over the world have directly invested in China, almost three quarters (73.29%) of the total FDI in the country has come from the Chinese community—namely, Hong Kong, Macao, Taiwan, and Singapore, comprising approximately four times as much as by Western multinationals. In Chapter 10, Luo attempts to explain the underlying rationale behind the dominance of Chinese community-funded FDI in China. The analysis is made from multiple perspectives—economic, cultural, and institutional—with each perspective containing multidimensional insights.

Chapter 11 analyzes the changes taking place in the financial system of China as it has evolved toward a more market-based system. Since 1978, financial reform has yielded a legal foundation for the central bank and commercial banks. Progress has been made in developing financial institutions, instruments, and securities markets. Reform in China has been gradual and pragmatic. In some respects it has been too cautious and delayed in timing. China has developed a large domestic bond market, but money market development has been limited. Many Chinese borrowing entities have gained favorable access to the international capital markets. Relative to bond issuance, the growth of equity securities has been limited. Offshore equities markets have been tapped with modest success. In this chapter, Lees reminds us that China faces several obstacles in developing its securities markets, including late enactment of appropriate legal infrastructure, lack of institutional investors, and perceptions of high risk. Hong Kong plays an important and special role for fund raising by Chinese enterprises. In 1998, Hong Kong's role is increasingly important, with it being the legal domicile for Chinese organizations known as the Red Chips and the use of the Hong Kong stock market for Chinese firms referred to as H shares.

Another critical issue in China's financial system has to do with foreign exchange reform. China's 1994 foreign exchange reforms have led to limited convertibility of renminbi under current account. China announced additional steps, in February 1996 and again in June 1996, to make renminbi more easily convertible. Full convertibility for current accounts was accomplished in 1996.

Convertibility for capital account transactions is still years away, however. Chapter 12 presents a review and an assessment of the development in China's emerging foreign exchange system. According to Liaw, further moves toward capital account convertibility will depend on the smooth transition of the current deregulation and political stability.

A central pillar to a decentralized economy is a rational, compulsory, and universal system of public finance. China has sought to develop a comprehensive modern system of taxation that ensures that everyone will make a contribution to the public good. Income, sales, products, services, land, imports, and exports are taxed. In Chapter 13, Gensler discusses the relationship between decentralization and taxation, overviews Chinese tax systems, and highlights tax factors for foreigners. In the ending part, Gensler also offers taxation trends and possible evolutions for China 2000.

The economic reforms and open-door policy of China have had a far-reaching influence on Chinese accounting systems. After establishing their Enterprise Accounting Standards on July 1, 1993, the Chinese accounting system is moving toward becoming international. In the near future, the Chinese accounting system is predicted to be part of the stream of international accounting and to influence the development of international accounting. In Chapter 14, Zhou and Yang analyze the past, present, and future development of accounting systems in China, which may help readers understand the Chinese accounting system in general.

Economic reform in China has been going on for almost two decades. The computerization of accounting is more difficult in China than in the West, partly due to the economic reform. In Chapter 15, Wang and Yang review the current development of accounting information systems in China and discuss its unique problems and prospects.

Human resource management, especially employee training and development, is undergoing changes and reforms in recent years. Its success affects not merely a firm's organizational performance but also changes the social environment. Focusing on past and current employee training practices in China's industrial enterprises, Zhu's Chapter 16 highlights the changes that have occurred during the transition of the economic system. These include the history of the training and development system in a highly centralized economy, how this system has been challenged during the reforms, and its current situation. She also offers her recent survey results with regard to the impact of the changes in this system. The chapter concludes with a discussion of functions of the trade unions in human resource management under current transitions.

China has long been a country shrouded in mystery. Although concerns over inflation, corruption, and stability fill the Chinese press today, although fears of political instability and institutional uncertainty exist in the minds of common Chinese and foreign investors, few observers expect a reversal of the various strategic policies that have emerged over the past 20 years. Economic forces point to a continuation of rapid economic integration of the Chinese economy with the outside world. One can expect that China will continue to move toward standard international trade and investment practices, although not without periodic reversals and significant regional discrepancies. This hinges, nevertheless, on whether China can preserve law and order in the post-Deng era. If China does manage to maintain stability, and it does continue its pragmatic policy of reform, then it is safe to assume that China will continue to prosper at the present pace.

It is interesting to note the situation of the Chinese economy relative to other Asian economies per the financial crisis originating in the fall of 1997. While the currencies of South Korea, Thailand, Malaysia, and Indonesia tumbled, China's and Hong Kong's economies were affected, but much less so. The Chinese currency is not convertible. Their foreign reserves in the spring of 1998 were over $100 billion. Hong Kong's currency is pegged to the U.S. dollar. The Crisis is expected to slow Hong Kong's economic growth to 4% to 5% and China's to about 8%—an enviable position relative to other Asian economies.

PART **I**

Emerging Business Issues
for Chinese Domestic Firms

chapter 1

Township and Village Enterprises in China

Strategy and Environment

YADONG LUO

J. JUSTIN TAN

ODED SHENKAR

One of the most distinctive features of China's transition to a market economy has been the role played by township and village enterprises (TVEs). TVEs refer to all those rural nonstate enterprises subordinate to township or village governments and owned and operated collectively. They represent an intermediate property form shaped by new pressures for efficiency and flexibility in rapidly changing environments in which market forces incrementally replace the state planning mechanism. TVEs, together with joint urban enterprises and joint rural enterprises, constitute collectively owned enterprises. According to the *Statistical Yearbook of China* (1995, pp. 363-365), there were 24.95 million TVEs and 120.18 million employees working in these organizations in 1994. In the same year, the share of total industrial output produced by TVEs was 30.46%, which drove collectively owned enterprises to surpass state-owned firms to become the dominant output contributor (*Statistical Yearbook of China,* 1995, p. 375). By 1995, almost half of the nation's total pretax profits were generated by TVEs (*Statistical Yearbook of China,* 1995, pp. 366, 391). In no other transitional economy have TVEs played such a dynamic role.

Weitzman and Xu (1993) attribute the success of TVEs to their internal institutional structure, which may facilitate cooperation through implicit contracts among community members locked into an ongoing relationship. Nee (1992) advances a similar interpretation, arguing that long-time community residents create forms of income sharing that may be optimal in the absence of an independent legal system. We suggest an alternative yet complementary view in this study: that the success of TVEs is largely due to their strategies in adapting to and configuring with the external competitive environment. Building upon Miles and Snow's (1978) framework, Tan and Litschert (1994) demonstrate in their study of predominantly Chinese state-owned firms that these firms respond to increased environmental uncertainties with conservative and risk-averse strategies. A more recent study by Tan (1996) suggests that Chinese privately owned firms tend to select proactive and risk-taking strategies in configuring for the complex, dynamic, and uncertain environment. It therefore appears that ownership type has a significant impact on environment-strategy configuration.

Given the increasing influence of TVEs in China's transitional economy, there has been little attention to the study of TVEs. From the transaction cost perspective (Williamson, 1985), ownership type may be considered a strategic variable directed at the corporate-level strategy of reducing costs associated with overcoming transaction difficulties, implying that the choice of ownership is the most important strategic consideration. In the Chinese management literature, Peng and Heath (1996) argue that many TVEs are actually private firms in disguise. By establishing partnerships with local governments, TVE entrepreneurs essentially use the organizational form as a "boundary-blurring" strategy in order to seek institutional protection. In addition, ownership type may play a significant role with regard to the environment-strategy configuration at the business level. Given the logic that the TVE is an effective uncertainty reduction form whose interorganizational relationship with the local government and elastic contracting mechanism facilitate continuity and efficient adaptation, we would expect that TVEs will adopt some distinctive strategies in response to industrial competition in the Chinese economy characterized by weak market structure, poorly specified property rights, and institutional uncertainty (Nee, 1992; Tan & Litschert, 1994). In this study, we address Chinese TVEs with a focus on firm strategic responses to competitive pressure during economic transformation. The basic premise of this study is that the complexity, dynamism, and hostility of the industrial environment influence TVE managers' perceptions of the competitive pressure, which in turn affects the firms' strategic orientations such as innovativeness, proactiveness, risk-taking behavior, and analysis. Unlike that of state firms, the market environment of TVEs is highly competitive (Jefferson, Rawski, & Zheng, 1992; Perkins, 1994). It is this industrial competition that constitutes a primary force underlying strategic decisions made by TVEs (Byrd, 1992; Naughton, 1992; Su, 1993). Thus, we assess the environment by focusing on the sector of industrial competition. Future research could advance studies on Chinese TVEs, especially with respect to strategy-environment-performance relations, by taking this study as a point of departure.

RESEARCH FOUNDATIONS AND HYPOTHESES

Management and Structure of TVEs

TVEs have rapidly emerged as a growing industrial force in China. As Table 1.1 shows, gross output produced by TVEs reached as high as 4,258.85 billion yuan in 1994, which represented 30.46% of the nation's total industry sector. By 1995, this sector had almost 10 times more TVEs than state-owned enterprises (*Statistical Yearbook of China*, 1995, p. 375). In 1994, 120.18 million people were employed by TVEs, almost three times the number of workers in state firms in the industry sector. Whereas approximately 70% of state firms experienced losses in the past years, TVEs' net profits and contributed taxes have increased progressively (see Table 1.1). The success and growth of TVEs are also reflected in high levels of key financial ratios, such as return on fixed assets, return on equity (funds), and return on sales (operating revenue; see Table 1.1).

TVEs operate outside the state plan and state control. Despite the "collective" label, TVEs themselves are not employee cooperatives: rather, they are established and controlled by township and village governments. Neither state owned nor privately owned, the TVE embodies a community property form, so that, in theory, the property belongs to all who live within the jurisdiction of the local government. This leaves township and village governments with the strongest claim over profits from TVEs, which soon become their major source of revenue through levies and revenue-sharing arrangements. Local governments also have the right to control residual income, dispose of assets, and appoint and dismiss managers (Byrd & Lin, 1989). Authority relations and compensation schedules are quite well specified. Township leaders are appointed by county officials, most often from outside the township in question. Their compensation is

TABLE 1.1 Descriptive Statistics of TVEs in China: 1989-1994

Item	1989	1990	1991	1992	1993	1994
General information						
Number of TVEs (millions)	18.69	18.50	19.09	20.79	24.53	24.95
Number of employees (millions)	93.67	92.65	96.09	105.81	123.45	120.18
Gross output (billion yuan)	742.84	846.16	1,162.17	1,797.54	3,154.07	4,258.85
Net value of fixed assets (billion yuan)	148.62	166.87	195.93	258.59	376.80	519.62
Net value of circulating funds (billion yuan)	189.01	224.47	292.50	406.38	561.87	845.89
Performance						
Total operating revenue (billion yuan)	482.16	521.86	655.60	1,004.09	1,742.21	2,508.90
Total net profits (billion yuan)	24.01	23.27	28.47	47.76	109.31	135.24
Taxes paid (billion yuan)	27.25	27.55	33.38	47.02	64.85	107.90
Total pretax profits (billion yuan)	30.10	28.98	35.28	57.22	178.40	222.57
Total wage bill (billion yuan)	58.07	60.68	70.65	95.71	132.39	165.05
Financial ratios						
After-tax return on fixed assets (%)	12.50	10.60	10.80	13.80	21.20	20.50
Pretax return on equity (funds) (%)	15.20	13.00	12.70	14.30	19.00	14.80
After-tax return on equity (funds) (%)	7.10	5.90	5.80	7.20	11.60	9.00
After-tax return on operating revenue (%)	5.00	4.50	4.30	4.80	6.30	5.40
Operating revenue on fixed assets (%)	251.00	237.00	249.60	289.90	337.60	379.40

SOURCE: Various years' *China Statistical Yearbook.*

governed by a "managerial contract" with explicit success indicators such as TVE output, sales, profits, and taxes paid. These township officials in turn appoint TVE managers, generally from the local township, and sign managerial contracts basing compensation on output and profits. It is true that there is no independent legal system to guarantee property rights, just as it is true that the overall structure of political power may lack legitimacy, but contingent upon the existing governmental structure, TVE property rights appear unambiguous.

Like hybrids in developed market economies, TVEs are an organizational form that "use resources and/or governance structures from more than one existing organization" (Borys & Jemison, 1989, p. 235). The interorganizational relationships between TVEs and local governments are bilaterally dependent. While TVEs constitute the primary source of revenues for the local governments, they also receive enormous assistance from their governments. This institutional arrangement, as Nee (1992) points out, represents a solution to the problem of weak market structure and incomplete market transition. Under transaction cost theory, this solution is a means to economize on transaction costs in interorganizational relationships when "parties to the transaction maintain autonomy but are bilaterally dependent to a nontrivial degree" (Williamson, 1991, p. 271). In other transitional economies, most new start-up businesses have severe difficulties getting access to capital, technology, information, scarce materials, and distribution channels, and as a result remain small, undercapitalized, and dependent on informal production factor markets (Roman, 1986). In contrast, township and village governments in China assist TVEs greatly in securing production factors, accessing infrastructure, arranging marketing channels, and getting higher-level government ratification if needed (Byrd & Lin, 1989). Moreover, local governments can better assess and diversify the risks of start-up businesses under their control. Government sponsorship serves to spread the risks incurred by start-ups, essentially by having the entire local community absorb the cost of failure. They also serve as finance intermediaries and guarantors of loans to individual TVEs. By underwriting a portion of the risk of entry, local governments help TVEs enter production with a larger size, starting with some mechanization and exploiting economies of scale. With local governments facilitating the flow of capital to rural enterprises, TVEs are also able to take advantage of China's relatively high household savings. All these roles played by the township and village governments reinforce TVEs' innovative and adaptive orientation.

Under the conditions of partial reform, TVEs have a better adaptive capacity to the rapidly changing environment because their structural location allows them to double-dip in the planning and market sectors of the economy. State enterprises enjoy favored access to state-allocated capital and factor resources regardless of performance; they operate inefficiently, under soft-budget constraints. Private firms operating under hard-budget constraints display higher productivity through economizing on production costs, yet their access to formal sources of capital and factor resources is least favorable. By contrast, TVEs enjoy a better fit between efficiency and access to resources. They operate in market environments with hardened budget constraints, benefit more from local governments' support, and have sufficient autonomy to reward employees and make strategic decisions (Weitzman & Xu, 1993). In addition, TVEs are able to hire temporary workers from nearby villages, who can be laid off and returned to farm work according to the firms' needs. Thus, TVEs enjoy greater flexibility in regulating the size of their human resources than either state firms that rely on permanent workers or private firms that lack support from local governments and state personnel agencies. That TVEs are an effective institutional adaptation to the Chinese economic environment can also be observed in product markets. Whenever product markets are established but asset markets are incomplete, TVEs allow local communities to translate control over scarce assets (especially land) into collective income. Moreover, TVEs could grow up as complements to state-owned firms, which often subcontract to TVEs, providing technology and equipment.

Because their property rights and management assignments are controlled by township and village governments, TVE managers' incentives are not identical to those of private owners. They must take into account the interests of the local community to some extent if they are to be effective in achieving a spectrum of economic and social indicators. Employment pressure from the local community, the presence of output and profit as an argument in the manager's compensation function, and fairly hard budget constraints constitute major factors underlying TVE managers' incentives to seek both efficiency and output-market expansion. Although TVEs can get help from local governments in accessing needed resources and marketing channels, such resources are limited and insecure. For this reason, they must turn to specialized markets to purchase many factory resources or to sell products. This often involves importing outside (domestic and foreign) investment and technologies to sustain TVEs' efficiency and expansion. This occurs not because the community instructs its agents to adopt this strategy, but rather because managers appointed by the local government are motivated to pursue both efficiency and expansion through well-stipulated management and compensation contracts (Jefferson et al., 1992).

In sum, TVEs' ownership structure provides institutional protection that buffers them from environmental disturbance, and their small size (relative to state firms) and internal flexibility predispose them to entrepreneurial ventures. Compared with managers of Chinese state-owned enterprises, managers of TVEs are equipped with greater prerogative and discretion. Consequently, the environment in which TVEs operate resembles to a large extent that of an entrepreneurial context.

Strategic Responses to Competitive Pressure

The alignment of an organization's strategic orientation with its environment is of paramount importance for the business's success. The information processing argument (Galbraith & Schendel, 1983) and the population ecology theory (Aldrich, McKelvey, & Ulrich, 1984) suggest that an organization's information processing system (in the form of hierarchical relationships and standard operating procedures) must be capable of accommodating both the variability and the uncertainty of its product-market environment. In the Chinese economy, the necessity for a strategy-environment fit can be greater because managerial discretion is highly constrained, strategic restructuring is fairly costly, and the industrial environment is enormously complex and turbulent (Child, 1994; Shenkar & Von Glinow, 1994).

The industrial environment in China is dynamic and complex (Luo, 1995); its influence is thus highly sustainable (Tung, 1982). As a result of structural transformation, most industries have been substantially decentralized or even privatized (Perkins, 1994). Efforts to revitalize and restructure Chinese industry are closely linked to the reform of pricing, public finance, ownership, and social welfare. Thus, the industrial environment has a critical impact on firm operations. Reform has meant an expansion not only of markets but also of industrial competition (Jefferson & Rawski, 1993). Naughton (1992) observes sharp reductions in the dispersion of profitability across Chinese industrial sectors. There is also evidence of convergence in financial returns to capital, labor, and materials across ownership types (Jefferson et al., 1992). These tendencies should be attributed to the decline and convergence of profit rates due to the continuing erosion of barriers that formerly protected state firms against competition from TVEs, private firms, and foreign businesses. Byrd (1992) finds that recent concentration ratios (market share of a few leading companies) for Chinese industry tend to fall considerably below comparable figures for the United States and Japan. These ratios even show a declining time trend (Su, 1993). Consequently, TVEs are now facing tremendous competitive pressure, not only from state-and privately owned enterprises, but also from foreign investors and other TVEs.

The strategic choice perspective suggests that a firm needs to have different strategic responses to adapt to different kinds of industrial competition (Miles & Snow, 1978). Organizational adaptability involves a firm's innovativeness, proactiveness, and riskiness (Miller & Friesen, 1983). These responses affect the firm's orientation in scanning, identifying, and capitalizing on emerging market opportunities, and its extensive capabilities to respond to market and contextual changes (Hambrick, 1983). As a hybrid strategic response between proactiveness and defensiveness, analysis strategy focuses both risk-adjusted efficiency and emerging market opportunities (Miles & Snow, 1978). Firms using this strategy defend existing product markets through efficiency-oriented strategies while cautiously penetrating new markets through intensified product/market innovation. Tan and Litschert (1994) find that Chinese managers' perception of industrial competition intensity significantly influences their firms' decision characteristics, including propensity for risk taking, innovativeness, proactiveness, and analysis.

TVEs tend to fare better than state enterprises in rapidly changing environments because of their strategic flexibility (Byrd, 1992). Economic reform brought about turbulence and transaction failure of the centrally planned mechanism (Tung, 1982). Such an environment brought about many niches that were not filled by the state planning mechanism. The existence of many unfilled niches in formerly centrally planned economies characterized by supply shortage (Roman, 1986), coupled with aggressive strategies (Nee, 1992), increase TVEs' chances for survival and growth. Meanwhile, the TVE structure has pre-positioned its entrepreneurs for speed and surprise, giving them the ability to react quickly to opportunities in the environment or proactively to outmaneuver the more established state firms (Vogel, 1989). Further, the interdependence with local governments creates transaction-cost and uncertainty-reduction advantages for TVEs and spurs the managers to be innovative and adaptive (Jefferson et al., 1992). Vogel (1989) reports that TVEs tend to be more aggressive and innovative than hierarchical state enterprises during transition.

From a competitive strategy perspective, Byrd and Zhu (1989) state that many TVEs tend to rush into newly discovered profit opportunities as quickly as possible because early entrants into a newly blossoming activity can earn very high, lightly taxed profits and can rapidly grow to substantial size. This is consistent with the strategy of imitation, because earlier imitators can still make high profits but with less risk than is taken by the first, pathbreaking entrants into the new activities (Jefferson et al., 1992). In addition, TVEs usually make rapid changes in product lines to take advantage of changing market opportunities. TVEs have shown great flexibility in developing new products and changing product lines quickly to avoid being stuck too long in industries that face declining market trends (Byrd & Zhu, 1989). Because of their low capital intensity, TVEs' assets can easily be switched to new activities, or, in Williamson's (1985) terminology, because asset specificity is low, TVEs often have a com-

petitive edge over their major rivals—state enterprises. This advantage rein-
forces TVEs' innovativeness and proactiveness in aligning with the increasingly
competitive and uncertain environment during transition. Tan and Litschert
(1994) have identified three dimensions in this environment: complexity, dynamism, and hostility. These three dimensions, as suggested by the information
uncertainty perspective, make up key factors affecting uncertainty (Lawrence &
Lorsch, 1967). Following the above line of reasoning, we propose that:

> H_1: *Among Chinese TVEs, a strategy of innovativeness is positively
> related to perceived environmental complexity (H_{1a}), dynamism (H_{1b}),
> and hostility (H_{1c}).*

> H_2: *Among Chinese TVEs, a strategy of proactiveness is positively
> related to perceived environmental complexity (H_{2a}), dynamism (H_{2b}),
> and hostility (H_{2c}).*

As noted earlier, TVEs represent an intermediary property form shaped by
increased competitive pressure. Hard budget constraints encourage them to
behave in accordance with the rule of the market (Perkins, 1994). In an environment characterized by weak market structures and unspecified property rights,
which makes market exchanges uncertain and transaction cost high, TVEs must
compete with other types of organizations, especially state firms, for scarce
resources. According to a resource dependency perspective, resource scarcity
affects the manager's perception of the task environment, which in turn influences risk-taking propensity (Miller & Friesen, 1983). Since TVEs have fewer
principal-agent conflicts, which facilitates managerial initiative, they have the
autonomy to respond to market signals and to determine riskiness involving
important investments and operations (Vogel, 1989).

TVEs' access to various critical resources and state-owned distribution
channels and marketing arrangements is at the bottom of the Chinese central
government's priority list. They have to be aggressive and willing to take risks
in order to configure with the industrial environment as well as the increased
industrial competition (Nee, 1992). While the state has substantially decentralized the national economy, it has not entirely relinquished its administrative
control over industry structure (Perkins, 1994). As a result, TVEs are not
structurally protected by the central government in acquiring production factors,
accessing infrastructure, and attaining government-instituted marketing assistance (Byrd, 1989). Yet, since TVEs lack both control over reliable information

and time to react under imperfect information concerning government policies and regulations, they have to accept and take risks when making strategic decisions. In a recent study, Xin and Pearce (1994) reported that Chinese TVEs manage scarcity (or hostility) by actively cultivating close personal relationships with their business connections in order to secure production factors, distribution channels, and institutional support. While state sectors are structurally protected, the TVEs often actively seek protection through "behavioral means." Apparently, this type of protection is loosely structured and often brings up numerous risks for participating TVEs (Nee, 1992). According to the above, the following relationship is predicted:

H_3: *Among Chinese TVEs, a strategy of risk taking is positively related to perceived environmental complexity (H_{3a}), dynamism (H_{3b}), and hostility (H_{3c}).*

Nevertheless, TVEs' risk-taking propensity may not be as high as that of purely private enterprises, which are found to behave essentially like prospectors (Tan, 1996). Unlike privately owned firms, TVEs must take such community benefits as workers' job security and local social welfare into strategy considerations (Jefferson et al., 1992). As noted above, the TVE sector's market-product environment is highly unstable and subject to fluctuations because of economic and administrative shocks (Perkins, 1994). Ease of entry, combined with strong pressures in local communities to develop TVEs as a means of employing surplus labor and generating revenues, can also be a source of uncertainties. The huge reserve army of rural labor available for relatively simple, labor-intensive activities means that violent downward movements in prices and profits are possible (Byrd & Lin, 1989). The weakness of market information networks and the lack of connections among local markets tend to exacerbate operation variations. These uncertainties and pressures make TVE managers more circumspect than their counterparts in private enterprises when making strategic decisions. Because TVEs are generally small, their ability to reduce contextual uncertainties and risks is fairly limited (Byrd & Zhu, 1989). These factors spur the managers to seek efficiency as well as stability. The dual objectives of efficiency and stability, according to the strategic choice paradigm (Miles & Snow, 1978), are a central characteristic of an analysis-oriented strategy. Jefferson and colleagues (1992) find that TVEs are more proactive and innovative than hierarchical state firms but less aggressive and risk taking than fully "marketized" private organizations in the complex, dynamic, and hostility environments. In light of the above, the following hypothesis states:

H₄: Among Chinese TVEs, an analysis-oriented strategy is positively related to perceived environmental complexity (H₄ₐ), dynamism (H₄ᵦ), and hostility (H₄c).

RESEARCH METHODS

Measurement, Questionnaire Design, and Pretest

Data used in this study were obtained through a survey of Chinese TVE managers in 1996. The questionnaire was adopted from a previous study of Chinese state and collective enterprises (Tan & Litschert, 1994). Briefly, environment was conceptualized as a multidimensional construct (Dess & Beard, 1984; Lawrence & Lorsch, 1967). Three dimensions of environmental attributes, namely environmental complexity, dynamism, and hostility, were investigated. For this study, the environment was viewed as a perceptual construct because the study deals with strategy that involves navigating within a chosen domain. It has long been recognized that how managers perceive their environment is more critical and relevant to variables subject to managerial control than are archival measures of the environment (Miller, 1988). Perceptual measures thus enable the researcher to view a firm's environment from the perspective of organizational members or key respondents (Boyd, Dess, & Rasheed, 1993). It has also been argued that perceptual measures make sense, because it is not the external reality but the way entrepreneurs think about reality that determines the outcome (Shaver & Scott, 1991). In addition, these measures of organizational environment have been validated and shown to correlate with objective measures with a high degree of reliability (e.g., Chandler & Hanks, 1993).

In the questionnaire, respondents were asked to rate, on a 7-point scale, their perception pertaining to criticality and hostility of the industrial competition (Pfeffer & Salancik, 1978), variability and predictability of the industrial competition (Lawrence & Lorsch, 1967), and heterogeneity and diversity of the industrial competition (Thompson, 1967). Based upon their responses, we measured the environment complexity by the average score of heterogeneity and diversity of the environment. Similarly, environment dynamism was the mean of variability and predictability, and environment hostility was the mean of criticality and hostility of the industrial environment.

As stated earlier, strategic orientations in this study include innovativeness, proactiveness, analysis, and risk taking (Lumpkin & Dess, 1996; Venkatraman,

1989). Respondents were asked to rank characteristics of each of these strategic orientations relevant to their particular firms on a 7-point scale. Specifically, respondents answered questions about whether or not they constantly seek to introduce new products or services into the market, whether or not they would move proactively to try to take the lead and to seize an opportunity, whether they preferred to analyze environmental conditions and alternatives carefully, and whether they preferred investments that had low risk and moderate return or those with high risk and high return. These measures were conceptually based and have been empirically validated in previous studies (e.g., Tan & Litschert, 1994; Venkatraman, 1989).

The questionnaire was first reviewed and revised by experts in strategic management and then subjected to a back-translation procedure to ensure validity in a cross-cultural setting (e.g., Adler, Brahm, & Graham, 1992). Consultation was sought on instrument development to obtain feedback on the quality of the instrument and any needed revisions. The pretest and survey were administered in Tianjin and Jiangsu provinces. We collected 12 double answers during the pretest of the questionnaire. The answers from the two respondents in the same firm exhibited a high level of interrater correlation, with the Guttman Split-Half Reliability Index ranging between .7 and .9. Results of personal interviews also provided added validation to responses in the questionnaire. After checking reliability, a subsequent questionnaire was sent to only one respondent in each sample firm.

Data and Measure Reliability

Two hundred ten TVE top managers in Tianjin and Jiangsu provinces were randomly selected as our respondents. Fifty-six questionnaires were collected, representing a response rate of 27%. Selected respondents were interviewed to collect pertinent information. The information collected exhibits a high level of consistency with questionnaire responses. This study followed the usual academic convention of leaving unidentified the individual organizations in the sample. Researchers who have used questionnaire surveys in China have reported that under anonymity, Chinese managers were more willing and more likely to provide accurate information (Adler, Campbell, & Laurent, 1989). We chose Jiangsu and Tianjin because they are locations where the most southern TVEs and the most northern TVEs, respectively, have been established (Byrd & Lin, 1989). The selection of the most representative province from the southern and northern regions could enhance the generalizability of the empirical results, as the two groups may have different strategic behaviors and operate in nonidentical environments (Byrd, 1989).

Reliability was tested using Cronbach's alpha coefficient. Generally, a value around .7 is considered adequate to conclude internal consistency (Nunnally, 1978). This guideline was met. The validity of the assumption of normality was tested, and results indicated that the normality assumption appears to be valid when applied to the data at hand. Multicollinearity was diagnosed by examining the variance inflation factors (VIF) for the predictors. The VIF values for the three predictors ruled out the possibility that multicollinearity is a serious problem in our study. These results are available from the authors.[1]

Descriptive statistics and Pearson correlation coefficients are presented in Table 1.2. The low correlation among the three measures of environmental characteristics offered a clear indication that they were distinct constructs, and that each as an independent variable would provide unique predictive power.

ANALYSIS AND RESULTS

Research hypotheses were tested using multiple regression. In the first equation, innovative strategy was predicted using the three environmental variables. As shown in Table 1.3, dynamism is positively related to innovativeness at a statistically significant level ($r = 0.32$, $p < 0.05$); thus hypothesis H_{1b} is supported. Environmental complexity is also positively related to innovativeness ($r = 0.27$), yet the effect is marginally significant ($p < 0.10$). Contrary to our hypothesis H_{1c}, environmental hostility carries a negative standardized regression estimate ($r = -0.16$) in relation to the strategic response (innovativeness), yet the relationship is not significant. This leads to a rejection of H_{1c}. It appears that environmental dynamism provides the strongest prediction of the degree of innovativeness, followed by environmental complexity. Hostility is not an important environmental factor affecting TVEs' strategic orientation. Our field study indicates that the process of developing competitive advantages or undermining those of rivals through innovation begins by understanding how better to satisfy customers. By discovering new ways to satisfy customers, the TVE can identify its next move to find a new niche.

Next, we examined the impact of industrial competition on the strategy of proactiveness. Although environmental hostility and complexity are found to be positively related to the dependent variable, the relationships are not significant

TABLE 1.2 Descriptive Statistics and Pearson Correlation Coefficients for TVEs
($N = 56$)

	M	SD	1	2	3	4	5	6	7
1. Complexity	4.66	0.64	1.00						
2. Dynamism	4.30	0.76	0.16	1.00					
3. Hostility	4.14	0.68	0.27*	0.42***	1.00				
4. Innovativeness	4.27	1.15	0.32*	0.26*	0.04	1.00			
5. Proactiveness	3.96	1.41	0.39**	0.10	0.15	0.60***	1.00		
6. Analysis	4.50	0.89	0.11	0.33**	0.18	0.22	0.10	1.00	
7. Risk-taking	4.09	1.12	0.49***	0.25	0.18	0.66***	0.75***	0.32*	1.00

$* p < 0.05; ** p < 0.01; *** p < 0.001.$

TABLE 1.3 Results of Multiple Regression for Township and Village Enterprises (Standardized Estimates β)

| | Dependent Variable | | | |
	1st Equation Innovativeness	2nd Equation Proactiveness	3rd Equation Risk-Taking	4th Equation Analysis
Independent variables				
Complexity	0.27 †	0.02	0.18	0.31*
Dynamism	0.32*	0.37**	0.46***	0.05
Hostility	−0.16	0.04	−0.04	0.03
R^2	0.17	0.15	0.27	0.12
F	3.49	3.12	6.33	2.27
p	0.05	0.05	0.001	0.10
N	56	56	56	56

† $p < 0.10$; * $p < 0.05$; ** $p < 0.01$; *** $p < 0.001$.

at the generally accepted level. The only independent variable that is significantly associated with proactiveness in the anticipated direction is environmental dynamism ($r = 0.37, p < 0.01$), thus providing support for H_{2b}. This result suggests that it is environmental dynamism, or variability of the industrial environment, rather than diversity or criticality of this sector that leads TVE entrepreneurs to respond proactively to industrial competition. The underlying implication is that TVEs need to respond aggressively to a dynamic environment in order to seize upon product-market opportunities that seem highly competitive and disappear quickly.

In the third equation, a set of hypotheses pertaining to risk taking was tested. As shown in Table 1.3, environmental dynamism has a significant impact on a TVE's risk taking in a positive way ($r = 0.46, p < 0.001$), lending support to H_{3b}. In contrast, perceived complexity of the industrial environment is not systematically related to a TVE's riskiness ($r = 0.18$). Environmental hostility is also not significantly linked with a TVE's risk-taking ($r = -0.04$). H_{3a} and H_{3c} are hence not supported. The regression analysis of this equation demonstrates that when the industrial environment is dynamic, the TVEs structurally protected by local governments tend to be adaptive and aggressive. This coincides with the notion in the Chinese management literature that a TVE's quasi-marketized structure often creates risk diversification advantages that encourage its managers to be less risk averse in searching for dynamic opportunities and transactions (Nee, 1992; Vogel, 1989).

Finally, the dependent variable, analysis orientation, was regressed on the variables of environmental attributes. Consistent with H_{4a}, it is found that environmental complexity is significantly and positively associated with analysis strategy ($r = 0.31$, $p < 0.05$). The impact of environmental dynamism and hostility also have a positive impact on a TVE's analysis orientation ($r = 0.05$ and $r = 0.03$, respectively), but it doesn't reach significant levels. This evidence does not lend support to H_{4b} and H_{4c}. These findings indicate that the perceived environmental complexity, or heterogeneity and diversity of the industrial environment, is systematically linked with TVEs' increased analysis orientation. This complexity leads TVEs to seek emerging product-market opportunities through deliberately analyzing the industrial environment and reducing unnecessary innovative costs and operational uncertainties. This empirical evidence corroborates our field study finding that many small TVEs in either Tianjin or Jiangsu appear to defend their existing product markets through efficiency-oriented strategies while cautiously penetrating new markets where suppliers, producers, buyers, and rivals interact with each other in a fairly complicated manner. Major results are summarized in Table 1.4.

DISCUSSION AND CONCLUSION

This research examined the configuration between strategic orientation and industrial competition for Chinese TVEs. TVEs are now becoming increasingly important for Chinese national economy and structural reform. In 1994, 120.18 million people worked in TVEs, which generated almost half of the nation's total fiscal income and contributed about one third of the nation's industrial output. The issue addressed in this study is, on the one hand, central to a better understanding of Chinese TVEs, and on the other hand, deficient in information about Chinese management; it therefore defines a gap to be filled. The key results suggest that the characteristics of industrial competition, a primary segment of Chinese industrial environment, have a deterministic and yet sustainable influence on TVEs' strategic orientation. It is found that TVEs respond strategically to different environmental dimensions such as complexity, dynamism, and hostility in different manners. These dimensions, as suggested by the information uncertainty perspective, make up key factors affecting industry structural uncertainty and competition intensity (Lawrence & Lorsch, 1967). They influence TVE managers' perceptions of competitive pressure, which in turn impact such strategic orientations as propensity for innovativeness,

TABLE 1.4 Summary of the Research Results

	Hypothesized (H) and Found (F) Regression Results Strategic Responses							
	Innovativeness		Proactiveness		Risk-Taking		Analysis	
Industrial environment	**H1**	**F**	**H2**	**F**	**H3**	**F**	**H4**	**F**
Complexity (a)	+	+	+	+/ns	+	+/ns	+	+
Dynamism (b)	+	+	+	+	+	+	+	+/ns
Hostility (c)	+	−/ns	+	+/ns	+	−/ns	+	+/ns

NOTE: ns = not significant.

proactiveness, risk taking, and analysis. Of the three environmental dimensions, complexity and dynamism of the industrial competition are found to have a systematically positive impact on TVEs' innovativeness, proactiveness, risk taking, or analysis. Hostility of the industrial environment is not significantly associated with any strategic orientations adopted by Chinese TVEs.

It is recalled that increased complexity of the industrial environment perceived by a TVE's managers leads to the firm's high innovativeness and high analysis. A competitive and complex industrial environment indeed puts great pressure on TVEs to perform well and is relatively unforgiving of mistakes. In such circumstances, price competition is intense in many TVE industries, and various forms of nonprice competition occur as well. This environment undoubtedly contributes greatly to the innovativeness, dynamism, and flexibility of the TVE sector. Innovation and differentiation are imperative business strategies for the success of TVEs in such an environment. Moreover, unlike many state enterprises, TVEs have no captive markets for their products. TVEs are hence largely outward-oriented in their product markets. In this situation, innovation turns out to be more imperative for survival and growth in the complex environment for TVEs. On the other hand, environmental complexity often implies structural uncertainty and being subject to fluctuations because of economic and administrative shocks. This is natural, since market adjustments had been weak or nonexistent for several decades in China. In these circumstances, it is critical for TVEs to analyze situations vigorously and to evaluate possible consequences thoroughly to obtain alternatives. Our field study in Jiangsu and Tianjin reveals that when the industrial environment is complex, TVEs tend to seek those product and market opportunities that have been shown to be promising.

It is also recapitulated that the dynamism of the industrial environment has a profoundly positive influence on TVEs' innovativeness, proactiveness, and risk taking. The goods markets that TVEs face have only just emerged, largely since the early 1980s. There has hence been instability and wide, sudden fluctuations, as well as numerous opportunities to make large profits. The state sector left many gaps where latent unfilled demand existed. The sharp rise in rural and urban personal incomes starting in the early 1980s also created new demand that state enterprises were, at least initially, not well placed to meet. In this dynamic environment, TVEs that enter the market early and aggressively, that seize upon market opportunities proactively, and that innovate products more quickly will have a high chance to prosper. Our field study finds that when a dynamic environment emerges, TVEs appear to make rapid changes in product lines to take advantage of changing market opportunities. In general, TVEs have shown both greater proactiveness and greater flexibility in developing new products and changing product lines to cope with a dynamic product-market environment than state firms have.

In conclusion, Chinese TVEs have been playing a pivotal role in national economic modernization and structural transformation. Reforms and experiments with varied forms of ownership and management in TVEs have already had a great demonstration effect on urban economic reforms and will continue to do so. This chapter presents one of the few systematic studies of TVEs' strategic behavior in the Chinese management literature. It demonstrates that TVEs behave as prospectors in configuring with a dynamic environment and as analyzers in aligning with a complex environment. In contrast to state-owned firms, which appear to act as Defenders (Tan & Litschert, 1994) in coping with complex and dynamic environments, TVEs have revealed significantly greater innovativeness, proactiveness, and risk taking when they encounter the same environments. It would be interesting to see if TVEs' strategic behavior will vary across industries and regions, because TVEs in different industries and locations confront heterogeneous task and institutional environments (Byrd & Lin, 1989), and are equipped with idiosyncratic organizational and entrepreneurial capabilities (Nee, 1992). These questions are proposed as an agenda for future research.

NOTE

1. Available from the authors: Yadong Luo, PhD, Department of Management, College of Business Administration, University of Hawaii at Manoa, Honolulu, HI 96822.

REFERENCES

Adler, N. J., Brahm, R., & Graham, J. L. (1992). Strategy implementation: A comparison of face-to-face negotiations in the People's Republic of China and the United States. *Strategic Management Journal, 13,* 449-466.

Adler, N. J., Campbell, N., & Laurent, A. (1989). In search of appropriate methodology: From outside the People's Republic of China looking in. *Journal of International Business Studies, 20,* 61-74.

Aldrich, H., McKelvey, B., & Ulrich, D. (1984). Design strategy from a population perspective. *Journal of Management, 10,* 67-86.

Borys, B., Jemison, D. B. (1989). Hybrid arrangements as strategic alliances: Theoretical issues in organizational combinations. *Academy of Management Review, 14,* 234-249.

Boyd, B. K., Dess, G. G., & Rasheed, A. M. A. (1993). Divergence between archival and perceptual measures of the environment: Causes and consequences. *Academy of Management Review, 18*, 204-226.

Byrd, W. A. (1992). *Chinese industrial firms under reform.* Cambridge, UK: Cambridge University Press.

Byrd, W. A., & Lin, Q. (1989). *China's rural industry: Structure, development, and reform.* New York: Oxford University Press.

Byrd, W. A., & Zhu, N. (1989). Market interactions and industrial structure. In W. A. Byrd & Q. Lin (Eds.), *China's rural industry: Structure, development, and reform* (pp. 85-111). New York: Oxford University Press.

Chandler, G. N., & Hanks, S. H. (1993). Measuring the performance of emerging businesses: A validation study. *Journal of Business Venturing, 8,* 391-408.

Child, J. (1994). *Management in China during the age of reform.* Cambridge, UK: Cambridge University Press.

Dess, G., & Beard, D. (1984). Dimensions of organizational task environments. *Administrative Science Quarterly, 29,* 52-73.

Galbraith, C., & Schendel, D. (1983). An empirical analysis of strategy types. *Strategic Management Journal, 4,* 153-173.

Hambrick, D. C. (1983). Some tests of the effectiveness and functional attributes of Miles and Snow's strategic types. *Academy of Management Journal, 26,* 5-26.

Jefferson, G. H., & Rawski, T. G. (1993). *A theory of economic reform.* University of Pittsburgh, Department of Economics, Working Paper No. 273.

Jefferson, G. H., Rawski, T. G., & Zheng, Y. (1992). Growth, efficiency, and convergence in China's state and collective industry. *Economic Development & Cultural Change, 40,* 239-266.

Lawrence, P., & Lorsch, J. W. (1967). Differentiation and integration in complex organizations. *Administrative Science Quarterly, 12,* 1-47.

Lumpkin, G. T., & Dess, G. G. (1996). Clarifying the entrepreneurial orientation construct and linking it to performance. *Academy of Management Review, 21*(1), 135-172.

Luo, Y. (1995). Business strategy, market structure and performance of international joint ventures: The case of joint ventures in China. *Management International Review, 35,* 241-264.

Miles, R. E., & Snow, C. C. (1978). *Organizational strategy, structure and process.* New York: McGraw-Hill.

Miller, D. (1988). Relating Porter's business strategies to environment and structure: Analysis and performance implications. *Academy of Management Journal, 31,* 280-308.

Miller, D., & Friesen, P. H. (1983). Strategy-making and environment: The third link. *Strategic Management Journal, 4,* 221-235.

Naughton, B. (1992). *Growing out of the plan: Chinese economic reform, 1978-1993.* New York: Cambridge University Press.

Nee, V. (1992). Organizational dynamics of market transition: Hybrid forms, property rights, and mixed economy in China. *Administrative Science Quarterly, 37,* 1-27.

Nunnally, J. C. (1978). *Psychometric theory* (2nd ed.). New York: McGraw-Hill.

Peng, M. W., & Heath, P. S. (1996). The growth of the firm in planned economies in transition: Institutions, organizations, and strategic choice. *Academy of Management Review, 21*(2), 492-528.

Perkins, D. (1994). Completing China's move to the market. *Journal of Economic Perspective, 8*(2), 23-46.

Pfeffer, J., & Salancik, G. R. (1978). *The external control of organizations: A resource dependence perspective*. New York: Harper & Row.

Roman, Z. (1986). Competition and industrial organization in the centrally planned economies. In J. Stiglitz & G. F. Mathewson (Eds.), *New developments in the analysis of market structure*. London: Macmillan.

Shaver, K. G., & Scott, L. R. (1991). Persons, process, choice: The psychology of new venture creation. *Entrepreneurship: Theory and Practices, 16*, 23-45.

Shenkar, O., & Von Glinow, M. A. (1994). Paradoxes of organizational theory and research: Using the case of China to illustrate national contingency. *Management Science, 40*(1), 56-71.

The statistical yearbook of China. (1995). China: State Statistical Bureau.

Su, N. (1993). *China's industrial policy during economic system transformation.* Paper delivered to an international Conference on Macroeconomic Management, Dalian, China.

Tan, J. (1996). Characteristics of regulatory environment and impact on entrepreneurial strategic orientations: An empirical study of Chinese private entrepreneurs. *Academy of Management Best Papers Proceedings, 1996*, pp. 106-110.

Tan, J. J., & Litschert, R. J. (1994). Environment-strategy relationship and its performance implications: An empirical study of the Chinese electronics industry. *Strategic Management Journal, 15*(1), 1-20.

Thompson, J. D. (1967). *Organizations in action.* New York: McGraw-Hill.

Tung, R. L. (1982). *Chinese industrial society after Mao.* Lexington, MA: Lexington Books.

Venkatraman, N. (1989). Strategic orientation of business enterprises: The construct, dimensionality, and measurement. *Management Science, 35*, 942-962.

Vogel, E. F. (1989). *One step ahead of China: Guangdong under reform.* Cambridge, MA: Harvard University Press.

Weitzman, M. L., & Xu, C. (1993). *Chinese township and village enterprises as vaguely defined cooperatives.* Mimeograph, Harvard University, April.

Williamson, O. E. (1985). *The economic institutions of capitalism.* Cambridge, MA: Harvard University Press.

Williamson, O. E. (1991). Comparative economic organization: The analysis of discrete structural alternatives. *Administrative Science Quarterly, 36*, 269-296.

Xin, K., & Pearce, J. L. (1994). *Guanxi: Good connections as substitutes for institutional support.* Paper presented at the annual meeting of the Academy of Management, Dallas, TX.

chapter 2

Private Businesses in China

Emerging Environment and Managerial Behavior

CHUNG-MING LAU
HANG-YUE NGO
CLEMENT KONG-WING CHOW

Entrepreneurial activities and private businesses had long been suppressed by the Chinese government before the economic reform in 1978. They are now back in the focus of the national economic policy. In the early stage of economic reform, private businesses were planned by the Chinese government as supplementary to the state sector and thus played a marginal role in the socialist economy. The Chinese government's initial objectives for encouraging the development of the private sector were limited to solving the serious unemployment problem created by the return of intellectuals to the cities from rural areas, and to relieving the chronic shortages of goods and services in cities (Chow & Tsang, 1994; Tsang, 1994a). Since the reform, however, the private sector has been booming and contributing significantly to the national

AUTHORS' NOTE: Acknowledgments: The authors would like to thank the University Service Center of the Chinese University of Hong Kong for providing the data for the 1991 survey, and for financial support from the Strategic Research Grant of the Chinese University of Hong Kong. We are also indebted to Siu-yun Lui and Maud Lee for help in data analysis and to Michael Fung for his helpful comments.

TABLE 2.1 Development of the Private Sector Economy

	Private Sector	State-Owned	Collective-Owned
Employment (millions)			
1990	1.37	43.64	18.76
1994	6.07	43.69	16.04
Number of enterprises (thousands)			
1990	6,176.0	104.4	1,668.5
1994	8,007.4	102.2	1,863.0
Fixed assets investment (in billion yuan)			
1990	100.1	291.8	52.9
1994	197.1	932.3	266.5
1995	238.1	1,082.2	297.8
Gross output value at current price (in billion yuan)			
1988	128.5	1,035.1	658.7
1990	233.7	1,306.3	852.3
1994	1,927.4	2,620.1	3,143.4

SOURCE: *China Statistical Yearbook, 1995: A Statistical Survey of China, 1996.*

economy in various ways. Given this growth rate, new and small private enterprises have been seen as a source of wealth creation and employment generation in China (Chow & Fung, 1996). To encourage the further development of the private sector, the government removed the negative social stigma attached to entrepreneurs as the exploiters of the working class through the proper legislation of private businesses. The positive role of private business in China is reaffirmed (Zhang, 1995). Thus, "enterprising culture" or "entrepreneurial spirit," which is relatively new to the Chinese under the socialist system, has developed quickly in urban areas (Chang & MacMillan, 1991; Chow, 1995).

Although the private economy makes up only a relatively small percentage of the national economy, it has great social and economic impacts on the whole country. As depicted in Table 2.1, the growth rate of the private sector is much higher than that of the other two sectors in terms of number of persons employed and output value. In 1994, the gross output value of the private sector was already 25% of the total output value of all sectors combined, reaching 1,927.4 million yuan. In the first 10 months of 1996, for instance, the number of private businesses in Shanghai grew by 29% over the previous year, with employment totalling 760,000, approximately one sixth of the employment in state-owned enterprises. Because of the major reforms in industrial structure and the employment system of state-owned enterprises, more and more workers have to leave the state sector. Part of these slack human resources have been gradually taken up by the private sector. In view of the above, the contribution of the private sector to the future development of the economy has significant importance.

The objective of this chapter is to survey the development and contribution of private businesses to the Chinese economy. The focus is on the roles of private businesses in the future of economic development. A review and analysis of three national surveys of the private business sector conducted in 1991, 1993, and 1995 are presented. The survey data provide a recent and systematic understanding of the major features of private businesses now in China. The managerial implications of private sector businesses are also explored.

DEVELOPMENT OF THE PRIVATE SECTOR

The development of the private sector (often called the "individual economy" in Chinese literature) is relatively gradual and is determined by the overall "evolutionary" economic reform program. In the early stage of economic reform, serious unemployment was one of the immediate issues that needed to be solved by the reformers. Opening up the private sector, which had gone extinct after the first decade of communist rule, was a viable option for absorbing unemployed workers at that time. The Chinese economy was reformed not by mass privatization but by grafting a variety of new non-state-owned economic organizations—like international joint ventures, private enterprises, state and collective jointly owned enterprises—onto the national economy so as to revitalize the whole system.

Private businesses, being a part of the nonstate sector, were initially expected to provide goods and services that had been neglected by the state and collective sectors, and to stimulate the two sectors to achieve greater efficiency through competition (Tsang, 1994a). In the early 1980s, the only private businesses allowed were those operated by an individual or a family. These are commonly known as *geti hu* in Chinese, which literally means "individual households." *Geti hu* are governed by a set of regulations promulgated by the State Council in 1987, replacing the old ones promulgated in 1981, 1983, and 1984 (Chow & Tsang, 1994; Tsang, 1994a). A *geti hu* is allowed to hire only one or two helpers and several apprentices. The total number of employees may generally not exceed seven. The scope of business has been gradually expanded to include manufacturing, handicrafts, retailing, wholesaling, goods and passenger transportation, repairing, food preparation, construction, and tourist accommodation (Zhang, Zhao, Yang, & Tung, 1992). The scale of operation is, however, substantially constrained by the restriction on labor employment. Because of this employment restriction, *geti hu* concentrate on personal services and retail sectors. For instance, a small food stall and a street corner retail shop operated solely by the owners are typical examples of *geti hu*.

As the private economy grew at a rapid pace, the employment restriction seriously affected the expansion and development of successful entrepreneurs. The State Council therefore promulgated regulations governing *siying qiye* (private enterprises) in 1988. A *siying qiye* is defined as a profit-making economic entity that employs at least eight persons and whose assets are owned by private individual(s). It may be in the form of a sole proprietorship, a partnership, or a limited liability company. These private enterprises are also allowed to set up joint ventures with foreign corporations. The only difference between these two forms of private businesses is the employment size restriction.

These new regulations have provided more growth opportunities for private businesses because there is little restriction of employment and scope of business on *siying qiye*. Given the boom in the manufacturing sector in China, most *siying qiye* engaged in light manufacturing industries in rural areas instead of in the retail sector where *geti hu* concentrated (Wu, 1991). Compared with state-owned enterprises, which are constrained by numerous government rules and regulations employing inputs and distributing their outputs, *siying qiye* enjoy much more flexibility in operations and the process of decision making. They actually behave like most private companies in other market economies, because they can acquire resources in the markets—such as employing workers by paying market wages—and can compete with all other enterprises in the marketplace. In addition, unlike state-owned enterprises, most *siying qiye* are small- and medium-sized firms actively managed by their owners. In the absence of separation of ownership and management, the agency costs are obviously much smaller in *siying qiye*. Owners will find it easier and less costly to monitor productivity and reduce the problems of shirking that are common in state-owned enterprises (Byrd & Lin, 1990; Weitzman & Xu, 1993; Yusuf, 1993a, 1993b).

There was a change in the national economic policy in 1992 when the economy was booming too quickly. The growth of infrastructure and real estate industries and the major development of big firms were suppressed by the so-called macro adjustment and control policy: A policy of tighter control over large firms but looser rules for small firms was adopted. As a result, private business was regarded as the key area of development in many provinces at a regional level. Several measures were taken to facilitate small businesses. For example, support was given in the areas of employment, business operations, licensing, taxation, and financing. In 1993, the number of industries in which private businesses cannot engage was reduced from more than 50 to only 35. Private businesses were also allowed to venture into high-technology industries, such as chemical, medical, biotechnology, and environmental areas, in early 1994. This change of national policy provided more opportunities for private businesses to participate in various markets.

THE ENVIRONMENT OF PRIVATE BUSINESSES

Unlike state-owned and collective enterprises, private businesses do not enjoy any institutional privileges or special assistance from the central or local governments. For example, state-owned enterprises can easily obtain inputs like raw materials, energy, and loans from the central government at subsidized prices. Private businesses have to rely on the open market to obtain these inputs, and thus pay a higher price. Because state banks generally offer loans more on the basis of political considerations than economic ones, private businesses have difficulty obtaining funding or loans from the government-owned banking system (McKinnon, 1994; Walder, 1991). Although the government has worked hard to enact many new laws and regulations so as to make the business environment more investor-friendly and to keep up with the rapid changes in the national economy, local governments may implement the central government's policy half-heartedly, owing to their regional interests. The vague and confused legal system in all areas of business operations, like employment, taxation, and even distribution logistics, also offers much leeway for local government bureaucrats to harass private entrepreneurs; for example, they may collect additional license fees and surcharges from private businesses. As a result, cultivating *guanxi,* a Chinese term that means "close connections," with local Communist Party cadres is the key for private entrepreneurs to solving supply, marketing, and financing problems (Tsang, 1994b; Young, 1989).

The political environment is, in general, still uncertain, and policies are changing fast. Thus, private businesses tend to plan and operate on a short-term basis. Consequently, long-term growth potential is sacrificed for short-term profits. In addition, private entrepreneurs still fear the loss of their private property in case of political backlashes. They thus hesitate to invest too much in their businesses under the threat of the "fat pig policy," a situation in which the state waits until businesses have become sizeable and then takes them over (Young, 1991).

Competitive Environment

For the past 15 years, competition has been the centerpiece of Chinese economic reform. The entire decade of industrial reform can be understood as an effort to "marketize" the industrial sector. McMillan and Naughton (1992) summarized the Chinese reform process into the following three stages: (a) massive entry of nonstate enterprises; (b) dramatic increase in competition; and (c) improvement in the performance of state-owned enterprises resulting from state-imposed market-like incentives. A major threat to the existence of many private businesses is competition from state-owned and collective enterprises.

Collective Enterprises. The collective enterprises that evolved from the cooperatives during the central planning era are the major competitors of private businesses. According to Weitzman (1993), these collective enterprises are actually the driving force behind the rapid economic growth. They are now the second largest sector of the national economy (after the state sector), constituting more than 40% of total industrial output. In addition, town and village enterprises (TVEs), most of which are collective-owned, are growing very fast. Small enterprises, which are the majority of nonstate enterprises, are also proven to be growing faster than their larger counterparts when firm size is measured by employment and value-added (Chow & Fung, 1996). Ngo, Lau, and Chow (1994) also found that the collective enterprises in Hubei province are in general more effective than state-owned enterprises on several performance measures.

Similar to private businesses, the collectives are mostly small- or medium-sized enterprises and are in the manufacturing and service industries. These collective enterprises and TVEs have to rely on the market to obtain their input factors. In addition, their products are sold in the market rather than being allocated by state planning. Finally, they are ultimately responsible for their own profits and losses. As a result, they are very much "marketized" and contribute substantially to improving the competitiveness of the economy. With an operation similar to private businesses but with stronger connections to the central and provincial governments, these firms have increased competitiveness in the economy.

International Joint Ventures. Since the opening up of the Chinese economy in 1978, China has been one of the hottest choices for foreign direct investment. Joint ventures were the only form of foreign investment allowed by the Chinese government until the early 1990s. According to Beamish (1993), no country had more equity joint venture formation than China during the 1980s. Although international joint ventures in China have been developing rapidly, their proportion is relatively small compared with domestic enterprises, because of numerous problems encountered, for example, government restrictions, the long and complicated negotiation process (De Bruijn & Jia, 1993; Eiteman, 1990), cultural differences, and communication problems (Beamish, 1993). International joint ventures, however, are more competitive in terms of technical sophistication and efficiency in the market. For example, Chow and Fung (in press) found that the technical efficiency of joint ventures in Shanghai is in general higher in comparison with other types of ownership. The international joint ventures' superiority in management skills, technology, and technical efficiency exert tremendous pressure on domestic enterprises in the marketplace.

State-Owned Enterprises. Jefferson and Rawski (1994) and Singh, Ratha, and Xiao (1993) show that profitability within the state industry is the lowest in provinces where the output of nonstate industry has grown more rapidly. In addition, Singh et al. also found that large provincial shares of nonstate industrial output are associated with higher levels of total factor productivity in state industry. This result suggests strong growth of the nonstate sector, which is dominated by collective enterprises and TVEs, and hence squeezes profits and motivates greater efficiency in the state sector. Because state-owned enterprises face so much pressure from nonstate enterprises, reform programs are implemented to boost their productivity and operational efficiency (Groves, Hong, McMillan, & Naughton, 1994).

The reform measures that are implemented in response to the challenges posed by nonstate enterprises include the following changes: (a) A higher degree of autonomy is given to an enterprise's manager in input, output, and pricing decisions; (b) a manager's rewards are linked to the enterprise's performance; (c) a bonus out of retained earnings is given to workers; and (d) more contract workers are employed to replace permanent workers so as to add flexibility to the labor force in an enterprise (Groves et al., 1994). In a recent economic committee meeting of the State Council, the major economic task in 1997 was the continued reform of state-owned enterprises ("Central Economic Committee Meeting," 1996). Economic efficiency is the major target of change through reforming the industry structure, enterprise autonomy, and, most important, the leadership and senior management staff of these enterprises. All these measures will inevitably increase their competitive power in the market and exert pressure on private businesses.

The other threat to private business is the entry barriers in some industries and markets. In the past, when China was under a planned economy, each industry was commonly dominated by a few giant, state-owned enterprises. Both product and factor markets were controlled by a few giant enterprises that had significantly reduced the scope of competition. When reforms are carried out, these giant enterprises may continue to dominate the product markets. Collusion among the giant enterprises is also likely to happen, and they may implement some anticompetitive schemes and entry barriers. For example, vertical integration is common among large state-owned enterprises and can be a significant source of entry barrier. This is because vertical integration deprives new nonstate enterprises of the sources of necessary materials for production. Thus, private businesses have to look for niche markets and make use of their small-scale flexibility to compete with the large enterprises.

CHARACTERISTICS OF PRIVATE BUSINESSES

Information on private businesses in China is fragmented. Not many reliable, systematic, and large-scale data collections have been made. Like many other China studies, firm-level data are not readily available. Researchers have to rely on published government statistical yearbooks to gain insights into economic situations. Occasionally, data collected by regional and provincial statistics bureaus, foreign trade departments, and other government agencies are released to outsiders through personal connections. It is thus very difficult to gain a full picture of the Chinese economy and firm characteristics, especially under reform. Nevertheless, three significant national surveys on the private sector have been conducted by different parties. The findings of these surveys are either published or released to research institutions outside China. The following is an analysis of the three surveys and its selected findings.

The first survey was conducted in 1991 by the State Economic System Reform Committee and State Industry and Commerce Administration. The survey covered a sample of both *geti hu* and *siying qiye* enterprises in all provinces. However, the raw data were originally not electronically coded. With the help of the University Service Center of the Chinese University of Hong Kong, part of the raw data were encoded electronically and ready for data analysis. The data set reported below consisted of 8,785 firms from more than 20 major provinces and municipalities. These firms were randomly selected from the original sample.

The second and third surveys were conducted by the Project Group for Research on Private Entrepreneurs in Contemporary China in 1993 and 1995, respectively. The Project Group is made up of researchers at the Chinese Academy of Social Sciences. The sample consisted of private enterprises (*siying qiye*) only, in contrast to the 1991 survey, which covered both groups in the private economy. The 1993 survey covered a sample of 1,700 enterprises selected randomly from all provinces and municipalities, with the assistance of industrial and commercial associations. A total of 1,440 responses was obtained. The 1995 survey was very similar to the 1993 one. A total of 3,025 enterprises were invited to participate, and 2,564 enterprises responded. Because the two surveys were designed for a longitudinal study of private businesses in China, data were by and large comparable.

The 1991 Survey

The 1991 survey had information about 5,907 *geti hu* and 2,878 *siying qiye,* covering many major provinces and municipalities. For example, Shanxi, Shandong, Henan, Zhejiang, and Guangdong each had over 400 *geti hu* represented. Shanghai, Shandong, Liaoning, Zhejiang, and Guangdong each had over 200 *siying qiye* included in the analysis sample. The rest were from all other provinces.

The profile of the owners of these sample enterprises is shown in Table 2.2. Most of the owners of these two types of private businesses were males (73.2% in *geti hu* and 89.5% in *siying qiye*). They were relatively young, with a majority in the age group 31 to 40 in both categories (33% and 39.3%, respectively). The pattern of political party affiliation was also very similar for the two groups.

Most of the owners had a high school standard education (close to 50% across the two groups). Given the relatively low university graduate population in China, this percentage was considered high; thus the owners were of high educational attainment. Most *geti hu* owners (74%) had been peasants; the percentage of peasants among the *siying qiye* was only 45%. The mean sizes of these businesses, measured in number of employees, were 3.5 (*geti hu*) and 17.0 (*siying qiye*). Most of them (51.6%) had been in business for less than 3 years at the time of survey.

Table 2.3 presents the managerial characteristics of these private business owners. A majority of them did not have any managerial experience before starting the business. Since most of these enterprises were small, the lack of

TABLE 2.2 Profile of Private Business Owners in 1991

	Geti Hu (%)	Siying Qiye (%)	Total (%)
Sex			
Female	1,577 (26.8)	301 (10.5)	1,878 (21.5)
Male	4,301 (73.2)	2,560 (89.5)	6,861 (78.5)
Total	5,878 (100)	2,861 (100)	8,739 (100)
Age			
20 or under	123 (2.1)	18 (0.6)	141 (1.6)
21-30	1,673 (28.6)	453 (16.0)	2,126 (24.4)
31-40	1,933 (33.0)	1,116 (39.3)	3,049 (35.1)
41-50	1,239 (21.2)	818 (28.8)	2,057 (23.7)
51-60	649 (11.1)	325 (11.5)	974 (11.2)
Over 60	241 (4.1)	107 (3.8)	348 (4.0)
Total	5,858 (100)	2,837 (100)	8,695 (100)
Political background			
Non-Party member	3,556 (76.1)	1,688 (71.5)	5,244 (74.6)
Party member	1,117 (23.9)	672 (28.5)	1,789 (25.4)
Total	4,673 (100)	2,360 (100)	7,033 (100)
Education			
Illiterate	439 (7.4)	58 (2.0)	497 (5.7)
Primary school	1,569 (26.7)	460 (16.1)	2,029 (23.2)
Junior high	2,828 (48.1)	1,373 (48.0)	4,201 (48.0)
Senior high	1,018 (17.3)	817 (28.4)	1,835 (21.0)
College/university	30 (0.5)	152 (5.5)	182 (2.1)
Total	5,884 (100)	2,860 (100)	8,744 (100)
Previous employment status			
Peasant	4,131 (74.0)	1,197 (45.3)	5,328 (64.8)
Unemployed	1,181 (21.2)	680 (25.7)	1,861 (22.6)
State-owned enterprises	237 (4.2)	289 (10.9)	526 (6.4)
Non-state-owned enterprises	18 (0.3)	14 (0.5)	32 (0.4)
geti hu or siying qiye	12 (0.2)	464 (17.6)	476 (5.8)
Total	5,579 (100)	2,644 (100)	8,223 (100)

managerial experience in an entrepreneurial set-up should not have been a major problem.

When asked about the motive for starting the business, most of the *geti hu* owners chose "for living" (63%) as the major reason. The corresponding percentage answering "for living" in *siying qiye* was only 39.2%. For the *geti hu* owners, the next most popular reason was "for earning more money" (only 21.6%). The most popular reasons for the *siying qiye* owners were "for achievement" (48.3%), "for the good of kinsman" (21.7%), and "for earning more money"

TABLE 2.3 Managerial Characteristics of Private Business Owners in 1991

	Geti Hu (%)	Siying Qiye (%)	Total (%)
Management experience			
No	5,292 (89.6)	2,220(77.1)	7,512 (85.5)
Yes	615 (10.4)	658 (22.9)	1,273 (14.5)
Total	5,907 (100)	2,878 (100)	8,785 (100)
Motive[a]			
For living	3,547 (63.0)	1,092 (39.2)	4,639 (55.2)
Achievement	823 (14.6)	1,345 (48.3)	2,168 (25.8)
Earn more money	1,218 (21.6)	530 (19.0)	1,748 (20.8)
For kinsman	849 (15.1)	603 (21.7)	1,452 (17.3)
For children	612 (10.4)	298 (10.7)	910 (10.8)
Total	5,628 (100)	2,783 (100)	8,411 (100)

NOTE: a. Respondents were allowed to choose more than one reason. Percentages are in terms of the total number of owners in the respective samples.

(19.0%). Since *geti hu* were of relatively smaller scale (no more than seven employees, according to regulations) than *siying qiye,* and were often started as a result of unemployment, it was natural and consistent that the owners had economic reasons behind the new start-ups. In contrast, *siying qiye* owners were more achievement-oriented. Economic reasons ranked only second and fourth.

In addition, the survey also asked the private business owners to describe the difficulties in their operations. Table 2.4 presents the major issues reported. The owners were asked to rank order a number of issues. The left-hand ("Most Important") columns for both *geti hu* and *siying qiye* in Table 2.4 show the percentage of owners who ranked the issue in question as the most important one. The right-hand columns ("Combined") give the combined percentages of owners who ranked the issue as the first, second, or third most important issue. The rank order of both columns within each category of owners is very similar. Between the two groups of owners there are marked differences, however, namely on the issues of financing and bad debts. These two issues were not that important among the *geti hu* owners, but were very critical for *siying qiye* owners.

When asked about the future, the owners listed a number of future plans (see Table 2.5). Most of the *geti hu* owners had no intention of changing the status quo, but more than half of *siying qiye* owners expressed the need for a change. Percentage-wise, the growth intentions of *siying qiye* owners were much higher. They also had a stronger incentive to cooperate with other enterprises and even with foreign firms. This was perhaps due to the fact that they had a larger operation and thus the capability to work with other firms.

TABLE 2.4 Difficulties Perceived by Private Business Owners in 1991

Issue	Geti Hu		Siying Qiye	
	Most Important (%)	Combined (%)	Most Important (%)	Combined (%)
Selling	20.7	40.6	17.3	41.6
Competition	11.9	36.5	5.9	22.9
Distribution channel	10.2	13.9	10.8	15.5
Heavy taxation	8.6	27.0	4.2	17.6
Bad debts	9.5	22.4	18.0	41.2
Financing	6.1	19.1	15.6	43.4

NOTE: All numbers are percentages of enterprises responding in each category. Some minor issues were not reported.

The 1993 and 1995 Surveys

The findings of the 1993 and 1995 surveys are analyzed together because they are of a similar nature and therefore comparable. The findings were based on reports published in Dai (1996) and Project Group (1995a, 1995b, 1996). The 1993 survey was based on data reported as of the end of 1992, and the 1995 survey was based on data reported at the end of 1994.

The two surveys were focused on *siying qiye* only. No *geti hu* were included in these surveys. Similar to the 1991 survey, most of the *siying qiye* owners were male (over 90%). The average age was 42.9 in the 1993 survey, and a majority

TABLE 2.5 Future Plans of Private Business Owners in 1991

	Geti Hu (%)	Siying Qiye (%)
Remain unchanged	69.4	47.2
Expand operation	16.8	34.1
Downsize operation	4.9	6.2
Change business direction	4.7	7.6
Close business	3.6	3.3
Work with state- or collective-enterprises	2.0	8.4
Horizontal merger	1.4	11.0
Cooperation with foreign company	0.3	8.4

NOTE: All numbers are percentage of enterprises responding in each category. Respondents were allowed to choose more than one item.

TABLE 2.6 Employment Characteristics of *Siying Qiye* in 1993 and 1995

	1993	*1995*
Mean number of employees	31	38
Median number of employees in selected industries		
Construction	40	47.6
Transportation	38	30.0
Food service	17	19.5
Manufacturing	40	51.2
Composition (%)		
Managers	6.6	8.9
Technicians	4.1	8.8
Front-line workers	89.3	82.3

of the 1995 survey owners were in the 41 to 45 age group (21.9%). The educational attainment of the owners was higher than in 1991, with 72% of them having completed junior or senior high school in 1993, and 73% in 1995. College- and postgraduate-trained owners accounted for 17.2% in 1993 and 18.4% in 1995.

In terms of form of business, as a whole, most were sole proprietorships. The percentages of sole proprietorships nationwide were 63.8% in 1993 and 55.8% in 1995. The percentages of partnerships and limited companies were very close in 1993, 16.0% and 16.5%, respectively. However, there was a higher percentage of limited companies in the 1995 survey, up to 28.5%. The distribution ratio varied among different parts of the country. For instance, limited companies accounted for more than 50% of those operating in major cities.

In terms of employees, Table 2.6 compares the figures of the 1993 and 1995 surveys. The mean numbers of employees for both periods were not very different; 31 in 1993 and 38 in 1995. The median number of employees in some selected industries (only those with the same classifications in the two surveys were listed) were roughly the same, with higher numbers in manufacturing and construction in 1995. In terms of the relative composition of the workforce, workers remained the major category, over 80%. However, the percentage of technicians in 1995 was double that of 1993, though the base number was small.

The difficulties that faced owners in 1993 and 1995 are listed in Table 2.7. A major difference between the 1993 and the 1995 surveys was the problem of selling. In 1993, only 27% of the respondents indicated that selling was an issue, while in 1995, over 45% of the respondents cited selling as a critical issue. In fact, this is the most problematic issue among those listed. The proportion of owners having difficulties in other areas remained roughly the same in both years. To a certain extent, this was due to the competition in the market and to immature marketing and distribution channels, as well. The 1995 survey asked about the reason(s) behind those difficulties. Market competition was clearly the most significant reason for explaining the selling problem. The breakdown of the reasons attributed by the owners revealed different aspects of the problems facing them. For instance, the problems of not enough operation space and financing were related to policy restrictions. Bureaucratic barriers were cited as the major reason for not enough electricity for operations and for transportation difficulties. Overall, market competition was the most significant reason perceived by these owners.

MANAGERIAL ISSUES

As suggested by the three surveys, a number of difficulties are commonly found in private businesses. Some of them are environmental and contextual issues and some are organizational and management issues. These issues affect the current operations and future growth of businesses. In order to remain in business, these enterprises have to develop strategies to cope with these difficulties. Some of these strategies have proven to be quite effective (Young, 1995).

Macro Environmental Issues

The first issue faced by private businesses is changing government policy. The role of private business was not formalized until 1988, and some of the new policies are on a trial basis, which also brings about confusion and uncertainties. Although the overall trend is toward liberalization, private businesses frequently face political risk. In fact, private businesses often grow beyond the bounds allowed by state regulations. Because local officials have the power to close down private firms for regulatory violations, they sometimes abuse their political power to gain benefits for themselves. They may, for example, extract economic rents from new private firms by invoking the threat of legal or policy violations. Even worse, they have harassed or closed private businesses when political winds turned in an anti-reform direction (Young, 1995).

To minimize these uncertainties, private business associations have been formed, notably the Self-Employed Laborers' Association (consisting mainly of

TABLE 2.7 Difficulties Facing *Siying Qiye* Owners in 1993 and 1995

| | Major Difficulties | | Reasons for Difficulties Faced in 1995 | | | | |
	1993	1995	Policy Restriction (%)	Market Competition (%)	Bureaucratic Barrier (%)	Firm-Specific Reason (%)	Other (%)
Operation space	44.9	40.7	42.8	8.0	19.2	24.5	5.4
Selling	27	45.5	11.2	76.0	3.8	5.7	3.3
Purchasing raw materials	25	28.5	20.9	47.4	5.0	18.1	8.7
Recruiting technical personnel	23.6	25.6	27.4	34.4	1.7	28.5	8.0
Transportation	18.5	16.2	22.8	11.7	33.2	21.8	10.4
Electricity	19.8	26.6	27.4	7.2	34.6	8.2	22.5
Recruiting managerial personnel	n/a	23.3	28.7	28.7	1.3	32.1	9.3
Financing	n/a	70.5	67.2	6.9	7.7	12.8	5.4

NOTE: All are percentages of respondents in respective surveys.
n/a = data not available.

geti hu) and the Industrial and Commercial Federation (consisting largely of *siying qiye*). The local branches of these associations represent their members and coordinate with local officials to formulate guidelines to reduce taxation, liberalize credit, and loosen restrictions on private business (Nevitt, 1996). These associations also provide legal services to their members. This kind of organizational linkage or alliance is a critical move to strengthen members' bargaining power. The trend of horizontal mergers and cooperation with state-owned and collective enterprises is also a good way to increase the buffer and reduce resource dependence.

Competition

Market force is both a major help and a major threat to private businesses. It is because of the move to a market-based economy that these enterprises can exist and flourish, but at the same time, market competition forces enterprises to pursue efficiency and effectiveness. Inefficient enterprises will be driven out of the market very quickly. Private businesses have to look for competitive edges in order to survive and grow.

Most enterprises (especially *geti hu*) usually have all of their production processes within a single plant, rather than specializing in a certain part of the production process. With a small scale of production, high-quality parts and an economy of scale are hard to achieve (Shen, 1993). As a result, these small enterprises can hardly upgrade their skills and technology because they have over-reached their production base. They may waste their limited resources in developing production procedures that do not give them any advantages.

Given the limited resources of any small- and medium-sized business, it is not efficient for these enterprises to conduct all production processes under one roof. Thus, it is important for the enterprises to search for and develop their competitive advantages and to specialize in them. One possible development direction is to acquire an entrepreneurial and innovative orientation. New product design and new product processes could be competitive advantages for private and small businesses. In addition, because large firms are not able to meet all the needs of a total market, niche markets could be identified. Private enterprises have the flexibility to meet the needs of many niche markets.

Resources

Private businesses are faced with a scarcity of resources. Operating within a socialist economy, in which many critical inputs are allocated only to state enterprises, private businesses often face severe supply shortages. In order to avoid production stoppage caused by a lack of scarce materials, some private businesses rely on black markets. Another common strategy is to build up *guanxi* (close connections) with the state bureau and large enterprises so as to secure supplies and to extend distribution networks (Siu, 1992).

One bottleneck for private economic activity is the limited access to basic services such as electricity, water, gas, and telephones (Nevitt, 1996). This was also confirmed by the three surveys. Even today, these services are administratively allocated. The lack of power-generation facilities in remote and rural areas is also critical to the development of enterprises. Because of their lack of formal association with state planning and administrative structures, private enterprises in urban areas have to rely on special pleading to gain access to these services, especially when they plan to expand their activities (Nevitt, 1996).

Insufficient capital poses another difficulty for private businesses. It is well documented that the reform of the financial system lags far behind reforms in other economic areas. The lending operations of banks are governed more by administrative directive than by business principles. The current policy is biased toward state enterprises, and private businesses thus have great difficulties in obtaining funds from banks. The 1995 survey indicated that the three major sources of initial business capital for private enterprises are personal savings, loans from friends or relatives, and personal loans from other people. Only 11.8% reported that their primary source of capital came from the banking system. Even for established private enterprises, the percentage of capital borrowed from banks remained low.

Thus, a major managerial problem facing private businesses is exploring means to acquire enough resources to maintain the operation. Establishing *guanxi* with important officials and suppliers is a key step in securing resources. Further, different forms of linkages among the enterprises, and even cooperation with state-owned enterprises, are also important.

Management Structure and Governance

As revealed by the 1995 survey, the organizational structure of private businesses is significantly different from that of state-owned enterprises. First, private businesses have a strong overlap of ownership and management. Most of the owners maintain tight control over their businesses, primarily through direct supervision. Only 3.1% are not involved in the management of their firm. For large private businesses, "management committees" and boards of directors have been set up to make long-range plans and major policies. It was reported in the 1995 survey that slightly more than 30% of the private enterprises have their own board of directors. Since the businesses are largely small-scale operations, this owner-management overlap is not a critical issue. As the businesses grow, however, especially in the case of partnerships or limited companies in *siying qiye,* a separation of ownership and management is necessary.

In decision making, private enterprises are characterized by a high centralization of power. In sole proprietorships, the power rests in the hands of the founder-owner. The 1995 survey reports that 95% of sole proprietors make decisions themselves or together with their managerial staff. Some of the managerial staff are indeed family members of the owner. In the case of partnerships and limited companies, most of the major decisions are discussed and made by the board of directors, over which the chief owner has a very strong influence. It is further observed that the greater the firm size, the wider will be the dispersion of power. This is basically consistent with the prediction of conventional organization theory, which suggests the needs for delegation and specialization for large firms. Moreover, for general management issues such as wage determination and personnel matters, managerial staff often have greater power in making the decisions. This kind of decision making presents the same governance problem faced by large corporations in the West.

This governance problem is twofold. The first problem is with the owner and chief officer in charge of operation and management, and the second is between the chief manager and the other senior management staff. When ownership and management are separate, the owners have to ascertain that chief managers are running the business with the interests of the owners in mind. However, managers have self-interests, too. With an emphasis on *guanxi* and linkages in developing a competitive edge, opportunistic behavior will likely take place. The solution lies in aligning the organization's interests with individual interests. This in turn will depend both on having an appropriate monitoring and control system, and on the reward system. Nevertheless, the control system cannot be at the expense of the flexibility inherent in private businesses and small firms.

Leadership and Human Resources

Other characteristics of management in private businesses are nepotism and favoritism, particularly in staff selection. It is reported that more than one third of workers in these firms were recruited through *guanxi*. In particular, about 30% of managerial staff have some kind of kinsman or family relationship with the owner. For that reason, a paternalistic style of leadership, which also reflects the influence of traditional Chinese culture, is widely adopted in private businesses.

This leadership style can create hazards in many situations. If, for instance, an incompetent family member is in charge of a major operation, or a strategy or a product is developed because it is the idea of an important family member, the result can be inefficiency and ineffective management of the enterprise. At the same time, the reputation of the founder may be harmed because of reliance on family members who have poor qualifications or competencies. However, the traditional Chinese culture is not overly critical of employing relatives in key positions. Thus, facing a social and economic dilemma, private enterprise owners may have difficulty finding competent family members to run the business. The tension grows stronger when the business becomes larger.

Concerning human resource management, private enterprises in general offer higher remuneration to workers than state-owned enterprises. This is because the private enterprises cannot provide high-cost fringe benefits such as housing, pensions, and social insurance (Ngo & Ng, 1996). However, workers in these firms are often required to work harder and longer. For example, in 1995, only 46% of private businesses offered medical insurance to workers, which is much lower than the national standards. Thus, the only motivation for people to join the business is the high wages they can earn, normally due to hard work. The higher monetary return is reinforced by the opportunity of better career advancement prospects in private businesses.

On the other hand, private enterprises have a higher proportion of workers under the "labor contract system" than the state- and collective-owned enterprises do (*China Labour Statistical Yearbook*, 1995). Under this employment system, labor and management are free to sign fixed-term contracts that stipulate their rights, duties, and benefits at work. Based on the performance of workers, the employment contracts can be terminated or renewed upon expiration. However, the system has been criticized on the grounds that due to the low unionization rate in the private sector, workers' rights are not sufficiently protected and workers are exploited on some occasions. The labor contract system allows enterprises to acquire needed human resources, but at the same time creates uncertainties for enterprise owners. This is because of employment issues and labor disputes arising from private employment (Ngo & Ng, 1996). The inefficient and incomplete labor laws in China also provide insufficient protection to employers.

The imperfect labor market is another issue. The Chinese labor market is characterized by imperfect information, and there is a limited supply of qualified technical and managerial staff. Private enterprises have difficulties attracting high-calibre people, especially in new start-ups. With the reform going on in the state sector, however, more and more technicians and managers are leaving the giant enterprises. As shown in the 1995 survey, private businesses employed a higher proportion of managerial and technical staff than before. Such an increase is expected to have a positive effect on the overall efficiency and competitiveness of private enterprises.

CONCLUSION

As China moves away from a rigid centrally planned economy through a series of market reforms, private enterprises are freer to operate throughout the country. With the relaxation of control, they can now enter some industries that were restricted in the past. In addition, private businesses have also benefited from a number of government measures. For example, when the government relaxed the price of many "small commodities" (household items), new markets became available to private commodity producers. They took advantage of this opportunity and expanded their scale of operations (Hodder, 1994). For that reason, the growth of private enterprises has been particularly impressive in light industrial sectors, in which economies of scale are not so important and the product market is competitive.

In addition, a higher rate of growth has been observed in inner provinces during past years, as shown in the 1995 survey. In order to correct the imbalance of development across regions, the Chinese government has encouraged the expansion of private enterprises in less-developed provinces. These inner and western provincial governments also offer favorable credit and taxation measures to stimulate private investment. With all these opportunities, it is expected that private businesses will play a critical role in the national economy in the coming decades.

In terms of total capital and output values within the private sector, *siying qiye* have surpassed *geti hu* as the dominant form of business. The successful private enterprises that have accumulated large amounts of capital and business experience strive to enlarge their scale of operation and to develop new technology. Another move is toward diversifying investments into different lines of business. According to the 1995 survey, 75% of private enterprises had enlarged or changed their initial scope of business. Some have even engaged in vertical integration. For example, it has been reported that in some rural areas private enterprises have established their own wholesale and retail trading networks (Gold, 1990) and that others have formed alliances or joint ownership with other enterprises (*Yearbook of the Huaren Economy,* 1995).

Thus, the initial stage of development has passed and large private corporations have emerged. These large private businesses are those that operate efficiently and in the right strategic directions. They are the key competitors of many state-owned firms. Their advantages are high adaptability and market sensitivity. With their flexibility in developing products to meet market needs, they are in a better position to grow and to contribute to societal needs. Yet with the rigorous reform undertaken by state-owned enterprises, they also face keen competition. As the economy continues to change toward a market orientation, both private and state enterprises face the same competitive environment. They each have to search for their own competitive edges and competencies.

In terms of internal management, many successful private businesses have to deal with the problems associated with the transition from small to large firms. The management of a small start-up is very different from that of a large corporation; it must deal with striving to streamline the decision-making process, the extent of decentralization, the organizing of different functions, and formulating growth strategies. In addition, with more people employed, interpersonal and employee relationships become more apparent. Human resource issues such as selection, promotion, and succession of both senior and middle management are eminent. These private business owners have to learn from the success stories of firms in the West and Hong Kong and adapt them to the Chinese context. The management challenges facing them are huge and remain to be explored and overcome.

REFERENCES

Beamish, P. W. (1993). The characteristics of joint ventures in the People's Republic of China. *Journal of International Marketing, 1,* 29-48.

Byrd, W. A., & Lin, Q. (1989). *China's rural industry: Structure, development, and reform.* New York: Oxford University Press.

Central economic committee meeting. (1996, November 25). *Wen Wei Po.* (newspaper, in Chinese)

Chang, W., & MacMillan, I. C. (1991). A review of entrepreneurial development in the People's Republic of China. *Journal of Business Venturing, 9,* 375-379.

China Labour Statistical Yearbook. (1995). Beijing: China Statistical Publishing House. (in Chinese)

Chow, C. K. W. (1995). Evaluating small business development in China's retail sector: An empirical analysis. *Journal of Small Business Management, 33*(1), 87-92.

Chow, C. K. W., & Fung, M. K. Y. (1996). Firm dynamics and industrialization in the Chinese economy in transition: Implications for small business policy. *Journal of Business Venturing, 11*(6), 489-505.

Chow, C. K. W., & Fung, M. K. Y. (in press). Firm size and performance of manufacturing enterprises in the People's Republic of China: The case of Shanghai's manufacturing industries. *Small Business Economics.*

Chow, K. W., & Tsang, W. K. (1994). Entrepreneurship in China: Development, functions and problems. *The International Small Business Journal, 23,* 63-77.

Dai, J. Z. (1996). A study of private enterprises and private enterprise owners in Mainland China. In S. K. Lau, P. S. Wan, M. K. Li, & S. L. Wong (Eds.), *New frontiers of social indicators research in Chinese societies* (pp. 493-526). Hong Kong: Hong Kong Asia-Pacific Research Institute.

De Bruijn, E. J., & Jia, X.-F. (1993). Transferring technology to China by means of joint ventures. *Research & Technology Management, 36,* 17-22.

Eiteman, D. K. (1990). American executives' perceptions of negotiating joint ventures with the People's Republic of China: Lessons learned. *Columbia Journal of World Business, 25,* 59-67.

Gold, T. B. (1990). Urban private business and social change. In D. Davis & E. F. Vogel (Eds.), *Chinese society on the eve of Tiananmen: The impact of reform* (pp. 157-178). Cambridge, MA: Harvard University Press.

Groves, T., Hong, Y., McMillan, J., & Naughton, B. (1994). Autonomy and incentives in Chinese state enterprises. *Quarterly Journal of Economics, 109,* 183-209.

Hodder, R. (1994). State, collective and private industry in China's evolving economy. In D. Dwyer (Ed.), *China: The next decades.* Essex, UK: Longman.

Jefferson, G. H., & Rawski, T. G. (1994). Enterprise reform in Chinese industry. *Journal of Economic Perspectives, 8*(2), 47-70.

McKinnon, R. I. (1994). Financial growth and macroeconomic stability in China, 1978-1992: Implications for Russia and other transitional economies. *Journal of Comparative Economics, 18*(3), 438-469.

McMillan, J., & Naughton, B. (1992). How to reform a planned economy: Lessons from China. *Oxford Review of Economic Policy, 8,* 130-143.

Nevitt, C. E. (1996). Private business associations in China: Evidence of civil society or local state power. *The China Journal, 36,* 25-43.

Ngo, H. Y., Lau, C. M., & Chow, L. K. (1994). Economic reform and enterprise effectiveness: The experience of Hubei province. *Hong Kong Journal of Business Management, 12,* 57-70.

Ngo, H. Y., & Ng, I. (1996). *One country, two systems of industrial relations? A comparison of China and Hong Kong.* Unpublished manuscript, Department of Management, Chinese University of Hong Kong.

Project Group for Research on Private Entrepreneurs in Contemporary China. (1995a, Summer). The group characteristics of the owners of private businesses in China. *Social Sciences in China,* pp. 61-69.

Project Group for Research on Private Entrepreneurs in Contemporary China. (1995b, Autumn). The operational status of private businesses in China. *Social Sciences in China,* pp. 5-14.

Project Group for Research on Private Entrepreneurs in Contemporary China. (1996). Data and analysis of the second national survey of private businesses in China 1995. In *Yearbook of private business economy 1996* (pp. 142-176). Beijing: China Industrial and Commercial Association. (in Chinese)

Shen, Y. L. (1993). *A study on the development strategies of the industrial structure of Shanghai.* Shanghai: Fudan University Press. (in Chinese)

Singh, I., Ratha, D., & Xiao, G. (1993). *Non-state enterprises as an engine of growth: An analysis of provincial industrial growth in post-reform China.* Working Paper, Transition and Macro Adjustment Division, World Bank.

Siu, W. S. (1992). Corporate entrepreneurs in the People's Republic of China: Problems encountered and respective solutions. *International Small Business Journal, 10*(4), 26-33.

A statistical survey of China. (1996). Beijing: China Statistical Publishing House. (in Chinese)

Tsang, E. W. K. (1994a). Ideology, policy and the private entrepreneur in China. *Journal of Asian Business, 10*(2), 1-19.

Tsang, E. W. K. (1994b). Threats and opportunities faced by private businesses in China. *Journal of Business Venturing, 9,* 451-458.

Walder, A. G. (1991). Local bargaining relationships and urban industrial finance. In K. Lieberthal & D. M. Lampton (Eds.), *Bureaucracy and policymaking in post-Mao China.* Berkeley: University of California Press.

Weitzman, M. L. (1993). Economic transition: Can theory help? *European Economic Review, 37,* 549-555.

Weitzman, M. L., & Xu, C. (1993). *Chinese township and village enterprises as vaguely defined cooperatives.* Mimeograph, Harvard University, April.

Wu, Y. (1991). Investigation on private business in Baodin Area. *Reform, 5,* 165-170.

Yearbook of the Huaren economy. (1995). Beijing: Chinese Academy of Social Sciences Press. (in Chinese)

Young, S. (1989). Policy, practice and the private sector in China. *Australian Journal of Chinese Affairs, 21,* 57-80.

Young, S. (1991). Wealth but not security: Attitude towards private businesses in China in the 1990s. *Australian Journal of Chinese Affairs, 25,* 115-137.

Young, S. (1995). *Private business and economic reform in China.* Armonk, NY: M. E. Sharpe.

Yusuf, S. (1993a). *Property rights and non-state sector development in China.* Unpublished manuscript, World Bank, Washington, D.C.

Yusuf, S. (1993b). *The rise of China's non-state sector.* Unpublished manuscript, World Bank, Washington, D.C.

Zhang, H. Y. (1995, Winter). The position of the private entrepreneur stratum in China's social structure. *Social Sciences in China,* pp. 29-36.

Zhang, X. D., Zhao, L. X., Yang, F. G., & Tung, C. G. (Eds.). (1992). *Policy and law advice of individual and private business.* Beijing: China Legal System Press. (in Chinese)

chapter 3

Environment-Strategy Configurations Among Ownership Types

J. JUSTIN TAN

Central to strategic management research are two assumptions pertaining to the role of strategic choice and environmental forces: whether strategic choice or environmental forces determine a firm's survival and success, and whether these two aspects are mutually exclusive (Astley & Van de Ven, 1983; Hrebiniak & Joyce, 1985). With regard to the first issue, representing the two extreme views are strategic choice (Child, 1972) and population ecology (Hannan & Freeman, 1989). The strategic choice view essentially argues that the effectiveness of organizational adaptation hinges on the dominant coalition's perceptions of environmental conditions and the decisions it makes concerning how the organization will cope with these conditions. The premises of this perspective are that strategy formation should be a controlled, conscious process of thought, and responsibility for that control and consciousness must rest with the top management team (e.g., Andrews, 1971).

Contrary to the strategic choice view, the population ecology view asserts that it is not realistic for management to carefully design and successfully implement adaptations to environmental change, because (a) members of an organization have diverse interests; (b) the connection between means and ends is uncertain; (c) the organization is also constrained by its existing form and scarce resources; and because of (d) bounded rationality and other internal and external constraints (Hannan & Freeman, 1989). These constraints limit choices available to management. The major implication of this perspective is that within a given population of organizations, some will by chance develop strategies more compatible with their existing and emerging environmental conditions than will their counterparts. Apparently, strategic choice and population ecology views have been considered as two mutually exclusive and competing explanations of organizational adaptations. Yet, regardless of these assumptions, a central issue common to both perspectives is the appropriate associations between the environment and strategy and their impact on performance (e.g., Lawless & Finch, 1989; Miller & Friesen, 1983).

In their attempt to reconcile strategic choice and population ecology views, Hrebiniak and Joyce (1985) presented a "revolutionary" (Lawless & Finch, 1989, p. 352) model that viewed choice and determinism as two aspects that can coexist at the two extremes of their respective continuum. Based on the interaction of the degrees of choice and determinism, a typology of organizational adaptation has been developed. The four scenarios described by these authors highlight four types of organizations that operate under different environmental attributes, and consequently develop distinct strategic profiles appropriate for each environmental condition. At one extreme of the continuum, environmental determinism is low and strategic choice is high. This group of organizations can adapt to environmental changes by carefully designing organization strategies. Their strategic orientations are characterized as aggressive and proactive. For firms operating under high environmental determinism and low strategic choice, strategic orientations are generally conservative, and innovation is low due to external constraints. Hrebiniak and Joyce also identified two other scenarios under which organizations face (a) high determinism and high strategic choice, or (b) low determinism and low strategic choice. Organizations in the former condition may be subject to greater environmental determinism, but at the same time they can exercise considerable strategic choice. For the last group of firms, those facing low determinism and low strategic choice, strategic adaptation is incremental and takes place by chance. The situation may exist where the firm faces external opportunities but lacks the internal strengths to capitalize on them.

Given these circumstances, it remains to be answered whether organizations operating under a certain environment adopt a consistent pattern of strategy configurations, and whether these configurations vary among organizations subject to different environmental constraints. In resolving these remaining issues, former centrally planned economies undergoing transition toward market-driven systems warrant particular attention. In those newly reformed centrally planned economies, such as the People's Republic of China (PRC) and Eastern

European countries, the shifts from central planning to more market-based economies around the world have typically not been as abrupt as industry deregulation, which has been the subject of voluminous studies. These changes are more likely to occur in stages, with certain segments undergoing transition while others are not (Tan & Litschert, 1994). In addition, the transition has given birth to a new diversity in organizational forms and a plurality of property ownership types, and has turned transition economies such as those of the PRC, the former Soviet Union, and other Eastern European countries that were previously dominated by state-owned enterprises into ones in which different organizational forms, including state-owned, collectively owned, private, foreign joint venture, and completely foreign-owned enterprises, coexist and compete (Peng, 1994). Firms exhibiting different ownership types are subject to different environmental constraints and vary significantly in their access to resources (Shenkar & von Glinow, 1994) and their ability to exercise strategic choice. Following the environment-strategy-performance paradigm (Venkatraman & Prescott, 1990), one would logically expect these firms to adopt different strategic postures that are consistent with their respective environments in order to achieve a fit, which is crucial for their survival and success. The existence of different environments thus offers an ideal context to test the Hrebiniak and Joyce (1985) framework on the environment-strategy relation.

In this chapter, I will examine the Hrebiniak and Joyce model in a transition economy among firms operating under different environmental constraints as a consequence of their differing ownership types. I will discuss the environment-strategy configurations among different ownership types from the strategic group perspective. In the following sections, I will first review literature regarding ownership, environmental constraints and firm strategic adaptations, and strategic group. I will then examine the environments under which four types of firms currently operate in the PRC and their respective decision-making characteristics. Following this discussion, I will introduce some propositions that are empirically testable.

THEORETICAL BACKGROUND

Ownership Type

Gedajlovic (1993) posits that ownership is a multidimensional concept. One dimension is based on the dispersion of stock ownership and represents a source of power that can be used to support or oppose management depending on how it is concentrated. McEachern (1975) has identified three forms of concentration: (a) owner managed, those for which stock ownership is concentrated among its managers; (b) management controlled, those for which stock ownership is dispersed among many shareholders; and (c) externally controlled, those for which stock ownership is concentrated among a few individuals who do not manage the firm.

However, the pattern of ownership and control does not completely explain the impact of ownership on strategic behavior. For instance, it does not adequately explain the impact of foreign and government ownership on financial performance (Gedajlovic, 1993). In this case, ownership influences organization governance structure, which in turn impacts exchange relationships with various environmental domains. Mascarenhas (1989) notes that an understanding of the relationship between ownership types and domain dimensions can help to reveal the underlying logic for an organization's activities and therefore can contribute to organization members' evaluations of business-level strategies.

In order to examine ownership as a contextual variable, a research setting characterized by a mixed economy composed of heterogeneous ownership types is necessary. Economic reform in China has turned an economy that was previously dominated by state-owned enterprises into one in which different organizational forms, including state-owned, collectively owned, private, and foreign joint ventures coexist and compete (Peng, 1994; Tan & Li, 1996). For instance, in the PRC, the percentage of tax revenue contributed by the state enterprises dropped from more than 90% in the late 1970s to less than 40% in the early 1990s, and even the state-controlled sectors are increasingly influenced by market forces ("When China Wakes," 1992). Lachman (1985) points out that most studies reporting differences in ownership types compared organizations with radically different task environments. In order to better control for multiple environmental variables, Shenkar and von Glinow (1994) recommend in their research of management issues in China that researchers compare "partially similar cases" (pp. 69). China's mixed economy not only offers such a setting, but heterogeneous ownership types can be found among firms in a single industry. These firms normally operate in a common task environment that limits the need to account for industry effects.

China's economic reform process officially began with the Communist Party Plenum of December, 1978; the changes that have taken place since then have been dramatic, exceeding the expectations of the most optimistic China watchers. Prior to the economic reform, the Chinese economy was basically self-sufficient, with state enterprises contributing more than 90% of tax revenue. During the first 10 years of the 1978 open-door policy, China's foreign trade rose by an impressive 300%, an unparalleled increase for any centrally planned economy and for most emerging economies of the world. During the same period, foreign investment reached more than 20 billion U.S. dollars, increasing at an average annual rate of about 30%. Although expectations were shattered by the "June Fourth Incident" in 1989, both trade and investment have continued to grow rapidly since 1989, with investment reaching more than U.S.\$6 billion in 1989 and 1990. In the first 9 months of 1994, foreign investments in China grew by 49%, compared with the same period the year before, and the level of foreign investment climbed to 22.72 billion U.S. dollars.

Meanwhile, collective and privately owned enterprises have also grown with astounding speed. In 1991, joint ventures and foreign subsidiaries, collective enterprises, and private enterprises together contributed 63% of tax revenue, compared to the state-owned enterprises' 37%, down from more than 90% 10 years ago. In the booming coastal provinces, such as Guangdong, collective and private enterprises produced 43% of the total industrial output in 1986 (Vogel, 1989, p. 456). As a result, over 50% of the Chinese state budget is now in the hands of officials in the provinces, despite efforts of the central government to recentralize fiscal control (Nee, 1992). Thus, the transition from a centrally planned economy toward a market economy, in conjunction with the existence of four ownership types in a single industry, offers a unique opportunity to investigate the effect of ownership on variables subject to managerial decision.

Ownership type represents a corporate-level decision regarding domain definition in China because firms can choose their ownership types, at least collective and private firms. For instance, some private firms choose to be classified as collective enterprises to gain legitimacy or resources, and both collective and private firms can team up with a foreign investor to become a joint venture. My focus in this chapter, however, is on the effect of ownership type on the environment-strategy configurations. Tan and Litschert (1994) found that firms in the Chinese electronics industry utilized distinctive business-level strategies that were significantly related to perceived environments. However, it was not determined whether or not environment-strategy configurations varied across ownership types. This setting thus offers an opportunity to examine the effects of four distinct ownership types on these configurations. The ownership types found in the setting are state owned, collectively owned, privately owned, and joint venture enterprises.

Environmental Constraints
and Strategic Adaptations

The environment is viewed as a multidimensional construct. Briefly, the environment has been conceptualized in terms of two distinct perspectives. The first perspective views the environment as a source of information (Duncan, 1972; Lawrence & Lorsch, 1967; Scott, 1987; Tung, 1979), and firms face more information uncertainty as the environment becomes more complex and dynamic (Thompson, 1967). The second perspective views the environment as a stock of resources (March & Simon, 1958; Scott, 1987), and firms become more resource dependent as the environment becomes less munificent and more hostile (Aldrich, 1979; Pfeffer & Salancik, 1978). Scott (1987) notes that uncertainty and dependency are viewed as problematic situations confronting organizations and as such are the focus of strategies and other mechanisms used to cope with environmental complexity, dynamism, and hostility. Tan and Litschert (1994), in a study of the Chinese electronics industry, found a relationship between these environmental dimensions and the orientation of business-level strategies.

It was argued above that domain navigation can be considered a surrogate for business-level strategy, because both concepts refer to the competitive positioning of a firm in its industry and task environment. Gedajlovic (1993) has also suggested that ownership structure may influence domain navigation. Therefore, it would seem intuitively reasonable to assume that ownership structure's influence on domain navigation (strategy) may be the result of its impact on management's perception of environmental complexity, dynamism, and hostility. For instance, state-owned firms are typically able to gain access to resources earlier than privately owned firms because of preferential treatment by the state. Such treatment may very well affect management's perception of the levels of complexity, dynamism, and hostility.

In my following discussion, the strategic choice perspective is used as the basis for the conceptualization of strategy. This construct is examined at the business level and defined as a patterned stream of decisions that focuses on a set of resource allocations that are employed in an attempt to reach a position consistent with a firm's environment (Mintzberg, 1973). The purpose of these decisions is to achieve a competitive advantage over industry rivals (Porter, 1980). It is argued that environmental pressure and structural constraints vary across different ownership types. Consequently, these differences among groups moderate the relationship between the environmental constraints and strategic adaptations by influencing management's perception of the level of environmental uncertainty, which in turn influences managerial decisions. It is further posited that the fit between the environment and strategy will have organizational performance implications (Venkatraman & Prescott, 1990).

Strategic Group

Groupings of competitors within an industry are often developed as part of the strategy formulation process. Competitive groupings provide rich information about a firm's competitive environment and strategic responses, and afford a level of analysis between that of the industry as a whole and the firm in isolation (Bogner & Thomas, 1993). A strategic group can be defined as a cluster of firms in an industry that face similar environmental conditions, share similar resources, and thus follow common strategies in making key decisions (Oster, 1994). It represents part of the substructure of an industry that may play a role in understanding performance difference among firms. In terms of analysis, the strategic group is a middle ground between the industry and the firm.

In the past 10 years, the strategic group concept has become an accepted element in the environmental analysis phase of strategy formulation. It developed from two separate viewpoints; one stemmed from industrial organization economics, the other from the strategic management discipline. In his study of the highly concentrated but highly competitive U.S. home appliance industry, Hunt (1972) noted that observed strategies of rivals fell into distinct patterns of behavior common to a subset of firms in the industry. He suggested that these strategy differences prevented the development of an industrywide oligopolistic consensus as prior organization economics research would predict. Thus, Hunt coined the term *strategic groups* to refer to firms displaying similar conduct along some key strategic dimensions. He implied that an industry is more likely to be composed of several strategic groups. Newman (1978) further noted that if firms' strategies differ persistently among direct market rivals, we can speak of strategic groups, each group consisting of firms "highly symmetric in their corporate strategies" (p. 417). Porter (1979) attempted to verify whether the elements of industry structure have a differential impact on the profitability of firms belonging to different strategic groups. To determine group membership, relative firm size was chosen as a proxy, by assuming that firm size is a summary measure of the strategies employed by firms. From this economic perspective, the group structure was seen as a primary reason for performance variations among industry members.

At the same time the strategic group studies were conducted at Harvard University, two dissertations were completed at Purdue University in which similar issues were addressed. In his first study, Hatten (1974) postulated that similarity in strategy could be gauged by assessing whether firms had similar profitability relationships, which differed significantly among groups. Patton (1976) replicated Hatten's research on heterogeneity in firm profitability relationships and found that different strategic groups did exist. As in Hatten's study, subsequent research by the Purdue group found that each strategic group has different estimated relationships and that industry-level estimates differed significantly from the group-level estimates (e.g., Hatten & Schendel, 1977; Hatten, Schendel, & Cooper, 1978; Schendel & Patton, 1978). This stream of research sought to focus on individual firms and their patterns of strategic decisions. Underlying this research were the strategic management assumptions of firm heterogeneity and a relationship between that heterogeneity and prior managerial decisions. A comprehensive review on strategic group literature can be found in McGee and Thomas (1986), and in Thomas and Venkatraman (1988).

For the strategic group concept to be of value to future research as well to practitioners, a set of constructs that allow better identification of strategic groups and an improvement of the analysis of research questions related to strategic groups is needed. By understanding the current strategic group postures of competitors, a manager may be able to predict varying competitors' strategic responses to future changes in the environment. Consequently, the study of strategic groupings will become a useful tool in the analysis of larger research questions (Bogner & Thomas, 1993). As Porter (1979) suggested, a strategic group is a group of firms competing in and responding to the environment on the basis of a similar combination of strategic dimensions in an industry at any point in time. Following this line of reasoning, I contend that the concept of strategic group has three major characteristics. First, a strategic group is composed of firms that follow similar strategic dimensions. Second, firms within a strategic group resemble one another more closely than they resemble firms outside the group. Third, firms within a strategic group are likely to respond similarly to environmental opportunities or threats. I further contend that firms within a strategic group share similar structural constraints, environmental pressures, and strategic responses, and consequently, certain configurations will emerge. Following the structure-conduct-performance paradigm, these configurations will have significant performance implications. These relationships are depicted in Figure 3.1. The development of environment-strategy configurations among ownership types in China is the subject of the following section.

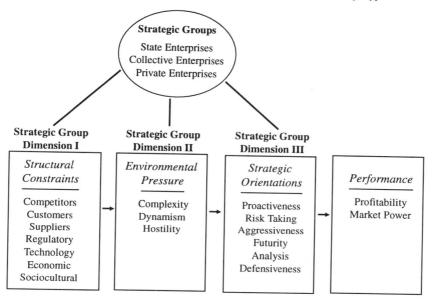

Figure 3.1. Ownership and Determinants of Strategic Group

AN EXAMINATION OF THE CHINESE CASE

In the PRC, the shift from central planning to more market-based economies has made the environment more favorable and thus allowed a variety of organizational forms to coexist. As a result, this transition has given birth to a new diversity in organizational forms and a plurality of property ownership types (Nee, 1992). The spectrum spans the continuum from the formal and hierarchical state-owned enterprises to small family-owned firms run by private entrepreneurs (Tan & Li, 1996), and also includes collectively owned, foreign joint venture, and completely foreign-owned subsidiaries. Even in a single industry, firms exhibiting different ownership types are subject to different environmental constraints, and vary significantly in their access to resources and their ability to exercise strategic choice (Tan & Li, 1996). Following the environment-strategy-performance paradigm (Venkatraman & Prescott, 1990), one would logically expect these firms to adopt different strategic postures that are consistent with their respective environments in order to achieve a fit, which is crucial to their survival and success. The existence of structural differences in environment-strategy configurations across ownership types in a single industry offers a unique opportunity to identify strategic groups.

The main purpose of this chapter is to examine and identify strategic groups among firms operating under different environmental constraints as a consequence of their differing ownership. I contend that the degree of managerial discretion, hence the latitude for strategic choice, will vary among ownership types due to constraints in organizational environments and from other sources (Bluedorn, Johnson, Cartwright, & Barringer, 1994). As a result, firms exhibiting the same ownership type will adopt similar strategies, which will vary across ownership types. It is expected that each ownership type will produce a definitive configuration that will in turn be presented as a specific set of propositions.

State-Owned Enterprises (SOEs)

In the Chinese electronics industry, the state-owned enterprises (SOEs) are structured quite differently from their typical Western counterpart (Henley & Nyaw, 1986). Many of their idiosyncrasies emerge directly from China's socialist tradition and are quite enduring. Thus, as a result of economic reform, SOEs have found themselves still a part of a bureaucratic command system but increasingly tied to an emerging market system. Firms must face these new conditions with an authority structure that lends a uniquely "Chinese" character to the organization (Perkins, 1994). On the bureaucratic command side, external rules typically take the form of civil service policies and rigid, hierarchical reporting requirements to government controllers (Shenkar & von Glinow, 1994). Managers are also commonly loaded down with objectives only partially related to market requirements. The objectives are often numerous, diverse, and intangible and include preserving declining industries and employment, subsidizing consumption, buttressing national security, and increasing the invisible resources of politicians (Aharoni, 1986; Perkins, 1994). Only after SOEs meet production and performance targets stipulated by the central plan can they produce goods/services for sale on the market. On the other hand, these firms continue to enjoy priority access to raw materials and capital allocated under the command system even though they now face increased competition from more market-oriented competitors. Although reforms have brought broader roles for factory directors and administrators through contractual management and responsibility systems that include "pay for performance," enterprise Communist Party secretaries continue to be an important factor in the organizations' authority structure. Their presence allows the Party to be an active participant in most enterprise decisions (Schermerhorn & Nyaw, 1991).

Because state enterprises are characterized by high governmental intervention and enormous administrative constraints, they are indeed not fully self-motivated organizations. This is compounded in important industries in which material supply, pricing policy, and distribution arrangement remain in the rigid state planning system (Luo, 1995). Firm growth in product diversification and business development is virtually constrained by the interference of various government institutions at the central, provincial, and/or city level (Jefferson, Rawski, & Zheng, 1992). Thus, local state firms maintain markedly lower levels of innovation and proactiveness than their rivals in other strategic groups operating in the same industry.

Previous studies of managers of Chinese SOEs have found that they share a common concern for security and are likely to avoid proactive and risk-taking decisions when faced with uncertain environments (Adler, Brahm, & Graham, 1992; Tan & Litschert, 1994). Because managers of SOEs are usually political appointees, they tend to be "extra conservative" (De Mente, 1989). Nee (1992) has also documented that managers of SOEs are more risk averse and less proactive than managers of private or collective enterprises. Their strategic orientations apparently resemble those of a Defender (Miles & Snow, 1978). Because the information uncertainty perspective posits that environmental complexity and dynamism are key dimensions affecting uncertainty (Lawrence & Lorsch, 1967; Thompson, 1967), I propose the following relationships:

Proposition 1: Chinese state enterprises operate under high environmental pressure and structural constraints that significantly limit strategic choice. As a result, these firms are more likely to adapt within a specified boundary with greater precaution. Their strategic orientations tend to be conservative and to resemble those of a Defender.

SOEs are classified as Strategic Group I in Figure 3.2.

Joint Venture Enterprises (JOEs)

The joint-venture option represents the most complex of the four ownership types that currently exist in China and when introduced may have a significant impact on industry structure (Harrigan, 1988). JOEs in the Chinese context were consistently composed of a domestic firm and a foreign partner. Ownership type of the domestic partner varied across the three types discussed above, while its foreign partner represented the unique and consistent dimension among

Firm Strategic Choice

		High	Low
	High	Group II: JOE Differentiated Choice Adaptation within constraints Primary orientation: Analyzer	Group I: SOE Minimum Choice Adaptation with conformity Primary orientation: Defender
Environmental Constraints	*Low*	Group III: POE Maximum Choice Adaptation by design Primary orientation: Prospector	Group IV: COE Incremental Choice Adaptation by chance Primary orientation: Networking

Figure 3.2. Environmental-Strategy Configuration and Strategic Group: A Classification Map

members of this ownership type. These organizations are also governed by jointly composed boards of directors that possess greater autonomy than those of typical domestic firms. Since strategic orientation is likely to emerge, in part at least, as a result of the interaction among partners and reflected in the board's decisions, several patterns appear possible. If domestic firms play a significant role in the decision process, as shown in Figure 3.1, then strategic orientation may vary with domestic ownership type. On the other hand, if the domestic firm plays a passive role in the decision process (Harrigan, 1988), strategic orientation may be determined primarily by the foreign partner. Recently, more and more multinational corporations have established wholly owned subsidiaries in the electronics industry. For instance, Motorola has set up a multibillion dollar operation to capitalize on China's lucrative cellular phone market. These wholly owned foreign subsidiaries are, however, excluded from this discussion.

Miles and Snow (1978) have suggested that multinational corporations often follow the Analyzer pattern "to the extent that they avoid the complexities involved in joint ventures and/or host-country production facilities" (p. 134). The very nature of decision-making characteristics and processes suggests that for joint ventures operating in a fast-changing and highly complex environment such as China, a critical task is to gather and analyze information. This is especially crucial when the relationship between joint venture enterprises and their various environmental elements is highly complex and particularistic, information is not codified, and regulations are not made explicit (Boisot & Child, 1988; Child & Lu, 1990). An environment characterized by uncodified information can promote noneconomic forms of opportunism, increase transaction costs, and prompt decision makers to be more cautious when making resource commitments (Boisot & Child, 1988). Thus, environmental scanning and coordination mechanisms are important to survival and growth. Consequently, this type of organization strikes a fine balance between the joint needs of adapting to environmental dictates and maintaining interdependent management. Whenever either of these tasks moves out of the limits for which established routines are available, the dominant coalition may become "overloaded" (Miles & Snow, 1978).

On the other hand, joint ventures are given more autonomy in making strategic decisions, and their resources and experience also give them the capabilities to adapt to the environmental pressure and structural constraints. These JOEs in China allocate most of their resources to a set of reasonably stable environments while at the same time conducting somewhat routinized scanning activities in a limited product-market area. They monitor market situations in the host country and carefully apply product and market innovations developed by headquarters. In most cases, R&D activities are conducted at the headquarters level and only mature products and well-known technologies are transferred to the host country. Much of the joint venture's success occurs through market penetration since the organization's basic strength comes from its traditional product-market base. This market development strategy allows the foreign investors to extend the product life cycle and to maximize returns on their R&D expenditure. From the standpoint of the foreign partners, this pattern of strategic posture is also grounded in the natural fear of creating potential competitors in the near future. They clearly follow the guiding principles delineated by Hisrich (1992): Follow the instructions given; do not take any initiative and make no proactive moves; do not be creative, do not make any mistakes, stay within your assigned position, and protect your turf (p. 525). This is especially true when facing a dynamic and complex environment. Thus, it may not be realistic to orient JOEs in a highly proactive and immensely innovative direction, because this orientation could lead to greater operational and contextual risks and higher innovative and adaptive costs in such an environment. The major strategic thrust of JOEs in such a context appears be to adapt to environments through incremental changes and sequential investments (Chang, 1995; Davidson, 1980). This evolutionary approach can be a lower-cost means of testing a foreign market considered too risky in terms of complexity, dynamism, and hostility for a full investment (Kogut & Zander, 1994). The risk factor hence makes multinational enterprise (MNE) subunits in an uncertain environment opt for mid-level innovative and proactive strategies. Miles and Snow (1978) explicitly suggest that

MNE subunits often follow the Analyzer strategy "to the extent that they avoid the complexities involved in host country production facilities" (p. 134). This strategy can make a subunit's managerial behavior directed toward efficiency and innovation more easily programmable (Bartlett & Ghoshal, 1987). Empirical evidence finds that JOEs in China allocate most of their resources to a set of reasonably stable environments while at the same time conducting routinized scanning activities in focused product-market areas (Luo, 1995; Shenkar, 1990). They closely monitor market situations in the country and carefully apply product and market innovations developed by headquarters (Beamish, 1993). Thus, JOEs in this context exhibit a pattern of strategic orientation consistent with Analyzers.

In sum, based on the above discussion, foreign joint ventures in China share the same corporate culture and reward system as their counterparts elsewhere, one that favors conservative decision making (Hisrich, 1992). They clearly exhibit a pattern of strategic orientation consistent with the strategy type categorized by Miles and Snow (1978) as Analyzer. Their major strategic thrust appears to be to adapt to foreign environments through cautious incremental changes. Therefore, it is expected that there exists a configuration of relationships between environmental characteristics and strategic orientations among joint ventures. However, lack of documented studies only justify hypotheses based on limited dimensions. With this in mind, the following statement is proposed:

Proposition 2: Chinese joint venture enterprises operate under high environmental pressure and structural constraints, yet their experience and access to critical resources significantly improve their strategic choice within those constraints. As a result, these firms are more likely to adapt to environmental constraints by following strategies similar to those of an Analyzer.

JOEs are classified as Strategic Group II in Figure 3.2.

Privately Owned Enterprises (POEs)

Aldrich and Wiedenmayer (1993) suggest that "environmental resources, or an environment's carrying capacity, set a limit on population density—the number and/or size of organizations competing for the same resources in a limited space" (p. 151). They also suggest that a change in political environment, especially a dramatic, one-of-a-kind historical event, is important because it may disrupt established ties between organizations and resources, freeing resources for use by new organizations. In the Chinese economy, a major consequence of the economic reform program is the resurgence of private entrepreneurship (Vogel, 1989), which first expanded in an area hard-line Communists found it difficult to oppose—among "youth awaiting employment" (Vogel, 1989). By 1974, many of the 994,000 young people sent to the countryside for "reeducation" in the late 1960s during the Cultural Revolution (1966-1976) had begun to return, but state enterprises and government offices, already overstaffed, had few openings. Leaders, fearing social unrest, knew change was urgently required in order to place thousands of youth, some of whom had been awaiting employment for several years. Allowing them to set up individual and collective enterprises to repair radio and TV sets or sell products for the SOEs seemed, even to many who opposed economic reform, a solution to the problem, and political opposition was not significant. Distasteful terms like *capitalist* were replaced by more attractive labels like "individual enterprise household" and, more recently, "entrepreneurs." More independent stalls and shops, almost always staffed by young people, had begun to reappear almost immediately after the end of the Cultural Revolution in 1976. By 1980, it was official policy that the monopoly of state enterprises had ended. Meanwhile, the government also encouraged individuals to lease and run some state-owned enterprises (Chang & MacMillan, 1991). To encourage larger enterprises in the private sector, a new attractive category, "private enterprise," was created in April 1988 for businesses with more than seven employees (Vogel, 1989). In 1992, the number of privately owned enterprises in communist China had reached 139,000, and some 2.32 million Chinese were employed in the private sector in 1992, an increase of 26% over 1991. For these young people who were socially, politically, culturally, and economically "displaced," entrepreneurial ventures seemed to be a desirable alternative. In a recent account of Chinese entrepreneurs, Tan (1993, 1996) reported that while the traditional hostility directed at private enterprises still exists in China, entrepreneurs have felt that the environment is not the most favorable one ever since the current political regime took power nearly 5 decades ago, and they do have the autonomy to make independent decisions. As discussed earlier, while the "objective" environment is relevant, it is what the decision maker perceives that enters the decision process.

The entrepreneurial context is characterized by turbulence and change, and entrepreneurial organizations tend to fare better than more stable firms in rapidly changing environments because of their strategic flexibility (Bird, 1989). Through searching for and even creating disequilibrium, and the "birth" and "death" of organizations in larger social and economic systems, entrepreneurs create chaos.

Economic reform brought about turbulence and transaction failure of the centrally planned mechanism. As Venkatraman, Van de Ven, Buckeye, and Hudson (1990) suggest, the probability of transaction failures is a product of the failure rate at the level of organizational population, as well as the kinds of transactions in which individual firms engage. Such an environment created many niches unfulfilled by the state planning mechanism and allowed entrepreneurs to perform two critical activities: connect different markets and answer market deficiencies. Knowing that government policies have historically been unpredictable, and that more favorable regulations may change at any time, private entrepreneurs simply identified a market niche for which demand could be easily met and filled the niche. The existence of many unfilled niches in former centrally planned economies characterized by shortage, coupled with aggressive strategies, increased an entrepreneur's chances for early survival, similar to what has been found in their Western counterparts (Romanelli, 1989). Meanwhile, the simple structure has pre-positioned the private entrepreneurs for speed and surprise, giving them the ability to react quickly to opportunities in the environment or proactively to outmaneuver the more established firms. As a result, the dynamic environment benefits consumers and gives smaller entrepreneurial firms a chance to disrupt the status quo and to destroy the competitive advantage of the more established firms.

Consistent with the traditional profile of entrepreneurs, it is generally expected that POEs respond rapidly and proactively to market opportunities even under the uncertain conditions characteristic of China's current mixed economy (Long, 1992). In addition, entrepreneurs tend to be overly optimistic in analyzing environmental information (Busenitz & Barney, 1994), particularly when they are relatively unfamiliar with the problem, substantial uncertainty exists, or both. While Bazerman (1986) and others have made suggestions about how to avoid the pitfalls of overconfidence, this may be difficult for entrepreneurs. Many of the solutions to their problems are simply not known in advance, and little information is generally available that would contradict their optimism. Perhaps more important, if entrepreneurs had a lower level of confidence in their decision-making ability, most new ventures would never be launched. Their overconfidence keeps them from being overwhelmed by the multiple hurdles they face (Busenitz & Barney, 1994). They pursue opportunity without concern for current resources or capabilities (Stevenson, Roberts, & Grousbeck, 1994), take great risks, and make decisions quickly even when information is not available (Bird, 1989). As one entrepreneur said, "If something is not explicitly prohibited, then move," and these entrepreneurs are indeed moving ahead quickly. These circumstances have led to the following proposition:

Proposition 3: Chinese private enterprises operate under relatively less environmental pressure and structural constraints, and these firms have the autonomy to make strategic choice. As a result, these firms are more likely to adapt to environmental constraints by following the Prospector strategy.

POEs are classified as Strategic Group III in Figure 3.2.

Collective-Owned Enterprises (COEs)

Unlike SOEs, most Chinese collective-owned enterprises (COEs) are established and run by local governments rather than by the central government's planning agencies, although in some cases SOEs are "passed down" to local governments to become collectives. Also, COEs are not as heavily subsidized by government budgets or by the banking system as SOEs. During the austerity after the June Fourth Incident in 1989, losses to state-owned firms soared, but none went bankrupt. Yet that same year, more collective-owned enterprises went out of business or were taken over, despite the fact that far more state-owned enterprises incurred losses ("When China Wakes," 1992). "Hard budget constraints" (Xin & Pearce, 1996) encourage efficiency and flexibility in contrast to state-owned and -directed companies, and these enterprises—to a greater extent than SOEs—must face incentives to behave in accordance with the rules of the market (Perkins, 1994).

COEs do contribute substantially to local government revenue, however, and this fact has created strong incentives on the part of local officials to ensure their success (Vogel, 1989). As a result, local governments typically assist COEs to secure reliable access to production factor resources, oversee local labor markets, appoint managers to COEs, serve as intermediaries in critical negotiations with banks for credit, fix local prices on select numbers of commodities, and approve and coordinate investment of extra budgetary funds under their control for projects proposed by COEs. In short, local governments may buffer COEs from unfavorable environmental conditions and provide the support and resources needed by COEs to compete effectively (Nee, 1992). One advantage of this interdependence between COEs and local governments has been the reduction of uncertainties during economic reform (Yusuf, 1994). Similar to SOEs, the COEs are structurally protected (Nee, 1992; Xin & Pearce, 1996). Since these COEs are jointly owned by local governments but produce products sold in competitive markets, such ownership structure gives them access to capital and raw materials and serves to protect them from debilitating interference.

Under these circumstances, Nee (1992) suggests that the COEs have an institutional advantage over both SOEs and private firms.

Furthermore, although the managers of COEs are often closely linked to local government, they also must be more responsive to the market than managers of SOEs because of the lack of subsidization by both the central government and the nation's banking system. Most COEs, especially the small firms, depend on resource exchange with their environment for survival and goal achievement. Of crucial importance are the costs of gathering and processing the information necessary to predict the future effects of today's strategic actions and to reduce conflicts between the organization and the environment. Under this unique circumstance, the Chinese COEs sought to include key stakeholders on their boards of directors in order to build a strategic network and to secure permanent cooperation within the network. In the Chinese context, such networking is a means of developing the advantages of specialization, and at the same time of reducing the cost of coordinating exchange. This is particularly important during China's transitional period, when the traditional mechanisms governing exchange have become inadequate for managing the increasing complexity. Internally, the COEs usually have a simple, centralized organizational structure. The strength of this kind of organization is an oral, direct management style, as well as top-management overview and direct control over the operating core of the firm. The informal strategic networks of these firms match this kind of organization (Perrow, 1986). Such networks, often connected with more personal relations of trust and affiliation between partners, give information and channels for resolving conflict, and are at the same time cheap to maintain. They can also more easily be cut off without sanctions and heavy exit costs. This networking strategy thus increases the interorganization's influence and control, and thereby secures the resources needed for survival and planning toward goal achievement (Pfeffer & Salancik, 1978).

In his extensive study of COEs conducted in Southern China, Vogel (1989) reported that firms characterized by this ownership type were more proactive and innovative than state sectors, and were willing to take risks in responding to environmental pressure and structural constraints. Tan and Li (1996) studied COEs located in Northern China, and their accounts reveal that the environmental constraints were lower than those reported by SOEs, similar to Vogel's findings. Their strategic orientations, on the other hand, did not fit into previously identified strategy types. In this case, the COEs adopted a strategy similar to that of subsidiaries of multinational corporations (MNCs), that is, Analyzer. However, this dominant strategy did not contribute to high performance, contrary to the environment-strategy-performance paradigm. Interestingly, some COEs adopted strategic orientations similar to those of a Defender, an orientation that is proposed as the predominant strategy for SOEs and that was positively related to COEs' performance. More recent studies of COEs indicate that in the Chinese context these firms may pursue growth through a networking strategy (Peng, 1997). As a trade-off for the absence of the institutional protection that is available to the SOEs, COEs face less constraints. They emulate the strategic initiatives of the JOEs in order to seek strategic advantage, yet they lack the experience and resources enjoyed by the JOEs. They strive to leave the shadow of the more powerful SOEs, but they cannot break away from their structural dependence on the SOEs. As a result, they make incremental changes and emulate those strategies that are shown to be effective. At the same time, they seek to build networks with stakeholders who have access to critical resources and, in the absence of institutional support, they strive to build structural protection. Under these circumstances, I propose the following statement:

Proposition 4: Chinese collective enterprises operate under relatively low environmental pressure and structural constraints, yet their lack of experience and critical resources significantly limit their strategic choice. As a result, these firms are more likely to make incremental changes and adopt only strategies that are shown effective. They will also pursue firm growth through a networking strategy.

COEs are classified as Strategic Group IV in Figure 3.2.

DISCUSSION AND CONCLUSION

The research on growth of firms in transitional economies is an area that is drawing growing attention from organizational theorists (Peng & Heath, 1996). In this chapter I identified a contextual variable—property ownership type—and examined its impact on variables subject to managerial decision in the Chinese transitional economy. The primary thesis of my discussion is that property ownership type provides richer, more predictively valid insights into the relationship between environmental constraints and firm strategic choice. Applying and extending the Hrebiniak and Joyce (1985) conception of the organization-environment relationship, it appears that firms in the Chinese setting seem to deal with their own concrete reality differently as their ownership type differs. When confronted with dramatic changes in their respective environments, firms respond strategically in a number of areas, such as willingness to take risk and motivation to innovate. Since ownership type is an organizational variable that is more transparent and readily available, it potentially represents a predictor variable that can be used to predict strategic group membership.

I believe there are several issues that can be studied in future research. First, future research should empirically test to what extent firm ownership can be used as a predictor of strategic group membership. As pointed out, most studies reporting differences in ownership types compared organizations with radically different task environments (Lachman, 1985). In order to identify strategic group membership, empirical studies should offer better control for multiple environmental variables. Consequently, researchers should attempt to collect data from within a single industry. As Shenkar and von Glinow (1994) recommend in their research on management issues in China, researchers should compare "partially similar cases" (p. 69). China's mixed economy not only offers such a setting, but heterogeneous ownership types can be found among firms in a single industry. By selecting firms that are of multiple ownership types but that compete within the same industry, it is possible to control for the industry effect. From a methodological standpoint, researchers can use a set of well-established organizational environment measures, such as complexity, dynamism, and resources scarcity; a set of strategy measures, such as proactiveness, risk taking, and innovation; and a set of firm performance measures, such as profitability and competitive position, to classify strategic group membership. If strategic groups do exist in a single Chinese industry setting, and the majority of group memberships can be predicted by ownership type, researchers as well as practitioners can then use ownership type to identify the strategic group membership of a particular firm. As a related matter, researchers should devote attention to examining the difference that strategic grouping makes in the actual strategy an organization uses.

Second, future research can examine the environment-strategy-performance paradigm within a single ownership type. For instance, while there is an emerging though limited interest in studying Chinese state, private, and joint-venture enterprises, little effort has been made to analyze the collective (including village and township) enterprises. In the Chinese context, collective enterprises are not institutionally protected, so they have to build structural protection. They try to escape the shadow of the state enterprises but cannot sever their dependency. At the same time, they try to emulate the joint ventures but lack the JOEs' prerogatives. This may offer an intriguing case to build new theories.

Finally, future research should investigate the impact of organizational culture and ideology on strategic grouping. Organizational culture and ideology, which represent a system of beliefs about the organization that is shared by its members and that distinguish it from other organizations, play a substantial role in group structure in the Chinese context. Virtually all organizations have some culture and ideology that condition their strategic responses to environmental changes; these organizations react to new opportunities in ways that reflect their goals. In the Chinese context, different organizational forms have different historical and ideological backgrounds. Such differences may result in quite different organizational capabilities for strategic groups operating within the same industry to take advantage of changes in the environment. As demonstrated in this study, strategic groups respond quite differently to common environmental events. As a result, the relative profitability and competitive position of particular strategic groups may change over time. Some may improve their performance, whereas others may not. The payoffs to particular strategic choices can vary considerably across groups.

REFERENCES

Adler, N. J., Brahm, R., & Graham, J. L. (1992). Strategy implementation: A comparison of face-to-face negotiations in the People's Republic of China and the United States. *Strategic Management Journal, 13,* 449-466.

Aharoni, Y. (1986). *The evolution and management of state owned enterprises.* Melrose, MA: Ballinger.

Aldrich, H. E. (1979). *Organizations and environments.* Englewood Cliffs, NJ: Prentice Hall.

Aldrich, H. E., & Wiedenmayer, G. (1993). From traits to rates: An ecological perspective on organizational foundings. In J. A. Katz & R. H. Brockhaus, Sr. (Eds.), *Advances in entrepreneurship, firm emergence, and growth* (pp. 145-195). Greenwich, CT: JAI.

Andrews, K. R. (1971). *The concept of corporate strategy.* Homewood, IL: Irwin.

Astley, W. G., & Van de Ven, A. H. (1983). Central perspectives and debates in organization theory. *Administrative Science Quarterly, 28,* 245-273.

Bartlett, C. A., & Ghoshal, S. (1987, November-December). Tap your subsidiaries for global reach. *Harvard Business Review,* pp. 87-94.

Bazerman, M. H. (1986). *Managerial decision making.* New York: John Wiley.

Beamish, P. W. (1993). The characteristics of joint ventures in the People's Republic of China. *Journal of International Marketing, 1*(2), 29-48.

Bird, B. J. (1989). *Entrepreneurial behavior.* Glenview, IL: Scott, Foresman.

Bluedorn, A. C., Johnson, R. A., Cartwright, D. K., & Barringer, B. R. (1994). The interface and convergence of strategic management and organizational environment domains. *Journal of Management, 20,* 201-262.

Bogner, W. C., & Thomas, H. (1993). The role of competitive groups in strategy formulation: A dynamic integration of two competing models. *Journal of Management Studies, 30,* 51-67.

Boisot, M., & Child, J. (1988). The iron law of fiefs: Bureaucratic failure and the problem of governance in the Chinese economic reforms. *Administrative Science Quarterly, 33,* 507-527.

Busenitz, L. W., & Barney, J. B. (1994). Biases and heuristics in strategic decision making: Differences between entrepreneurs and managers in large organizations. *Academy of Management Best Papers Proceedings.*

Chang, S. J. (1995). International expansion strategy of Japanese firms: Capability building through sequential entry. *Academy of Management Journal, 38,* 383-407.

Chang, W., & MacMillan, I. C. (1991). A review of entrepreneurial development in the People's Republic of China. *Journal of Business Venturing, 6,* 375-379.

Child, J. (1972). Organization structure, environment, and performance—The role of strategic choice. *Sociology, 6,* 1-22.

Child, J., & Lu, Y. (1990). Industrial decision-making under China's reform 1985-1988. *Organization Studies, 11,* 321-351.

Davidson, W. H. (1980). The location of foreign direct investment activity: Country characteristics and experience effects. *Journal of International Business Studies, 12,* 9-22.

De Mente, B. L. (1989). *Chinese etiquette and ethics in business.* Lincolnwood, IL: NTC Business Books.

Duncan, R. B. (1972). Characteristics of organizational environments and perceived environment uncertainty. *Administrative Science Quarterly, 17,* 313-327.

Gedajlovic, E. (1993). Ownership, strategy and performance: Is the dichotomy sufficient? *Organization Studies, 14,* 731-752.

Hannan, M. T., & Freeman, J. (1989). *Organizational ecology.* Cambridge, MA: Harvard University Press.

Harrigan, K. R. (1988). Joint venture and competitive strategy. *Strategic Management Journal, 9,* 141-158.

Hatten, K. J. (1974). *Strategic models in the brewing industry.* Unpublished doctoral dissertation, Purdue University.

Hatten, K. J., & Schendel, D. E. (1977). Heterogeneity within an industry: Firm conduct in the U.S. brewing industry 1952-1971. *Academy of Management Journal, 20,* 97-113.

Hatten, K. J., Schendel, D. E., & Cooper, A. C. (1978). A strategic model of the United States brewing industry. *Academy of Management Journal, 21,* 592-610.

Henley, J. S., & Nyaw, M. K. (1986). Introducing market forces into managerial decision-making in Chinese industrial enterprises. *Journal of Management Studies, 23,* 635-656.

Hisrich, R. D. (1992). Joint ventures: Research base and use in international markets. In D. L. Sexton & J. D. Kasarda (Eds.), *The state of the art of entrepreneurship* (pp. 520-559). Boston: PWS-Kent.

Hrebiniak, L. G., & Joyce, W. F. (1985). Organizational adaptation: Strategic choice and environmental determinism. *Administrative Science Quarterly, 30,* 336-349.

Hunt, M. S. (1972). *Competition in the major home appliance industry 1960-1970.* Unpublished doctoral dissertation, Harvard University.

Jefferson, G. H., Rawski, T. G., & Zheng, Y. (1992). Growth, efficiency, and convergence in China's state and collective industry. *Economic Development & Cultural Change, 40,* 239-266.

Kogut, B., & Zander, U. (1994). Knowledge of the firm and the evolutionary theory of the multinational enterprise. *Journal of International Business Studies, 24,* 625-646.

Lachman, R. (1985). Public and private sector differences: CEOs' perceptions of their role environments. *Academy of Management Journal, 28,* 671-680.

Lawless, M. W., & Finch, L. K. (1989). Choice and determinism: A test of Hrebiniak and Joyce's framework on strategy-environment fit. *Strategic Management Journal, 10,* 351-365.

Lawrence, P., & Lorsch, J. W. (1967). Differentiation and integration in complex organizations. *Administrative Science Quarterly, 12,* 1-47.

Long, N. (1992). There are more and more millionaires in China. *China Times Weekly, 23,* 74-76.

Luo, Y. (1995). Business strategy, market structure, and performance of international joint ventures: The case of joint ventures in China. *Management International Review, 35,* 241-264.

March, J. G., & Simon, H. A. (1958). *Organizations.* New York: John Wiley.

Mascarenhas, B. (1989). Domains of state-owned, privately held, and publicly traded firms in international competition. *Administrative Science Quarterly, 34,* 582-579.

McEachern, W. A. (1975). *Managerial control and performance.* Lexington, MA: D. C. Heath.

McGee, J., & Thomas, H. (1986). Strategic groups: Theory, research and taxonomy. *Strategic Management Journal, 9,* 139-156.

Miles, R. E., & Snow, C. C. (1978). *Organizational strategy, structure and process.* New York: McGraw-Hill.

Miller, D., & Friesen, P. H. (1983). Strategy-making and environment: The third link. *Strategic Management Journal, 4,* 221-235.

Mintzberg, H. (1973). Strategy-making in three modes. *California Management Review, 16,* 44-53.

Nee, V. (1992). Organizational dynamics of market transition: Hybrid forms, property rights, and mixed economy in China. *Administrative Science Quarterly, 37,* 1-27.

Newman, H. H. (1978). Strategic groups and the structure-performance relationship. *Review of Economics and Statistics, 60,* 417-427.

Oster, S. M. (1994). *Modern competitive analysis* (2nd ed.). New York: Oxford University Press.

Patton, G. R. (1976). *A simultaneous equation model of corporate strategy: The case of the U.S. brewing industry.* Unpublished doctoral dissertation, Purdue University.

Peng, M. W. (1994). Organizational changes in planned economies in transition: An eclectic model. *Advances in International Comparative Management, 9,* 223-251.

Peng, M. W. (1997). Firm growth in transitional economies: Three longitudinal cases from China, 1989-96. *Organizational Studies, 18*(3), 385-413.

Peng, M. W., & Heath, P. S. (1996). The growth of the firm in planned economies in transition: Institutions, organizations, and strategic choice. *Academy of Management Review, 21*(2), 492-528.

Perkins, D. (1994). Completing China's move to the market. *Journal of Economic Perspective, 8*(2), 23-46.

Perrow, C. (1986). *Complex organizations: A critical essay* (3rd ed.). New York: Random House.

Pfeffer, J., & Salancik, G. R. (1978). *The external control of organizations: A resource dependence perspective.* New York: Harper & Row.

Porter, M. E. (1979). The structure within industries and companies' performance. *Review of Economics and Statistics, 1,* 214-227.

Porter, M. E. (1980). *Competitive strategy: Techniques for analyzing industries and competitors.* New York: Free Press.

Romanelli, E. (1989). Environments and strategy of organization start-up: Effects on early survival. *Administrative Science Quarterly, 34,* 369-387.

Schendel, D. E., & Patton, G. R. (1978). A simultaneous equation model of corporate strategy. *Management Science, 24,* 1611-1621.

Scott, W. R. (1987). *Organizations: Rational, natural, and open systems* (2nd ed.). Englewood Cliffs, NJ: Prentice Hall.

Schermerhorn, J. R., Jr., & Nyaw, M. K. (1991). Managerial leadership in Chinese industrial enterprises. In O. Shenkar (Ed.), *Organization and management in China: 1979-1990* (pp. 9-21). Armonk, NY: M. E. Sharpe.

Shenkar, O. (1990). International joint ventures' problems in China: Risks and remedies. *Long Range Planning, 23*(3), 82-90.

Shenkar, O., & von Glinow, M. A. (1994). Paradoxes of organizational theory and research: Using the case of China to illustrate national contingency. *Management Science, 40*(1), 56-71.

Stevenson, H. H., Roberts, M. J., & Grousbeck, H. I. (1994). *New business ventures and the entrepreneur* (4th ed.). Homewood, IL: Irwin.

Tan, J. (1993). *Perceived environment, strategic orientation, ownership effect and performance implications in a transition economy: An empirical study in the People's Republic of China.* Unpublished doctoral dissertation, Virginia Tech.

Tan, J. (1996, Fall). Regulatory environment and strategic orientations: A study of Chinese private entrepreneurs. *Entrepreneurship Theory and Practice,* pp. 31-44.

Tan, J., & Li, M. (1996). Effect of ownership types on environment-strategy configuration in China's emerging transitional economy. *Advances in International Comparative Management, 11,* 217-250.

Tan, J., & Litschert, R. J. (1994). Environment-strategy relationship and its performance implications: An empirical study of the Chinese electronics industry. *Strategic Management Journal, 15*(1), 1-20.

Thomas, H., & Venkatraman, N. (1988). Research on strategic groups: Progress and prognosis. *Journal of Management Studies, 25,* 537-555.

Thompson, J. D. (1967). *Organizations in action.* New York: McGraw-Hill.

Tung, R. L. (1979). Dimensions of organizational environments: An exploratory study of their impact on organizational structure. *Academy of Management Journal, 22,* 672-693.

Venkatraman, N., & Prescott, J. E. (1990). Environment-strategy coalignment: An empirical test of its performance implications. *Strategic Management Journal, 11,* 1-23.

Venkatraman, S., Van de Ven, A. H., Buckeye, J., & Hudson, R. (1990). Starting up in a turbulent environment: A process model of failure among firms with high customer dependence. *Journal of Business Strategy, 5,* 277-295.

Vogel, E. F. (1989). *One step ahead of China: Guangdong under reform.* Cambridge, MA: Harvard University Press.

When China wakes: A survey of China. (1992, November 28). *The Economist.*

Xin, K., & Pearce, J. L. (1996). Guanxi: Connections as substitutes for formal institutional support. *Academy of Management Journal, 39*(6), 1641-1658.

Yusuf, S. (1994). China's macroeconomic performance and management during transition, *Journal of Economic Perspective, 8,* 71-92.

chapter 4

Firm Growth via Mergers
and Acquisitions in China

MIKE W. PENG
YADONG LUO
LI SUN

As a major strategy for firm growth, mergers and acquisitions (M&As) have been examined extensively in the West. However, very little research has been done on M&As in China. For example, none of the comprehensive collections of papers on management and organization issues in China edited by Brown and Porter (1996), Child and Lu (1996), Davies (1995), Kelley and Shenkar (1993), and Shenkar (1991) had any coverage of M&As. This is not surprising given that it was only in the late 1980s that M&As started to take place in that country. In recent years, M&As have become an increasingly common strategy used not only by Chinese enterprises seeking expansion (Lai, 1995; Sun, 1995), but also by foreign firms interested in direct entry (Ho, 1996). According to many observers, M&As will become one of the "hot" business issues in China in the next century, thus necessitating more scholarly attention.

Attempting to fill a gap in our understanding of an issue of such growing importance, this chapter focuses on a basic question: What are the characteristics

AUTHORS' NOTE: This research was supported in part by a Research and Faculty Development Grant, a Research Relations Grant, and a CIBER Grant from the University of Hawaii. We thank Trevor Buck, Orlan Lee, Yuan Lu, and Agnes Peng for their helpful comments.

of M&A activities in China to date? Two well-known M&A cases will be used as illustrative examples. The approach we take is interdisciplinary, drawing on research in management, finance, economics, sociology, and law, as well as China studies. We start with a brief review of existing research on M&As in the West, then examine the development of M&As in China since the 1980s. Two case studies are then analyzed. Finally, implications for researchers, practitioners, and policymakers in China and abroad are discussed.

PRIOR RESEARCH ON MERGERS AND ACQUISITIONS

Thousands of M&As have occurred in developed economies since the turn of the 20th century. A comprehensive review of the literature is beyond the scope of this chapter. Our brief review is intended only to provide some baseline information upon which one can evaluate M&As in China.

Firm Growth via M&As

Research on the growth of the firm in the West has identified three major strategic choices for growth: (a) Undertaking internally driven, generic expansion; (b) conducting M&As; and (c) developing trust-based network relationships (see Peng & Heath, 1996, pp. 495-499, for a state-of-the-art review). A strategy of growth via M&As is often necessary, since very few firms are able to grow based entirely on their internal development, and trust-based networks (or collusion) often break down (Penrose, 1959; Powell, 1990; Yip, 1982). The rationale is that as the firm grows larger, it will have more complex relationships with its suppliers, buyers, and other transaction parties; these complicated exchange relationships may cause transaction failure, thus necessitating the acquisition of other firms in order to bring some of these relationships under control—hence the term "internalization" (Williamson, 1985). Through M&As, the firm grows larger, gains more market power, enters new markets, and reduces risks (Anslinger & Copeland, 1996). Both the economics-based transaction cost perspective (Williamson, 1985) and the sociology-based resource dependency perspective (Pfeffer & Salancik, 1978) offer essentially the same arguments as to why M&As are a viable growth strategy. Yet despite the consensus on the necessity of M&As, different disciplines have different views on the role of M&As in the modern economy.

A Positive View of M&As

Most financial economists hold a positive view of M&As. When an outsider acquires an "inefficient" firm, the acquired firm is expected to enhance its efficiency and improve its performance, thus "benefiting shareholders, society, and the corporate form of organization" (Jensen, 1987, p. 102). The theoretical underpinning behind this perspective is agency theory, which focuses on the conflict of interest between principals and agents (Jensen & Meckling, 1976). Since Berle and Means's (1932) pioneering work, a large literature has grown to describe the separation of ownership and control in modern Western corporations (Fama, 1980). The firm is conceptualized as a nexus of agency contracts between shareholders as principals and managers as agents. Over time, top managers (agents) gain more control of the firm due to their superior expertise and information about the firm, despite the nominal control of the corporation by shareholders (Mizruchi, 1983). Instead of maximizing shareholders' wealth, top managers often pursue a different set of objectives and agendas in order to maximize their own power, prestige, and wealth (Marris, 1964; Williamson, 1964). Therefore, they often engage in activities such as overdiversification, empire building, and on-the-job shirking that are at odds with shareholders' interests (Jensen, 1987). Over the long run, these agency problems lead to inefficiency, which hurts the value of the firm and shareholders' wealth.

Such a conflict of interest between shareholders (principals) and managers (agents) calls for remedies. The first remedy is to employ boards of directors to safeguard shareholders' interests. However, boards are often not effective because they are usually nominated and influenced by top managers (Mizruchi, 1983). As a result, the external financial market through M&As, as a second remedy, disciplines top managers in a way that internal control mechanisms such as boards of directors have been unable to do. Such a financial economics perspective is best expressed by Jensen (1987):

> The market for corporate control [via M&As] . . . is the arena in which alternative management teams compete for the rights to manage corporate resources. . . . [Existing] managers often have trouble abandoning strategies they have spent years devising and implementing, even when those strategies no longer contribute to the organization's survival. It is easier for new top-level managers with no ties to current employees or communities to make changes. . . . When the internal processes for change in large corporations are too slow, costly, and clumsy to bring about the required restructuring or change in managers effectively, the capital markets do so through the market for corporate control. (p. 106)

Jensen and Ruback (1983) and Smith (1986) reviewed the literature and found that, on average, target firms' stocks jump 20% to 30% surrounding the M&A event, a significant increase. Acquiring firms' stocks experience a 0 to 4% increase, an insignificant increase. On balance, the sheer increase of target shareholders' wealth has been regarded as a strong piece of evidence in support of the performance-enhancing effect of M&As.

In summary, the financial economics perspective views M&As as mechanisms to discipline inefficient firms run by managers unable or unwilling to improve performance. As a result, M&As enhance efficiency and performance, and hence generate wealth.

A Doubtful View of M&As

Not all economists share the financial economics perspective. Industrial organization (IO) economists, as well as strategic management researchers, have questioned this view. Two IO economists, Ravenscraft and Scherer (1987), presented the most powerful evidence to refute the financial economics view. They investigated more than 5,000 M&As that occurred in the United States between 1950 and 1975 and found significant declines in postmerger profitability for *all* types of mergers except two—tender offers and mergers of equal-sized firms. Five possible explanations were suggested: (a) "Hubris" on the part of acquiring firms' management, which failed to anticipate difficulties in integrating two merged companies; (b) inadequate incentives for target firms' senior management, who become line managers after the M&A; (c) mistakes caused by the lack of experience of the new management in the target firm's industry; (d) problems latent in the target firm, some of which were not fully understood by the new management; and (e) plain bad luck (Caves, 1989; Ravenscraft & Scherer, 1987; Roll, 1986). In short, IO economists argued that the M&A-related gains found by financial economists are mostly "perceived" benefits that boosted target firms' stock prices during a short window surrounding the M&A event; these benefits, if any, tend to dissipate over time.

Since the primary motive for acquiring firms through M&As is to pursue a strategy of growth through diversification (Salter & Weinhold, 1979), strategic management researchers have also made significant contributions to the literature. Their research focuses on what kind of M&A strategy, that is, related or unrelated diversification, results in better performance (Ramanujam & Varadarajan, 1989). Following Rumelt (1974), many strategists have found that, on average, related diversifiers have higher levels of performance compared with unrelated diversifiers (Bettis & Hall, 1982; Chatterjee & Lubatkin, 1990; Lubatkin, 1987;

Montgomery, 1985; Palepu, 1985; Singh & Montgomery, 1987). It is believed that the closer the acquired firms' businesses are to the core skills of the acquirer, the better the post-M&A performance. Unrelated diversification, on the other hand, can easily result in lackluster performance due to the lack of synergy between the two merging firms (Markides, 1995; Rumelt, 1974; Schleifer & Vishny, 1991).

Why, despite the theoretical superiority of the unrelated diversification strategy, have the vast majority of M&As, including many related ones, have experienced profitability losses as found by Ravenscraft and Scherer (1987)? Strategy researchers argued that relatedness and synergy, however sound theoretically, can be too loosely defined (Barney, 1988), resulting in "imagined synergies" (Porter, 1987) or "illusionary fit" (Lubatkin, 1987). As such, managers are often unable to implement the M&A strategy effectively (Ilinitch & Zeithaml, 1995; Jemison & Sitkin, 1986; Prahalad & Bettis, 1986). Jones and Hill (1988) further argued that due to the increased needs for coordination with the acquired firm, a related diversifier has to incur high bureaucratic costs, thus further complicating the already difficult implementation process. Finally, Hitt, Hoskisson, Johnson, and Moesel (1996) suggested that firms using M&As to access innovations have less incentive to innovate on their own, thus hurting their long-run innovation capabilities. On balance, strategy research has been inconclusive as to how firm growth via M&As can actually enhance efficiency, and this area of research continues to be characterized by a "growing confusion" (Reed & Luffman, 1986).

In summary, IO economists and strategy researchers have doubts about the performance-enhancing effects of M&As. While acknowledging the theoretical rationale for M&As, such as synergy, they are not so sure about how these benefits can actually be acquired.

A Negative View of M&As

Whereas financial and IO economists are interested in the impact of M&As on the overall economy and strategy researchers concentrate on M&As' impact on a given firm, a third school of thought, mostly growing out of sociological, organizational, and behavioral research, focuses on M&As' impact on individuals. Given the tremendous amount of turmoil and uncertainty generated by M&As, it is not surprising that this sociological perspective has a negative view of M&As.

According to this view, M&As are employed by powerful elites such as shareholders, investment bankers, and corporate raiders to exert their control over economic resources (Perrow, 1986). As a result, employees' and other stakeholders' interests are generally ignored. These writers focus on employees' typical feelings of conflict, tension, alienation, stress, loss of trust and productivity, concerns about financial and job security, and a host of other human resource problems (Buono & Bowditch, 1989; Schweiger & Walsh, 1990). Moreover, it is found that not only employees experience these problems; managers, who normally belong to the elite group, also have to endure similar problems, resulting in abnormally high turnover, especially among acquired firms (Walsh, 1988).

These researchers suggested that calculations for "strategic fit" in M&As, such as synergy, typically outweigh considerations for "organizational fit," and it is the lack of organizational fit that has resulted in many M&A failures (Haspeslagh & Jemison, 1991; Jemison & Sitkin, 1986). Therefore, they argued that great weight should be given to organizational and cultural compatibility between the two merged firms (Buono & Bowditch, 1989). How actually to implement these tactics, however, remains to be seen.

In summary, the sociological perspective focuses on the human costs of M&As, which leads to a negative view on these activities. However, these studies tend to fall at the opposite end of the extreme they criticize: "Although they provide an antidote to the financial or strategic perspective on acquisitions, . . . they let organizational issues outweigh an acquisition's strategic potential and consider integration issues primarily from the standpoint of whether individuals accept the new situation" (Haspeslagh & Jemison, 1991, p. 306).

Summary

While the necessity for firm growth via M&As has been acknowledged, scholars disagree on the role of M&As in the modern economy. Financial economists embrace a positive view on M&As. IO economists and strategy researchers cast doubts on such a view. Sociologists, together with organizational behavior and human resource specialists, paint a quite negative picture of M&As. Overall, the interdisciplinary debate on M&As is inconclusive. It is worth noting, however, that almost all prior research on M&As has been conducted in developed economies where the existence of financial markets for M&As has been taken for granted. How M&As work in China immediately becomes a huge question when one considers the infant financial markets and the lack of capital market law there. We turn to the challenges of M&As in China in the next section.

MERGERS AND ACQUISITIONS IN CHINA

Because M&A activities are inherently affected by the constraints of the particular institutional environment in which firms operate (North, 1990), it is important to note the institutional environment of China's economic reforms (Peng & Heath, 1996; Shenkar & Von Glinow, 1994). The rise of M&As since the 1980s is not an isolated incident; rather it is institutionally embedded in the expansion of China's economic reform efforts (Jefferson & Rawski, 1994).

Background

The pre-reform industrial structure in China was characterized by rigid central planning and extensive government control of state-owned enterprises (SOEs) (Perkins, 1994). With little autonomy and accountability, managers were not concerned about firm performance. As a result, the need to "grow" by exercising strategic choice was minimal for SOEs, and the notion of "strategizing" was foreign to these managers (Peng, 1997b; Tan & Litschert, 1994). In other words, SOE managers as agents of the state during the pre-reform era did not pursue the fundamental interests of the state (principal), namely development of the economy (Granick, 1990). As a result, SOE performance was grossly inadequate, thus necessitating reforms aimed at solving these agency problems.

A great deal of change has occurred since the reforms started in 1978 (Child, 1994). Chinese writers regarded the emergence of M&As as the "third wave" in industrial reform efforts (Lai, 1995, p. 95). Both of the first two "waves" were designed to solve agency problems at SOEs. The first wave was decentralization of managerial responsibility to the plant level so that administrative superiors would not interfere extensively with managerial decisions. However, the line between administrative and managerial responsibilities, without a legal and regulatory regime spelling out the boundaries of property rights, was too hard to draw, thus resulting in continuous intervention from the top and continued lack of accountability on the part of managers (Peng, 1996). As a result, the second wave, a management responsibility system, was unleashed (Child, 1994). This system also proved to be limited, however, since top managers engaged in extensive short-term maximizing behavior during their contract period in fear that policy changes would prove to be tentative once the contract expired (Boisot & Child, 1988; Lai, 1995, p. 144). Despite some improvement due to these two waves, the vast majority of SOEs continued to be plagued by lackluster performance, draining a huge amount of subsidies from the state ("Wake-Up Call," 1996; Wu, 1996).

M&As: The Third Wave

Against this background, M&As became the "third wave" to restructure SOEs. The initial motivation for such M&As was an effort by the government to use strong SOEs to rescue failing SOEs. The first M&As were arranged by the Baoding city government in Hebei province in 1984 (Lai, 1995, pp. 33, 337-338). These were considered to be a compromise measure to avoid poorly performing firms' bankruptcy, which was considered by the government to be politically and socially unacceptable.[1] Soon, this wave was felt in many parts of the country. According to official statistics, 6,226 firms acquired 3,966 others during the 1980s, transferring 8.2 billion yuan-worth of assets and reducing 522 million yuan of losses (Lai, 1995, p. 107). In the 1990s, the scale and scope of M&As intensified, resulting in 10,000 transactions in 1994 alone (Sun, 1995, p. 4).[2]

However, most M&As in the 1980s were not initiated by the acquiring firms seeking growth and expansion. Rather, government agencies at different levels had to search, persuade, and in some cases order strong firms to "take over" weak ones. As a result, managers at profitable enterprises had a strong incentive to just break even, in fear of being "asked" by administrative superiors to take over ailing firms (Peng, 1997b; Xiao, 1991). Moreover, once these forced M&As—similar to arranged marriages—were undertaken, some merged firms were unable to compete in the increasingly competitive market, a result very familiar to post-M&A researchers in the West (e.g., Caves, 1989; Hitt et al., 1996; Ravenscraft & Scherer, 1987).

The key problem that emerged in these so-called M&As was the lack of a clearly defined legal and regulatory property rights framework, which made it difficult for a market for M&As to emerge (Peng, 1994; Peng & Heath, 1996). In the 1980s, the government imposed a "three no change" policy governing M&As: No change (a) in affiliation relationships with government agencies, (b) in ownership structure, and (c) in fiscal and tax remittance channels (Peng, 1997b; Wu, 1990). Led by Wuhan in 1988, dozens of "M&A markets" were established in major cities. Nationwide, there were 122 such "markets" by 1993 (Sun, 1995, p. 118). However, these were no more than matchmaking agencies run by the government in search of willing (or reluctant) parties to take over nearly bankrupt firms. For the government, the fundamental motivation was to avoid the massive layoffs that would be generated by bankrupt firms (Sun, 1995, p. 121). This motive was at odds with that of many profitable firms being forced to acquire others, namely seeking better economic efficiency and performance. In order to achieve growth, these firms might want to engage in M&As, but the targets would not be those assigned by the government (Peng, 1997b).

In summary, instead of a strategy for firm growth, M&As emerged as a solution to performance problems at weak firms in the 1980s. The lack of "strategic factor markets" (Barney, 1986)—or the "market for corporate control" (Jensen, 1987)—resulted in continuous intervention by the government and in reluctant parties to M&As.

Recent Developments

M&As in China entered a new chapter when the Shanghai and Shenzhen Stock Exchanges were established in 1990 and 1991, respectively (Lau & Johnstone, 1995; Xia, Lin, & Grub, 1992). For the first time, Chinese firms were able to acquire other firms' stocks through direct purchase on the stock exchanges, thus allowing for M&As based on acquiring firms' own initiative. These activities, together with the government-run "M&A markets," led to a diverse range of merger activities in the 1990s. Chinese writers grouped different kinds of M&As into eight categories in an order of increasing sophistication (Lai, 1995, pp. 108-110):

1. *Intra-industry M&As:* These are mostly M&As arranged through a government body, usually an industrial bureau in charge of the particular industry. Acquiring firms may not be interested in the particular target, and administrative orders may be used to "facilitate" these M&As.

2. *Inter-industry M&As:* Acquiring firms are usually interested in certain attributes of the target, such as land, plant, and/or distribution channels. Compared with the previous mode, the element of government intervention in inter-industry M&As is weaker and the element of "strategizing" is stronger on the part of the acquiring firms.

3. *Intra-regional M&As:* Arranged by local or regional governments, these M&As may be intra- or inter-industry. However, due to extensive local protectionism, the choice of acquisition targets is limited by the jurisdiction of the particular government, thus depressing acquiring firms' strategic choice.

4. *Inter-regional M&As:* This more aggressive M&A strategy is believed to promote more economies of scale and inter-regional trade. The government is less involved, and acquiring firms have a stronger sense of "strategizing."

5. *Intra-ownership M&As:* These involve only firms in the same ownership group; most pertain to M&As involving SOEs and M&As involving collective firms.

Among these, the government was initially extensively involved in SOE-only M&As. Recently, however, the government gradually distanced itself. These M&As can be intra-industry, inter-industry, or intra-regional, but rarely inter-regional.

6. *Inter-ownership M&As:* This is one of the recent developments and may involve collective and foreign-invested firms acquiring SOEs. It is still politically sensitive. The element of "strategizing" is very strong in these M&As.

7. *International M&As:* This was started by the Liaoning Provincial Government in 1989, which auctioned off 33 near-bankrupt SOEs to international bidders. Increasingly, foreign investors found that it was possible to "buy a piece of industry" in China (Ho, 1996). Currently, most target firms are small and midsize SOEs and collective firms. Large SOEs, many of which incur tremendous losses, are still off limits to foreign investors. On the other hand, exceptionally strong Chinese firms, such as Capital Steel, have also started to move abroad to acquire foreign firms (Lai, 1995, pp. 419-421; Ye, 1992; Zhang & Van den Bulcke, 1996).

8. *Open-market M&As:* This refers to acquiring firms through the stock exchanges in Shanghai and Shenzhen. The government plays a minimal role here, and the element of the "market" is the strongest. It is through this form that China's first hostile takeover battles were fought.

In summary, M&As in China in the 1990s have featured a diversity of forms, within and across industrial, regional, ownership, and national boundaries. Amid growing pains, a more comprehensive legal and regulatory framework has been gradually put in place, allowing for more sophisticated modes of M&As, such as international and open-market acquisitions, to take place. While the government is still involved in some M&As, it does not necessarily have to intervene in many others. As a result, a true M&A market, through the establishment of stock exchanges, has started to emerge, and firm growth via M&As have become possible for some Chinese enterprises.

TWO CASE STUDIES

Given that most readers may be unfamiliar with the processes of M&As in China, in this section we will use two well-known cases to illustrate different modes of M&As. The first reports China's first SOE M&A involving a full buyout. The second case focuses on the first hostile takeover battle in China.

Case 1: Beijing Gear Box Takes Over
Chaoyang Manufacturing (1987)

This was the first buyout case involving two SOEs in China, and was widely reported and discussed (Lai, 1995, pp. 321-325). Previous M&As had been arranged by the government; though assuming the assets and debts of the target firms, the acquiring firms usually did not pay for these assets. The acquiring firm in this case was the Beijing Automobile Gear Box Factory (hereafter Beijing Gear Box). It was the market leader in the automobile ball bearing industry, with 55% market share in China. With 87 million yuan in fixed assets, its annual pretax profits averaged an impressive 30 million yuan in the late 1980s. Among the top 13 firms in the industry, Beijing Gear Box generated more tax revenues than the rest of the 12 firms combined. More than 450 of its 6,000 employees were R&D (research and development) and engineering staff. By all accounts, this was one of the strongest and best-run SOEs. The top management articulated a clear vision for the growth of the firm: "Safeguard the Beijing market, dominate China, and go global." In order to attain its ambitious goals, it needed to grow, especially in the area of production capacity. By 1987, it reached a point where its physically constrained production facilities would not allow it to reach these goals. It had to rent a site at a high price in a suburb of Beijing in order to expand its production. Room for further generic expansion was limited.

The target firm was Chaoyang Manufacturing Factory (hereafter Chaoyang Manufacturing), which had extreme difficulties competing in the market. Its product line drifted from electronic components to souvenir bottoms, and its products were mostly stockpiled in the warehouse. While it had 836,000 yuan in fixed assets, losses amounted to 510,000 yuan in 1986. By 1987, all its production capacity was idle, and its 157 employees—who had very little to do—were paid only 70% of their salary. Without an infusion of capital and management expertise or a declaration of bankruptcy, it would have to continue to rely on subsidies from its administrative superior, Chaoyang District Government. However, Chaoyang Manufacturing had something that Beijing Gear Box needed, namely well-established production facilities in a suburb of Beijing that would make further expansion possible.

The initial negotiations between the two firms concentrated on forming an enterprise network whereby Beijing Gear Box would invest in Chaoyang Manufacturing in exchange for access to the latter's production facilities. As a way to bypass the "three no change" policy imposed by the government, cooperation through enterprise networks was the prevailing method for firm growth among different firms in China; it allowed for interfirm collaboration without formal transfer of ownership (Peng, 1997b; Peng & Heath, 1996). Chaoyang Manufacturing's previous collaboration with other enterprise networks had not been successful, however, and it worried about being taken advantage of by the stronger partner. Beijing Gear Box, on the other hand, worried about how to protect its investment in case the collaboration broke down. As a result, the negotiations shifted to discussions about a possible takeover of Chaoyang Manufacturing by Beijing Gear Box.

Since Chaoyang Manufacturing was administratively controlled by the Chaoyang District Government, and Beijing Gear Box belonged to the Beijing Automobile Corporation, a takeover would violate one of the "three no change" policies governing M&As in the 1980s, namely, no change in affiliation relationships with government agencies. After negotiations involving the two firms and the Chaoyang District Government, the district government decided to sell Chaoyang Manufacturing to Beijing Gear Box for a price of 5.05 million yuan, almost six times the fixed assets of Chaoyang Manufacturing. Thus, the first M&A involving a buyout occurred in China.

This case is interesting because the element of "strategizing" is evident. Rather than entering a forced marriage arranged by the government, Beijing Gear Box had a clear set of goals it intended to achieve. Acquiring Chaoyang Manufacturing would help achieve these goals. After one year, Beijing Gear Box's pretax profits increased 200,000 yuan. Former employees of Chaoyang Manufacturing were able to become a part of the workforce at Beijing Gear Box and improve their earnings. Finally, the Chaoyang District Government got completely rid of a "black hole" that had sucked in an endless stream of subsidies and so found itself a lot richer than before. This case was widely regarded as one of the institutional innovations in the reform era, which could lead toward real M&As based on acquiring firms' own initiatives, instead of administratively arranged M&As.

A number of problems emerged, however. First, the lack of a property-rights-based legal and regulatory framework was a major obstacle. Parties to this deal undertook the transaction without legal protection. The notary public office refused to certify the documents, citing the lack of legal precedents. Second, despite some preliminary work in asset appraisal and financial auditing, lack of financial disclosure resulted in Beijing Gear Box's postmerger "discovery" of additional debts incurred by its acquired target. Third, the Chaoyang District Government, after obtaining the payment from Beijing Gear Box, did not know how to use this money because there were no guidelines on how to use the proceeds of SOE sellouts. Instead of channeling the money for productive purposes, a special account had to be set up to await instruction from higher authorities. Fourth, there was no information on whether former managers at Chaoyang Manufacturing were disciplined. The usual practice of the government was to reassign these managers to new posts, which would hardly prevent agency problems on the part of these managers. Finally, although the merger was based on Beijing Gear Box's initiatives, the involvement of the government was extensive. Since none of the involved firms was traded in the financial market, the issue of the acquisition's impact on stock prices was irrelevant. In short, the market for M&As was not there yet.

Case 2: The Baoan-Yanzhong Hostile Takeover Battle (1993)

As the first hostile takeover battle in China, the Baoan-Yanzhong hostile takeover caught considerable practitioner, media, and academic attention in China (Lai, 1995, pp. 365-376). It involved two firms organized as corporations with shares traded on the Shanghai and Shenzhen Stock Exchanges. Though the predecessors of these firms were SOEs, they became publicly owned corporations by issuing stocks on the open market. As a result, the state was no longer the principal of these firms; shareholders who were interested in the growth of their wealth became the principals. This case clearly demonstrated the maturity of the Chinese firm and the emergence of a market for corporate control via M&As.

The target firm was Yanzhong Enterprises Limited (hereafter Yanzhong), a Shanghai-based firm producing computer and electronic accessories, stationery, and household goods. It was one of the first firms listed on the Shanghai Stock Exchange, and its total capitalization was 30 million yuan by the end of 1992. In that year, its sales reached 13.88 million yuan, and pretax profits were 3.52 million yuan. Its profitability level relative to total assets was considered low by Chinese standards (2.83% for return on assets and 6.80% for net profit margin; see Table 4.1). Nevertheless, its return on equity was reasonably high (20.62%). In asset management, the company revealed a high level of efficiency in inventory management, accounts receivable management, and total asset management. As shown in Table 4.1, relevant ratios in asset management all indicated satisfactory levels. A major problem appeared in the firm's liquidity and solvency. According to our computation based on the firm's financial statements, both current ratio and quick ratio were quite low (1.36 and 1.26, respectively). Although book-based debt-to-assets and debt-to-equity ratios were not at the high-risk level, the actual numbers of these ratios were expected to be much higher, because, like many other firms in China, Yanzhong relied heavily on accounts payable to meet its short-term financing needs.

TABLE 4.1 Key Financial Ratios of Shanghai Yanzhong in 1992

Ratios	1992
Profitability	
Gross profit margin	15.21%
Net profit margin	6.80%
Return on assets	2.83%
Return on equity	20.62%
Liquidity	
Current ratio	1.36
Quick ratio	1.26
Inventory to working capital	0.25
Leverage	
Debt-to-assets ratio	0.27
Debt-to-equity ratio	0.37
Asset Management	
Inventory turnover	5.80%
Fixed-asset turnover	1.98%
Accounts receivable turnover	4.64%

SOURCE: Authors' calculation based on the firm's balance sheet and income statement in 1992.

The acquiring firm was a Shenzhen-based conglomerate, Baoan Enterprises (Group) Limited (hereafter Baoan). Listed on the Shenzhen Stock Exchange, this firm had a total capitalization of 264 million yuan by the end of 1992. Baoan is active in a number of fields, such as real estate development, high-tech industries, domestic trading, and international trading. Geographically, the firm had a presence in Shanghai, Beijing, Wuhan, Changchung, Hong Kong, and New York. As one of the best-known conglomerates in Southern China, its 1992 sales were 773.36 million yuan, and pretax profits were 259.16 million yuan. Headed by a group of aggressive managers, the firm pursued a strategy of product and regional diversification in order to achieve growth. Its stated goal was to become a strong multinational corporation. It was unthinkable, according to its managers, that a China-based multinational had not established a strong presence in such a major Chinese city as Shanghai; the Yanzhong acquisition would be a major step in that direction.

Before initiating the battle, Baoan did its homework. It focused on Yanzhong for four reasons. First, Yanzhong's unsatisfactory performance resulted in a low share price of its stocks, traded at 8.1 yuan per share in July 1993. Second, Yanzhong's weak capitalization base led Baoan to believe that, with its war chest of cash reserves, it would be possible to take over the target. Third, Yanzhong's corporate charters had no anti-takeover clauses, which legally permitted it to be taken over. Finally, Baoan believed that Yanzhong had strong potential after significant restructuring that could contribute to Baoan's portfolio of businesses. In short, Yanzhong was an ideal target for Baoan's seeking expansion in Shanghai. Baoan's top management ordered three subsidiaries to be the "front-line soldiers" of this takeover battle, Baoan Shanghai Company, Baoan East China Health Products Company, and Shenzhen Longgang Electronics Company.

During September 1993, Yanzhong's share price started to rise in active trading on the Shanghai Stock Exchange, despite the general lack of trading activities. It reached 8.8 yuan on September 14 and 10.47 yuan on September 29. Rumors and takeover speculation intensified, particularly since nobody had yet filed a report with the China Securities Regulatory Commission. Such a report was required when any investor accumulated 5% or more of the shares in a company.[3] Very few people knew that Baoan already controlled 10.6% of Yanzhong's shares. These shares were bought separately by three subsidiaries of Baoan, and none of these three crossed the 5% threshold. Due to their lack of experience, top management at Yanzhong were not alarmed by the steady increase in volume and share price for its shares on the Shanghai Stock Exchange.[4]

The "attack" was launched on September 30, when three subsidiaries of Baoan used a blitzkrieg tactic to increase their control of Yanzhong from 10.6% to 15.98% within a few hours. All together, Baoan spent over 1 billion yuan for 4.79 million Yanzhong shares. The final hours of trading saw Yanzhong's share price rise to an unusually high level of more than 40 yuan per share. Since they already controlled enough shares of Yanzhong, two of Baoan's subsidiaries even sold 246,000 shares back to the public for profit. By 11:15 a.m., trading of Yanzhong's shares was stopped by the Exchange, and Baoan filed a report with the China Securities Regulatory Commission, which was broadcast live via a large computer screen at the Exchange: "Since today, our company has controlled more than 5% of the shares of Yanzhong." Yanzhong's managers were stunned when this "declaration of war" reached them.

For M&A researchers and observers in the West, the following scenarios would be very familiar: Yanzhong struggled to resist the takeover, and Baoan continued to apply pressure. Yanzhong was lucky that October 1 and 2 were China's National Day holidays, and its managers were able to use this time to attempt to formulate an anti-takeover strategy. With financial advisors from Hong Kong, Yanzhong faced three options: (a) Repurchase the stock that Baoan had garnered, which would result in more debt; (b) find a "white knight" that might possibly take the same action, but in a much less brutal fashion; (c) attack Baoan on the grounds of technicality in that it failed to report to the authorities immediately after it acquired more than 5% of Yanzhong's shares; instead it waited until it had 15.98% of the shares.

Baoan's managers, on the other hand, used language that might be frequently heard from such corporate raiders in the West as James Goldsmith (Deitzer, Krigline, & Peterson, 1990; Wansell, 1987). First, they stressed that maximizing shareholders' wealth was the fundamental purpose of the corporate form of organization, which, in China, was a recent institutional innovation that started in the late 1980s. They pointed out that anti-takeover measures such as repurchase of the shares would only result in losses to the shareholders. Second, they stated that they were interested in restructuring Yanzhong to help it focus on realizing its potential. Finally, they revealed that they were not "hostile" to Yanzhong; in fact, they planned to retain most middle management—however, they did not say anything about how they would treat the top managers at Yanzhong.

The high drama continued on October 6, when a team of top managers from Baoan held a meeting with their counterparts at Yanzhong's headquarters. The Baoan team demanded board representation because their company was now the largest shareholder in Yanzhong. The Yanzhong team, on the other hand, argued that they were not willing to settle, given the alleged illegality of Baoan's late reporting, until the China Securities Regulatory Commission investigated the case. Afterwards, both sides held separate press conferences, starting a new "media war." Baoan even leaked a new "shadow cabinet" for Yanzhong's top management team, pointing out who the new managers would be and where the old managers would have to go.

On October 22, the China Securities Regulatory Commission announced its rulings: (a) Baoan was fined 1 million yuan for failing to report its intention after crossing the 5% threshold; (b) Baoan's profits, generated by selling 264,000 shares back to the public on September 30, were to be given to Yanzhong; and (c) Baoan would not be allowed to purchase more Yanzhong shares until November 4. The Chinese media, however, considered Baoan as the real winner, both in terms of corporate reputation and of financial strength. Within a few weeks, Baoan became a household name in Shanghai and other parts of China. Yanzhong's management, on the other hand, had to learn the lesson that if they could not improve corporate performance and share price, the firm might become a takeover target again, and they might lose their jobs.

This case was fascinating because it resembled familiar features of M&As in the West, on the one hand, and retained some uniquely Chinese characteristics, on the other hand. This case is much more sophisticated than the previous one, and the element of "strategizing" is very strong: The entire takeover was planned and carried out by Baoan's top management, using military terminology such as front-line actions, logistics, stealth attack, and blitzkrieg. The stated objective was to restructure Yanzhong for the purpose of maximizing shareholder wealth. As found in financial economics research in the West, Yanzhong's shareholders experienced substantial gain when the share price rose by almost five times in 2 months (July to September 1993). Since the takeover was not completed, it was difficult to assess post-M&A performance. The case, however, indicated the emergence of a functioning financial market in which takeover battles could be fought. Thus, the stock exchanges in China did start to resemble Western financial markets as "the arena in which alternative management teams compete for the rights to manage corporate resources" (Jensen, 1987, p. 106). From reluctant M&As arranged by the government in the 1980s, M&As in China have come a long way to enable strong firms such as Baoan to flex their muscles in order to achieve growth.

This case was also a significant test for China's fledgling legal and regulatory framework governing the operations of financial markets. Although any investor accumulating more than 5% of the shares of a single company was required to file a report with the authorities, no hostile acquirer had done this prior to this case. Moreover, the law was ambiguous, which led to Baoan's liberal interpretation that as long as each of its three subsidiaries did not cross the 5% threshold, it did not have to report. The law became clearer after the China Securities Regulatory Commission issued its rulings, finding that Baoan erred on technical grounds.

DISCUSSION

Having reviewed prior research on M&As in the West, the development of M&As in China, and two well-known cases, it becomes possible to evaluate the viability of firm growth via M&As, as well as the role of M&As in restructuring the Chinese economy.

The Viability of Firm Growth via M&As

Our previous research suggested that given the underdevelopment of strategic factor markets such as the financial markets in China, "the route for firms to grow through mergers and acquisitions would be treacherous" (Peng & Heath, 1996, p. 512). We did note that there were many "M&As" that were politically motivated "consolidations" arranged by the government in an effort to rescue failing firms (Peng, 1997b). As a result, strong firms resented being "asked" by their superiors to take over weak ones. One manager we interviewed said: "We are really fed up with these so-called 'acquisitions' which are the Ministry's euphemism for 'bailout.' . . . Do we like to acquire other firms? You bet we do, if we are able to select our own acquisition targets which we believe will help us build our firm" (Peng, Luo, Shenkar, & Harwit, 1997).

While the previous waves of reform efforts, such as decentralization and management responsibility system, had their limits, the third wave, namely M&As, was believed to be able largely to solve agency problems at SOEs and boost their performance. The M&As in the 1980s did not fulfill such a promise. According to many observers, many early M&As in the 1980s were not true M&As ("The Next Hot Spot," 1995). Local governments acted as "boards of directors" and restructured thousands of these firms (Walder, 1995). As our two case studies highlight, however, things are rapidly changing in China's transitional economy. Since Beijing Gear Box's buyout of its target in 1987, it has become possible to acquire other firms directly, based on the acquiring firm's own initiative. With Baoan's revolutionary attempt to take over Yanzhong in 1993, a new era of M&As in China started that allows for firm growth via M&As.

The rise of real M&As can be a promising way to restructure China's large number of lackluster SOEs and discipline their managers. Facing persistently poor performance due to extensive agency problems at SOEs, Chinese researchers and policymakers have since the early 1990s shown a great deal of interest in the "modern enterprise system," which is the Chinese term for the corporate form of organization in the West (Zhang, Yuan, & Hua, 1994). When SOEs are transformed into publicly owned corporations, managers can be held accountable for their performance, as reflected in the share price of the companies' stocks. As the Baoan-Yanzhong case illustrated, if managers at the target firm are not performing well, the firm runs the risk of being taken over by an outsider, and managers face the real danger of being replaced. Gone are the old days—like the 1980s—when managers at the acquired firms would be automatically reassigned by the government. Thus, the M&As in the 1990s, operated through financial markets, are gradually beginning to fulfill this promise of disciplining agency problems at SOEs and providing incentive for performance improvement.

On the other hand, while open-market M&As have become possible in the mid-1990s, such opportunities are limited. By the end of 1994, there were only 289 firms listed on the Shanghai and Shenzhen Stock Exchanges (Dong & Hu, 1995, p. 24). These firms were a small fraction of the 100,000 SOEs and the millions of collective enterprises. Apparently, most of the 10,000 M&A deals that occurred in 1994 (Sun, 1995, p. 4) were not undertaken through the financial markets, indicating the coexistence of several of the modes of M&As we described in the "Recent Developments" section. Therefore, it is important to note the government's continued interest and presence in many of these M&A deals, while acknowledging the emergence of M&As as a growth strategy based on acquirers' own initiatives.

Research Implications

Given that M&As are a recent phenomenon in China, there has been very little rigorous research on this important topic. Most Chinese writings on this subject have been "thought pieces," with little connection to the M&A literature in the West (see Sun, 1995, for an exception). Western researchers, on the other hand, have yet to appreciate the complexity and intricacies of M&As in China. This is unfortunate, because (a) the importance of M&As in China's reform efforts calls for improved understanding of this phenomenon; (b) the increased interest among foreign firms in using M&As as an entry strategy into China also necessitates more knowledge about these activities; and (c) finally, the Chinese experience may help shed light on how M&As can be used to restructure and discipline firms in other transitional economies, such as Eastern Europe and the post-Soviet republics (Peng, 1997b).

Given that research on M&As has always been an interdisciplinary enterprise, researchers from multiple disciplines can jointly advance our understanding of this important issue. For strategic management researchers, in-depth investigation of M&A strategies in China can yield insights into a core question in strategy research: What kind of diversification strategy via M&As results in the best performance? (Hitt et al., 1996; Rumelt, 1974). For organizational researchers interested in the growth of the firm (Penrose, 1959), a growth strategy via M&As can be viewed as a strategic choice that is believed to be superior to the other two choices, namely internal expansion and network building (Peng, 1994, 1997b; Peng & Heath, 1996; Peng et al., 1997). The more behavior-oriented management researchers can probe into the psychology of Chinese managers initiating M&As, thus helping to answer a question that has intrigued organizational behavior scholars and human resource managers for decades, namely: What is the motivation to manage? (Miner, Chen, & Yu, 1991). Finally, for international management researchers interested in successful entry in China, how M&As can help foreign entrants establish their presence in China can be a fascinating area of inquiry (Luo, 1995, 1997; Peng, 1995, 1997a).

For financial and IO economists, the debate about the role of M&As in a modern economy can be extended to China. While financial economists such as Jensen (1987) may regard the gains of shareholder wealth in takeover cases such as Baoan-Yanzhong as new evidence of the positive role of M&As, IO economists such as Ravenscraft and Scherer (1987) might say, "Wait until the dust settles." It is important to caution that M&As may not be a panacea for all firms, given the persistent findings of the loss of long-run competitiveness in post-M&A firms in the West (Caves, 1989; Hitt et al., 1996; Ravenscraft & Scherer, 1987). Since M&As are such a recent phenomenon, longitudinal data on post-M&A performance in China have been rarely reported. Further research in this area is clearly needed.

For sociological researchers with a negative view on M&As, further research in China may help advance their case (Schweiger & Walsh, 1990). Without exaggerating, one can argue that the Chinese government shares this view for political reasons. Despite the widespread lackluster performance of thousands of SOEs, the government is still obsessed with avoiding large-scale shutdowns and layoffs, which can create social problems threatening to the stability of the regime ("Wake-Up Call," 1996). The initial interest in arranged M&As in the 1980s was a direct result of this thinking. As competition intensifies in the Chinese economy, however, real M&As aiming at disciplining inefficient firms have started to occur, thus necessitating an increasing number of layoffs. How to minimize the human costs of M&As (Buono & Bowditch, 1989) appears to be a topic that will resonate well among Chinese officials and managers.

Finally, for legal and institutional researchers, how China creates an increasingly sophisticated legal and regulatory framework is a classic case of institution building in a transitional economy (North, 1990; Watson, 1989). While most branches of law in China have been underdeveloped, corporate law has been one of the least developed (Kirby, 1995). In the early 1980s, however, some researchers noted that we "may be optimistic about the formation and growth of contract law in China" (Lee, 1983, p. 215). Such a prediction seems to be borne out by the more than 500 pieces of economic legislature China has promulgated since 1979, many of which are the first of their kind in Chinese legal history, including Accounting Law, Bankruptcy Law, Contract Law, Corporate Law, and Joint Venture Law (Clarke, 1991; Potter, 1995). Nevertheless, a lot more work remains to be done since a comprehensive and credible legal infrastructure is a prerequisite for an increasing number of M&As to take place through the financial markets (Peng, 1994). Fundamentally, only through independent legal and regulatory institutions can the separation of the state and the firm become a reality in China (Peng, 1996, in press).

In summary, M&As in China offer fascinating grounds for testing existing theories and developing new ones (Shenkar & Von Glinow, 1994). While researchers from different backgrounds have their own disciplinary focus, one issue that intrigues scholars across disciplinary boundaries is: Do M&As come in waves? This is true, for example, in the case of the United States, with four documented waves historically (and maybe a current ongoing one) (Barney, 1997; Stearns & Allan, 1996). Whether M&As will occur in waves in China remains to be seen. However, given the Chinese conceptualization of M&As as the third "wave" in industrial reform efforts, that may well be the case.

Practical Implications

A number of implications can be drawn for policymakers and practitioners. For policymakers, sustained institution-building efforts are necessary. Currently, the regulations governing the Shanghai and Shenzhen Stock Exchanges are found to be "overlapping, repetitive, clumsy, ill-organized and poorly-drafted" (Lau & Johnstone, 1995, p. 130). It is not even clear which regulations are legally binding, and rules are not necessarily followed. Moreover, many of the current regulations are not comprehensible to foreigners. Foreign direct investment via mergers and acquisitions will be of great value not only to the target Chinese firms but also for the modernization of Chinese industry as a whole. M&As with transnational investors can enhance productivity through re-innovation, improve economic efficiency through reengineering, reduce bureaucratic costs through restructuring, and increase solvency through the injection of cash flow. From the policy-making perspective, the government should, on the one hand, create and maintain a stable, transparent, and consummate institutional environment for both domestic and foreign investors, and on the other hand, avoid overcontrol by foreign investors in those industries that are strategically vital to the national economy (Luo, in press).

The long-anticipated official sanction of the central government was issued on November 14, 1993, when it passed the landmark document *A Resolution on Several Issues in Establishing a Socialist Market Economy* that formally acknowledged the value and legitimacy of private enterprises and endorsed more liberal reform measures for SOEs and collective enterprises (Dong & Hu, 1995, p. 20). As a major agenda for Chinese policymakers, the establishment of an operational-level policy system on the issue seems the key to the success of the development of mergers and acquisitions at the current stage. In addition, the harmonization of nationwide policies is important because, as a result of decentralization, various local governments tend to have interfered in firm behavior and enacted a number of region-specific rules and regulations on M&As that are in conflict with those of the central government.

For practitioners, mergers and acquisitions provide many more opportunities for business development and firm growth. Through M&As, relevant parties can optimize their economies of scale or scope and can maximize their financial or operational synergies. To accomplish these goals, it is important for these organizations to assess and analyze the degree of interfirm complementarity or indivisibility in needs, motivations, resources, capabilities, skills, knowledge, and experience. This complementarity has been recognized as the primary determinant of the success of M&A activities. In today's China, interfirm fit in financial structure and strength, technological capability and orientation, organizational skills and development, and marketing expertise and experience is particularly of utmost importance for the firms, because these skills or strengths constitute distinctive competitive advantages ensuring their survival and growth in the nation (Luo, 1996b).

For foreign investors, investing in China has always been a challenge, especially given the many unfamiliar open and secret regulations (Carver, 1996). Traditionally, foreign investment was limited to establishing joint ventures (JVs) or wholly owned subsidiaries (WOSs) in China, which required some transfer of management and technology (Luo, 1996a; Peng, 1997a, 1997c). In contrast, investing in China through M&As is a purely financial activity that offers several advantages. First, the investor may choose to attend to the target firm's operations, as in the case of JVs and WOSs, but the investor does not necessarily have to do so. As a result, M&As not only allow corporate investors to enter China, but also allow general investors to gain entry through holding companies, as in the case of many Hong Kong-based companies. Second, cash flow may be generated in a shorter time than in the case of a JV or WOS, since the acquired firm, by definition, does not have to be built from scratch. Finally, M&A deals may be more attractive than JVs or WOSs because M&As offer immediate access at little or no cost to such resources as land, ready-made distribution channels, and skilled labor—even when target firms have been losing money (Dong & Hu, 1995, p. 20).

CONCLUSION

M&As are an integral part of any market economy, enhancing economic efficiency by reallocating and recombining corporate resources for better use. From a modest start as the government's compromise measure to avoid firms' bankruptcies, M&As have been undertaken by Chinese firms for more than a decade during the reform era. Outside observers may not agree that the initial M&As were real M&As since they were all arranged by the government. In recent years, however, real M&As have started to emerge, based on acquiring firms' strategic objectives for growth via M&As.

As the Chinese economy continues its drive toward a market orientation, it is safe to predict that M&As will become an increasingly important strategy for firm growth in China. Currently, we still know very little about these activities, especially their long-run impacts. Because more people and firms exist in China than in any other country, no managerial, financial, economic, or sociological theory can claim to establish validity without exploring its implications in that country (Boyacigiller & Adler, 1991; Shenkar & Von Glinow, 1994). Given the sheer size of the Chinese economy and the rise of M&As in recent years (Overholt, 1993), it will be difficult to dismiss their behavior as outliers that can be ignored by discipline-based mainstream researchers. As we have illustrated, a significant amount of future research is necessary to further our understanding of this "hot" business issue in China in the next millennium.

NOTES

1. The Bankruptcy Law was passed by the National People's Congress in 1986 and took effect in 1988 (Watson, 1989). In 1988, the heavily debt-ridden Shenyang Anticorrosion Chemical Plant became the first SOE in China to be declared bankrupt. Employees threatened a sit-in strike, and the local officials were terrified. Officials eventually convinced another profitable SOE to "take over" the bankrupt company, including all its employees and outstanding debts ("Bankruptcy Law," 1988).

2. In comparison, there were 55,000 M&A deals in the United States in the 1980s, valued at just under $2 trillion (Hitt et al., 1996, p. 1084). The 1980s witnessed the fourth and largest merger wave in U.S. history (Stearns & Allan, 1996). However, some observers argued that there is an ongoing, fifth merger wave, starting in the mid-1990s, that surpasses the level of the 1980s wave. In 1994, there were 5,800 M&As in the United States, valued at $344 billion, beating the previous record of $336 billion in 1988 (Barney, 1997, p. 437). This comparison indicates that if one looks at the number—rather than the value—of M&A deals, there is indeed a huge M&A wave in China.

3. This requirement is the same as the Form 13-D requirement of the Securities and Exchange Commission in the United States.

4. Even if Yanzhong's top managers had been alarmed, they would still have the difficulty of sorting out and identifying one particular buyer or group of buyers as a potential corporate raider. This is not a specifically Chinese problem, but a worldwide problem for target firm management.

See, for example, the case of Goldsmith's hostile takeover of Goodyear Tire on the New York Stock Exchange in 1986 (Deitzer, Krigline, & Peterson, 1990).

REFERENCES

Anslinger, P. L., & Copeland, T. E. (1996). Growth through acquisitions: A fresh look. *Harvard Business Review, 74*(1), 126-135.

Bankruptcy law to go into effect in November. (1988, July 28). *China Daily,* p. 2.

Barney, J. B. (1986). Strategic factor markets: Expectations, luck and business strategy. *Management Science, 32,* 1231-1241.

Barney, J. B. (1988). Returns to bidding firms in mergers and acquisitions: Reconsidering the relatedness hypothesis. *Strategic Management Journal, 9,* 71-78.

Barney, J. B. (1997). *Gaining and sustaining competitive advantage.* Reading, MA: Addison-Wesley.

Berle, A. A., & Means, G. C. (1932). *The modern corporation and private property.* New York: Macmillan.

Bettis, R. A., & Hall, W. K. (1982). Diversification strategy, accounting determined risk, and accounting determined return. *Academy of Management Journal, 25*(2), 254-264.

Boisot, M., & Child, J. (1988). The iron law of fiefs: Bureaucratic failure and the problem of governance in the Chinese economic reforms. *Administrative Science Quarterly, 33,* 507-527.

Boyacigiller, N., & Adler, N. J. (1991). The parochial dinosaur: Organizational science in a global context. *Academy of Management Review, 16,* 262-290.

Brown, D. H., & Porter, R. (Eds.). (1996). *Management issues in China: Vol. 1. Domestic enterprises.* London: Routledge & Kegan Paul.

Buono, A. F., & Bowditch, J. L. (1989). *The human side of mergers and acquisitions: Managing collisions between people and organizations.* San Francisco: Jossey-Bass.

Carver, A. (1996). Open and secret regulations and their implication for foreign investment. In J. Child & Y. Lu (Eds.), *Management issues in China: Vol. 2. International enterprises* (pp. 11-29). London: Routledge & Kegan Paul.

Caves, R. E. (1989). Mergers, takeovers, and economic efficiency. *International Journal of Industrial Organization, 7,* 151-174.

Chatterjee, S., & Lubatkin, M. (1990). Corporate mergers, stockholder diversification, and changes in systematic risk. *Strategic Management Journal, 11*(4), 255-268.

Child, J. (1994). *Management in China during the age of reform.* Cambridge, UK: Cambridge University Press.

Child, J., & Lu, Y. (Eds.). (1996). *Management issues in China: Vol. 2. International enterprises.* London: Routledge & Kegan Paul.

Clarke, D. C. (1991). What's law got to do with it? Legal institutions and economic reform in China. *UCLA Pacific Basin Law Journal, 10,* 1-76.

Davies, H. (1995). *China business: Context and issues.* Hong Kong: Longman.

Deitzer, B. A., Krigline, A. G., & Peterson, T. (1990). Goodyear Tire and the Goldsmith challenge. In L. Digman (Ed.), *Strategic management* (2nd ed., pp. 630-653). Chicago: Irwin.

Dong, J. L., & Hu, J. (1995, December). Mergers and acquisitions in China. *Economic Review of the Federal Reserve Bank of Atlanta*, pp. 15-29.

Fama, E. (1980). Agency problems and the theory of the firm. *Journal of Political Economy, 88*, 288-298.

Granick, D. (1990). *Chinese state enterprises*. Chicago: University of Chicago Press.

Haspeslagh, P. C., & Jemison, D. B. (1991). *Managing acquisitions: Creating value through corporate renewal*. New York: Free Press.

Hitt, M. A., Hoskisson, R. E., Johnson, R. A., & Moesel, D. D. (1996). The market for corporate control and firm innovation. *Academy of Management Journal, 39*(5), 1084-1119.

Ho, H. (1996, January-February). Buying a piece of PRC industry. *The China Business Review*, pp. 34-37.

Ilinitch, A. Y., & Zeithaml, C. P. (1995). Operationalizing and testing Galbraith's center of gravity theory. *Strategic Management Journal, 16*(5), 401-410.

Jefferson, G. H., & Rawski, T. G. (1994). Enterprise reform in Chinese industry. *Journal of Economic Perspectives, 8*(2), 47-70.

Jemison, D. B., & Sitkin, S. (1986). Corporate acquisitions: A process perspective. *Academy of Management Review, 11*, 145-163.

Jensen, M. C. (1987). The free cash flow theory of takeovers: A financial perspective on mergers and acquisitions and the economy. In L. Browne & E. Rosengren (Eds.), *The merger boom* (pp. 102-143). Boston: Federal Reserve Bank of Boston.

Jensen, M. C., & Meckling, W. H. (1976). Theory of the firm: Managerial behavior, agency cost, and ownership structure. *Journal of Financial Economics, 11*, 5-50.

Jensen, M. C., & Ruback, R. (1983). The market for corporate control: The scientific evidence. *Journal of Financial Economics, 11*(5), 5-50.

Jones, G. R., & Hill, C. W. L. (1988). Transaction cost analysis of strategy-structure choice. *Strategic Management Journal, 9*, 159-172.

Kelley, L., & Shenkar, O. (Eds.). (1993). *International business in China*. London: Routledge & Kegan Paul.

Kirby, W. C. (1995). China unincorporated: Company law and business enterprise in twentieth-century China. *Journal of Asian Studies, 54*(1), 43-63.

Lai, Y. (Ed.). (1995). *Zhongguo qiye jianbin quanshu* [Enterprise mergers and acquisitions in China: A complete book]. Beijing: China Economics Press.

Lau, A., & Johnstone, L. (1995). The development of China's financial markets: The Shenzhen Stock Exchange. In H. Davies (Ed.), *China business* (pp. 117-136). Hong Kong: Longman.

Lee, F. O. (1983). Formation of contract and contract law through multinational joint ventures: Indonesia, China and the Third World. *The International Lawyer, 17*(2), 257-281.

Lubatkin, M. (1987). Merger strategies and stockholder value. *Strategic Management Journal, 8*, 39-54.

Luo, Y. (1995). Business strategy, market structure, and performance of international joint ventures: The case of joint ventures in China. *Management International Review, 35*, 241-264.

Luo, Y. (1996a). Evaluating strategic alliance performance in China. *Long Range Planning, 29*(4), 532-540.

Luo, Y. (1996b). Partner selection and international joint venture performance: Chinese evidence. *Academy of Management Best Papers Proceedings, 1996*, pp. 161-165.

Luo, Y. (1997). Global strategy and performance of foreign-invested enterprises in China. *Group and Organization Management, 22*(1), 87-116.

Luo, Y. (in press). Industry attractiveness, firm competence, and international investment performance in a transitional economy. *Bulletin of Economic Research.*

Markides, C. C. (1995). Diversification, restructuring and economic performance. *Strategic Management Journal, 16,* 101-118.

Marris, R. (1964). *The economic theory of managerial capitalism.* London: Macmillan.

Miner, J. B., Chen, C.-C., & Yu, K. C. (1991). Theory testing under adverse conditions: Motivation to manage in the People's Republic of China. *Journal of Applied Psychology, 76*(3), 343-349.

Mizruchi, M. S. (1983). Who controls whom? An examination of the relation between management and board of directors in large American corporations. *Academy of Management Review, 8,* 426-435.

Montgomery, C. A. (1985). Product market diversification and market power. *Academy of Management Journal, 28,* 789-798.

The next hot spot for M&A: Shanghai. (1995, March 13). *Business Week,* p. 56.

North, D. (1990). *Institutions, institutional change and economic performance.* New York: Norton.

Overholt, W. H. (1993). *The rise of China: How economic reform is creating a new superpower.* New York: Norton.

Palepu, K. (1985). Diversification strategy, profit performance and the entropy measure. *Strategic Management Journal, 6,* 239-255.

Peng, M. W. (1994). Organizational changes in planned economies in transition: An eclectic model. *Advances in International Comparative Management, 9,* 223-251.

Peng, M. W. (1995). Foreign direct investment in the innovation-driven stage: Toward a learning option perspective. In M. Green & R. NcNaughton (Eds.), *The location of foreign direct investment* (pp. 29-42). London: Avebury.

Peng, M. W. (1996). Modeling China's economic reforms through an organizational approach: The case of the M-form hypothesis. *Journal of Management Inquiry, 5*(1), 45-58.

Peng, M. W. (1997a). The China strategy: A tale of two firms. In C. Hill (Ed.), *International business* (2nd ed., pp. 107-118). Chicago: Irwin.

Peng, M. W. (1997b). Firm growth in transitional economies: Three longitudinal cases from China, 1989-96. *Organization Studies, 18*(3), 385-413.

Peng, M. W. (1997c). Winning structures. *The China Business Review, 24*(1), 30-33.

Peng, M. W. (in press). The state, the firm, and economic performance: A review from the midpoint. *China Review International.*

Peng, M. W., & Heath, P. S. (1996). The growth of the firm in planned economies in transition: Institutions, organizations, and strategic choice. *Academy of Management Review, 21*(2), 492-528.

Peng, M. W., Luo, Y., Shenkar, O., & Harwit, E. (1997, January). The growth of the firm in China: An information-processing perspective. *Proceedings of the Hawaii International Conference on Systems Sciences* (CD/ROM), Maui.

Penrose, E. T. (1959). *The theory of the growth of the firm.* New York: John Wiley.

Perkins, D. (1994). Completing China's move to the market. *Journal of Economic Perspectives, 8*(2), 23-46.

Perrow, C. (1986). *Complex organizations: A critical essay* (3rd ed.). New York: Random House.

Pfeffer, J., & Salancik, G. R. (1978). *The external control of organizations.* New York: Harper Row.

Porter, M. E. (1987, May-June). From competitive advantage to corporate strategy. *Harvard Business Review,* pp. 43-59.

Potter, P. B. (1995). Foreign investment law in the People's Republic of China: Dilemmas of state control. *The China Quarterly,* No. 141, pp. 155-185.

Powell, W. W. (1990). Neither market nor hierarchy: Network forms of organization. *Research in Organizational Behavior, 12,* 295-336.

Prahalad, C. K., & Bettis, R. A. (1986). The dominant logic: A new linkage between diversity and performance. *Strategic Management Journal, 7,* 485-501.

Ramanujam, V., & Varadarajan, P. (1989). Research on corporate diversification: A synthesis. *Strategic Management Journal, 10,* 523-551.

Ravenscraft, D. J., & Scherer, F. M. (1987). *Mergers, sell-offs, and economic efficiency.* Washington, DC: Brookings Institution.

Reed, R., & Luffman, G. A. (1986). Diversification: The growing confusion. *Strategic Management Journal, 7,* 29-36.

Roll, R. (1986). The hubris hypothesis of corporate takeovers. *Journal of Business, 59,* 197-216.

Rumelt, R. P. (1974). *Strategy, structure, and economic performance.* Boston: Harvard Business School, Division of Research.

Salter, M. S., & Weinhold, W. S. (1979). *Diversification through acquisition.* New York: Free Press.

Schleifer, A., & Vishny, R. (1991). Takeovers in the '60s and the '80s: Evidence and implications. *Strategic Management Journal, 12*(Winter special issue), 51-59.

Schweiger, D., & Walsh, J. P. (1990). Mergers and acquisitions: An interdisciplinary view. *Research in Personnel and Human Resource Management,* pp. 41-107.

Shenkar, O. (Ed.). (1991). *Management and organization in China, 1979-90.* New York: M. E. Sharpe.

Shenkar, O., & Von Glinow, M. A. (1994). Paradoxes of organizational theory and research: Using the case of China to illustrate national contingency. *Management Science, 40*(1), 56-71.

Singh, H., & Montgomery, C. A. (1987). Corporate acquisition strategies and economic performance. *Strategic Management Journal, 8,* 377-386.

Smith, C. W. (1986). Investment banking and the capital acquisition process. *Journal of Financial Economics, 15,* 3-29.

Stearns, L. B., & Allan, K. D. (1996). Economic behavior in institutional environments: The corporate merger wave of the 1980s. *American Sociological Review, 61,* 699-718.

Sun, L. (Ed.). (1995). *Gongsi goubin yu chanquan jiaoyi* [Corporate buyouts, mergers, and property-rights transactions]. Beijing: China Chamber of Commerce Press.

Tan, J. J., & Litschert, R. J. (1994). Environment-strategy relationship and its performance implications: An empirical study of the Chinese electronics industry. *Strategic Management Journal, 15*(1), 1-20.

Wake-up call for China's state sector. (1996, September 12). *Far Eastern Economic Review,* pp. 62-69.

Walder, A. G. (1995). Local governments as industrial firms: An organizational analysis of China's transitional economy. *American Journal of Sociology, 101*(2), 263-301.

Walsh, J. P. (1988). Top management turnover following mergers and acquisitions. *Strategic Management Journal, 9,* 173-183.

Wansell, G, (1987). *Tycoon: The life of James Goldsmith.* New York: Macmillan.

Watson, G. (1989). Business law in the People's Republic of China. *American Business Law Journal, 27,* 315-374.

Williamson, O. E. (1964). *The economics of discretionary behavior: Managerial objectives in a theory of the firm.* Englewood Cliffs, NJ: Prentice Hall.

Williamson, O. E. (1985). *The economic institution of capitalism.* New York: Free Press.

Wu, C. (1990). Enterprise groups in China's industry. *Asia Pacific Journal of Management, 7*(2), 123-136.

Wu, Y. (1996). *Productive performance in Chinese enterprises.* New York: St. Martin's.

Xia, M., Lin, J. H., & Grub, P. D. (1992). *The re-emergence of securities market in China.* Westport, CT: Quorum.

Xiao, G. (1991). Managerial autonomy, fringe benefits, and ownership structure: A comparative study of Chinese state and collective enterprises. *China Economic Review, 2*(1), 47-73.

Ye, G. (1992). Chinese transnational corporations. *Transnational Corporations, 1*(2), 125-133.

Yip, G. S. (1982). Diversification entry: Internal development versus acquisition. *Strategic Management Journal, 3,* 331-345.

Zhang, H., & Van den Bulcke, D. (1996). International management strategies of Chinese multinational firms. In J. Child & Y. Lu (Eds.), *Management issues in China: Vol 2. International enterprises* (pp. 141-164). London: Routledge & Kegan Paul.

Zhang, H., Yuan, Z., & Hua, M. (1994). *Xiandai qiye zhidu* [The modern enterprise system]. Shanghai: Fudan University Press.

PART II

Emerging Business Issues
for Foreign Firms in China

chapter 5

International Joint Ventures in China

Interpartner Characteristics, Dynamics, Opportunities, and Challenges for the New Century

AIMIN YAN

Since the late 1980s, China has been the leading destination country in the world for direct foreign investment. International participation in China's economic development has played an increasingly important role in the country's reform programs. According to a report by the Chinese government (*China Daily,* December 31, 1996), as of November 1996 a total of 281,298 foreign investment enterprises had been approved, with a registered capital investment of U.S.$462.4 billion and actual injected capital of $171.8 billion. These international enterprises have contributed an increasing share (approximately 15%) to China's annual national production and have employed a significantly large Chinese work force (about 14 million).

AUTHOR'S NOTE: The author gratefully acknowledges the support he received in the preparation of this chapter from the Center for Research in Conflict and Negotiation at Penn State University; the Human Resource Policy Institute, the Asia Institute; and the Asian Management Center at Boston University.

The rapid proliferation of foreign business ventures in China and the miraculous development of the Chinese economy in the past two decades have attracted increasing attention from Western management researchers. Scholars argue that the Chinese economic reform has provided an invaluable natural experimental setting for Western researchers to observe and study system transformation at both the macro or national level and the micro or corporate level (Child, 1991; Pearson, 1991; Peng & Heath, 1996). Child (1991) suggests that the rapid growth of international joint ventures (IJVs) and other business partnerships presents an interesting and challenging opportunity to examine international alliances in an institutional context that is new and unfamiliar to Western management scholars.

However, previous research on international joint ventures in China has limited its focus to either interpreting the political, legal, and economic policies of the government in respect to direct foreign investment or to reporting individualistic, descriptive accounts of specific joint ventures. Although in-depth, significant theoretical and empirical studies of international joint ventures in China have started to accumulate, much prior work on the topic (and probably on China-related topics in general) suffers from superficiality, Western ethno-centric stereotypes, and outdated anecdotes. This is not surprising, given the country's large national territory and significant cross-regional differences; its culture, language, and political ideology, radically different from those in the West; its modern history of being closed to the rest of the world for more than three decades; and, most important, the high dynamism and unpredictability during its system transformation.

More specifically, departing from the tradition of "mainstream" international business research, most studies of international joint ventures in China have been conducted by considering only the multinational joint venture sponsor's per-spective. The role of the local partner has been underemphasized, and the relational characteristics and dynamic interactions between the partners have been neglected by previous research. For example, what are the prototypical relationships between the partners before they team up for a joint venture? By what means do the joint venture partners contact each other for the first time to start the alliance-forming process? What are the specific strategic objectives and expectations of the foreign and the local partner with respect to the partnership, and how do the partners' strategies change over time? How do the partners differ in their contributions of critical resources and expertise to the joint venture? How do the foreign and the local partners share management control over the joint venture's operation? Although there are rich anecdotal evidence and dramatic but unconfirmable war stories, as well as speculations and inferences offered by various "China hands," many of these basic but important questions have remained empirically unanswered.

This chapter focuses particularly on the formation dynamics of international joint ventures in China. The findings reported here were derived from the author's doctoral dissertation study as well as his pre- and post-dissertation research on the topic. In this chapter, I first provide a brief review of the literature on Chinese joint ventures on which this research was grounded. Then both qualitative and quantitative data are presented to illustrate several key characteristics and interpartner relationships found in a large sample of manufacturing joint ventures between the United States and China. Finally, I update the reader by identifying and analyzing several recent trends and issues that are creating new opportunities as well challenges for the formation and management of international joint ventures in China in the upcoming century.

STREAMS OF RESEARCH ON JOINT VENTURES IN CHINA

Conducting in-depth research on international joint ventures in China has proved to be a challenging task. First, the significant differences between the Chinese and the Western political and economic systems, as well as cultures and languages, have prevented most Western researchers from gaining an in-depth understanding of international business partnerships in China (Tung, 1982). Second, research by scholars in China is unavailable to Western researchers. The subject has been new to researchers in China; therefore, scholarly research on international joint ventures reported even in the Chinese language is limited. Language barriers and methodological differences, among other factors, may also have prevented an East-West exchange on this subject. Third, because of the tradition of political economy and government control, reliable data sources on international joint ventures in China are not publicly available, rendering data collection extremely difficult (Daniels, Krug, & Nigh, 1985). Although a thorough and rigorous review of the relevant literature is certainly beyond the scope of the current chapter, I provide below a partial sketch of the development of research on this subject over the past two decades for the interested reader's further reference.

Previous research on international joint ventures in China consists of four streams of work that emerged more or less in chronological order. First, immediately following China's adoption of its open-door policy, a large number of studies focused on the political, economic, and legal environments in China for direct foreign investment, with a particular interest in government policy making and policy changes over time (e.g., Campbell, 1988; Ho, 1990; Mathur & Chen, 1987; Pearson, 1991; Stoltenberg & McClure, 1987; Tung, 1982). For example, Pearson (1991) draws on the perspectives of Chinese politics and international political economy to explain why the Chinese prefer equity joint ventures. She argues that joint ventures represent an ideal form for absorbing foreign capital, which both satisfies the needs of Chinese and eases their concerns: On the one hand, Chinese leaders were attracted by badly needed foreign capital to spur economic development; on the other hand, they were reluctant to allow Western capitalists to flood into China with wholly owned businesses because they feared loss of state control over the country's development path, loss of political independence, and possible foreign contamination of their socialist ideology. Focusing on the impact of the local political and economic environments on international joint ventures, Shan (1991) examined how the level of environmental uncertainty and the joint venture's dependence on its infrastructure affect the foreign partner's investment decisions. His findings suggest that the higher the level of uncertainty and the higher the degree of the joint venture's dependence on local transactional relationships, the less capital foreign firms tend to inject into their joint ventures. Child and Markoczy (1991) investigated the Chinese system transformation and its impact on the behavior of the Chinese managers in international joint ventures. They identified several contextual factors (industrial governance, level of industrialization, national culture, and resistance to change) that determine the modes of learning of Chinese managers in adapting to Western management practices.

A second stream of literature on Chinese joint ventures consists of case descriptions and individual experiences, typically appearing in practitioner journals or popular books by participants in joint venture negotiations or joint venture managers (e.g., Hendryx, 1986, on Tianjin Otis Elevator and O'Reilly, 1988, on Heinz's ventures), reporters (e.g., Mann's 1989 book on Beijing Jeep), and academic researchers (Campbell, 1988; Newman, 1992b; Schnepp, Von Glinow, & Bhambri, 1990). For example, based on interviews conducted with both the U.S. and the Chinese partners, Schnepp et al. (1990) provide rich details about several technology transfer deals conducted in the context of U.S.-China joint ventures. Mann's (1989) book, although slightly gloomy, depicts a comprehensive picture of Beijing Jeep, one of the earliest foreign joint ventures in China, traces the venture from the initial negotiations to the Tian-An-Men incident in 1989, and documents rich details about the ups and downs in the rough journey of the venture's development. These accounts of Chinese joint ventures, however, are primarily descriptive in nature.

Scholarly work exploring the motivation and strategic objectives of the foreign and the local partners represents the third stream of research on Chinese joint ventures. This research focuses on the inherent motivations that drove the partners to join forces and the problems and challenges associated with the significant differences in the foreign and the local partners' strategic expectations (Daniels et al., 1985; Shenkar, 1990; Teagarden, 1989). For example, Daniels et al. (1985) reported that U.S. companies are most interested in the huge Chinese market and the potential for low-cost sourcing, while the local partner is eager to learn foreign technology and to generate exports in exchange for hard currency. In comparing Chinese IJVs with those in other developing countries, Beamish (1993) reported a commonality between the two groups with many dimensions, such as the major reasons for creating joint ventures and the preferred ownership and parent control structures.

Finally, a fourth stream of research on Chinese joint ventures that emerged relatively recently is engaged in a search for the key factors in joint venture success in China. For example, Newman (1992a) suggests that "focused" joint ventures with a limited scale of operations, product lines, and targeted markets are more likely to perform well. Others reported that interpartner trust building and local networking were found critical to joint venture success (Davidson, 1987; Newman, 1992b; Yan & Gray, 1994). Using a cross-sectorial sample of Chinese joint ventures over the 1988-1991 period, Luo's (1996) dissertation research examined the relationship between the foreign partner's investment strategies and joint venture performance. The results of this research reveal that the timing of investment, industry selection, and local partner selection are among the most important factors in joint venture performance. Other factors, such as interpartner split-sharing arrangements, firm location, product diversification, and project-type selection and the interactive effects among these factors were also found to impact the various dimensions of venture performance. Yan and Gray (1994) indicated a strong positive relationship between the quality of the interpartner working relationship and the venture's performance, measured as the perceived extent to which both partners' founding objectives are achieved. In addition, a direct, positive relationship was found in their study between the level of management control exercised by a partner and the level of achievement of its founding objectives. More recently, Child, Yan, and Lu (1997) have examined and confirmed the strong effect of ownership structure on parent control structure in a cross-country and cross-sectorial sample of foreign joint ventures in China.

These different streams of previous research founded the useful ground on which the two studies reported in this chapter were designed and conducted. In the next section, I describe these studies and report research results.

THE STUDIES

The results reported in this chapter are based on two empirical studies, a qualitative comparative case study of four joint ventures and a quantitative survey study in which data were collected from 90 joint ventures. Both studies were focused on manufacturing joint ventures created between American and Chinese firms. American joint ventures were chosen because the United States has represented one of the largest sources of foreign investment in China (The Economic Intelligence Unit, 1994; The U.S.-China Business Council, 1990). I limited my studies to manufacturing partnerships because (a) about 70% of U.S. joint ventures in China are involved in manufacturing (The U.S.-China Business Council, 1990); and (b) I wanted to avoid extraneous variation that might be derived from combining manufacturing with service ventures. Previous scholars (e.g., Chowdhury, 1988) suggest that international alliances in manufacturing sectors are substantially different from those in service industries, such as hotels and restaurants. I elected to undertake both qualitative and quantitative approaches to enhance the rigor and richness of the research.

Comparative Case Studies

The case studies included four joint ventures in industries ranging from electronic equipment and peripherals (Office Aid), industrial control equipment (IndusCon), personal hygiene products (Daily Product), and pharmaceuticals (BioTech Ltd.). For each case study, data were collected through in-depth personal interviews with multiple executives of both the U.S. and Chinese partners, as well as the managers of the joint ventures. My informants at the parent companies are senior executives who either were personally involved in the initial negotiations for the venture or were directly responsible for overseeing the joint venture's operation. Interviewees from the joint ventures include the general manager, the deputy general manager, and some key functional managers. Except for one joint venture, three or more informants were interviewed for each partnership. The key characteristics of the four joint ventures are summarized in Table 5.1.

TABLE 5.1   Major Characteristics of the Joint Ventures in the Case Studies

Joint Venture	Office Aid	IndusCon	Daily Product	BioTech Ltd.
Product	Electronic office equipment	Industrial process control	Personal hygiene products	Pharmaceuticals
Length of negotiation in years	4	3	2	3
Formation	1987	1982	1981	1982
Total investment in millions of dollars	30	10	2.85	10
U.S.–China equity shares	51:49	49:51	50:50	50:50
Duration in years	30	20	20	15
Product market	Mainly local; small % for export	Local, import substitution	50% for export	Mainly local; small % for export
Parents' objectives:				
United States	Profit	Business growth	Learn how to do business in China	Market
	Market share	Market penetration	Establish credibility	Profit
	Low-cost sourcing	Profit	Profit	
			Business expansion	
People's Republic of China	Technology and management	Import substitution	Profit	Technology
	Export for foreign exchange	Manufacturing technology	Export for foreign exchange	Gain management expertise
		Upgrade suppliers' technology	Technology	Business expansion
			Growth	

The Survey Study

Based on the findings in the comparative case studies, a survey was conducted among a population of 279 U.S.-China manufacturing joint ventures whose addresses were available in the U.S.-China Business Council's (1990) directory. The questionnaire was prepared in both the English and the Chinese languages. The Chinese version of the questionnaire was mailed to the Chinese general

TABLE 5.2 Industrial Sectors Represented in the Sample *

Industry Sector	Number of Joint Ventures	Percentage
Chemicals	16	17.78
Electronics	14	16.56
Miscellaneous light industry	13	14.44
Food and agriculture	10	11.11
Miscellaneous industrial equipment	10	11.11
Metals	6	6.67
Medical	5	5.56
Building materials	5	5.56
Telecommunications	4	4.44
Engineering services	3	3.33
Resources	3	3.33
Transportation	1	1.11
Total	**90**	**100.00**

NOTE: * The categories are those suggested by the U.S.-China Business Council (1990).

manager or deputy general manager of the joint venture; the English version was sent to the American general manager or deputy general manager. In addition, a separate questionnaire was sent to the U.S. parent company. I administered the questionnaires in China as a collaborative effort with the business school of a Chinese university. We secured support from the municipal governments of several Chinese cities in which a large number of the targeted joint ventures were located.

Respondents at 90 joint ventures completed and returned the questionnaire (response rate of 32.3%). For 68 ventures (75.6% of the sample), the respondents were top executives (the venture's chairman, president, general manager, or deputy general manager). For 13 ventures (14.4%), the respondents were assistant general managers or chief staff members. For the remaining 9 ventures (10.0%), a lower-level manager or the general manager's administrative/business assistant responded to the questionnaire. From 27 joint ventures in the sample, two responses to the questionnaire were generated, typically one from the Chinese general manager and the other from the expatriate general manager. Respondents from 55 joint ventures (61.1%) had personally participated in the initial negotiations that led to the formation of the partnership.

The 90 joint ventures in the quantitative sample were formed between 1982 and 1992. Although all joint ventures in the sample are manufacturing or engineering partnerships, they fall into 12 industrial sectors (see Table 5.2). The majority of the joint ventures (71%) operated within five industrial sectors: chemical materials or products, electronic components or equipment, light industry manufacturing, food processing and agricultural products, and miscellaneous industrial equipment.

RESULTS

In this section, results derived from both studies are reported. In each subsection, I first present the quantitative results generated from the survey study. These are then discussed in light of the richer qualitative data from the comparative case studies.

Descriptive Characteristics

The joint ventures in the quantitative sample varied considerably with respect to their geographic locations, date of formation, size, ownership structure, and contracted length of incorporation. The sample represents joint ventures located in 17 of the 30 Chinese provinces and municipalities. They were formed between February 1982 and May 1992, with an average age of 5.7 years. During these 10 years, U.S.-China joint ventures witnessed a rapid proliferation. The joint ventures in the sample varied significantly in size as measured by the total amount of capital investment. The sample contains both very small and very large companies, ranging from $100,000 to $232,000,000 in registered total assets. The joint ventures include a wide range of ownership structures, from 16% to 90% U.S. ownership. By and large, older joint ventures tend to have an equal or majority ownership by the Chinese partner. However, an increase in foreign ownership over time was observed in newer ventures. This general pattern mirrors policy changes by the Chinese government during this period of time from limiting and constraining to allowing and encouraging in-depth foreign participation in China's economic development. For example, during the negotiations that eventually led to the formation of Daily Product in 1991, the U.S. partner asked for, but failed to receive, a majority holding in the joint venture because of the local partner's objection. As a result, a 50:50 partnership was created. Ten years later, however, this same U.S. company was able not only to form a second joint venture in China, in which it owns 70% equity, but also to use the new joint venture as a holding company to take shares in the old one.

In this way, ownership control by the U.S. company over both ventures was consolidated. The U.S. partner in Office Aid adopted a similar strategy. In 1995, it formed two new joint ventures in China in which it holds majority ownership. Moreover, it had established its wholly owned holding company in Beijing to control and coordinate all its joint venture operations in China.

With respect to the length of contract, both the case and the survey studies demonstrate an increase in the length of the contracted term of joint ventures over time. In the case studies, the three older joint ventures, formed in 1981 or 1982, had a contracted term of 15 or 20 years, but the one that was formed in 1987 was contracted for 30 years, the maximum length of contract legally allowed at that time. The joint ventures in the survey sample varied from 10 to 50 years. Again, data from this larger sample suggest that newer joint ventures have a longer term of expected duration than older ones. This trend reflects China's relaxation of the legal restriction on the length of a joint venture's contracted term over time. In 1991, the legally allowed length of contract was increased from 30 to 50 years and, upon mutual agreement, can be further extended. The longer planned lives for newer joint ventures may also signify an increased level of confidence of the foreign investors in doing business in China and their longer-term commitment to their business ventures in the country. Table 5.3 summarizes the descriptive characteristics of the ventures in the sample.

In summary, both the qualitative and the quantitative samples are cross-sectorial and cover a wide range of U.S. manufacturing joint ventures in China in terms of the industries represented, the geographical locations in China, the years of formation, the size of capital investment, and the ownership structure between the foreign and the local partners. Thus, I am optimistic about the representativeness of the samples and the reliability of the results.

Founding Negotiations

Previous observers have pointed out that business negotiations with partners in Asian countries, particularly those from China or Japan, are significantly longer than most Western executives anticipate. Our data show that the average length of time that elapsed between the first contact among the partners and closing the deal (signified by signing the joint venture contract) ranged between 2 and 84 months, with an average of 16.3 months ($SD = 13.8$). Generally, the larger the joint venture size, the longer the negotiation. This is not a surprise because the levels of complexity and financial risks increase exponentially as the venture's potential scale of operations increases. Another key factor contrib-

TABLE 5.3 Descriptive Characteristics of the Quantitative Sample

Characteristic	Range	Mean	S.D.
Formation period	February 1982-May 1992		
Average age	1-10 years	5.66	2.14
Total investment	$.10-232.00 million	6.18	8.88
U.S. ownership	16%-90%	43.85	14.66
Length of contract	10-50 years	17.00	6.70

uting to the additional length of negotiation time needed for large joint ventures is associated with the governmental approval process. Typically, each local government at the municipal or the provincial level is authorized to approve joint ventures whose total capital investment does not exceed a maximum amount determined by the central government. For projects larger than the authorized size, which varies from one municipality/province to another, approval by the central government in Beijing has to be obtained. Examination and approval by higher governmental bureaucracies not only increase the length of pending time, but often also precipitate issues that call for renegotiations. The fact that negotiations for a joint venture take an average of more than a year should not be a surprise, given the geographical distance and radical differences in cultures and languages between the partners. For example, the case studies suggest that the partners usually make multiple across-the-Pacific trips to visit each other's facilities during the negotiation, and in each and every case, the Chinese partner's superiors in the responsible governmental offices either participated in these visits or made separate trips to the U.S. partner's headquarters. In addition, the case studies show that, because of the language barriers, all joint venture negotiations had to be conducted through interpreters, which significantly increased the amount of time for negotiation. The lack of knowledge about international business negotiations on the Chinese side and the unfamiliarity with the Chinese negotiation styles and decision processes on the foreign partner's side also prolong the negotiation process. For example, the head negotiator of the U.S. team for the Office Aid joint venture had a hard time identifying who his counterpart was on the Chinese negotiation team; as he recalled,

> It was a struggle for us in the first several rounds of negotiation. We couldn't tell who the Chinese head negotiator was. My colleagues and I made a guess: "The guy in white socks must be the one!"—because at that time not all Chinese

families could afford a washing machine to keep white socks white. Subsequently, we found we were right! It sounds funny, but is not at all a joke.

For joint ventures formed in the earlier years, a high level of political risk, bureaucratic red tape, lack of experience by the Chinese government as a matchmaker, and mutual skepticism and distrust between the would-be partners characterized most joint venture negotiations. For example, when the American parent company of Office Aid, a manufacturer of high-technology electronic equipment, first contacted the central government in Beijing for a Chinese partner, it was matched with a shipyard located in an inner province. "The government officials believed that anyone who can bend steel sheets would be able to manufacture our steel-shelled equipment," the American head negotiator commented. The dream for a partnership predictably dissipated because the local shipyard neither had any knowledge of international joint ventures nor had produced anything electronic. Months had been wasted before the U.S. company returned to Beijing and was eventually matched with a negotiable Chinese partner in a coastal city. Negotiation times for two subsequent joint ventures, however, both formed in 1995 by the same U.S. firm, were significantly shortened. It took only 8 months to close both deals.

Means of First Contact

The most frequent means of initial contact among the potential joint venture partners included direct contacts with each other, arrangements made by the various agencies of the Chinese government, or matches arranged or mediated by a third-party broker. Both our interview and survey data suggest that the use of government agencies for selecting a local partner was much more common for older joint ventures than for those that were formed more recently. As a matter of fact, all four joint ventures in our case studies, to a varying extent, were formed with the assistance of Chinese government agencies in selecting the local partner. Sometimes the local government agencies even perform the role of a champion in joint venture projects by initiating the joint venture idea, hunting for and matching foreign or local partners, facilitating negotiations, and smoothing the way through to formation of the joint venture. Daily Product's story demonstrates this. In 1980, when the first American symphony orchestra visited China as a bilateral cultural exchange program, the future U.S. partner in Daily Product was one of the corporate sponsors. As a result, an executive of the U.S. firm was

TABLE 5.4 Means of First Contact Between Partners

Means of First Contact	Frequency of Use	Percentage
Direct contact between partners	44	42.72
Via Chinese government	31	30.10
Via broker/middleman	23	22.33
Other	5	4.85
TOTAL:	103*	100.00

NOTE: * The total number exceeds 90 because several joint ventures reportedly used more than one means of contact.

invited to visit Beijing while the orchestra was performing there. During his stay in the Chinese capital, he was approached by Chinese government officials from the Ministry of Light Industry who were interested in importing technology or equipment from the U.S. firm. The U.S. executive explained to the Chinese officials that his company was not a vendor of technology or equipment but would be interested in forming a joint venture facility in China. The government officials were very enthusiastic about the proposal and subsequently arranged for a group of managers from the U.S. firm to visit all four Chinese manufacturers of the proposed product as candidates for a local joint venture partner.

The role that Chinese government agencies play in bridging the gap between joint venture partners has diminished since 1987, presumably because of the emergence of alternative channels. Newer joint venture deals were found to be more frequently mediated by third-party brokers or by direct contact between the partners themselves. Although Chinese Americans or various business agencies in Hong Kong have played a major role in bridging the gap between the U.S. and the Chinese partners, in quite a few cases, the U.S. partners in established joint ventures in China played the role of a third party in assisting newcomers to find a local Chinese partner. Other means of contact were also reported in this study, albeit they were used much less frequently. These included accidental meetings between executives and connections through personal contacts (e.g., through relatives). Table 5.4 reports the means of first contact between the partners.

Pre-Venture Relationship

Partners in more than half (56.3%) of the joint ventures in the survey sample had no business relationships with each other prior to the joint venture negotia-

TABLE 5.5 Pre-Venture Relationships Between Partners

Pre-Venture Relationship	Number of Joint Ventures	Percentage
No relationship	54	56.25
Buyer-seller relationships	14	14.58
Marketing agreement	6	6.25
Technology licensing agreement	3	3.13
R&D partnership	7	7.29
Other	12	12.50
TOTAL:	96*	100.00

NOTE: * The total number exceeds 90 because some joint ventures reported more than one type of pre-venture relationship between the partners.

tions. In three out of the four joint ventures in our case studies, the partners were strangers before the negotiations started and the relationship was initiated by making cold calls. This result should be expected because China has been in a self-contained environment, insulated from the rest of the world for more than three decades. Before 1978, China was very much a closed economic system and maintained few relationships with the Western business world. Nevertheless, 43.7% of the participating joint ventures in our survey sample were built on prior business relationships of various types between the partners, ranging from previous buyer-seller relationships to some sort of contractual partnerships. For example, the U.S. partner of IndusCon had been exporting to China for several years preceding the joint venture negotiation with one of its Chinese customers that a representative first met in a new product exhibition. Table 5.5 lists the different types of pre-venture relationships between joint venture partners.

Strategic Objectives of the Partners

My studies generated a comprehensive list of strategic objectives of joint venture sponsors. These objectives, as summarized in Table 5.6, delineate the motivations and strategic expectations of the American and the Chinese partners, respectively.

The two dominant objectives for American firms included earning a profit and penetrating business markets in China. The leading strategic objective of the Chinese partner, however, was to acquire or to learn advanced Western technology. Earning a profit was the second most important goal of the Chinese. My

TABLE 5.6 Strategic Objectives of Partners

Strategic Objectives of U.S. Partners	Frequency	Percentage
Earn a profit in China	79	87.78
Penetrate the Chinese market	73	81.11
Pursue business growth	41	45.56
Develop a base for low-cost sourcing	40	44.44
Establish a presence in China	32	35.56
Build credibility and reputation	26	28.89
Establish a base to access Asia market	23	25.56
Learn how to do business in China	9	10.00
Other	2	2.22

Strategic Objectives of Chinese Partners	Frequency	Percentage
Acquire/learn advanced technology	87	96.67
Earn a profit	70	77.78
Acquire/learn management expertise	61	67.78
Earn foreign exchange through export	47	52.22
Substitute import by manufacturing locally	42	46.67
Pursue business growth	23	25.56
Develop technology for Chinese suppliers/users	15	16.67
Other	4	4.44

case studies, however, suggest that, until very recently, profitability was a goal much less important than technology to the Chinese partners. Acquisition of Western management expertise and promotion of export were also important Chinese objectives. Overall, the two sets of objectives of the partners show more differences than similarities. However, because both partners regarded profitability as one of the most important goals, this overlap in strategic interests may have provided sufficient common ground for initial success. Moreover, a high level of complementarity between the two sets of partner objectives is also evident. The objectives of market penetration and business growth pursued by the U.S. partner and the learning-oriented goals, that is, acquisition of Western technology and management expertise, of the Chinese partner are radically different, but they can be achieved simultaneously. As an interviewee at IndusCon's U.S. parent noted,

The joint venture represents a win-win situation. We have the technology and certain know-how. The Chinese partner knows how to make things happen in China. You put the two together right, it works.

Potential conflict in the partners' strategic interests can also be expected. For example, conflict occurred in three out of the four joint ventures in our case studies. The U.S. partner was primarily interested in penetrating the local Chinese market (the objective second in importance for the U.S. partner in the survey sample), while the Chinese partner expected the joint venture to be a major vehicle for export (the objective fourth in importance for the Chinese partner as revealed in the survey). The case data also suggest that mutual compromise between the partners served as a typical solution to such a conflict. A practical and viable strategy observed across the cases is a joint decision between the partners that divides the joint venture's products into those designated for the Chinese market and those for export.

Some Chinese sponsors perceived their U.S. partner as reluctant to export the joint venture's product because of its concerns for potential internal competition within its own international operational network. Some U.S. firms, however, had to persuade their Chinese partners that the joint venture's products manufactured in China were not technologically competitive for global markets. This was the situation encountered by Office Aid. The U.S. partner is a multinational conglomerate whose primary interest was to develop the local market in China through the joint venture. The Chinese partner, however, was interested in exporting the joint venture's product because it was under pressure to pay back its loans in hard currency. An expedient solution to the conflicting interests was reached between the partners in which the U.S. parent company bought back a small percentage of the joint venture's products at an internal transfer price and sold them in its South American markets. As a matter of fact, economically, the joint venture conducted this export business at a loss, which subsequently created a number of serious problems between the partners. The Chinese partner accused its U.S. partner of skimming off the joint venture's profit because the Americans were making money by exporting the joint venture's products. The U.S. partner, however, argued that exporting was the Chinese partner's idea, and the U.S. company could not do it free. The quarrel between the partners prompted by their contrasting objectives seriously undermined interpartner trust and left a lasting negative imprint on the interpartner relationship. To deal with these problems, the partners agreed to develop jointly a couple of new products at the joint venture that were exclusively for export. In this effort, several Chinese engineers from the venture were brought to the United States to join the new product development team at the American partner's headquarters. As a matter of fact, the first new product for export manufactured by the joint venture was well received in the South American and other Third World country markets. Both the U.S. and the Chinese partners assessed the project as very successful. Interestingly, as the foreign exchange shortage situation in China improved subsequently, the Chinese partner dropped "earning foreign exchange" as one of its most important objectives for the joint venture, which had once created both crises and new business opportunities for the joint venture.

Conflict in partners' objectives can also occur in joint ventures whose U.S. parent wants a quick payback for investment and whose local parent prefers to reinvest profits in the partnership. IndusCon represents an example of successful resolution of this potential conflict. Formally written in the joint venture's incorporating contract, the U.S. partner made an explicit commitment that it would not remit a penny to the United States in the joint venture's first 5 years of operation. Both partners agreed that all profits generated in the first 5 years would be reinvested. This initial commitment by the U.S. partner impressed the Chinese and helped create a positive perception on the Chinese side that the U.S. firm was sincere, considerate, and committed to the partnership's long-term interests. IndusCon had been able to generate a high level of consensus and a superior working relationship between the partners, and it demonstrated very solid performance over the 14 years of operation up to 1996, when the most recent update interviews were conducted at the joint venture for the current study.

Partner Resource Contribution

In addition to the financial capital the sponsors inject into joint ventures, six categories of other critical resources were identified in my studies. These noncapital resources include technology and know-how, management expertise, local knowledge and political clout, raw-material procurement channels, product distribution and marketing channels, and service support for the joint venture's products. I saw a consistent, complementary pattern with respect to the types of noncapital resources committed by the partners (see Table 5.7). Predictably, the U.S. firms contributed more than their local partners in technology (product design, manufacturing know-how, and special equipment), marketing channels for exporting the venture's product, and channels for importing materials that the joint venture needed from the international market. In contrast,

TABLE 5.7 Partner Resource Contributions

	U.S. < Chinese Number of JVs (%)		U.S. = Chinese Number of JVs (%)		U.S. > Chinese Number of JVs (%)	
Technology	16	(17.8)	7	(7.8)	67	(74.4)
Management expertise	40	(44.4)	11	(12.2)	37	(41.1)
Marketing channels						
(Local)	54	(60.0)	17	(18.9)	19	(21.0)
(Export)	13	(14.4)	37	(41.1)	38	(42.2)
Material procurement						
(Local)	64	(71.1)	18	(20.0)	8	(8.9)
(Import)	18	(20.0)	20	(22.2)	52	(57.8)
Political clout	58	(64.4)	19	(21.1)	13	(14.4)
Operational support	52	(57.7)	22	(24.4)	16	(17.8)

the Chinese partner contributed more in providing local distribution channels; procuring local content; building relationships and consolidating political clout; and rendering technical, maintenance, and customer services for the joint venture's products. With respect to their contribution to the joint venture's managerial expertise, the partners contributed approximately equally. The case studies suggest that the U.S. partner tended to contribute more in the "harder" areas of management, including managing technology, production, quality control, and information systems; the Chinese partner contributed more expertise in the "softer" areas, such as management of personnel and labor relations, administration, and management of relations with local government agencies. In other areas, for example, purchasing, distribution, and accounting, managerial expertise was contributed by both partners in a relatively balanced manner.

However, partner contributions in resources and expertise tend to change over time as a result of partner learning, alterations in the partners' policies, or changes in the environment. For example, the U.S. partner of Office Aid preferred a joint venture to a wholly owned option when it first went to China in order to acquire the expertise of a potential local partner, as the venture's first American expatriate general manager suggested during an interview in 1991:

As a foreign company, who will you see for water? For electricity? Who will you talk to for the right employees you need? In a country full of uncertainty, you need a local partner at least to start with. I was against the wholly-owned scenario from the outset even though we might have had that option then.

Four years later, however, the same executive, in the position of the U.S. company's general manager for China operations, single-handedly created two more U.S.-majority joint ventures and was involved in the establishment of the wholly owned holding company. In an interview in 1996, he made the following comments:

> I believe Office Aid now, as an American company, knows how to do business in China. Over the years, we have learned a great deal in doing business in that country. We have piggybacked on our partner's initial dealers network and built our own. We have developed very good relationships with Chinese government officials, including the former mayor of this city now the head of the State. . . . My advice for everybody is that you go alone if you can, or at least you should avoid a 50:50 joint venture whenever possible.

At IndusCon, a shift in technology transfer policies within the U.S. sponsoring company significantly changed its technological input into the joint venture. A recent acquisition of the American firm by a British company made several important adjustments in the foreign partner's attitude toward the joint venture in China. Over a period of more than 10 years, the U.S. parent firm had transferred new product designs and the associated technology to the joint venture in China on a regular basis based upon an agreement that such a transfer can be made as long as it is approved by the joint venture's board of directors. After the ownership of the U.S. company changed hands, the new owner quickly changed the policy. As a result, the rate of new product transfers to the joint venture slowed down, which exerted a negative influence on the relationship between the partners and prompted tough rounds of renegotiations.

Nomination of Key Personnel

The 1979 version of the Chinese Joint Venture Law stipulates that the joint venture's chairman of the board of directors must be a Chinese regardless of the ownership structure of the joint venture. This requirement was subsequently removed in the 1990 amendment to the law. Although most chairmen of the board in Chinese joint ventures are not directly involved in the venture's operational matters, there are exceptions. For example, BioTech Ltd.'s chairman acted as the chief executive officer of the joint venture, and the U.S. partner-nominated president reported to him on a regular basis. The U.S. partner in Office Aid perceived the role of the joint venture's Chinese chairman very differently. The joint venture's first expatriate general manager described it as follows:

> I think, it is part of the goodwill in a country where you are operating. The chairman never should be a foreigner. Chairmen always should be local. Even if it is a 90:10 joint venture, the 10% local partner should be the chairman of the board. . . . Also, the title of the chairman of the board should bring some influence. A foreigner that has the title but is not on site will never do any good.

Supporting this argument, I found that few joint ventures formed after the 1990 amendment to China's Joint Venture Law had installed a foreign chairman of the board, even in joint ventures with a foreign majority ownership, although, at least theoretically, they could have chosen to do so.

With respect to the composition of the board of directors, the Chinese partners were found to nominate more board members than the U.S. partner did (see Table 5.8). Obviously, this configuration directly reflects the ownership structure of the joint ventures in which 45 (50%) have a Chinese majority while 20 (22.2%) are equally owned partnerships. However, it is important to point out that my quantitative analysis suggests that the correlation between partner ownership and the nomination of the board members is far from perfect ($r = .6043$).

The nomination of management personnel for a joint venture is usually decided between the partners upon the board's approval. In contrast to the minority position of the U.S. partners at the board of directors level, in 50 (55.6%) joint ventures in the sample, the U.S. partner nominated an expatriate executive to fill the venture's chief executive position, and the Chinese partner provided candidates for deputy or assistant positions. At the functional management level, a consistent pattern was observed in which expatriate managers took charge in the harder areas of operation, such as engineering, manufacturing, and marketing, whereas local managers took positions in the softer functions, such as human resources, public relations, servicing, and general administration. This division of labor at the managerial level certainly corresponds to the observed structure of resource mix and distinct competencies of the foreign and the local partners, as discussed earlier in this chapter. At an overall level, a tendency of foreign domination in management and operation is apparent in the joint ventures in this study. This suggests that whenever both partners share management responsibilities for the joint venture's operation, the American partner is likely to exercise a higher level of control than the Chinese partner.

TABLE 5.8 Nomination of Key Personnel

	More Chinese Members	Equal	More U.S. Members
Board of Directors	48 (53.3%)	33 (36.7%)	9 (10.0%)
General Manager	Chinese Nominated 40 (44.4%)		U.S. Nominated 50 (55.6%)

Summary

The results from the case studies and the survey provide insights into several key characteristics of U.S.-China manufacturing joint ventures and interpartner configurational relationships, as well as their changes over time. Among the findings of the research are: (a) Lengthy negotiations precede each joint venture agreement, especially for large-scale projects. However, shorter negotiations have been found in newer joint ventures. (b) Most partnerships are formed between partners with no prior relationships by cold calls. (c) Direct contact and mediation by Chinese government agencies are the dominant means of first contact between the partners. Third-party brokers, such as business or legal consulting companies in Hong Kong, China, and the United States, are becoming increasingly active in bridging the gap between potential joint venture partners. (d) There were significant differences in the partners' expectations and strategic objectives. Whereas the American firms are most interested in the Chinese local market and a profit, the overwhelming majority of the Chinese sponsors formed joint ventures to acquire advanced Western technology and management expertise and to pursue export opportunities for hard currency. However, partners' founding objectives are subject to change over time, which, in many cases, can create new dynamics between the partners in terms of their interdependency, conflict, and trust-building. (e) There exists a clear and distinctive pattern in the types of resources that the foreign and the local partners contribute to the joint venture and a high level of interpartner resource complementarity. However, partner resource contributions and their strategic importance to the venture are likely to change over time as a result of interorganizational and environmental changes and/or interpartner learning. (f) Finally, although an overwhelming majority of joint ventures are equipped with a Chinese chairman of the board of directors, stronger operational and managerial control is exercised by executives nominated by the foreign partner. In the next section, I identify several new trends and issues that may have critical implications for forming and managing equity joint ventures in China.

PROSPECTS OF THE NEW CENTURY: OPPORTUNITIES AND CHALLENGES

It is arguable that China represents one of the most dynamic countries in the world today. Having closely traced the new development in China with respect to direct foreign investment and joint ventures, and having made frequent trips to the country in the past 7 years, I have often been surprised by significant changes. It is a challenging task to predict what exactly will happen in China in the next century. However, based on my recent observations, below, I identify several new trends that may have significant implications for forming and managing international joint ventures in China in the upcoming century, therefore deserving the attention of joint venture researchers as well as practitioners.

Changes in Interpartner Relational Characteristics

As was highlighted early in this chapter, several salient changes have occurred over time with respect to the interpartner relational characteristics in joint ventures in China. For example, recent evidence suggests that the Chinese partners are becoming increasingly attracted by financial returns, and the desire for hard currency is losing motivation power. It is arguable that learning technology for modernization through joint venturing may remain only a quasi-political goal of the Chinese partner. As a result of the recent proliferation of economic pragmatism in China, making a profit is quickly moving to the top of the list of the Chinese joint venture partner's strategic interests, replacing the objective of obtaining advanced Western technology. Technology may still remain a top objective in the Chinese central government's priority, but the more autonomous business enterprises and government officials at the local provincial or municipal levels tend to treat technology more or less as only a means to derive financial returns. This shift in the Chinese partner's strategic objectives may have significant effects on both the existing joint ventures and partnerships yet to be formed. It can bring changes in the venture's strategic mission, as well as in the relationships between the partners. To a certain extent, this implies that the Chinese partner is moving closer to the foreign partner by sharing the same strategic expectations. The converging goals between the partners may significantly decrease interpartner conflict and opportunism, thereby enhancing venture performance. However, the increased compatibility of Chinese enterprises with international firms will potentially gain the Chinese more alternative partners to cooperate with, which may give rise to increased competition among international players in China.

China recently reported that, up to November 1996, its foreign exchange reserve had reached $1.023 billion, the second highest in the world next to Japan (*China Daily,* December 31, 1996; January 15, 1997). At the macro level, the Chinese government has significantly relaxed its state control over foreign exchange; at the corporate level, the Chinese joint venture partners have gradually removed earnings in hard currency as an important objective, as witnessed in the Office Aid case study. I envision that these changes will have three important effects on joint ventures. First, the promise to export the joint venture's product will diminish in power as a bargaining chip for the international partner in negotiating with the local government for preferential treatment. Second, the foreign and the Chinese partners will converge in their strategic interests in the joint venture, which may have a positive effect on performance. The decision on where to sell the venture's product, in the international or the local market, has been an area in which interpartner disagreements and controversies frequently occurred, but now it is no longer a serious concern. Finally, decreased Chinese interest in export may send bad news to potential international partners who intend to derive heavy returns by buying back the joint venture's product at internal transfer prices, as the U.S. parent of Office Aid did.

Changes in the Multinational Partner's China Strategies

A significant change has been observed recently in the multinational partners' overall China strategies in which they strive for a higher level of control over their joint ventures and for an increased degree of integration among their overall operation in China. There are two major factors contributing to this aggressive drive for control by the foreign joint venture sponsors. First, the lifting of the Chinese government's restriction on foreign ownership and governance structures has made these changes legally possible. Over a period of a decade, the highly positive effect of foreign invested businesses on China's economic development has convinced the Chinese government and eased its initial concerns about the possibility of loss of control or of ideological contamination. Therefore, some important policy changes have been undertaken, one of which is an increased tolerance toward foreign-majority ownership in joint ventures.

Although not strictly defined by law, the Chinese government's previous preference for equally shared ownership to foreign-majority ownership in equity joint ventures created an overwhelming majority of 50:50-structured joint ventures. For the past several years, the number of foreign-majority joint ventures has rapidly increased. At the same time, the 1991 amendment to the joint venture law has allowed joint ventures to install a foreign chairman. These changes in government policy provide the legal and institutional backgrounds against which the multinationals' attempts to increase control are legitimately proposed. Second, many multinational firms have grown their joint ventures in China both in number and scale of operation to such a point that an overall strategy and a coordination structure are needed to integrate these different ventures/operations. For example, when BCG, a British conglomerate manufacturer of industrial gases, formed its first joint ventures in China, each venture was designated to serve a regional market. Because of the vast territory of the country, cross-joint venture competition had never been a concern at all until recently. Now the company is operating more than a dozen joint ventures in China. At least occasionally, these sister joint ventures have engaged in competition against each other, which has caught the attention of the foreign parent and prompted actions undertaken to consolidate its overall control.

The multinational firms' attempt to increase control over their joint ventures has been made by pursuing a variety of strategies, two of which are observed most frequently: renegotiating for an increase in ownership, and creating majority- or wholly owned holding companies. Increase or proposal for increase in the foreign partner's equity holding occurred in three out of the four joint ventures in this case study. IndusCon changed its ownership structure from 49:51 (American:Chinese) to 51:49. Although the change is hardly large in terms of absolute scale (2%), the shift of the symbolic majority positions carries much more significance. In Office Aid, the U.S. partner has been more aggressive, attempting to increase its control at both the individual joint venture level and the level of its overall operation in China. A wholly owned holding company was founded in Beijing in 1995, and reconfiguration of the first joint venture was completed in 1997, in which the ownership structure was changed from 51:49 (American:Chinese) to 65:35. At Daily Product, the U.S. partner set up a second joint venture in 1996 in which it holds a majority control, and it used this new venture to take shares in the old, 50:50-structured venture. Therefore, the U.S. partner's overall control has been strengthened.

The foreign parent's consolidation of control over joint ventures may signify a landmark event in the history of direct foreign investment in China. It represents a significant step in which the Chinese business environment is upgraded toward maturity and internationalization. The Chinese market is no longer a clean slate of competition isolated from the rest of the world. As a result, fierce competition among international firms in China looms large. Meanwhile, the attempt for increased control over their joint ventures indicates that the early entrants into China have put an end to their initial strategy, that is, going to China to test the local market or simply to establish a presence in the country. Now they are getting serious. They are starting to take advantage of being the early entrants by building entry barriers against newcomers. However, the consolidation effort by the foreign joint venture partners is not conducted without resistance. In the next section, I discuss the reactions by the Chinese government and the local joint venture partners.

Changes in the Bargaining Power Structure

Significant changes have occurred in the relative bargaining power balance between the international partner and the local government/partner. In the early years of the open-door policy, China was eager to attract foreign investors. Accordingly, favorable taxation policies and other preferential treatment were offered by the central and/or the local government to the joint venture early birds. Over time, as more and more international firms flew into China forming joint ventures or wholly owned foreign subsidiaries, many of these incentive offers have been reduced or eliminated. Especially in the more developed regions, such as the coastal areas, the local government has perceived a substantial increase in its bargaining power in negotiating with prospective foreign joint venture partners. A government official in a coastal city commented in a recent interview:

> Originally it was us who pulled them [the foreign firms] here to make deals. So, they were very picky about us. . . . Now it's our turn, because it is them who want to team up with us. We have to compare at least three foreign candidates to decide with which one to form a joint venture.

Although it probably is the experience of most joint ventures in China that the local government interference in the joint ventures' affairs, particularly in the operation and management areas, has been minor or minimal, this does not imply that the government would give up its influence on strategically critical issues. For example, the increased number of foreign wholly owned holding companies has captured significant attention by the government policymakers. Several times since 1996, government media (e.g., *China Daily*) have made it a topic for front page commentaries where it is argued that the emerging foreign holding companies are presenting a potential threat to Chinese domestic enterprises. The current policy allows a holding company to be established only when the foreign company is concurrently operating at least three separate joint ventures in China. The function of holding companies is also being subjected to significant constraints. It is my prediction that not only will the existing constraints for holding companies remain for a relatively long period of time, but that new and more detailed regulation measures are likely to be stipulated.

Local governments and the Chinese joint venture partners are highly reluctant to reduce their ownership holdings in joint ventures, particularly when joint ventures significantly outperform the wholly owned domestic divisions of the Chinese partner. Therefore, the Chinese stakes in, and returns from, the joint venture become extremely critical. For example, in the Office Aid joint venture, the renegotiation around the proposed increase in the U.S. partner's ownership was extremely painful. After many rounds of bargaining over a period of more than 2 years, in late 1996 the partners eventually reached an agreement to change the U.S. partner's symbolic majority (51%) to a substantial majority (65%). However, not long after the American negotiators had returned home, they were told that the municipal government vetoed the agreement for unexplained reasons. After another round of painful negotiation and lobbying, the proposed change in ownership structure was eventually institutionalized in 1997.

CONCLUSION

The research results reported in this chapter offer empirical data on several important characteristics of the negotiation and formation of international joint ventures in China. Whereas the survey data may provide potentially generalizable insights, the longitudinal comparative case studies may be especially valuable to enhance understanding of how interpartner characteristics dynamically evolve over time as changes occur in the joint venture's environment and/or in the parent company's strategies. Finally, the new trends identified in the chapter may serve as useful clues for future research as well as for practitioners who are involved in or interested in joint ventures in China.

After several years of tough but low-key negotiations, in 1997 McDonald's reached the final settlement of its dispute with the municipal government of Beijing regarding the relocation of the former's largest restaurant in the Chinese capital. The controversy started when the local government contracted with a giant Hong Kong real estate developer to build a business center (to be named

The Oriental Plaza) in the larger area in which the restaurant was built under a 20-year lease of the piece of land. The settlement, which involves a payment by the city's government to McDonald's of approximately $12 million (RMB 100 million Yuan), ended a years-long, highly publicized negotiation. The relocation of the restaurant per se (the new site is less than 100 meters away, according to the report) and the amount of compensation involved are far less significant than the political implications of the case, in my view. As the first high-profile case in which a Chinese government ended up compensating a foreign company, it carries an encouraging message for foreign investors and businesses.

As the turn of the century approaches, several major events have occurred or are expected to happen, not the least significant of which are the recent transition of Hong Kong back to China and China becoming a member of the World Trade Organization. These events potentially have significant impacts on international business ventures in the country. According to Hong Kong Basic Law, Hong Kong investors will continue to be treated as "foreign" by the Central government when they initiate investment projects on the mainland. After joining the World Trade Organization, it is expected that China will further remove entry barriers to service industries, the agriculture sector, and certain state-controlled manufacturing industries. This removal will help foreign investors more effectively and efficiently enter and operate in this vast market.

REFERENCES

Beamish, P. W. (1993). Characteristics of joint ventures in the People's Republic of China. *Journal of International Marketing, 1*(1), 29-48.

Campbell, N. (1988). *A strategic guide to equity joint ventures in China*. Elmsdale, NY: Pergamon.

Child, J. (1991). A foreign perspective on the management of people in China. *The International Journal of Human Resource Management, 2*(1), 93-107.

Child, J., & Markoczy, L. (1991). *Host country managerial behavior in Chinese and Hungarian joint ventures: Assessment of competing explanations*. Working paper, University of Aston, England.

Child, J., Yan, Y., & Lu, Y. (1997). Ownership and control in Sino-foreign joint ventures. In P. W. Beamish & J. P. Killing (Eds.), *Cooperative strategies: Asian Pacific perspectives* (pp. 181-225). San Francisco: New Lexington Press.

Chowdhury, M. A. J. (1988). *International joint ventures: Some interfirm-organizational specific determinants of success and failure—A factor analytic exploration*. Unpublished doctoral dissertation, Temple University, Philadelphia.

Daniels, J. D., Krug, J., & Nigh, D. (1985, Summer). U.S. joint ventures in China: Motivation and management of political risk. *California Management Review*, pp. 46-58.

Davidson, W. H. (1987). Creating and managing joint ventures in China. *California Management Review, 24*(4), 77-94.

The Economic Intelligence Unit. (1994). *Country report: China, Mongolia* (3rd quarter). London: Author.

Hendryx, S. R. (1986). Implementation of a technology transfer joint venture in the People's Republic of China: A management perspective. *Columbia Journal of World Business, 21*(1), 57-66.

Ho, A. K. (1990). *Joint ventures in the People's Republic of China.* New York: Praeger.

Luo, Y. (1996). *Foreign parent investment strategies and international joint venture performance: China evidence.* Unpublished doctoral dissertation, Temple University, Philadelphia.

Mann, J. (1989). *Beijing Jeep.* New York: Simon & Schuster.

Mathur, I., & Chen, J. S. (1987). *Strategies for joint ventures in the People's Republic of China.* New York: Praeger.

Newman, W. H. (1992a). Focused joint ventures in transforming economies. *Academy of Management Executive, 6*(1), 67-75.

Newman, W. H. (1992b, Fall). Launching a viable joint venture. *California Management Review,* pp. 68-80.

O'Reilly, A. J. (1988, Spring). Establishing successful joint ventures in developing nations: A CEO's perspective. *Columbia Journal of World Business,* pp. 65-71.

Pearson, M. M. (1991). *Joint ventures in the People's Republic of China: The control of foreign direct investment under socialism.* Princeton, NJ: Princeton University Press.

Peng, M. W., & Heath, P. S. (1996). The growth of the firm in planned economies in transition: Institutions, organizations, and strategic choice. *Academy of Management Review, 21*(2), 492-528.

Schnepp, O., Von Glinow, M. A., & Bhambri, A. (1990). *United States-China technology transfer.* Englewood Cliffs, NJ: Prentice Hall.

Shan, W.-J. (1991). Environmental risks and joint venture sharing arrangements. *Journal of International Business Studies, 22*(4), 555-578.

Shenkar, O. (1990). International joint ventures' problems in China: Risks and remedies. *Long Range Planning, 23*(3), 82-90.

Stoltenberg, C. D., & McClure, D. W. (1987). The joint venture and related contract laws of Mainland China and Taiwan: A comparative analysis. *Georgia Journal of International and Comparative Law, 17*(1), 45-97.

Teagarden, M. B. (1989). *Sino-U.S. joint venture effectiveness.* Unpublished doctoral dissertation, University of Southern California.

Tung, R. L. (1982). *U.S.-China trade negotiations.* Elmsdale, NY: Pergamon.

The U.S.-China Business Council. (1990). *Special report on U.S. investment in China.* Washington DC: China Business Forum.

Yan, A., & Gray, B. (1994). Bargaining power, management control, and performance in United States-China joint ventures: A comparative case study. *Academy of Management Journal, 37,* 1478-1517.

chapter 6

International Joint Ventures in China

Industry Structure and Its Performance Implications

YADONG LUO

A major challenge today for multinational corporations (MNCs) is how organizations become competent and attain sustained superior performance in the global marketplace. When expanding globally, MNCs are likely to achieve higher performance than firms operating domestically (Morck & Yeung, 1991), because the former benefit from the industry structure variance between the host and home country by investing those distinct resources that can enhance firms' competitive advantages vis-à-vis rivals in indigenous markets (Porter, 1986). It is recognized that industry structure imperfections in foreign markets constitute a dominant factor that not only makes foreign direct investment (FDI) preferable to trade or licensing (Contractor & Lorange, 1988), but also determines the relative attractiveness of some host countries over other host countries and the home country itself (Dunning, 1979). In general, empirical evidence tends to support an existence of systematic linkage between MNC performance and structural variables in the market economy context (Caves & Mehra, 1986; Kogut & Singh, 1988; Mitchell, Shaver, & Yeung, 1993; Willmore, 1994; Yu & Ito, 1988). However, there has been inadequate empirical research on this issue pertaining to complex, dynamic, and uncertain environments such as transitional economies. This is a serious gap, especially because these economies have in recent years become major hosts of MNCs' direct investment. The industry structure in transitional economies is different from that in market economies with respect not only to the degree of imperfection but also the structural uncertainty and information transparency (Newfarmer & Marsh, 1992). The current industry structure transformation in these economies, where some sectors are privatized and others are not, contributes to added complexity and underlines the distinct dynamic of these structures (Rawski, 1994). This study seeks to examine the relationship between industry structure attributes and international expansion performance in the environment of a transitional economy.

Most previous studies analyzed the industry structure-MNC performance relationship at the corporate or firm level (e.g., Morck & Yeung, 1991; Newfarmer & Marsh, 1992). As a result, this relationship has not been well understood at the business-unit level. Morrison and Roth (1992) and Rumelt (1991) state that theoretical or statistical work seeking to identify the degree of attractiveness of the industry for a participating business must use the business unit, or even less-aggregated entities, as the unit of analysis, because contextual factors including structural conditions directly impact operations and performance of business units. The present study, therefore, intends to address the issue at the business-unit level.

When entering transitional economies, MNCs are most likely to opt for the international equity joint venture (IJV) as the preferred form of business unit (Harrigan, 1988). The rationale for this choice derives from strategic considerations such as uncertainty reduction, indigenous resource or knowledge acquirement, local market expansion, or evasion of compulsory rules by host governments (Contractor & Lorange, 1988; Hennart, 1988; Kogut, 1988). Although the analysis of IJV performance in transitional economies has commanded considerable attention in IJV literature (Beamish, 1993; Shan, 1991), few systematic attempts have been made to examine the effect of industry structure variables on IJV performance in this context. This is indeed a very complicated research question because both industry structure and IJV performance are multidimensional constructs (Kogut & Singh, 1988) and fairly unstable in dynamic environments (Child, 1994).

In sum, the purpose of this study is to explore the impact of industry structure variables on the performance of IJVs operating in a transitional economy. In light of the particular importance of China as one of the largest dynamic economies, fastest-growing markets, and biggest FDI recipient in the world, this study uses China as the analytical context. The underlying premise of this study is that industry structure in transitional economies significantly influences IJVs' overall performance (multivariate effect), and different structural attributes idiosyncratically influence IJVs' unidimensional performance (univariate effect). This study may be of interest for both theory and practice. It sought to establish whether there was a systematic linkage between the host country industry structure and IJV performance in an emerging economy, an assumption that, although largely untested, is critical to theories of FDI and IJV. It may also have implications for the global strategy paradigm, because industry is an important driver of global strategy (Yip, 1994). Given the similarities in the inherent characteristics of the long-standing industrial policies pursued by many formerly centrally planned economies in transition (Child & Lu, 1990), the results of the present study are expected to hold to some extent for other transitional economies.

THEORETICAL CONSIDERATIONS AND HYPOTHESES

A widely accepted conceptual framework in industrial organization holds that structural conditions determine the behavior and subsequent performance of a firm (Bain, 1959). In an economy unfettered by structural imperfection of output, profit rates across industries should fall to some equilibrium rate reflecting the risk-adjusted marginal efficiency of capital (Hay & Morris, 1979). In the presence of structural imperfections, however, inter-industry variations in profitability abound because entry barriers prevent new competition and expanded output (Scherer & Ross, 1990). In a similar vein, the industry structure paradigm in the strategy literature maintains that competitive advantages and interfirm differences in efficiency cannot persist over a long time period unless structural imperfections are present (Porter, 1980, 1986; Teece, Pisano, & Shuen, 1991). Porter (1991) also notes these strong industry effects on the selection of business-level strategies. A large body of research in corporate business portfolios studies concurs and points out the importance of industry structure variables in explaining performance (Bettis & Mahajan, 1985; Christensen & Montgomery, 1981; Montgomery, 1985).

From an international perspective, when the industry structure of a host country is imperfect, FDI will flow in as a direct response if entry barriers are low (Hymer, 1976; Yu & Ito, 1988).[1] Firms in oligopolistic industries in the host country enjoy the advantages of economies of scale and control of supply that give them market power (Caves, 1971; Yu & Ito, 1988). This power allows them to overcome the disadvantages of being foreign and to compete with local competitors in host countries where they have FDI facilities (Brewer, 1993). Direct investment tends to involve market conduct that extends the recognition of mutual market dependence—the essence of oligopoly—beyond national boundaries (Teece, 1985). Likewise, it tends broadly to equalize the rate of return on capital (equity) throughout a given industry in all the countries in which production actually takes place (Willmore, 1994). This common profit rate, however, may exceed a "normal" or competitive one since persistent oligopoly—nation- or worldwide—is marked by various barriers to entry of new firms and, perforce, to the inflow of capital (Caves, 1971; Teece, 1985).

MNCs entering planned economies in transition are likely to confront a higher level of barriers. This holds especially true for high profitability industries that generally remain state-owned and are not undergoing privatization. In order to prevent foreign investors from fully controlling these industrial sectors while encouraging them to bring in advanced technologies to modernize these sectors, host governments in these economies often impose an equity ceiling on FDI (Buckley & Casson, 1992). As a result, foreign investors in these industries have to use the IJV as the entry mode and the form of business-unit identity (Brewer, 1993). More important, the IJV form can help foreign investors in all industries attain benefits from structural imperfections of indigenous industries. Factor markets in these economies are virtually in their infancy since it is the government-instituted system that often controls the allocation of relatively scarce factors in the national economy (Child & Lu, 1990). Under these circumstances, a local partner can greatly assist the foreign investor in meeting the demand for local production factors such as human resources, strategic information, land, and raw materials. In addition, markets for proprietary and nonproprietary know-how are far from well established (Nee, 1992). International licensing is thus often superseded by making direct investments. Due to the lack of local networks in distributing final products made by proprietary knowledge, foreign investors often need collaboration with local firms. These structural factors contribute to the dominance and prevalence of the IJV as an entry mode for FDI and the form of MNCs' business-unit identity in these economies.

In transitional economies, the operation of local firms, particularly state-owned ones, is extensively influenced by numerous government decisions in addition to government industrial policies (Roman, 1986). These decisions may include labor allocation, investment, material supply, price controls, and performance target, among others (Rawski, 1994). Local firms obtain resources and distribute products through the combination of government plan and market activity (Nee, 1992). In contrast, IJVs and other types of foreign businesses in these economies occupy the market-oriented extreme of the industrial system

(Jefferson, Rawski, & Zheng, 1992). This extreme enables us to link IJV performance to industry structure in the absence of controlling the above government decisions. The operation of all local and foreign businesses, however, is inevitably impacted by the government's industrial policies that are reflected in the movement of multiple structure attributes (McGee, 1988).

Despite great improvements in recent years, industry structure in most transitional economies remains one of the bottlenecks hampering economic development (Roman, 1986). The main characteristics of industry structure in these economies include the following: First, there is an immense difference in after-tax profitability across industries, due primarily to the long-rooted industry structure imperfections and cumbersome consolidation tax system (Jia, 1991). Second, there is also a fundamental difference in sales growth across industries, due mainly to government industrial policy that allows only some sectors to be decentralized and privatized (Katrak, 1991). Third, a major structural "headache" is that the central governments of these economies have to control the ownership of state firms' assets while allowing firms to be acquired by or merged with domestic or foreign investors (Child, 1994). The higher-asset-intense industries thus are subject to greater government interference (Rawski, 1994). In other words, inter-industry variations in asset intensity can lead to treatment variations for firms in different industries. Fourth, growth of the number of firms in an industry is enormously idiosyncratic across industries. Controlling the number of new firms established in the industry is a predominant means for governments to monitor structural development (Jefferson et al., 1992). This entry barrier consequently leads to the heterogeneity of competition vigor in different industries. Fifth, industry structure is highly uncertain, arising mainly from the transformative nature of the national economy and the experimental nature of an array of new industrial policies (Jenkins, 1991). These structural characteristics urged the selection of the following structure attributes to be examined in this study: (a) industry profitability, (b) industry sales growth, (c) industry asset intensity, (d) growth of number of firms in an industry, and (e) industry structure uncertainty.

The efficiency paradigm in industrial organization economics and resource-based theory in strategic management both suggest that firms have different types of resources and capabilities (Mahoney & Pandian, 1992; McGee, 1988) and that these resources and capabilities can be used to achieve two types of economic benefits: (a) cooperative and strategic or (b) competitive and financial (Hoskisson, Hill, & Kim, 1993). For IJVs, cooperative and strategic benefits accrue from sharing highly specialized resources that are complementary between partners (Blodgett, 1992; Hagedoorn & Schakenraad, 1994; Parkhe,

1991). Competitive and financial benefits are achieved from increasing econo-mies of scale, learning effect, risk reduction, or global integration synergies (Ghoshal, 1987; Harrigan, 1988; Kogut, 1988). These benefits of different aspects necessitate a multidimensional approach to assess IJV performance. To develop further the relationship between industry structure variables and multi-dimensional performance of IJVs in the transitional economy environment, the following sections will examine the effects of specific structural variables on concrete dimensions of IJVs based on the Chinese context.

Industry Profitability

Industry profitability constitutes one of the major industry drivers of a firm's global strategy (Yip, 1994; Yu & Ito, 1988) and one of the key environmental traits affecting cooperative strategies and subsequent performance of the firm (Harrigan, 1985). Inter-industry variance in profitability has been an enduring characteristic of the Chinese economy, due in major part to government inter-vention (Tung, 1982).[2] The breadth and depth of the removal of government-in-duced asymmetries in an industry during the transition stage depend largely upon the industry's profit level (Jefferson et al., 1992). In order to keep inflation surge and market fluctuations at a minimum, the Chinese government first lifted central control over low-profitability industries where transaction price was usually close to the market equilibrium position (Rawski, 1994). Consequently, lower-profitability industries moved more quickly toward the position of market equilibrium, and competitive entry by more efficient rivals first took place in these industries (e.g., textile and light industries). At the same time, continued government hindrance in business entry remained in high-profitability industries (e.g., medical and pharmaceutical, petroleum processing, and raw chemical materials; Grub & Lin, 1991). This hindrance resulted in appreciable barriers to new entry and enabled existing firms, including IJVs in the industry, to keep their market power and advantageous competition position (Shenkar, 1990).

Not surprisingly, whenever a particular industry in the host country displays sustained high profitability over the years, foreign investors in the industry are expected to pursue this profitability by devoting their competencies to the production in local sites and marketing in the host country rather than exporting to home or international markets (Child, 1994; Jenkins, 1991). This strategic orientation could enable IJVs in the industry to exploit more economic benefits from the indigenous market growth and industry profitability (Yip, 1994). In addition, as noted above, when operating in high-profitability industries, firms are likely to confront more government intervention and hindrance. Moreover, because the price departure from market-determined equilibrium in high-profitability industries is greater than that in low-profitability industries, the latent or potential market fluctuations in the former industries are likely to be greater than those in the latter industries (Roman, 1986; Scherer & Ross, 1990). Thus:

H_{1a}: In the Chinese context, ceteris paribus, an IJV's accounting return and local sales are positively related to the profitability of the industry in which the IJV participates.

H_{1b}: In the Chinese context, ceteris paribus, an IJV's export sales and risk reduction are negatively related to the profitability of the industry in which the IJV participates.

Industry Sales Growth

Industry sales growth constitutes a key component of market attractiveness for IJVs. Growth serves as an indicator of disequilibrium and industry evolution (McGee, 1988). Porter (1980) argues that rapid industry growth ensures a strong financial performance for incumbents even though new entrants take some market share. Because industry sales growth is also interrelated with market demand and customer traits as well as volatility of competitive behavior, the form, focus, and duration of a firm's cooperative strategies and venture success will vary from industry to industry (Caves & Mehra, 1986; Harrigan, 1988; Kogut & Singh, 1988). In the Chinese economy, some industry sectors are undergoing transition while others are not (Nee, 1992). When a sector is freed from government control over market supply, rapid market growth will usually ensue for the sector (Hay & Morris, 1979; Katrak, 1991). This takeoff is reflected in a surge in industry sales growth, which is in turn likely to be mirrored in the sales growth of existing IJVs in the industry, ceteris paribus. However, when the local market for a particular industry appears to grow dramatically, it is reasonable to expect that IJVs will pursue local market expansion rather than export growth because, as prior studies have demonstrated, the predominant strategic objective of transnational investors entering developing countries or transitional economies is to acquire market share in growing industries (Beamish, 1993; Buckley & Casson, 1992). Thus:

H_{2a}: In the Chinese context, ceteris paribus, an IJV's accounting return and local sales are positively related to the sales growth of the industry in which the IJV participates.

H₂b: In the Chinese context, ceteris paribus, an IJV's export sales are negatively related to the sales growth of the industry in which the IJV participates.

Industry Asset Intensity

Industry asset intensity refers to an industry's average level of total fixed assets that must be maintained in order to start production and carry out operations (Hay & Morris, 1979). This intensity constitutes a plausible indicator for capital requirements, a proxy for entry barriers, and a determinant of economies of scale (Bain, 1959). The imperfect capital market argument in industrial organization studies contends that firms in an industry that requires a large initial capital investment can obtain monopolistic profits in the long run because few truly qualified competitors can enter the industry (Scherer & Ross, 1990) and because exit barriers created by substantial resource commitments may not be fully recoverable (Caves, 1971). Although interindustry mobility turns out to be higher during transition than pretransition in China, high asset intensity discourages entry of new firms into the industry, thus leading to high concentration and collusive pricing behavior in the industry (Jefferson et al., 1992). As a result, IJVs in a high-asset-intensity industry are likely to have high profitability.

Nevertheless, oligopolistic rivalry due to entry barriers arising from high capital requirement in a transitional economy is played out in an uncertain, ever-changing environment (Tan & Litschert, 1994). While the evolution of this environment permits managers to learn about market conditions and competitors' intentions, it also presents the constant danger that a rival will undercut the existing pricing structure in search of competitive advantage (Rawski, 1994). Moreover, high-asset-intensity industries are subject to more government interferences because the state seeks to control the ownership of state-owned firms' assets in the course of privatization (Child, 1994). Thus IJVs in these industries are expected to have more operational risks.

A high-asset-intensity industry usually requires foreign investors to commit a great deal of investing capital or other distinctive resources (Kogut & Singh, 1988). According to the efficiency paradigm in industrial organization, a firm's distinctive competence uniquely positions the firm with respect to the factor markets and justifies the choice of its product-market position in the industry (McGee, 1988). When contributing their distinctive resources to local asset-intensive industries (i.e., capital- or technology-intensive ones), IJVs manifest their long-term commitment to indigenous production and local market expansion. This complies with the notion in the Chinese IJV literature that IJVs in capital- or technology-intensive industries tend to be local-market-oriented while those in labor-intensive industries seem export-oriented (Beamish, 1993; National Council, 1991). Therefore, an IJV's export performance is predicted to be negatively related to the asset intensity of industry in which the IJV operates. Thus:

H₃ₐ: In the Chinese context, ceteris paribus, an IJV's accounting return is positively related to the asset intensity of the industry in which the IJV participates.

H₃ᵦ: In the Chinese context, ceteris paribus, an IJV's export sales and risk reduction are negatively related to the asset intensity of the industry in which the IJV participates.

Growth of Number of Firms in an Industry

In examining the degree of competition in an industry in market economies, the most widely used measure is the leading firm concentration ratio (e.g., CR4 for the United States, CR5 for the United Kingdom, CR3 for Germany). However, this ratio is neither applicable nor available in China because the degree of inequality of firms' share in an industry does not necessarily reflect the vigor of competition, as a consequence of government intervention and the "state-owned" identity of leading firms (Tung, 1982).

Following the decentralization and privatization of most industry sectors that had been unable to meet market demand, the number of firms in these now-more-competitive industries has grown drastically, and this growth constitutes a good proxy for competition intensity in the transition phase.[3] Industrial organization theory suggests that this competition intensity is positively related to the number of firms in the industry (Hay & Morris, 1979; McGee, 1988). Therefore, the increase in the number of firms in an industry is expected to boost competition in the industry, lessen the difference of firms' profitability among industries, and slow down the average growth rate of local sales for individual firms (Jenkins, 1991; Katrak, 1991).

Whenever a host industry appears to be highly competitive as a result of an increase in the number of firms in the industry, IJVs are likely to shift their focus from local market development to production factor exploitation via export

(Davidson, 1980; Ghoshal, 1987). This strategic choice may result in high export sales for the IJVs (Stern, 1975; Yip, 1994). Thus:

H$_{4a}$: In the Chinese context, ceteris paribus, an IJV's accounting return and local sales are negatively related to the growth of number of firms in the industry in which the IJV participates.

H$_{4b}$: In the Chinese context, ceteris paribus, an IJV's export sales are positively related to the growth of number of firms in the industry in which the IJV participates.

Industry Structure Uncertainty

An important feature of planned economies in transition is the dynamic nature of industry structure (Child, 1994; Roman, 1986). The degree of decentralization and privatization and the stage of structure transformation differ enormously across industries. Consequently, the level of structural uncertainty varies immensely according to industry. Unlike structural uncertainties in market economies that often arise due to market force fluctuations, structural uncertainties in transitional economies such as China are attributable mainly to the change of host government rules and policies (Child & Lu, 1990; Nee, 1992). Under these circumstances, it is difficult for firms to avoid the uncertainties derived from changing rules and policies because these are beyond the control of the firms (Kobrin, 1982; Root, 1988). In addition, it is reported that there is a greater information imperfection in transitional economies than in market economies (Nee, 1992). This compounds structural uncertainty, which further increases the business risks facing IJVs (Beamish, 1993). Moreover, industry conditions in this context change so rapidly that it is extremely difficult for firms to keep up, thus creating a situation that mimics organizational inertia (Tan & Litschert, 1994). Under these circumstances, a high-uncertainty industry is likely to yield more operational instabilities for the firm. Thus, it is expected that firms in highly uncertain industries confront more operational risks.

According to the IJV theory, foreign ventures can reduce vulnerability to industry structure uncertainty by minimizing reliance on local settings (Killing, 1983). In their effort to do so, foreign investors can decrease the portion of local purchase, distribution, and marketing and can accordingly increase the portion of export business (Davidson, 1980). It thus can be hypothesized that when the local industry structure is unstable or turbulent, IJVs are likely to have high export performance. Thus:

H$_{5a}$: In the Chinese context, ceteris paribus, an IJV's risk reduction is negatively related to the structure uncertainty of the industry in which the IJV participates.

H$_{5b}$: In the Chinese context, ceteris paribus, an IJV's export sales are positively related to the structure uncertainty of the industry in which the IJV participates.

Control Variables

It is clear that IJVs in the same industry achieve widely different levels of success. These firm-level actions can be traced to the firm's strategy, resources, or commitments (Hennart & Park, 1994; Porter, 1991; Tallman & Shenkar, 1994). In examining the relationship between industry structure and IJV performance, this study isolates relevant firm-level factors as control variables. These variables include *equity distribution, type of projects, length of operation,* and *venture size.*

First, as an element of entry strategy and a sign of resource commitment (Hennart, 1988), an IJV's equity distribution could impact the ability and propensity of an IJV to influence contextual factors, including structural elements. This is because the sharing arrangement influences bargaining power vis-à-vis local partners, extent of control over the IJV, and degree of local dependence (Kogut, 1988; Shan, 1991). Equity distribution is therefore treated as a control variable in this study.

Second, FDI theory maintains that the positions of investors from dissimilar nations along the political, economic, and cultural dimensions in the investment sequence will improve as investors become more knowledgeable about local conditions through direct experience (Harrigan, 1985; Kogut & Zander, 1994). In international business, Parkhe (1991) and Yu (1991) demonstrate that under a dynamic and uncertain environment, the interaction between learning effect and contributed competencies as the source of a foreign subsidiary's efficiency or competitive advantage is intensified. As a proxy for learning and experience, length of operation may hence facilitate the contributions of an IJV's competence to the venture success in an indigenous setting. Looking at the issue from another angle, Wernerfelt and Karnani (1987) suggest that in an uncertain environment, operation length is an important component of competitive strategy because it involves a trade-off between acting early and acting later after the uncertainty has diminished. Length of operation is hence included in the study as another control variable.

The third control variable is labeled type of project, referring to the nature of project orientations such as import-substitution, export-oriented, technologically advanced, or domestic-oriented. This variable links an investor's distinctive competence and a host country's industry structure, labor cost, raw material supply, and the like. The resource-based view suggests that a firm could achieve rents as a result not only of controlling better resources, but also of its ability to make better use of its resources. The ability thus constitutes its distinctive competence (Mahoney & Pandian, 1992). When investing abroad, the overall pattern of resource usage is reflected by project-type selection. In addition, the governments in some transitional economies, such as China's, treat various types of projects differentially, according to policy objectives oriented toward bringing in advanced technology and generating foreign exchange earnings. As a result, type of project is likely to affect an IJV's accessibility to, and treatment in, local industries.

Finally, IJV size is widely recognized as affecting the venture's market power over competitors (Kogut & Singh, 1988; Yu, 1991) and its risk-taking capability in the host country (Blodgett, 1992). IJV size is also an important investment strategy variable influencing not only the ability to generate financial or operational synergies but also the capability of accessing markets in transitional economies (Beamish, 1993). IJV size is therefore incorporated in the model as a fourth control variable.

RESEARCH METHODS

Research Setting

The data were collected from the People's Republic of China during a pivotal time in the transition stage. China officially opened its doors to foreign investment in 1979. Between then and the end of 1995, Chinese authorities approved the establishment of more than 258,444 FDI projects involving $393.04 billion in foreign capital. About 120,000 ventures, representing $133.04 billion in investment, commenced operations (*Foreign Investment in China,* 1996). The formation and operation of these ventures have played a major role in shaping the new economic environment and have turned China into the second largest FDI absorbing country in the world, behind only the United States. Among FDI entry modes, the IJV form remains dominant and accounted for 52.02% of total FDI value in 1994 (*Bulletin of Ministry of Foreign Trade and Economic Coop-*

eration [MOFTEC], 1995a, p. 13). Among economic sectors, the manufacturing sector leads with 54.94% of total FDI in 1994 (MOFTEC, 1995b, p. 11).

As in other formerly centrally planned economies, industry structure in China prior to economic transition was characterized by high concentration (relatively small numbers of enterprises) and by the limited freedom of action permitted to these enterprises. This system causes widespread poor performance in many industries. During the transitional stage, particularly in recent years, the performance of Chinese industry has improved remarkably.[4] This is the result of the increased competition and growing financial pressures that have accompanied a gradual and still incomplete shift from a planned economy to a market economy. In industry, the transition from plan to market started with commodities and has now begun to penetrate the allocation of land, labor, and capital. The share of industrial products sold through markets now exceeds 85% (Rawski, 1994). Few firms remain immune from competition. The degree of concentration is low and declining. Competition from manufactured imports has expanded, and barriers to domestic trade are increasingly porous. IJVs and other types of foreign businesses have played an important role in enhancing nationwide competition and pushing the economy forward to the market orientation.

Data

Industry data were collected from four consecutive editions of the *China Statistical Yearbook* (industry section), compiled by the State Statistical Bureau of China, covering the years 1988 through 1991. This time frame is appropriate because (a) it lies in the middle of economic transition in the country and is an overall operating rather than start-up phase nationwide as far as foreign investment is concerned. The government policies, rules, and regulations concerning foreign investment were much more exhaustive during the period, and (b) as Scherer and Ross (1990) note, measuring the industry structure-firm performance relation requires a time period long enough to avoid short-term effects of the business cycle but not so long that the underlying structural parameters will have changed. In the Chinese economy literature, Jefferson et al. (1992) and Jia (1991) both use a 4-year period to examine the performance effect of industry structure. The present study uses a 4-year length as well.

The firm-specific financial data regarding IJVs in China is available only from the local authorities, such as commissions of foreign economic relations and trade, foreign exchange administrations, and taxation bureaus. In this study, cross-sectional data for 117 IJVs operating in industry sectors[5] from 1988 through 1991 in Jiangsu Province were obtained from the Provincial Commission of Foreign Economic Relations and Trade, where I once worked as a department head. These sample IJVs were formed by the end of 1986.[6] Specifically, the data about relevant financial figures were obtained from the balance sheets and income statements that the IJVs submitted to the above Commission. These statements were audited by independent certified public accountants before they were submitted. The sample IJVs' investment information, including length of operation, equity distribution, and type of project, was obtained from the *Directory of Foreign-Invested Enterprises in Jiangsu Province* (1992 edition), compiled by the above Commission.

Jiangsu ranks second in China in terms of GDP and FDI absorption, surpassed only by Guangdong province. The policies, rules, and measures adopted in the province vis-à-vis FDI have been widely applied elsewhere in the country.

Measurement

IJV Performance. It is recognized that IJV performance studies have suffered considerably from the comparability and reliability of alternative performance measures (Geringer & Hebert, 1991). Prior research observed significant differences in the operationalization of IJV performance. Three broad categories of IJV performance measures used in prior studies include (a) traditional financial return, such as ROI (return on investment) and ROA (return on assets) (Hagedoorn & Schakenraad, 1994); (b) IJVs' instability (Killing, 1983; Kogut, 1988); and (c) subjective assessment of a parent's satisfaction with an IJV performance (Beamish, 1993). Each of these measures has its own limitations and cannot reflect all facets of IJV performance.

In the present study, the following principles have guided the selection of appropriate IJV performance measures. First, all single measures can reflect only certain aspects of firm performance, and no single measure can capture the diverse goals of IJVs. Therefore, multidimensional performance measures should be used. Second, the performance measurement must be in harmony with the strategic roles of IJVs. In IJV literature, the commonly accepted roles of IJVs include efficiency, market growth, cost-minimization (via export), and risk reduction.[7] Based on the above considerations, four measures are finally selected and will be utilized to evaluate IJV performance in this study. They are *return on investment, local sales/investment, export sales/investment,*[8] and *operational risk index.*

Because the number of IJVs listed in the Chinese stock exchanges is exceedingly small (no sample firm in this study has been listed in the exchanges) and foreign investors are even subject to restrictions in purchasing the so-called B shares (common stocks denominated in foreign currencies) of the existing joint stock companies, stock market-based measurement of risk[9] is neither appropriate nor available in a Chinese case study. As a result, this study employs accounting-based risk measurement to reflect a firm's operation variability. In the strategic management literature, accounting-based risk is commonly measured by the standard deviation of accounting return such as ROA (Amit & Livnat, 1988; Bettis & Mahajan, 1985), because the standard deviation or its square, the variance, is a standard measure of dispersion and hence operational risk (Amit & Livnat, 1988). This study also uses the standard deviations of IJV performance measures during the 1988-through-1991 period to compute operational risk of IJVs. However, earlier studies in the literature failed to capture the variations of multiple performance measures. In contrast, this study computes the standard deviations of all four performance measures. Further, because the multiplication of standard deviations of multiple performance measures could be very large (extreme scores) for some observations in a dynamic environment, thus leading to skewed distributions, this study uses the geometric average instead of simple multiplication of measures' standard deviations (for a detailed calculation, see Table 6.1 and the Appendix). Researchers in the accounting literature also use this approach to assess a firm's operational risk (e.g., Choi, Ghosh, & Kim, 1991). Table 6.1 shows the measurement or calculation of criterion variables (multidimensional performance of IJVs), predictor variables (industry structure attributes), and control variables (firm characteristics). The measurement of industry structure attributes is further illustrated below.

Industry Structure Attributes. Industry profitability is measured by the industry's ROA, which is computed by the industry's total after-tax profits divided by total assets in the industry. According to the Chinese industry accounting system, total assets are composed of circulating assets (different from "current assets" defined by the U.S. GAAP [generally accepted accounting principles]) and fixed assets, and the amount of circulating assets always equates with that of circulating funds (the former are treated as so-called capital application while the latter are viewed as "capital source"). As a result, the value of total assets of an industry was obtained by adding up the fixed assets and circulating funds of the industry, both figures being provided in the *China Statistical Yearbook*.

As shown in Table 6.1 and the Appendix, industry sales growth was calculated using a compound growth rate covering 1988 through 1991. The data on industry sales were obtained from the *Yearbook*.

Industry asset intensity is measured by the net value of fixed assets. The *Yearbook* provides both the total cross-value of fixed assets and the aggregate

TABLE 6.1 Variable Measurement and Calculation

Variable	Measurement and Calculation[a]	Data Source
Criterion variables		
Return on investment (*ROI*)	Net income after tax/total investment (%)	Firm's financial statement[b]
Local sales *(SALE)*	Local sales revenue/total investment (%)	Firm's financial statement
Export (*EXPORT*)	Export value/total investment (%)	Firm's financial statement
Operational risk (*RISK*)	[Std(ROI)Std(SALE)Std(EXPORT)]$^{1/3}$	Own calculation[c]
Predictor variables		
Industry profitability (*INDPRO*)	Industry's after-tax ROA (%)	*China Statistical Yearbook*
Industry sales growth (*INDSAG*)	Industry's compound growth rate of sales	*China Statistical Yearbook*[d]
Industry asset intensity (*INDASS*)	Industry's fixed assets (net value, in billion yuan)	*China Statistical Yearbook*
Growth of number of firms in an industry (*INDNUM*)	Industry's compound growth rate of the number of firms	*China Statistical Yearbook*[e]
Industry structure uncertainty (*INDUNC*)	[Std(INDPRO)Std(INDSAG)Std(INDASS)Std(INDNUM)]$^{1/4}$	Own calculation[f]
Control variables		
Length of operation (*LENGTH*)	Number of years from IJV formation through end of the performance examination year	*Directory of FIEs*[g]
Equity distribution (*EQUITY*)	Equity owned by a foreign investor (%)	*Directory of FIEs*
Type of projects (*TYPE*)	Dummy variable, TYPE 1: 1 if technology-advanced, 0 otherwise; TYPE 2: 1 if export-oriented, 0 otherwise; TYPE 3: 1 if domestic-oriented, 0 otherwise	*Directory of FIEs*
Firm size (*SIZE*)	IJV's total assets (in $ million)	Firm's financial statement

NOTE: a. Except *RISK, INDSAG, INDNUM, INDUNC, EQUITY,* and *TYPE,* other variables are entered in SAS (CARDS) after being averaged.
b. Jiangsu Provincial Commission of Foreign Economic Relations and Trade released the firms' financial information to the researcher.
c, d, e, f. The computation steps are detailed in the Appendix.
g. *Directory of Foreign-Invested Enterprises in Jiangsu Province* (1992 edition), compiled by China Jiangsu Provincial Commission of Foreign Economic Relations and Trade.

value of accumulated depreciation for each industry. Based on this source, the net value of fixed assets for each industry was obtained by deducting accumulated depreciation from the cross-value of fixed assets.

The *Yearbook* reveals the number of firms in each industry, including both local Chinese firms and foreign-invested enterprises. The growth of number of firms in each industry was measured by computing the industry's compound growth rate covering the period 1988 through 1991. The computation of this attribute is further explained in the Appendix.

Finally, industry structure uncertainty is measured by the geometric average of standard deviations of all other structural variables examined in the present study (see Table 6.1 and the Appendix). This way of operationalizing industry structure uncertainty is appropriate because standard deviation is a common measure of variability, and industry structure is a multidimensional construct. Using the geometric average, instead of a simple multiplication of structure attributes' standard deviations, could remove the possible skewness of distribution because simple multiplication of large standard deviations results in extreme scores that may be concentrated on one side of the mean (Cooley & Lohns, 1971).

When an IJV involves multiple industries, all the structure attributes of industry j in which the IJV participates are multiplied by the proportion of firm sales in the industry (P_j) and aggregated for the firm. That is,

$$\text{Industry Structure Attribute } (I_i) = \Sigma (I_{ij} * P_j).$$

Analytical Approach

This study employs the general linear models procedure (GLM) to run a multivariate regression (MANOVA) using SAS software. The combination of a MANOVA statement and GLM procedure provides the best analytical approach for the significance test wherever criterion variables are highly correlated, and whenever both multivariate and univariate analyses of variance are needed (Hair, Anderson, Tatham, & Black, 1992; *SAS/STAT User's Guide,* 1990, chap. 24). Both the Pearson correlation coefficients (see Table 6.2) and Bartlett's test of sphericity (Cooley & Lohns, 1971) (Bartlett's = 242.67, $p < 0.001$) indicate that the criterion variables are highly correlated; a multivariate technique is hence appropriate for analyzing the data. In addition, GLM can allow researchers to specify any degree of interaction and nested effects, incorporate both categorical and continuous variables in the same model, and offer tests of hypotheses regardless of the extent of confounding (*SAS/STAT User's Guide,* 1990, chap. 24).

TABLE 6.2 Descriptive Statistics and Correlation Coefficient ($N = 117$)

Variable	Mean	S.D.	1	2	3	4	5	6	7	8	9	10	11	12	13	14	15
1. ROI	13.37	7.37	1.00														
2. SALE	41.93	18.32	0.81***	1.00													
3. EXPORT	9.06	11.74	0.25**	-0.19	1.00												
4. RISK	3.11	4.35	0.22**	0.30**	0.10	1.00											
5. INDPRO	3.52	3.88	0.41***	0.32***	-0.20*	0.19*	1.00										
6. INDSAG	23.73	9.19	0.35***	0.36***	-0.24**	0.14	0.44***	1.00									
7. INDASS	25.99	16.06	0.26**	0.08	-0.21*	0.18	0.10	0.05	1.00								
8. INDNUM	2.48	4.31	0.26**	0.31***	-0.23*	0.29**	0.52***	0.63***	0.13	1.00							
9. INDUNC	7.18	8.33	0.17	-0.15	0.10	0.45***	0.39***	0.48***	0.10	0.31***	1.00						
10. LENGTH	7.36	1.51	0.23*	0.26**	0.15	-0.27**	0.05	0.09	-0.04	0.07	0.04	1.00					
11. EQUITY	34.36	8.25	0.13	0.11	-0.11	-0.20*	-0.08	0.06	0.09	0.11	0.21*	-0.16	1.00				
12. TYPE I	0.22	0.38	0.15	0.09	-0.13	-0.23*	0.20*	0.38***	0.49***	-0.12	-0.07	0.11	0.22*	1.00			
13. TYPE II	0.42	0.49	0.11	-0.39***	0.36***	-0.23*	-0.31***	-0.47***	-0.12	0.06	0.26**	0.10	-0.15	-0.27**	1.00		
14. TYPE III	0.21	0.36	0.08	0.18	-0.40***	0.22*	0.17	0.19*	0.08	0.14	0.17	0.04	0.12	-0.21*	-0.15	1.00	
15. SIZE	5.23	5.86	0.15	0.03	-0.09	-0.12	0.20*	0.06	0.38***	-0.08	-0.05	0.12	0.10	0.29**	-0.02	0.11	1.00

* $p < 0.05$; ** $p < 0.01$; *** $p < 0.001$.

RESULTS

Results described in Table 6.2 reveal a high level of standard deviations of industry structure variables, confirming the dynamic and uncertain nature of industry structure in China. IJV performance also displays a high level of variance across firms. Findings concerning the underlying relationship between structural variables and IJV performance are presented and discussed next.

Conforming to my hypothesis, the examination demonstrates that industry profitability (*INDPRO*) affects IJVs' overall and unidimensional performance at a significant level. As shown in Table 6.3, the multivariate effect of industry profitability on a firm's overall performance is statistically significant ($F = 2.76$, $p = 0.023$). This structural variable also has a significantly positive univariate influence on IJVs' return on investment ($F = 8.32$, $p = 0.005$) and local market expansion ($F = 19.10$, $p = 0.001$), and a strong but negative impact on IJVs' export ($F = 7.01$, $p = 0.011$) and risk reduction ($F = 3.47$, $p = 0.066$). H_{1a} and H_{1b} are hence supported. This evidence suggests that industry profitability in China vigorously affects all the dimensions of venture performance and has a heterogenous direction, according to the dimension considered. In addition, it is found that the interaction between industry profitability and firm size (*SIZE*) is important for IJVs' accounting return (Table 6.3). Since *SIZE* is interacted with the predictor (*INDPRO*) but not significantly related to the criterion, according to the definition by Sharma, Durand, and Gur-Arie (1981),[10] firm size moderates the form (not the strength) of the relationship between industry profitability and firm profitability.

As shown in Table 6.3, industry sales growth (*INDSAG*) has a significant multivariate impact on IJVs' overall performance ($F = 2.40$, $p = 0.045$). The study also observes that industry sales growth is significantly and positively associated with IJVs' profitability ($F = 6.85$, $p = 0.013$) and local market growth ($F = 3.68$, $p = 0.060$) but negatively related to a venture's export growth in a significant fashion ($F = 3.16$, $p = 0.080$). H_{2a} and H_{2b} are therefore supported. This finding demonstrates that when host industries seem to flourish, IJVs appear to participate actively in the local expansion at the expense of exports.

It was hypothesized that industry asset intensity is positively related to IJVs' profitability but negatively associated with IJVs' export and risk reduction. The test results reveal that, although industry asset intensity (*INDASS*) has no apparent multivariate effect on IJVs' overall performance, it is systematically linked with some dimensions of venture performance. As shown in Table 6.3,

TABLE 6.3 MANOVA and GLM Tests for Effect Significance of Industry Structure Attributes on IJV Performance[a]

Sources of Variance	Multivariate F^b	Univariate F^c	Type I SS^d	$Pr > F$	r_s Sign[e]	Hypotheses Results
INDPRO	2.76			0.023		
ROI		8.32	165.57	0.005	+	H_{1a} Supported
SALE		19.10	1,690.35	0.001	+	H_{1a} Supported
EXPORT		7.01	118.47	0.011	−	H_{1b} Supported
RISK		3.47	35.39	0.066	+	H_{1b} Supported
INDSAG	2.40			0.045		
ROI		6.85	136.31	0.013	+	H_{2a} Supported
SALE		3.68	325.68	0.060	+	H_{2a} Supported
EXPORT		3.16	53.40	0.080	−	H_{2b} Supported
RISK		1.36	13.87	0.250	+	—
INDASS	1.44			0.222		
ROI		3.41	67.86	0.071	+	H_{3a} Supported
SALE		0.58	51.33	0.448	+	—
EXPORT		4.60	77.74	0.034	−	H_{3b} Supported
RISK		3.01	30.70	0.089	+	H_{3b} Supported
INDNUM	1.85			0.114		
ROI		3.16	62.88	0.079	+	H_{4a} Rejected
SALE		4.92	435.42	0.029	+	H_{4a} Rejected
EXPORT		2.70	45.63	0.102	−	H_{4b} Rejected
RISK		1.62	16.52	0.207	+	—
INDUNC	2.00			0.089		
ROI		1.06	21.09	0.307	+	—
SALE		2.29	202.66	0.133	−	—
EXPORT		1.20	20.28	0.270	+	H_{5b} Rejected
RISK		11.02	112.40	0.001	+	H_{5a} Supported

industry asset intensity has a significant and positive influence on firms' ROI ($F = 3.41$, $p = 0.071$) and a noticeably negative effect on firms' export ($F = 4.60$, $p = 0.034$) and risk reduction ($F = 3.01$, $p = 0.089$). H_{3a} and H_{3b} are thereby supported. Moreover, MANOVA and GLM tests reveal that the interaction between industry asset intensity and project-type selection (technologically advanced) has a significant influence on IJVs' accounting return, suggesting that the coupling between industry selection and resource allocation is important to investment success.

The test suggests that growth of number of firms in an industry has no significant multivariate impact on IJVs' overall performance. Strikingly, how-

TABLE 6.3 Continued

Sources of Variance	Multivariate F^b	Univariate F^c	Type I SS^d	$Pr > F$	r_s Sign^e	Hypotheses Results
LENGTH [6]	2.28			0.055		
ROI		3.67	73.03	0.059	+	
SALE		3.11	275.23	0.083	+	
RISK		4.43	45.18	0.039	−	
INDUNC*						
LENGTH[7]	0.85			0.527		
SALE		3.00	265.50	0.089		
RISK		3.60	36.72	0.062		
INDASS*TYPE I	0.58			0.711		
ROI		2.83	56.32	0.096		
INDUNC*EQUITY	1.25			0.299		
RISK		4.19	42.74	0.044		
INDPRO*SIZE	1.15			0.346		
ROI		4.06	80.79	0.047		

NOTEs: a. The SAS model: $Y_i = X_j + C_k + X_j'X_j'' + X_jC_k$, where Y_i stands for performance measures, X_j structure attributes, C_k control variables, $X_j'X_j''$ interactions among structure attributes, and X_jC_k interactions between industry attributes and control variables. The tests results are reported using a format suggested by Hair et al. (1992, p. 187).
b. Although with different criteria values, F and p statistics for a predictor variable are exactly same among Wilks's Lambda, Pillai's Trace, Hotelling-Lawley Trace, and Roy's Greatest Root.
c. GLM statistics: (1) model for Y_1-ROI: $F = 2.69$, $p < 0.001$, $R^2 = 0.58$; (2) model for Y_2 – SALE: $F = 5.10$, $p < 0.001$, $R^2 = 0.78$; (3) model for Y_3— EXPORT: $F = 3.70$, $p < 0.001$, $R^2 = 0.67$; (4) model for Y_4 – RISK: $F = 4.36$, $p < 0.001$, $R^2 = 0.70$. All the statistics for the above SAS model run by GLM and by separate regression analysis of variance are same.
d. Degree of freedom for each source of variance is 1, thus a source's mean square is equal to its Type I SS.
e. Sign of the standardized regression coefficients.
f & g. Only those control variables and predictor-control variable interaction terms that are significantly ($p < 0.10$) related to overall or unidimensional criterion variables are listed in this table. Since we did not conceptually establish the effect of interactions among structure attributes on performance, this effect is not reported in the table.

ever, Table 6.3 provides evidence contradicting my hypothesis: Growth of number of firms in an industry (*INDNUM*) is positively—rather than nega-tively—related to ventures' profitability and local market expansion, and the association is significant ($F = 3.16$ and $p = 0.079$ for ROI; $F = 4.92$ and $p = 0.029$ for SALE). Moreover, contrary to the stated hypothesis, this structural variable is found to have a marginally significant and negative influence on firms' export performance ($F = 2.70$, $p = 0.102$). H$_{4a}$ and H$_{4b}$ are thereby rejected. This result indicates that high growth of number of firms in a particular industry could signal great potential or the existence of business opportunities in the industry, once the numerous government-instituted interventions are eliminated as the transition stage progresses. Under these circumstances, a greater number of entrants would take the plunge into the industry in search of abnormal economic returns (Beamish, 1993; Grub & Lin, 1991). The above evidence also suggests that when a specific industry appears to prosper in a transitional economy, IJVs tend to enter the industry to seek local market expansion rather than to pursue high export performance.

Industry structure uncertainty (*INDUNC*) is found to be important to IJVs' overall performance according to the test result ($F = 2.00, p = 0.089$). Complying with the earlier prediction, industry structure uncertainty is positively related to operational risk, and thus negatively related to risk reduction, at a significant level ($F = 11.02, p = 0.001$). This lends support to H_{5a}. Indeed, structural uncertainty can often be traced to government's direct hindrance and the instability of its industrial policies (Rawski, 1994). This sort of risk is more difficult to avoid or is even inavertable because it is of a political or sovereign nature (Kobrin, 1982; Root, 1988). On the other hand, statistical evidence demonstrates that there is no significant linkage between structural uncertainty and IJVs' export performance ($F = 1.20, p = 0.270$), leading to a rejection of H_{5b}. Strong motivations in expanding the Chinese market and seeking long-term economic benefits may lead foreign investors to emphasize the local market rather than export, though they are more vulnerable to structural uncertainties. Further, Table 6.3 suggests that an IJV's length of operation (*LENGTH*) and its equity distribution (*EQUITY*) influence the form of the relationship between structural uncertainty and the venture's performance in a significant way. Length of operation also independently affects the major aspects of IJV performance.

DISCUSSION

Building upon the theoretical foundations of industrial organization, strategic management, and FDI/IJV frameworks, this study investigates the systematic relationships between industry structure attributes and IJV performance in the transitional economy environment. The exploratory character of this work demands a brief discussion of its main findings as well as some directions for future research.

This study finds that industry profitability has a significant impact on IJVs' overall performance. It also has a strongly positive effect on firms' efficiency and local market expansion but a negative effect on firms' export and risk reduction. This linkage demonstrates that industry attractiveness constitutes an important source for explaining variations of firm performance. The trade-offs between firm profitability and risk reduction, and between local market expansion and export growth, support a theoretical tenet in IJV literature that IJV performance evaluation should correspond to the venture roles prestipulated by parent firms (Davidson, 1980).

It is observed that industry sales growth is important for IJVs' overall performance. It is also positively related to IJVs' profitability and domestic sales growth but negatively associated with firms' export in a significant way. This evidence confirms that, when local industry conditions are favorable, IJVs' strategic aim necessitates local market growth at the expense of export (Killing, 1983). When these conditions appear unfavorable, IJVs can benefit from cost minimization through exploiting indigenous factor benefits (Ghoshal, 1987).

It was found that industry asset intensity has no significant effect on IJVs' overall performance but has a modest and positive influence on firm's profitability and a negative influence on firm's export and risk reduction. This finding, based on the Chinese context, is consistent with the observations by Bettis (1981) and Scherer and Ross (1990) for firms in the developed market economies that asset intensity or capital requirement is positively correlated with firms' profit as well as risk levels. A good fit between distinctive resource contribution (i.e., project-type selection) and industry selection is also found to be critical to IJVs' efficiency.

This research demonstrates that growth of number of firms in an industry has a significantly favorable influence on IJVs' profitability and local market expansion. Previous studies in industrial organization research based on the developed market economies observed that the higher the growth of number of firms in an industry, the lower the economic efficiency that firms in the industry could accomplish, ceteris paribus (Hay & Morris, 1979; Phillips, 1976). In contrast, the present study observes a positive function for the relation. Indeed, when government-instituted control over industry supply is lifted during transition, high growth of number of firms in an industry appears to signal industry growth rather than simply increased competition. In other words, it seems that "emerging economies" are aptly named, since the explosion in the number of participants in newly competitive industries does not exhaust its potential. In order to truly appreciate the significance of this finding, it may be necessary to test the robustness of the relationship over time. The rapidly expanding Chinese economy together with the existence of a pent-up demand, long stifled by ideologically based government interventions, may help explain the inability of producers in newly competitive industries to fully exploit market possibilities. The major question is whether this phenomenon is ephemeral in nature and thus time- and place specific. The answer is not readily apparent and may be disclosed only after additional tests in China at a later date or in other transitional economies.

Similarly, although market-economy-based studies found that there was not necessarily a causality between industry structure uncertainty and operational risks facing firms (Scherer & Ross, 1990), this study shows a positive relationship between the two, implying that macro environmental factors may outweigh micro firm factors in an economy in transition. As suggested earlier, this may derive from the nature of industry structure uncertainty. If, as it is very probable, uncertainty is attributable mostly to government policies, no single firm can escape the risks of rule changes and their consequences. It remains to be seen whether the association of industry structure uncertainty with operational risks will be sustained over time. Indeed, over the past few years, the Chinese government has relinquished control over a growing number of industries. Eventually, as the transition toward a market economy is completed, public policy may cease to be a source of uncertainty. It cannot be ruled out that future tests would uncover a fading relationship between uncertainty and risk, thus lending support to the generalizability of results based on studies conducted in the context of advanced market economies. Until then, researchers and investors should exercise caution when appraising industry structure uncertainty in transitional economies.

This study also demonstrates that length of IJV operation, a control variable in this study, not only significantly interacts with industry structure uncertainty but also has an independent and significant effect on an IJV's overall performance and a sizably favorable impact on the IJV's unidimensional performance. Indeed, a greater length of IJV operation in a transitional economy enables the firm to attain the advantages of earlier timing of entry and those of the learning effect (Harrigan, 1985). From China's transitional economy perspective, these findings confirm the argument in the global strategy paradigm that international expansion is a process of knowledge development (Kogut & Zander, 1994).

Overall, the results demonstrate that industry structural variables are important for the overall and unidimensional performance of IJVs and that this importance varies, in terms of direction or magnitude, depending on the structural characteristics considered. It suggests that industry structure in a dynamic environment is at least partly exogenous for the performance of participating IJVs. This evidence supports a key notion in the global strategy paradigm that industry structure characteristics constitute an important driver of global strategy as well as international performance (Porter, 1991; Yip, 1994). Fundamental differences in the effect that different structure attributes have on IJVs overall as well as unidimensional performance confirm an important assumption in the FDI and IJV theories that the alignment of an IJV's strategic orientation to its industrial environment is of paramount importance for the IJV's stability and profitability (Harrigan, 1985; Kogut & Singh, 1988). What this study did not address, and was not designed to address, are the questions of (a) the effect of all related firm-level factors on IJV performance and the relative importance between firm- and industry-level factors in relation to venture performance, and (b) the moderating effect of a local partner's resource position and the characteristics on the structure-IJV performance relations. These questions are areas worthy of examination. As business strategy perspective maintains, firm-level factors determine the unique endowments, positions, and strategies of individual businesses, hence constituting an essential source of performance drivers (Prahalad & Hamel, 1990; Rumelt, 1991). Moreover, it has been noted that industry-level drivers and firm-level drivers are strongly interrelated in the course of international expansion (Yip, 1994). Local partner selection, on the other hand, can influence the accessibility of prospective industries, the overall mix of available skills and resources, and short- and long-term variability of IJVs (Hamel, 1991; Parkhe, 1991). These questions are proposed as an agenda for future research.

CONCLUSION

This study examines the multivariate and univariate effects of industry structure attributes on the multidimensional performance of IJVs operating in China. The principal findings suggest that industry structure variables in a transitional economy have not only a significant influence on IJVs' overall performance but also a strong impact on various aspects of IJV performance. In addition, the study reveals fundamental differences in the effect that different structure attributes have on IJVs' performance. Moreover, each individual attribute impacts differentially on the various dimensions of IJV performance. Overall, this study observes some similarities in the structure-performance relationship between a transitional economy and the developed market economies with respect to such structural variables as industry's profitability, sales growth, and asset intensity. Nevertheless, in two areas—industry structure uncertainty and growth of number of firms in an industry—the relationships diverge according to the context. Apart from these findings, the multidimensional approach to IJV performance is validated as pertinent and promising by the results, as it can capture the heterogeneous impacts of predictor variables on the various aspects of performance, clarify the trade-offs that are often involved, and underline the importance of IJVs' strategic role in identifying relevant performance dimensions.

NOTES

1. There are two closely related and overlapping types of market imperfections. One emphasizes industry structure as a source of market power (Hymer, 1976), the other focuses on transaction costs as barriers to international trade and licensing (Dunning, 1979). This study examines the effect of the former on IJV performance.

2. Market economies also have government involvement. The difference between the two types of economies is not the involvement itself but the type and degree of involvement. According to macroeconomics, governments in market economies interfere in economic development primarily using "two hands": fiscal and monetary. Governments in transitional economies, however, use "three hands" to that end: administrative, fiscal, and monetary, among which the "administrative" plays the most prominent part in intervening in economy operations (Roman, 1986).

3. Wherever the degree of competition is not reflected in the increase in the number of firms (i.e., few government-controlled state firms still dominate the industry), IJVs are generally not permitted to enter (Child, 1994; Shenkar, 1990).

4. Based on the test of Cobb-Douglas production function, some researchers (e.g., Jefferson et al., 1992) find that, despite great improvements in Chinese industry, there still exist slightly decreasing returns to scale, unitary elasticity of substitution between labor and capital, slow technical progress, and low economic efficiency during the transition. These results suggest that the industrial policy should focus on pursuing intensive development by promoting technical progress and increasing productivity.

5. Instead of being personally collected from the sample firms, the data are obtained from the Commission where I once worked as a department head. Foreign researchers who attempt to access this resource for scholarly purposes can obtain it through consulting with numerous local state-owned international consulting companies.

6. Considering the heterogeneity of structure attributes between these sectors and industry sectors, this study is not designed to examine the relations of service and agriculture sectors' structure to firm performance. It would be a worthy effort to explore this issue, however, because many foreign investors, particularly Asian multinationals, have recently oriented toward the service sector, and the Chinese government encourages FDI in the agriculture sector during its ninth 5-year plan period. This issue needs to be taken up by future research.

7. Interpartner learning represents one of a parent firm's objectives in forming an IJV (Hamel, 1991; Osborn & Baughn, 1990), and the acquisition of local knowledge is an enabling device for the foreign partner to operate autonomously (Beamish & Inkpen, 1995). In light of the fact that

this learning effect often directly contributes to the monetary or nonmonetary performance of individual parent firms rather than those of IJVs, this study did not use a learning measure for IJV performance. As Beamish and Inkpen (1995) claim, once a foreign partner has acquired local knowledge from the local partner, the rationale for cooperation will disappear.

8. This study defines local sales or export as a percentage of total investment rather than total sales (local sales + export). The logic behind this is twofold: First, using total sales as a denominator to define local sales or export can reflect only the structure or orientation of sales (local sales vs. export), not actual performance. Two firms may have the same local sales percentage in total sales, but the real value of local and total sales could be substantially different between the firms. Second, using total investment as a denominator can control the investment size effect in an IJV's market expansion. In fact, this computation indicates a firm's investment turnover (similar to asset turnover) in local and international settings.

9. Market-based risk measure, namely systematic risk or β, is usually estimated using an ordinary least squares regression of the form:

$$R_{jt} = \alpha_j + \beta_j R_{mt} + \varepsilon_{jt},$$

where R_{jt} is the return on the security of firm j on day t, and R_{mt} is the equally weighted market return on that day.

10. According to Sharma et al. (1981), the moderator is referred to as a *homologizer,* which modifies the strength of relationship between criterion variables and predictor variables, if it is not significantly related to the criterion and does not interact with the predictor; if it interacts significantly with the predictor and is related to the criterion, it is a *quasi-moderator,* which modifies the form of the relationship; if it is interacted with the predictor but not related to the criterion, it is called a *pure-moderator,* which impacts the form of the relationship.

REFERENCES

Amit, R., & Livnat, J. (1988). Diversification and the risk-return trade-off. *Academy of Management Journal, 31,* 154-166.

Bain, J. S. (1959). *Industrial organization.* New York: John Wiley.

Beamish, P. W. (1993). The characteristics of joint ventures in the People's Republic of China. *Journal of International Marketing, 1*(2), 29-48.

Beamish, P. W., & Inkpen, A. C. (1995). Keeping international joint ventures stable and profitable. *Long Range Planning, 28*(3), 26-36.

Bettis, R. A. (1981). Performance differences in related and unrelated diversified firms. *Strategic Management Journal, 2,* 379-393.

Bettis, A. R., & Mahajan, V. (1985). Risk/return performance of diversified firms. *Management Science, 31,* 785-799.

Blodgett, L. L. (1992). Factors in the instability of international joint ventures: An event history analysis. *Strategic Management Journal, 13,* 475-482.

Brewer, T. L. (1993). Government policies, market imperfections, and foreign direct investment. *Journal of International Business Studies, 24,* 101-120.

Buckley, P. J., & Casson, M. C. (1992). Multinational enterprises in less developed countries: Cultural and economic interactions. In P. J. Buckley (Ed.), *Studies in international business.* New York: St. Martin's.

Bulletin of Ministry of Foreign Trade and Economic Cooperation (MOFTEC). (1995a). People's Republic of China. Issue No. 1 (Serial No. 25).

Bulletin of Ministry of Foreign Trade and Economic Cooperation (MOFTEC). (1995b). People's Republic of China. Issue No. 2 (Serial No. 26).

Caves, R. E. (1971). International corporation: The industrial economies of foreign investment. *Economica, 38,* 1-27.

Caves, R. E., & Mehra, K. (1986). Entry of foreign multinationals into U.S. manufacturing industries. In M. E. Porter (Ed.), *Competition in global industries.* Boston: Harvard Business School Press.

Child, J. (1994). *Management in China during the age of reform.* Cambridge, UK: Cambridge University Press.

Child, J., & Lu, Y. (1990). Industrial decision-making under China's reform, 1985-1988. *Organization Studies, 11,* 321-351.

China statistical yearbook. (Annual). Beijing: State Statistical Bureau.

Choi, J., Ghosh, D., & Kim, Y. (1991). Optimum cash balance for international firms. *Advances in Working Capital Management, 2,* 36-51.

Christensen, H. K., & Montgomery, C. A. (1981). Corporate economic performance: Diversification strategy versus market structure, *Strategic Management Journal, 2,* 327-343.

Contractor, F. J., & Lorange, P. (1988). The strategy and economic basis for cooperative venture. In F. J. Contractor & P. Lorange (Eds.), *Cooperative strategies in international business.* Toronto: Lexington Books.

Cooley, W. W., & Lohns, P. R. (1971). *Multivariate data analysis.* New York: John Wiley.

Davidson, W. H. (1980). The location of foreign direct investment activity: Country characteristics and experience effects. *Journal of International Business Studies, 12,* 9-22.

Dunning, J. H. (1979). Explaining changing patterns of international production: In defense of the eclectic theory. *Oxford Bulletin of Economics and Statistics, 41,* 269-296.

Foreign investment in China. (1996). China Foreign-Invested Enterprises Association, 96(4), Serial No. 41, p. 20.

Geringer, J. M., & Hebert, L. (1991). Measuring performance of international joint ventures. *Journal of International Business Studies, 22,* 253-267.

Ghoshal, S. (1987). Global strategy: An organizing framework. *Strategic Management Journal, 8,* 425-440.

Grub, P. D., & Lin, L. (1991). *Foreign direct investment in China.* New York: Quorum.

Hagedoorn, J., & Schakenraad, J. (1994). The effect of strategic technology partnering: Interorganizational modes of cooperation and sectoral differences. *Strategic Management Journal, 14,* 371-385.

Hair, J. F., Anderson, R. E., Tatham, R. L., & Black, W. C. (1992). *Multivariate data analysis* (3rd ed.). New York: Macmillan.

Hamel, G. (1991). Competition for competence and inter-partner learning within international strategic alliances. *Strategic Management Journal, 12*(Special issue), 83-104.

Harrigan, K. R. (1985). *Strategies for joint venture success.* Lexington, MA: Lexington Books.

Harrigan, K. R. (1988). Joint ventures and competitive strategy. *Strategic Management Journal, 9,* 141-158.

Hay, D. A., & Morris, D. J. (1979). *Industrial economics.* London: Oxford University Press.

Hennart, J. F. (1988). A transaction cost theory of equity joint ventures. *Strategic Management Journal, 9,* 361-374.

Hennart, J. F., & Park, Y. (1994). Location, governance, and strategic determinants of Japanese manufacturing investment in the United States. *Strategic Management Journal, 18,* 419-436.

Hoskisson, R. E., Hill, C. W. L., & Kim, H. (1993). The multidivisional structure: Organizational fossil or source of value? *Journal of Management, 19,* 269-298.

Hymer, S. H. (1976). *The international operations of national firms: A study of direct foreign investment.* Cambridge: MIT Press.

Jefferson, G. H., Rawski, T. G., & Zheng, Y. (1992). Growth, efficiency, and convergence in China's state and collective industry. *Economic Development & Cultural Change, 40,* 239-266.

Jenkins, R. (1991). The impact of foreign investment on less developed countries: Cross-section analysis versus industry studies. In P. J. Buckley & J. Clegg (Eds.), *Multinational enterprises in less developed countries* (pp. 111-130). London: Macmillan.

Jia, L. (1991). A quantitative analysis of Chinese industrial structure and technological change: Production functions for aggregate industry, sectorial industries and small scale industry. *Applied Economics, 23,* 1733-1740.

Katrak, H. (1991). Market rivalry, government policies and multinational enterprise in developing countries. In P. J. Buckley & J. Clegg (Eds.), *Multinational enterprises in less developed countries* (pp. 92-110). London: Macmillan.

Killing, J. P. (1983). *Strategies for joint venture success.* New York: Praeger.

Kobrin, S. J. (1982). *Managing political risk assessment.* Berkeley: University of California Press.

Kogut, B. (1988). Joint ventures: Theoretical and empirical perspectives. *Strategic Management Journal, 9,* 319-332.

Kogut, B., & Singh, H. (1988). Entering the U.S. by joint venture: Competitive rivalry and industry structure. In F. J. Contractor & P. Lorange (Eds.), *Cooperative strategies in international business.* Lexington, MA: Lexington Books.

Kogut, B., & Zander, U. (1994). Knowledge of the firm and the evolutionary theory of the multinational corporation. *Journal of International Business Studies, 24,* 625-646.

Mahoney, J., & Pandian, J. R. (1992). The resource-based view within the conversation of strategic management. *Strategic Management Journal, 13,* 363-380.

McGee, J. S. (1988). *Industrial organization.* Englewood Cliffs, NJ: Prentice Hall.

Mitchell, W., Shaver, J. M., & Yeung, B. (1993). Performance following changes of international presence in domestic and transition industries. *Journal of International Business Studies, 24,* 647-669.

Montgomery, C. A. (1985). Product-market diversification and market power. *Academy of Management Journal, 25,* 789-798.

Morck, R., & Yeung, B. (1991). Why investors value multinationality. *Journal of Business, 64,* 165-187.

Morrison, A. J., & Roth, K. (1992). A taxonomy of business-level strategies in global industries. *Strategic Management Journal, 13,* 399-417.

National Council for U.S.-China Trade. (1991). *Special report on U.S. investment in China.* Washington, DC: Department of Commerce.

Nee, V. (1992). Organizational dynamics of market transition: Hybrid forms, property rights, and mixed economy in China. *Administrative Science Quarterly, 37,* 1-27.

Newfarmer, R., & Marsh, L. (1992). Industry structure, market power and profitability. *Industrial Series Paper No. 63,* The World Bank, Washington, D.C.

Osborn, R. N., & Baughn, C. C. (1990). Forms of interorganizational governance for multinational alliances. *Academy of Management Journal, 33,* 503-519.

Parkhe, A. (1991). Interfirm diversity, organizational learning, and longevity in global strategic alliances. *Journal of International Business Studies, 22,* 579-601.

Phillips, A. (1976). A critique of empirical studies of relations between market structure and profitability. *Journal of Industrial Economics, 24,* 241-249.

Porter, M. E. (1980). *Competitive advantage: Techniques for analyzing industries and competitors.* New York: Free Press.

Porter, M. E. (1986). *Competition in global industries.* Boston: Harvard Business School Press.

Porter, M. E. (1991). Towards a dynamic theory of strategy. *Strategic Management Journal, 12,* 95-117.

Prahalad, C. K., & Hamel, G. (1990). The core competence of the corporation. *Harvard Business Review, 90,* 79-91.

Rawski, T. G. (1994). Chinese industrial reform: Accomplishments, prospects, and implications. *American Economic Review, 84,* 271-275.

Roman, Z. (1986). Competition and industrial organization in the centrally planned economies. In J. Stiglitz & G. F. Mathewson (Eds.), *New developments in the analysis of market structure.* London: Macmillan.

Root, F. R. (1988, Fall). Environmental risks and the bargaining power of multinational corporations. *International Trade Journal,* pp. 111-124.

Rumelt, R. P. (1991). How much does industry matter? *Strategic Management Journal, 12,* 167-185.

SAS/STAT user's guide. (1990). (Version 6, 4th ed.). Cary, NC: SAS Institute.

Scherer, F. M., & Ross, D. (1990). *Industrial market structure and economic performance* (3rd ed.). Boston: Houghton Mifflin.

Shan, W. J. (1991). Environmental risks and joint venture sharing arrangements. *Journal of International Business Studies, 22*(4), 555-578.

Sharma, S. R., Durand, M., & Gur-Arie, D. (1981). Identification and analysis of moderator variables. *Journal of Marketing Research, 18,* 291-300.

Shenkar, O. (1990). International joint ventures' problems in China: Risks and remedies. *Long Range Planning, 23*(3), 82-90.

Stern, R. M. (1975). Testing trade theories. In P. B. Kenen (Ed.), *International trade and finance.* Cambridge, UK: Cambridge University Press.

Tallman, S. B., & Shenkar, O. (1994). A managerial decision model of international cooperative venture formation. *Journal of International Business Studies, 25,* 91-114.

Tan, J. J., & Litschert, R. J. (1994). Environment-strategy relationship and its performance implications: An empirical study of the Chinese electronics industry. *Strategic Management Journal, 15,* 1-20.

Teece, D. J. (1985). Multinational enterprises, internal governance, and industrial organization. *American Economic Review, Papers and Proceedings, 75,* 233-238.

Teece, D. J., Pisano, G., & Shuen, A. (1991). *Dynamic capabilities and strategic management.* Working paper, University of California at Berkeley.

Tung, R. L. (1982). *Chinese industrial society after Mao.* Lexington, MA: Lexington Books.

Wernerfelt, B., & Karnani, A. (1987). Competitive strategy under uncertainty. *Strategic Management Journal, 8,* 187-194.

Willmore, L. (1994). Determinants of industrial structure: A Brazilian case study. In J. H. Dunning (Ed.), *Transnational corporations: Market structure and industrial performance* (United Nations Library on Transnational Corporations, Vol. 15, pp. 96-129). New York: United Nations.

Yip, G. S. (1994). Industry drivers of global strategy and organization. *The International Executive, 36*(5), 529-556.

Yu, C.-M. J. (1991). The experience effect and foreign direct investment. *Weltwirtschaftliches Archiev, 126,* 561-579.

Yu, C.-M. J., & Ito, K. (1988). Oligopolistic reaction and foreign direct investment: The case of the U.S. tire and textile industries. *Journal of International Business Studies, 19,* 449-460.

APPENDIX:
Computation of Firm's Operational Risk
and Industry's Structure Uncertainty,
Sales Growth, and Growth of Number of Firms

1. Steps in Calculating Each IJV's Operational Risk
   a. Compute arithmetic means of an IJV's ROI (**ROI**), local sales (**SALE**), and export (**EXPORT**) during the period 1988-1991, respectively;
   b. Compute standard deviations (Std) of the IJV's **ROI, SALE,** and **EXPORT,** respectively;
   c. Compute geometric average of the IJV's performance standard deviations, that is:

$$[\text{Std(ROI)Std(SALE)Std(EXPORT)}]^{1/3}$$

2. Steps in Calculating Each Industry's Structure Uncertainty
   a. Compute arithmetic means of an industry's profitability (**INDPRO**), sales growth (**INDSAG**), asset intensity (**INDASS**), and growth of number of firms in the industry (**INDNUM**) during the period from 1988 to 1991, respectively;
   b. Compute standard deviations (Std) of various industry structure attributes respectively for each industry;
   c. Compute geometric average of standard deviations for each industry obtained in Step 2b:

$$[\text{Std(INDPRO)Std(INDSAG)Std(INDASS)Std(INDNUM)}]^{1/4}$$

3. Steps in Calculating Each Industry's Sales Growth
   a. Compute each year's annual growth rate (R) during from 1988 to 1991, that is, R_{89}, R_{90}, and R_{91};
   b. Compute the compound growth rate for the period as follows:

$$[(1 + R_{89})(1 + R_{90})(1 + R_{91})]^{1/3} - 1$$

4. Steps in Calculating Each Industry's Growth of Number of Firms
   a. Compute each year's annual growth rate (r) during 1988-1991, that is, r_{89}, r_{90}, r_{91};
   b. Compute the compound growth rate for the period as follows:

$$[(1 + r_{89})(1 + r_{90})(1 + r_{91})]^{1/3} - 1$$

chapter 7

International Joint Ventures in China

Environment-Strategy-Performance Relations

YADONG LUO

J. JUSTIN TAN

The relationship between a multinational corporation's (MNC) headquarters and its foreign subsidiaries has recently shifted in focus from control to strategic orientation because orientation is an efficient "mid-range" instrument linking global integration and local responsiveness (Doz & Prahalad, 1991; Duysters & Hagedoorn, 1995; Golden, 1992). The global strategy literature asserts that the alignment of an interorganizational network to its uncertain global environment is critical for international expansion (Ghoshal, 1987; Morrison & Roth, 1992; Yip, 1995). Jarillo and Martinez (1990), Shan (1991), and Carpano, Chrisman, and Roth (1994) demonstrate that there is a linkage between a firm's strategic profile and its external context, and that this linkage has significant implications for international performance in an uncertain environment. This corroborates the notion in resource-based theory that the resource-deployment strategy can be far more important than the resource itself in a complex and dynamic context (Wernerfelt & Karnani, 1987).

Since competition in the global marketplace occurs at the business-unit level (Porter, 1986), it is important for MNCs to establish a good coupling between a foreign subsidiary's strategic orientation and its external context in the host country (Bartlett & Ghoshal, 1989). In recent years, MNCs have turned increasingly to the use of international joint ventures (IJVs) as the form of business unit in their search for sustained global competitive advantage in a dynamic environment such as emerging economies (Beamish, 1993; Buckley & Casson, 1992; Shama, 1995). This leads to a greater need to construct the strategy-environment relationship for IJVs operating in this context. IJVs there can serve as (a) an eclectic choice, when the transaction costs involved are too high to use market mechanism but not high enough to form a hierarchy (Hennart, 1991; Williamson, 1991); (b) an entry mode to improve market position and maximize profits through either a defensive posture blocking competitor entry or collusive arrangements enhancing market power (Contractor & Lorange, 1988; Kogut, 1988); or (c) an optimal tool to learn tacit or organizationally embedded knowledge (Hamel, 1991; Kogut, 1988).

Despite its importance, however, the environment-strategy linkage and its performance implications for IJVs have not been adequately studied. As a result, the understanding of the manner in which a MNC formulates an IJV's strategic orientation, which in turn drives the venture's performance, is incomplete. This issue warrants investigation because in confronting heterogenous-to-home external environments (Brewer, 1993) and involving complex interfirm organizational structure (Osborn & Baughn, 1990) an IJV needs a preformulated strategic posture that can govern and facilitate its role accomplishment (Harrigan, 1985). According to the neo-contingency framework (Sorge, 1991), this necessity seems reinforced when an IJV operates in a complex and dynamic environment, because organizational strategic choice virtually determines the IJV's exposure to uncertain environmental components that impact firm performance (Miller, 1992). As a step toward this goal, this study aims to examine the environment-strategy relationship and its performance implications for IJVs operating in a highly uncertain environment. The basic premise of this study is that the nature of host environment dimensions such as complexity, dynamism, and hostility has a strong and sustainable influence over the choices of an IJV's strategic orientation (e.g., futurity, proactiveness, riskiness, and innovativeness), and such an influence also has profound implications for the IJV's performance.

As emerging economies are considerably dynamic and uncertain, on the one hand, and are major hosts of IJVs, on the other hand, they may be an ideal setting for the analysis of the above research question. Typically, reforms in these economies have continued unabated, and their pace has even accelerated in recent years (Child, 1994), contributing to a surge in IJV activity. This activity has in turn profoundly transformed these economies to the point that they are today major players in the global integration of international business (Luo, 1995). In light of the particular importance of China as the world's largest emerging economy and fastest-growing market, this research uses China as its analytical context.

In the remainder of the chapter, the first section elucidates the theoretical issues. The following section is devoted to the hypothesis development. Methodological issues are addressed in a subsequent section. The next section presents and discusses major findings of the study. Possible theoretical and practical implications are also highlighted.

THEORETICAL FOUNDATIONS

Strategic Orientation

In contrast to freestanding single-business firms, the strategic context of IJVs within diversified MNCs is substantially influenced by the role and corresponding orientation the business is intended to play in the corporate portfolio (Beamish & Banks, 1987; Hambrick, MacMillan, & Day, 1982). IJVs are rarely equally attractive candidates for either long-term market share building or short-term maximization of profits and cash flow. This stems from several reasons: (a) the markets in which different IJVs compete are often differentially attractive (Porter, 1991); (b) different IJVs possess different competitive strengths (Harrigan, 1985); and (c) different local partners of IJVs have heterogenous attributes, thus leading to idiosyncratic "complementarity" between the partners (Buckley & Casson, 1988). Consequently, an MNC must decide explicitly or implicitly which strategic orientation its IJVs will pursue.

It has been noted that competitive advantage in a global environment can be sought through organizational adaptability as well as rigidity (Ghoshal & Bartlett, 1990; Wright, Kroll, Pray, & Lado, 1995). Organizational adaptability corresponds to a proactive, innovative, future-oriented, and risk-taking strategic orientation (Child, 1972; Miller & Friesen, 1983; Sorge, 1991). Building on Miles and Snow's (1978) framework, proactive IJVs can be defined as Prospectors. They concentrate on scanning, identifying, and capitalizing on emerging market opportunities beyond an MNC's network, and maintain and bear the costs and risks inherent in extensive capabilities for responding to market and contextual changes in the host setting. Organizational rigidity corresponds to a nonadaptive, defensive, and risk-aversive strategic orientation (McKee, Varadarajan, &

Pride, 1989). IJVs with this orientation can be referred to as Defenders (Miles & Snow, 1978). They are rigid, noninnovative, and shortsighted ventures. They deliberately reduce innovative and adaptive costs and risks by selecting a stable and narrowly defined product or market domain, or by merely exploiting internalization benefits within an MNC's network. Berg, Duncan, and Friedman (1982) and Killing (1983) find that, in the context of an advanced economy, proactive IJVs pursue local market expansion at the expense of high operational risk and innovation cost, whereas defensive IJVs focus on production cost minimization, using host manufacturing sites as export platforms. As a hybrid strategy between proactiveness and defensiveness, analysis strategy may be an appropriate choice for those IJVs seeking both risk-adjusted efficiency and emerging market opportunities (Stopford & Wells, 1972). These IJVs can be labeled Analyzers; Analyzers defend existing product markets through efficiency-oriented strategies while cautiously penetrating new markets through intensified product/market innovation (Miles & Snow, 1978). In other words, in one sphere, they emphasize efficiencies, and in the other sphere, they emphasize product or process innovations in response to competitors and emerging market opportunities (Hisrich, 1992). These IJVs are market driven on either host, home, or international markets. Their futurity, innovativeness, and risk-involvement lie in the middle, between Prospector IJVs and Defender IJVs. Hence, Analyzer IJVs exhibit characteristics of both Prospectors and Defenders (Miles & Snow, 1978, 1986).

The information processing argument (Galbraith & Schendel, 1983) and population ecology theory (Aldrich, McKelvey, & Ulrich, 1984) suggest that the organization's information processing system (in the form of hierarchical relationships and standard operating procedures) must be capable of accommodating both the variability and the uncertainty of the subunits' product-market environments. Corroborating this argument, global strategy paradigm maintains that local responsiveness and internal differentiation in a complex and heterogenous environment may be more important than globally integrative optimization (Doz & Prahalad, 1991). Once an IJV's strategic orientation is determined, its foreign parent firm needs to formulate a subsidiary-level international strategy to match with the subsidiary's orientation (Ghoshal & Bartlett, 1990; Jarillo & Martinez, 1990). The international strategy at this level directly affects the resource deployment and power authorization within the network, thus influencing the implementation of an IJV's strategic orientation (Ghoshal, 1987; Yip, 1995). Because proactive IJVs carry out most of the functions of the value chain in a manner that is relatively independent of their parents or of other subsidiaries, these ventures seem to need an autonomous international strategy (Bartlett &

Ghoshal, 1989; Ghoshal & Nohria, 1989). In contrast, defensive IJVs may need a receptive international strategy, because they are highly integrated with the rest of the diversified MNCs and few of the functions of the value chain are performed in the host country (Bartlett, 1986; Jarillo & Martinez, 1990). Because many activities of Analyzer IJVs are located in the host countries and are carried out in close coordination with the rest of the MNCs, Analyzer IJVs may need an active international strategy formulated by parent firms (Jarillo & Martinez, 1990).

Environment Dimensions

The particularist approach of analyzing specific dimensions of uncertain environment in isolation from other dimensions has recently come under criticism (Miller, 1992; Oxeheim & Wihlborg, 1987). Duncan (1972) suggests that the environment be viewed as a multidimensional construct. Broadly, the external environment may be perceived along two dimensions: (a) the source of impact (e.g., regulatory, competitors, suppliers, and customers); and (b) the nature of impact (complexity, dynamism, and hostility) (Dess & Beard, 1984; Miller, 1992; Tan & Litschert, 1994). These dimensions virtually represent the host-societal profile, which is fairly tacit, ambiguous, complex, cumulative, and history dependent (Barney, 1991); their influence is thus highly sustainable (Mueller, 1994). Moreover, the above dimensions depend upon and reinforce each other in a complex way. Impact sources constitute the environmental segments. In each of these segments, environmental complexity, dynamism, and hostility may be identified (Scott, 1987; Tan & Litschert, 1994).

The impact of host regulatory and industrial environments on an IJV's decision characteristics and organizational behavior is fairly vigorous and direct (Brewer, 1993). In an uncertain host environment, regulatory factors (e.g., IJV laws, FDI [foreign direct investment] policies, taxation and financing regulations, foreign exchange administration rules, threat of nationalization, earnings repatriation, and price controls) may outweigh macroeconomic and technological factors (Aggarwal & Agmon, 1990). As some studies suggest (e.g., Agmon, 1985), regulatory environment should also include the threats and opportunities associated with potential or actual changes in the political system because changes in governments do not necessarily result in changes in government policies affecting foreign business operations (Root, 1988), nor does political stability preclude policy uncertainty (Kobrin, 1982). The effect of such policy uncertainty may be significant in formerly centrally planned economies undergoing transition, such as the former Soviet republics, Eastern European countries, and China. Recent studies set in China report that the regulatory sectors have significant impact in shaping managerial decision making (Tan, 1996; Tan & Litschert, 1994). While regulatory forces are generally viewed as part of the institutional environment (Meyer & Rowan, 1977; Scott, 1987), their influence is more direct in transitional economies.

While there is a rather extensive literature on the general environment in relation to IJV formation and operations, the industry-level environment effect has not been fully explored (Luo, 1995). According to Porter's (1979) five forces model, customers, suppliers, and competitors (i.e., existing and potential competitors in the same and substitute industries) all shape competition in the industry. Similarly, Miller (1992, in his integrated environment management framework, categorizes industry environment into an input dimension (i.e., suppliers), a product dimension (i.e., customer), and a competitive dimension (i.e., competitors). In this study, our focus is on the regulatory sector and industry-level environment sectors that directly influence firm performance, including competitors, customers, and suppliers.

Conceptual and empirical studies in strategic management have identified several environmental dimensions in each of the above segments, which include dynamism (Dess & Beard, 1984), complexity (Child, 1972; Tung, 1979), and hostility (Miller & Friesen, 1978; Venkatraman & Prescott, 1990). Environmental complexity and dynamism have been closely linked to the information uncertainty perspective (Lawrence & Lorsch, 1967; Tan & Litschert, 1994), while hostility has been tied to the resource dependence perspective (Pfeffer & Salancik, 1978). The perspectives offer a better understanding of the impact of each environmental dimension on the formulation of a firm's strategy. An important notion in IJV literature is that, when environment is complex and dynamic, the rationale behind IJV formation is intensified because a local partner can assist greatly in searching, scanning, interpreting, and examining information in the host context (Harrigan, 1985; Parkhe, 1993). The bargaining power model in the literature also suggests that the possession or control of critical resources by a MNC in the form of either de jure (dominant equity position) or de facto (dominant managerial or technological position) constitutes power in interpartner cooperation, which lessens the IJV's dependence on, hence its vulnerability to, the local hostile environment (Geringer & Hebert, 1989; Root, 1988; Shan, 1991; Yan & Gray, 1994). In addition, environmental complexity, dynamism, and hostility affect an IJV management's perception of the host country uncertainty, which in turn influences such strategic decision characteristics as propensity for risk taking, futurity, and proactiveness or defensiveness (Killing, 1983). It is further posited that the fit between environmental dimensions and strategic orientation may lead to better IJV performance (Bartlett & Ghoshal, 1989; Jarillo & Martinez, 1990).

Fit Between Strategy and Environment

The alignment of an IJV's strategic orientation to its uncertain host environment is of paramount importance for the venture's success (Buckley & Casson, 1992; Morrison & Roth, 1992). The environment-strategy paradigm asserts that there must be an appropriate fit between strategy-making behavior and the nature of the environment to ensure effective selection of strategies (Miller & Friesen, 1983; Tan & Litschert, 1994). Similarly, the global strategy literature indicates that it is essential for MNC subsidiaries to have distinctive strategic orientations to be coupled with the local environment in order to exploit critical environmental resources in the host country (Ghoshal, 1987; Porter, 1986; Yip, 1995). For IJVs, interpartner complementary competence alone cannot guarantee the venture's success because the performance effect of competence depends on the requirements of, and the degree of its fit with, the host environment (Beamish & Banks, 1987; Harrigan, 1985; Kogut & Singh, 1988). According to the strategic choice perspective (Miles & Snow, 1986), when IJVs operate in a highly dynamic environment, the importance of this fit is reinforced (Collis, 1991; Luo, 1995). The degree of fit, as institutionalization theory suggests, spurs the IJV to adopt patterns of behavior and activity that are appropriate to its environment. A series of IJV studies based on developing countries verify that when managerial discretion is constrained in the indigenous setting, the environment-strategy alignment plays a larger role in determining IJV performance (Dang, 1977; Gold, 1991; Lall, 1987; Luo, 1995). In such circumstances, an IJV's management must be able to scan and interpret the environment and make decisions appropriate for both internal arrangement and external alignment (Lecraw, 1984; Lyles, 1988).

The necessity for the strategy-environment fit is expected to be magnified in the context of an emerging economy (Child, 1994; Luo, 1995). Environmental dimensions affect fundamental management philosophies and principles and trigger a genuine review of corporate business operations (Tan & Litschert, 1994). An IJV's survival and expansion in this context depend on its ability to understand the environment and react in time to permit necessary organizational adjustments (Shenkar, 1990). According to the neo-contingency model, a good coupling between strategic orientation and environment conditions in a turbulent context can enable the IJV to maximize the economic rents from the interaction between "societal effect" and "organizational effect" (Mueller, 1994).[1] This coupling also helps to better exploit a local partner's advantages in accessing distribution channels, obtaining insightful information, bettering the relationship with the local government, and reducing environmental risks in the context (Beamish, 1993). Shan (1991) and Teagarden and Von Glinow (1990) suggest that prearranged strategic orientation by both parties can reduce the local partner's opportunism and boost its collaborative incentive.

HYPOTHESIS DEVELOPMENT

The strategic behavior perspective of IJV theory suggests that firms establish IJVs to maximize economic rents through market expansion and market position improvement (Gomes-Casseres, 1989; Harrigan, 1988). Such improvement is assumed since IJVs are deemed to create partner synergies in the marketplace, deter competitive market entry, and capture more positive externalities (Contractor & Lorange, 1988; Kogut, 1988). Kumar (1995) and Luo (1996) observed a significantly favorable impact of a local partner's market share and industrial experience on the IJV's goal accomplishment. Moreover, dynamic and uncertain economies often offer more investment opportunities and business potentials that firms can preempt (Porter, 1986; Wernerfelt & Karnani, 1987). Shama (1995) finds that U.S. investors enter the newly independent states, Baltic states, and Eastern European countries in search of local market share. Similarly, Shenkar (1990) and the National Council (1991) find that Western parent firms seek market expansion and growth in China. These arguments and evidence suggest that the Defender strategy may be too conservative to be adopted by MNCs seeking global competitive advantages.

However, it is also not realistic to orient IJVs toward a highly proactive and immensely innovative direction, because this orientation could lead to vast operational and contextual risks and enormous innovative and adaptive costs for IJVs in a complex, dynamic, and hostile environment (Shan, 1991; Wright et al., 1995). Theoretically, IJVs are often formed because of important risk factors that induce a high degree of interfirm cooperation (Harrigan, 1988; Osborn & Baughn, 1990). The risk may become so high that even large MNCs join hands to share the development risk and have to use a larger joint market over which to amortize the costs (Contractor, 1990; Stopford & Wells, 1972). This complies with the learning model of FDI theory, which suggests that foreign direct investment in an uncertain environment is a gradual and sequential process (Davidson, 1980). The major strategic thrust of investors in such a context seems to be to adapt to foreign environments through incremental changes. In addition, transaction cost perspective of IJV theory asserts that IJVs can be a lower-cost means of testing a foreign market considered too risky in terms of complexity, dynamism, and hostility for a full investment (Hennart, 1991; Kogut, 1988). As an inherently riskier strategic orientation, therefore, Prospector may not be a right choice for IJVs in an uncertain environment. Rajagopalan and Finkelstein (1992) further demonstrate that the risk associated with Prospector strategies increases outcome uncertainty and operation instability. This contradicts the rationale underlying the formation of IJVs. In light of the above paragraphs, it is expected that there exists a configuration of relationships between environmental characteristics (i.e., complexity, dynamism, and hostility) and Analyzer strategies among IJVs in an uncertain context.

Along these lines, Miles and Snow (1978) suggest that MNCs often follow the Analyzer strategy "to the extent that they avoid the complexities involved in IJVs and/or host country production facilities" (p. 134). When an IJV operates in a rapidly changing and highly complex environment, a critical task is to gather and analyze information (Child, 1994). This is especially crucial when the relationship between IJVs and their various environmental elements is highly complex, dynamic, and particularistic; when information is not codified; and when regulations are not made explicit (Root, 1988). A host environment characterized by uncodified information can promote noneconomic forms of opportunism (Williamson, 1991), increase transaction costs (Pan, 1996), and prompt IJV managers to be more cautious when making resource commitments (Gomes-Casseres, 1989). This characteristic of the environment spurs IJVs to have more discretion than Prospectors but less than Defenders. In such an uncertain context, an Analyzer strategy can make an IJV's managerial behavior toward efficiency and innovation more easily programmable (Berg et al., 1982). The dual nature of this strategy also reduces the likelihood of outright failure and creates upper limits to success, hence leading IJVs to face only moderate outcome uncertainty (Miles & Snow, 1978).

Empirical evidence finds that IJVs in emerging economies such as China allocate most of their resources to a set of reasonably stable environments while at the same time conducting somewhat routinized scanning activities in a limited product-market area (Shan, 1991; Shenkar, 1990). They monitor market situations in the host country and carefully apply product and market innovations developed by headquarters (Beamish, 1993). In most cases, R&D activities are conducted at the headquarters level and only mature products and well-known technologies are transferred to the host country (Shama, 1995). Much of the IJV's success occurs through market penetration because the organization's basic strength comes from its traditional product-market base. This market development strategy allows the foreign investors to extend the product life cycle and to maximize returns on their technological and organizational skills (Teagarden & Von Glinow, 1990).[2] From the standpoint of the foreign partners, this pattern of strategic posture is also grounded in the natural fear of creating potential competitors in the local market (Kumar, 1995). Thus, IJVs in this context clearly exhibit a pattern of strategic orientation consistent with Analyzer strategy. Following the above line of reasoning, the following relationships are predicted:

H$_{1a}$: Among IJVs in an emerging economy, environmental complexity is positively related to an Analyzer strategy.

H$_{1b}$: Among IJVs in an emerging economy, environmental dynamism is positively related to an Analyzer strategy.

H$_{1c}$: Among IJVs in an emerging economy, environmental hostility is positively related to an Analyzer strategy.

Hambrick (1983) finds that alternative strategies are related to variations in performance.[3] Miller and Friesen (1983) and Venkatraman and Prescott (1990) demonstrate that the appropriate environment-strategy configuration will lead to high performance. As noted above, Analyzer IJVs maintain a stable domain wherein they not only can operate with relative efficiency but also identify, through market scanning and research, emerging opportunities (Miles & Snow, 1978, 1986). Such IJVs emphasize output improvements and differentiation through innovation and advertising or other promoting efforts (Luo, 1995). Their outputs may allow them to charge above average industry prices or at least to avoid damaging price competition (Buzzell & Gale, 1987). Businesses that combine efficiency with improvements or innovations may have levels of return higher than their industry average (Miles & Snow, 1986).

As stated earlier, there is no strict market focus for Analyzer IJVs; they can sell in the local market or export to home or a third country. Rather, the clear-cut feature of this type of IJV lies in its competence contribution and market flexibility. Contractor (1990) observes that Analyzer IJVs are viewed more favorably by the host government and bear a lower political risk, because these IJVs are likely to generate more foreign exchange earnings through export than Prospector IJVs and to bring more appropriate technologies than Defender IJVs. In China, for example, the central government bestows the following benefits on this type of IJV: (a) reduction in land-use fees; (b) exemption from the profit remittance tax; and (c) priority status for obtaining water, electricity, transportation, and communication services. These benefits are expected to have a favorable influence on an Analyzer IJV's performance. In light of the above, the following relationships are predicted:

H₂: Among IJVs in an emerging economy, an Analyzer strategy is related to higher performance.

RESEARCH DESIGN

Research Setting

This study was set in the People's Republic of China during a pivotal time in the transition stage. China officially opened its doors to foreign investment in 1979. From that point through the end of 1995, Chinese authorities approved the establishment of more than 258,444 FDI projects involving $393.04 billion in foreign capital. About 120,000 ventures representing $133.04 billion in investment commenced operations (*Foreign Investment in China,* 1996). The formation and operation of these ventures have played a major role in shaping the new economic environment and have turned China into the second largest FDI-absorbing country in the world, behind only the United States. Among FDI entry modes, the IJV form remains dominant, accounting for 52.02% of total FDI value in 1994 (*Bulletin of Ministry of Foreign Trade and Economic Cooperation* [MOFTEC], 1995, p. 13). As China becomes progressively integrated into the world economy, the relevance of Western models becomes a practical matter as much as a theoretical issue (Shenkar & von Glinow, 1994; Tan & Litschert, 1994). Since China differs from Western countries in a wide array of aspects such as culture, society, and political and economic systems, it potentially represents the most serious challenge to the managerial paradigm developed and empirically tested primarily in the West, and thus presents grounds to refine and test existing management theories and to develop new ones (Shenkar & von Glinow, 1994).

Data used in this study were obtained through a survey of managers of IJVs operating in Northern China. The questionnaire was adopted from Tan and Litschert (1994). The questionnaire, designed for their study of top managers in

Chinese state and collective enterprises, was subjected to validity tests and shown to be an effective and reliable instrument.

Measurement

In this study, environment was conceptualized as a multidimensional construct (Dess & Beard, 1984; Lawrence & Lorsch, 1967). Three dimensions of environmental attributes—namely, environmental complexity, dynamism, and hostility—were investigated. These dimensions affect IJV managers' perception of uncertainty, which in turn influences strategic decision characteristics similar to those of a Prospector, a Defender, or an Analyzer (Miles & Snow, 1978). For this study, the environment was viewed as a perceptual construct because the study deals with strategy that involves navigating within a chosen domain. It has been long recognized that the manner in which managers perceive their environment is more critical and relevant to variables subject to managerial control than are archival measures of the environment (e.g., Hambrick, 1983). Perceptual measures thus enable the researcher to view a firm's environment from the perspective of organizational members or key respondents (Venkatraman & Prescott, 1990). It has also been argued that perceptual measures make sense because it is not the external reality but the way entrepreneurs think about reality that determines the outcome (Rajagopalan & Finkelstein, 1992). In addition, these measures of organizational environment have been validated and shown to correlate with objective measures with a high degree of reliability (e.g., Chandler & Hanks, 1993).

In the questionnaire, respondents were asked to rate, on a 7-point scale, their perception pertaining to criticality and hostility of competitors, suppliers, customers, and regulatory sectors (Pfeffer & Salancik, 1978), variability and predictability of these sectors (Lawrence & Lorsch, 1967), and heterogeneity and diversity of these sectors (Thompson, 1967). Hostility was then measured by the average score of criticality and hostility measures. Similarly, dynamism was the mean of variability and predictability, and complexity was the mean of heterogeneity and diversity.

Strategy was also measured as a multidimensional construct (Miles & Snow, 1978; Venkatraman & Prescott, 1990). Respondents were asked to rank characteristics of strategic orientations that were relevant to their particular firms, such as futurity, proactiveness, riskiness, analysis, and defensiveness, on a 7-point scale. These measures were conceptually based and have been empirically validated in previous studies (e.g., Tan & Litschert, 1994).

In addition, a set of questions was included in the questionnaire to measure the subjective evaluation of performance, which comprises after-tax returns on sales and on assets, sales growth, and competitive position. These measures of performance are widely used in the PRC. The response format was a 5-point scale (bottom 20% to top 20% in the industry). The overall performance score in our study was a mean of the above composite measures. The latest research suggests that the use of subjective measures of firm performance relative to competitors is particularly desirable in studying emerging businesses (Chandler & Hanks, 1993). The subjective, self-reporting approach was appropriate not only because financial and accounting data were not readily available in China, but also because these measures of organizational environment and performance have been validated and shown to correlate with objective measures with a high degree of reliability (Chandler & Hanks, 1993). In addition, firm size was included in this study as a control variable, measured by the number of employees.

Data Collection

The questionnaire was first reviewed and revised by experts, and then subjected to a back-translation procedure to ensure validity in a cross-cultural setting. Consultation was sought on instrument development to obtain feedback on the quality of the instrument and any necessary revisions. The pretest and survey were administered in several cities in Northern China.

Sixty high-level IJV managers who were directly involved in operations were randomly selected; 51 participants completed and returned the questionnaire. Selected respondents were interviewed to collect pertinent information. The information collected exhibits a high level of consistency with questionnaire responses.

This study followed the usual academic convention of leaving unidentified the individual organization in the sample. Researchers who have used questionnaire surveys in China have reported that under conditions of anonymity, Chinese managers were more willing (and more likely) to provide accurate information (Adler, Cambell, & Laurent, 1989).

Reliability of Measures

Reliability was tested using Cronbach's alpha coefficient. Generally, a value around 0.7 is considered adequate to conclude internal consistency (Nunnally,

1978). This guideline was met. The validity of the assumption of normality was tested, and results indicated that the normality assumption appears to be valid when applied to the data at hand. Multicollinearity was diagnosed by examining the variance inflation factors (VIF) for the predictors. The VIF values for the three predictors ruled out the possibility that multicollinearity could become a problem in our study. These results are available from the authors. Descriptive statistics and correlation coefficients were presented in Table 7.1.

DATA ANALYSIS AND RESULTS

LISREL modeling was used as the primary productive data analysis method for our research. This approach enabled us to study the whole theoretical framework as developed, instead of just testing each hypothesis regarding environment-strategy configuration separately (Bagozzi & Phillips, 1982). The indicators for overall model fit would provide support for the conceptual framework (Jöreskog & Sörbom, 1988). In addition, by analyzing the total effect of environmental attributes and strategies on firm performance, we anticipate being able to derive some useful insights regarding the desirability of environmental challenges to IJVs operating in a transitional economy, an important topic that has so far either been taken for granted or looked at on only a limited basis. For example, strategic management literature assumes that greater environmental challenges are healthy for businesses. Porter (1991) also suggests that competitive pressure helps improve industry competitiveness. Empirically, what is required is a systematic analysis of how various environmental challenges may actually contribute to performance, either directly or indirectly, and in the aggregation. From looking at the direct, indirect, and total effects of environmental attributes on profit, we derived some tentative conclusions related to this crucial aspect.

During our data analysis stage, we introduced nonzero paths for all environment-strategy relations, for specific strategy-performance relations, and for all environment-performance relations. Two considerations led us to estimate only the causal relations without the measurement model part of a typical full LISREL analysis. First, our analysis focused on the causal relations identified in our theoretical exposition. Also, our sample size was only moderate by the conventional standard (Jöreskog & Sörbom, 1988). Since construct reliability and validity assessments had been performed in advance, we concentrated on analyzing identified causal relations.

TABLE 7.1 Descriptive Statistics and Correlation Coefficients

	N	Mean	S.D.	1	2	3	4	5	6	7	8
1. Complexity	51	4.57	0.36	1.00							
2. Dynamism	51	4.52	0.35	0.94***	1.00						
3. Hostility	51	4.58	0.33	0.87***	0.88***	1.00					
4. Prospector	51	4.34	0.91	-0.39***	-0.44***	-0.46***	1.00				
5. Analyzer	51	4.62	0.78	0.44***	0.33**	0.46***	-0.40***	1.00			
6. Defender	51	3.99	1.11	0.36***	0.42***	0.37***	-0.70***	0.24*	1.00		
7. Size	47	1.49	0.66	-0.07	-0.11	0.03	0.02	-0.15	0.07	1.00	
8. Performance	51	2.99	0.91	0.57***	0.46***	0.65***	-0.45***	0.68***	0.36***	0.07	1.00

$* p < 0.05$; $** p < 0.01$; $*** p < 0.001$.

TABLE 7.2 LISREL Analysis Results *

Relationship	Coefficients	T Statistics
Complexity → Prospector	0.39	1.04
Complexity → Analyzer	**0.84**	**2.32**
Complexity → Defender	−0.36	−0.93
Dynamism → Prospector	−0.46	−1.18
Dynamism → Analyzer	**−0.94**	**−2.52**
Dynamism → Defender	0.71	1.78
Hostility → Prospector	−0.41	−1.46
Hostility → Analyzer	**0.54**	**2.05**
Hostility → Defender	0.06	0.21
Prospector → Performance	−0.06	−0.58
Analyzer → Performance	**0.35**	**3.49**
Defender → Performance	0.15	1.67
Complexity → Performance	**0.76**	**2.66**
Dynamism → Performance	**−1.05**	**−3.58**
Hostility → Performance	**0.91**	**4.32**
Goodness of Fit		0.89
Root Mean Sq. Residual		0.11

NOTE: * Bold numbers are significant paths.

Table 7.2 summarizes the key findings of our LISREL analysis. We first report the empirical analysis results according to the hypotheses advanced earlier, and then discuss additional findings.4

Hypothesis 1a states that IJVs will cope with environmental complexity by adopting an Analyzer strategy. This hypothesis is supported by a positive relationship between complexity and an Analyzer strategy (0.84). We also hypothesized a positive association between environmental hostility and an Analyzer strategy. Statistical results indicate that the firms tend to deal with increased hostility through increased analysis orientation (0.54), thus H_{1c} was also supported. On the other hand, Hypothesis 1b suggested a positive relation between dynamism and an Analyzer strategy. Statistical results revealed a negative relationship (−0.94), suggesting that the IJVs dealt with dynamism with reduced Analyzer activity. Thus Hypothesis 1b is rejected. Overall, the IJVs do seem to opt for an Analyzer strategy as their prime response to environmental challenges. As Table 7.2 indicates, we included Prospector and Defender strategies in the model but these were not preferred strategies under the current environment.

The dominant strategic orientation we hypothesized for IJVs in China, an Analyzer strategy, appears to make a positive contribution to firm performance (0.35). This finding supports our strategy-performance relationship (H_2). In addition, from a path analysis perspective, we find that poorer performance appears to be caused by increased dynamism (−1.05). Interestingly, the statistical analysis also reveals that firm performance seems to be positively related to increased hostility (0.91) and complexity (0.76), all at significant levels. This evidence demonstrates that various environment dimensions affect IJV performance idiosyncratically. While an environment's dynamism has a negative impact on firm performance, its complexity and hostility may imply superior market position in which higher performers often face a more hostile competitive environment or operate in more complex industries (Luo, 1995). While environmental complexity presents major challenges for Chinese domestic firms (Tan, 1996; Tan & Litschert, 1994), IJVs are more troubled by the dramatic changes that China is currently undergoing. Overall, IJVs in China seem to survive and prosper in light of environmental challenges as reflected in environmental complexity and hostility. While the impact of environment on firm performance was not hypothesized, these findings seem to point out clearly that a challenging environment may actually be beneficial for firms that implement carefully planned strategies.

To put the key findings identified so far into perspective, the statistical analysis shows a clear association between environmental conditions and their respective strategic orientations. For the IJVs in our sample, the squared multiple correlations for the three strategy types, that is, Prospector, Analyzer, and Defender, are 0.24, 0.31, 0.19, respectively, and for firm performance, the coefficient is 0.66. The squared multiple correlations are similar to R^2, and theoretically represent the strength of environment and strategy relationship in our case. Our study indicates that the IJVs seem to adjust their predominant strategy (Analyzer) when dealing with environmental challenges. Also, for these firms environmental challenges in general seem to be healthy conditions for their success. As we reported earlier, the environmental attributes produce an overall positive impact on firm performance.

DISCUSSION AND CONCLUSION

Based on the context of a high uncertainty economy (China), this study examined the environment-strategy configuration and its performance implications for international joint ventures. The issue addressed here is, on the one hand, central to a better understanding of IJV strategy and performance, and on the other hand, is indicative of a deficiency in the IJV literature and therefore defines a gap to be filled. The primary findings suggest that IJVs exhibit distinctive strategies in such a context, and that these strategies are significantly associated with perceived environmental complexity, dynamism, and hostility. More specifically, managers' perceptions of increased environmental complexity and hostility are found to be positively related to an Analyzer strategy. Proactive and defensive strategies are either negatively or nonsignificantly linked with contextual uncertainty. Moreover, Analyzer strategy is positively and significantly related to an IJV's overall performance. IJV success hinges to a significant extent on the good fit between its strategic orientation and the nature of the host country environment.

It is found that perceived complexity (heterogeneity and diversity) and hostility (criticality and hostility) of competitors, customers, suppliers, and regulatory environments are positively associated with an IJV's Analyzer strategy in a significant fashion. This strategy-environment alignment has a profoundly favorable influence on IJV performance. Indeed, environmental diversity and criticality imply both market opportunities and threats from competitors, buyers, suppliers, and government authorities in the host country. These contextual conditions drive IJVs to seek both risk-adjusted efficiency and emerging opportunities. They are innovative but not highly proactive; they are adaptive but not highly risk taking. Moreover, they are circumspect but not totally defensive; they pursue efficiency but are not fully dependent upon cost minimization through export. Analyzer IJVs' futurity, innovativeness, and riskiness lie in the middle, between Prospectors and Defenders. Their dual market orientation (i.e., seeking both local market and export advantages) not only mitigates IJVs' dependence on local settings, thus reducing their business uncertainties, but also has a superior position in achieving internalization as well as internationalization benefits.

Contrary to environmental complexity and hostility, environmental dynamism (variability and predictability of competitors, buyers, suppliers, and regulatory sectors) is negatively associated with analysis-orientation and positively associated with defensive-orientation of IJVs (see Table 7.2). High variability and unpredictability of task as well as institutional environments consolidate an IJV's risk aversion. This evidence coincides with previous studies on Chinese management that suggest that the uncertainty and unpredictability of the Chinese institutional environment, particularly the regulatory sector, constitute the most important contextual factor explaining the variance of firms' performance and leading them deliberately to select a stable and narrowly defined product or market domain (Tan, 1996; Tan & Litschert, 1994).

This research observed fundamental differences in the effect that different environmental dimensions have on an IJV's strategies as well as its performance. Environmental complexity and hostility are positively related to IJV performance, whereas environmental dynamism has a negative influence on venture performance. This implies that high diversity and criticality of environmental sectors perceived by IJV managers may mirror business potentials from which the ventures can benefit. In contrast, perceived uncertainty and unpredictability of environment sectors may indicate the level of contextual risks facing IJVs. The findings of the present study suggest that it is imperative to use a multidimensional approach to assess the strategy-environment configuration and its performance effect. Using specific dimensions of uncertain environment in isolation from others appears inappropriate because they are unable to capture the heterogeneous effects of different environmental dimensions on either strategy formulation or operational outcome.

Both Prospector and Defender strategies are found to be either negatively or nonsignificantly related to environmental dimensions and IJV performance. Prospective orientation often leads to great operational and contextual risks and high innovative and adaptive costs in an uncertain environment such as China. When the perceived host environment is highly uncertain, this orientation is apparently contradictory to the underlying objective that IJVs pursue risk reduction. In an alternative vein, defensive orientation often makes IJVs unable to seize upon preemptive opportunities and business potentials in the host country. This orientation is hence contrary to the rationale that an IJV is a vehicle of market expansion, particularly in emerging economies (Beamish, 1993; Luo, 1995; Shenkar, 1990). An analysis orientation appears to be the best strategic choice for IJVs in aligning with the complex and uncertain environment and in attaining their inherent advantages and potential benefits.

This work enriches the IJV theories in the following areas. First, it establishes that an IJV's performance is significantly influenced by its strategic orientation, and an analysis orientation is the best strategic posture in an uncertain environment. Second, it confirms that the alignment of IJV strategies to the host country environment is critical to the venture's success (Contractor, 1990; Harrigan, 1985). Perceived environmental complexity, dynamism, and hostility have a strong and sustainable influence over the choices of an IJV's strategic orientations in futurity, proactiveness, riskiness, and innovativeness. Third, it underlines the multidimensional nature of the host country environment facing IJVs. Different environmental dimensions affect IJV strategies and performance idiosyncratically. This necessitates more sophisticated and vigorous analyses of an IJV's local responsiveness, industry selection, information processing, and competence deployment.

This study has important managerial implications for international executives, particularly those interested in investing or marketing in emerging economies. First, it is important for transnational investors to establish a good coupling between an IJV's strategic orientation and its contextual conditions. This orientation formulation has replaced conventional control as a major instrument balancing an MNC's headquarters and its foreign subsidiaries, including IJVs. Second, hybrid strategy (Analyzer) and dual-emphasis market orientation (both local and export markets) can facilitate the accomplishment of both internalization and internationalization advantages for IJVs in an uncertain environment. The Chinese evidence presented by this study suggests that hybrid strategy between proactive and defensive orientations will spur efficiency growth and market expansion from structural transformation. Third, foreign investors need to assess individual dimensions of the local environment taken separately rather than taken as a whole, because various environment dimensions such as complexity, dynamism, and hostility influence IJV strategy and performance heterogeneously. Thus, the configuration of IJV strategy with local environments is a complicated matrix rather than a one-dimensional linkage. The lessons from China demonstrate that diversity and criticality of environment sectors are much more conducive to IJV performance than variability and predictability of these sectors. Since the nature of environmental dimensions could be industry-specific and region-specific, international executives should correctly identify the nature of the host country environment based upon the particular dynamics of the selected industry and geographical market. This will in turn help them improve strategy formulation, resource dispersal, and output control.

Despite some contributions to the literature and practice, this research has several limitations that should be addressed in future research. First, the sample IJVs studied here may not be fully representative of all IJVs in China. In order truly to appreciate the robustness and generalizability of the empirical results reported here, future work needs to use a larger sample or more representative firms. The lessons drawn from China could possibly be extended to other emerging economies; however, this needs to be empirically verified. In addition, an IJV's motives need to be captured in the empirical model because they may influence the IJV's strategic orientation. Similarly, a local partner's objective in IJV formation and its strength in technological, operational, and organizational skills must be controlled when examining the strategy-environment-performance relationships. The degree of congruence in strategic motivations of IJV formation and the degree of complementarity in rent-generating skills between foreign and local partners are areas worthy of investigation because they are likely either independently to impact IJV performance or to moderate the relationship between IJV strategy and performance. Furthermore, future research should investigate the possible moderating effect of equity distribution between partners because this affects bargaining power and IJV control from each side, thus influencing the venture's process of strategy formulation and implementation. Finally, as China and other emerging economies are highly dynamic, more valuable insights into the dynamic relationships among strategy, environment, and performance can be gained from additional studies that trace IJV strategy-environment configurations and performance implications over time. Taking this study as a point of departure, future research should be devoted to longitudinal comparisons on this issue.

NOTES

1. An "organizational effect" may arise against a "societal effect" (Mueller, 1994). This could be possibly true via technological skill diffusion and organizational skill diffusion. As argued by both strategic management theorists and the internalization theory school, an MNC is a relatively effective mechanism for transferring knowledge via IJVs across borders (Bartlett & Ghoshal, 1989). However, this effect is likely to be deterred when IJVs operate in a hostile, complex, and dynamic environment, because contextual and structural impediments hinder its dissemination (Sorge, 1991).

2. A resource-dependence perspective maintains that in a complex and dynamic environment, an IJV's ability to reduce its dependence on local settings and increase its bargaining power over the host government relies on the distinctiveness of its invested competence (Pfeffer & Salancik, 1978; Prahalad & Hamel, 1990). MNCs often contribute organizational skills, international distribution channels, and technological skills to Analyzer IJVs as distinctive competencies.

3. Resource-based theory suggests that different firms benefit from different types of resources and that these resources can be used to achieve two types of economic advantages: (a) cooperative and strategic or (b) competitive and financial (Wernerfelt & Karnani, 1987). This study measures IJV performance focusing on the latter. As interfirm cooperative or learning effect often directly contributes to performance of individual parent firms rather than that of IJVs, this study does not use a learning measure for IJV performance. As Beamish and Inkpen (1995) have claimed, once a foreign partner has acquired local knowledge from the local partner, the rationale for cooperation disappears.

REFERENCES

Adler, N. J., Cambell, N., & Laurent, A. (1989). In search of appropriate methodology: From outside the People's Republic of China looking in. *Journal of International Business Studies, 20,* 61-74.

Aggarwal, R., & Agmon, T. (1990). The international success of developing country firms: Role of government-directed advantage. *Management International Review, 30*(2), 163-180.

Agmon, T. (1985). *Political economy and risk in world financial markets.* Lexington, MA: Lexington Books.

Aldrich, H., McKelvey, B., & Ulrich, D. (1984). Design strategy from a population perspective. *Journal of Management, 10,* 67-86.

Bagozzi, R. P., & Phillips, L. W. (1982). Representing and testing organizational theories: A holistic construal. *Administrative Science Quarterly, 27,* 459-489.

Barney, J. (1991). Firm resources and sustained competitive advantage. *Journal of Management, 17,* 99-120.

Bartlett, C. A. (1986). Building and managing the transnational: The new organization challenge. In M. Porter (Ed.), *Competition in global industries* (pp. 367-404). Boston: Harvard Business School Press.

Bartlett, C. A., & Ghoshal, S. (1989). *Managing across borders.* Boston: Harvard Business School Press.

Beamish, P. W. (1993). The characteristics of joint ventures in the People's Republic of China. *Journal of International Marketing, 1*(2), 29-48.

Beamish, P. W., & Banks, J. C. (1987). Equity joint ventures and the theory of the multinational enterprises. *Journal of International Business Studies, 17,* 1-16.

Beamish, P. W., & Inkpen, A. C. (1995). Keeping international joint ventures stable and profitable. *Long Range Planning, 28*(3), 26-36.

Berg, S. V., Duncan, J., & Friedman, P. (1982). *Joint venture strategies and corporate innovation.* Cambridge, MA: Oelgeschlager.

Brewer, T. L. (1993). Government policies, market imperfections, and foreign direct investment. *Journal of International Business Studies, 24,* 101-120.

Buckley, P. J., & Casson, M. C. (1988). The theory of cooperation in international business. In F. Contractor & P. Lorange (Eds.), *Cooperative strategies in international business* (pp. 31-34). Lexington, MA: Lexington Books.

Buckley, P. J., & Casson, M. C. (1992). *Multinational enterprises in less developed countries: Cultural and economic interactions.* In P. J. Buckley (Ed.), *Studies in international business.* New York: St. Martin's.

Bulletin of Ministry of Foreign Trade and Economic Cooperation (MOFTEC). (1995). People's Republic of China. Issue No. 1 (Serial No. 25).

Buzzell, R. D., & Gale, B. T. (1987). *The PIMS principles: Linking strategy to performance.* New York: Free Press.

Carpano, C., Chrisman, J., & Roth, K. (1994). International strategy and environment: An assessment of the performance relationship. *Journal of International Business Studies, 25,* 639-656.

Chandler, G. N., & Hanks, S. H. (1993). Measuring the performance of emerging business: A validation study. *Journal of Business Venturing, 8,* 391-408.

Child, J. (1972). Organizational structure, environment and performance: The role of strategic choice. *Sociology, 6,* 1-22.

Child, J. (1994). *Management in China during the age of reform.* Cambridge, UK: Cambridge University Press.

Collis, D. J. (1991). A resource-based analysis of global competition: The case of the bearings industry. *Strategic Management Journal, 12*(Special issue), 49-68.

Contractor, F. J. (1990). Contractual and cooperative forms of international business: Towards a unified theory of modal choice. *Management International Review, 30*(1), 31-54.

Contractor, F. J., & Lorange, P. (1988). The strategy and economic basis for cooperative venture. In F. J. Contractor & P. Lorange (Eds.), *Cooperative strategies in international business.* Toronto: Lexington Books.

Dang, T. (1977). *Ownership, control, and performance of the multinational corporation: A study of U.S. wholly-owned subsidiaries and joint ventures in Philippines and Taiwan.* Unpublished doctoral dissertation, University of California, Los Angeles.

Davidson, W. H. (1980). The location of foreign direct investment activity: Country characteristics and experience effects. *Journal of International Business Studies, 12*, 9-22.

Dess, G., & Beard, D. (1984). Dimensions of organizational task environments. *Administrative Science Quarterly, 29*, 52-73.

Doz, Y., & Prahalad, C. K. (1991). Managing DMNCs: A search for a new paradigm. *Strategic Management Journal, 12*(Special issue), 145-164.

Duncan, J. (1972). Characteristics of organizational environments and perceived environmental uncertainty. *Administrative Science Quarterly, 17*, 313-327.

Duysters, G., & Hagedoorn, J. (1995). Strategic groups and inter-firm networks in international high-tech industries. *Journal of Management Studies, 32*, 359-381.

Foreign investment in China. (1996). China Foreign Invested Enterprises Association, *96*(4), Serial No. 41, pp. 20-22.

Galbraith, C., & Schendel, D. (1983). An empirical analysis of strategic types. *Strategic Management Journal, 4*, 153-173.

Geringer, J. M., & Hebert, L. (1989). Control and performance of international joint ventures. *Journal of International Business Studies, 20*, 235-267.

Ghoshal, S. (1987). Global strategy: An organizing framework. *Strategic Management Journal, 8*, 425-440.

Ghoshal, S., & Bartlett, C. A. (1990). The multinational corporation as an interorganizational network. *Academy of Management Review, 15*, 603-625.

Ghoshal, S., & Nohria, N. (1989). Internal differentiation within multinational corporations. *Strategic Management Journal, 10*, 323-338.

Gold, D. (1991). The determinants of foreign direct investment and their implications for host developing countries. *CTC Reporter, 31*, 21-24.

Golden, B. R. (1992). SBU strategy and performance: The moderating effects of the corporate-sbu relationship. *Strategic Management Journal, 13*, 145-158.

Gomes-Casseres, B. (1989). Ownership structure of foreign subsidiaries: Theory and evidence. *Journal of Economic Behavior and Organization, 11*, 1-25.

Hambrick, D. C. (1983). Some tests of the effectiveness and functional attributes of Miles and Snow's strategic types. *Academy of Management Journal, 26*, 5-26.

Hambrick, D. C., MacMillan, I. C., & Day, D. L. (1982). Strategic attributes and performance in the bcg matrix: A PIMS-based analysis of industrial product business. *Academy of Management Journal, 25*, 510-531.

Hamel, G. (1991). Competition for competence and inter-partner learning within international strategic alliances. *Strategic Management Journal, 12*(Special issue), 83-104.

Harrigan, K. R. (1985). *Strategies for joint venture success.* Lexington, MA: Lexington Books.

Harrigan, K. R. (1988). Joint ventures and competitive strategy. *Strategic Management Journal, 9*, 141-158.

Hennart, J. F. (1991). The transactions cost theory of joint ventures: An empirical study of Japanese subsidiaries in the United States. *Management Science, 37*(4), 483-497.

Hisrich, R. D. (1992). Joint ventures: Research base and use in international markets. In D. L. Sexton & J. D. Kasards (Eds.), *The state of the art of entrepreneurship* (pp. 520-559). Boston: PWS-Kent.

Jarillo, J. C., & Martinez, J. I. (1990). Different roles for subsidiaries: The case of multinational corporations in Spain. *Strategic Management Journal, 11,* 501-512.

Jöreskog, K. G., & Sörbom, D. (1988). *LISREL 7: A guide to the program and applications.* Chicago: SPSS.

Killing, J. P. (1983). *Strategies for joint venture success.* New York: Praeger.

Kobrin, S. J. (1982). *Managing political risk assessment.* Berkeley: University of California Press.

Kogut, B. (1988). Joint ventures: Theoretical and empirical perspectives. *Strategic Management Journal, 9,* 319-332.

Kogut, B., & Singh, H. (1988). Entering the U.S. by joint venture: Competitive rivalry and industry structure. In F. J. Contractor & P. Lorange (Eds.), *Cooperative strategies in international business.* Lexington, MA: Lexington Books.

Kumar, B. N. (1995). Partner-selection-criteria and success of technology transfer: A model based on learning theory applied to the case of Indo-German technical collaborations. *Management International Review, 35*(Special issue), 65-78.

Lall, S. (1987). Transnational, domestic enterprises and industrial structure in host LDCs: A survey. *Oxford Economic Papers,* pp. 217-248.

Lawrence, P., & Lorsch, J. W. (1967). Differentiation and integration in complex organizations. *Administrative Science Quarterly, 12,* 1-47.

Lecraw, D. J. (1984, Spring/Summer). Bargaining power, ownership, and profitability of transnational corporations in developing countries. *Journal of International Business Studies, 15*(1), 27-43.

Luo, Y. (1995). Business strategy, market structure, and performance of international joint ventures: The case of joint ventures in China. *Management International Review, 35,* 241-264.

Luo, Y. (1996). Partner selection and international joint venture performance: Chinese evidence. *Academy of Management Best Papers Proceedings, 1996,* pp. 161-165.

Lyles, M. A. (1988). Learning among joint venture sophisticated firms. *Management International Review* (Special issue), pp. 85-97.

McKee, D. O., Varadarajan, R., & Pride, W. M. (1989). Strategic adaptability and firm performance: A market-contingent perspective. *Journal of Marketing, 53*(3), 21-35.

Meyer, J. W., & Rowan, B. (1977). Institutionalized organizations: Formal structures as myth and ceremony. *American Journal of Sociology, 83,* 340-363.

Miles, R. E., & Snow, C. C. (1978). *Organizational strategy, structure, and process.* New York: McGraw-Hill.

Miles, R. E., & Snow, C. C. (1986). New concepts for new forms. *California Management Review, 28*(3), 66-73.

Miller, K. D. (1992). A framework for integrated risk management in international business. *Journal of International Business Studies, 23*(2), 311-331.

Miller, D., & Friesen, P. H. (1978). Archetypes of strategy formulation. *Management Science, 24,* 921-933.

Miller, D., & Friesen, P. H. (1983). Strategy-making and environment: The third link. *Strategic Management Journal, 4*, 221-235.

Morrison, A. J., & Roth, K. (1992). A taxonomy of business-level strategies in global industries. *Strategic Management Journal, 13*, 399-417.

Mueller, F. (1994). Societal effect, organizational effect and globalization. *Organization Studies, 15*(3), 407-428.

National Council for U.S.-China Trade. (1991). *Special report on U.S. investment in China.* Washington, DC: Department of Commerce.

Nunnally, J. C. (1978). *Psychometric theory* (2nd ed.). New York: McGraw-Hill.

Osborn, R. N., & Baughn, C. C. (1990). Forms of interorganizational governance for multinational alliances. *Academy of Management Journal, 33*, 503-519.

Oxeheim, L., & Wihlborg, C. G. (1987). *Macroeconomic uncertainty: International risks and opportunities for the corporation.* New York: John Wiley.

Pan, Y. (1996). Influences on foreign equity ownership level in joint ventures in China. *Journal of International Business Studies, 27*, 1-26.

Parkhe, A. (1993). Strategic alliance structuring: A game theoretic and transaction cost examination of interfirm cooperation. *Academy of Management Journal, 36*, 794-829.

Pfeffer, J., & Salancik, G. R. (1978). *The external control of organizations: A resource dependence perspective.* New York: Harper & Row.

Porter, M. E. (1979, March-April). How competitive forces shape strategy. *Harvard Business Review,* pp. 35-44.

Porter, M. E. (1986). *Competition in global industries.* Boston: Harvard Business School Press.

Porter, M. E. (1991). Towards a dynamic theory of strategy. *Strategic Management Journal, 12*, 95-117.

Prahalad, C. K., & Hamel, G. (1990). The core competence of the corporation. *Harvard Business Review, 90*(May/June), 79-91.

Rajagopalan, N., & Finkelstein, S. (1992). Effects of strategic orientation and environmental change on senior management reward systems. *Strategic Management Journal, 13*, 127-142.

Root, F. R. (1988, Fall). Environmental risks and the bargaining power of multinational corporations. *International Trade Journal,* pp. 111-124.

Scott, W. R. (1987). *Organizations: Rational, natural, and open systems* (2nd ed.). Englewood Cliffs, NJ: Prentice Hall.

Shama, A. (1995). Entry strategies of U.S. firms to the newly independent states, Baltic states, and Eastern European countries. *California Management Review, 37*(3), 90-109.

Shan, W. (1991). Environmental risks and joint venture sharing arrangements. *Journal of International Business Studies, 22*, 555-578.

Shenkar, O. (1990). International joint ventures' problems in China: Risks and remedies. *Long Range Planning, 23*(3), 82-90.

Shenkar, O., & Von Glinow, M. A. (1994). Paradoxes of organizational theory and research: Using the case of China to illustrate national contingency. *Management Science, 40*(1), 56-71.

Sorge, A. (1991). Strategic fit and the societal effect: Interpreting cross-national comparisons of technology, organization and human resources. *Organization Studies, 12*(2), 161-190.

Stopford, J. M., & Wells, L. T. (1972). *Managing the multinational enterprise.* New York: Basic Books.

Tan, J. J. (1996). Characteristics of regulatory environment and impact on entrepreneurial strategic orientations: An empirical study of Chinese private entrepreneurs. *Academy of Management Best Papers Proceedings, 1996,* pp. 106-110.

Tan, J. J., & Litschert, R. J. (1994). Environment-strategy relationship and its performance implications: An empirical study of the Chinese electronics industry. *Strategic Management Journal, 15,* 1-20.

Teagarden, M. B., & Von Glinow, M. A. (1990). Sino-foreign strategic alliances types and related operating characteristics. *International Studies of Management and Organization, 20*(1/2), 99-108.

Thompson, J. D. (1967). *Organizations in action.* New York: McGraw-Hill.

Tung, R. L. (1979). Dimensions of organizational environments: An exploratory study of their impact on organizational structure. *Academy of Management Journal, 22,* 672-693.

Venkatraman, N., & Prescott, J. E. (1990). Environment-strategy coalignment: An empirical test of its performance implications. *Strategic Management Journal, 11,* 1-23.

Wernerfelt, B., & Karnani, A. (1987). Competitive strategy under uncertainty. *Strategic Management Journal, 8,* 187-194.

Williamson, O. E. (1991). Comparative economic organization: The analysis of discrete structural alternatives. *Administrative Science Quarterly, 36,* 269-296.

Wright, P., Kroll, M., Pray, B., & Lado, A. (1995). Strategic orientations, competitive advantage and business performance. *Journal of Business Research, 33,* 143-151.

Yan, A., & Gray, B. (1994). Bargaining power, management control, and performance in united states-china joint ventures: A comparative case study. *Academy of Management Journal, 37,* 1478-1517.

Yip, G. S. (1995). *Total global strategy: Managing for worldwide competitive advantages.* Englewood Cliffs, NJ: Prentice Hall.

8

Technology Transfer to China

Environmental Considerations and Emerging Management Practices

MARIS G. MARTINSONS
CHOO-SIN TSENG

The People's Republic of China (PRC) has been making a concerted effort to reform and modernize its economy since the late 1970s. After a prolonged period of socioeconomic isolation and technological stagnation, its *open-door policy* has attracted considerable amounts of foreign capital and an inflow of new production and management technology. Recent policy initiatives have also stimulated the indigenous development of technological applications.

Despite this progress, industrial and commercial activities in the PRC continue to use comparatively primitive product and process technologies, particularly when compared to those employed by areas such as the military (Yin, 1990; Zhao, 1995). Businesses in China have commonly concentrated on lowering production costs, developing new markets, and possibly acquiring new hardware rather than stimulating technological innovation. The introduction of machine tools, flexible manufacturing systems (FMSs), and similarly mundane manufacturing technologies remain newsworthy, while few business process reengineering efforts have been reported (see "China to Speed Up," 1995; Jiang, Wang, & Sun, 1993; Xia, 1995).

Foreign direct investment (FDI) into the PRC has primarily entered low-technology sectors of the economy, such as light industry, textiles, and hotels, rather than more technology-intensive industries like computer component manufacturing, energy production, and telecommunications (*Bulletin of Ministry of Foreign Trade and Economic Cooperation* [MOFTEC], 1995; Stewart, 1988, p. 168; Zhao, 1995). By 1993, FDI in the information technology (IT) industry in China had reached only U.S.$300-400 million (Hui & McKown, 1993).

Some 2,500 domestic enterprises have moved into the 52 technology development zones that were created by the High-Technology Research and Development Initiative. However, there has been little diffusion of advanced technology into the overall Chinese economy ("Techno-China," 1993). Not surprisingly, the effect of *science-technology input* is reported to be relatively modest in the PRC (Wan & Deng, 1995; Zhao, 1995). The ability of Chinese enterprises to satisfy evolving domestic demands and to compete in the global marketplace continues to be severely constrained by a lack of technological sophistication.

Technological innovation is now imperative across much of the Chinese economy, but this will be both very costly and very difficult. The magnitude and nature of the required effort have prompted the Chinese authorities actively to seek foreign sources of technology and other outside assistance (Woodward & Liu, 1993; Zhang, 1992). Significantly, the technologies that are to be transferred will have to fit specific situations rather than be state-of-the-art. The ability to assimilate the most advanced imported technologies is limited to a small number of Chinese enterprises.

As in the former Soviet Union, internal politics have pushed many of the most talented and creative individuals into the relatively noncontroversial environment of science and technology. An overwhelming majority of university graduates are employed in the public sector. By 1990, the PRC had more than half a million scientists and engineers working in 15,000 research institutions and over 1,000 universities and technical colleges (Deng, 1990). However, their collective strength is in basic research with a focus on theoretical explorations.

The emphasis on applied research and development may be expected to increase as China becomes more prosperous (Ratchford, 1994; Wingrove, 1995). Some universities in China have already created commercial arms to leverage their scientific expertise while international exchange programs and research cooperation with other countries is growing (Hu, 1990). Despite these promising developments, the percentage of those with science and technology backgrounds in China who have experience with business process innovation or new product development remains very small.

The continuing macroeconomic changes and the substantial numbers of well-educated people do make the PRC an attractive destination for technology transfer. Chinese scientists can be expected to apply their expertise to the engineering, design, production, and servicing of technology-based products. As a result, some firms have already relocated some of their business operations into China; about 3 million workers in Guangdong province were employed by Hong Kong-owned businesses by 1993 (Clifford, 1993). Service companies, including Cathay Pacific Airlines and several financial service firms, have shifted large parts of their back-office activities from Hong Kong into southern China. Meanwhile, the manufacturing transplants typically have hundreds of local engineers among their thousands of production workers (Kraar, 1993).

Much of the potential for mutually beneficial technology transfer to the PRC remains unrealized. Opportunities for cooperation between foreign and Chinese researchers are also expected to increase, especially in the areas of biotechnology, electronics, and IT management (Ratchford, 1994). Those seeking to participate are likely to benefit from our consideration of the environmental considerations for technology transfer and the technology management practices that are emerging in China.

This chapter draws from an expanding literature on technology in China and makes use of primary data that was partly collected during 3 days of intensive discussions with senior managers from seven higher-technology joint ventures. The foreign partners in the focal ventures were Squibb Pharmaceuticals, Ingersoll-Rand, Xerox, Printronics, Bell Telephone, Johnson Products, and Schindler Elevator. Each venture had been operating for several years, and its technology transfer process was considered largely successful by both partners. The problems that had been overcome, and those that lingered, were considered. We begin by examining the regulatory environment for transferring technology to China. Subsequently, the relationships and situational factors that facilitate transfer processes are considered.

TECHNOLOGY TRANSFER REGULATIONS

The Beijing government has exercised care to ensure that technology transferred into the PRC is both advanced and able to be successfully integrated into the recipient industry. It does not want the country to become a dumping ground for outdated technology. Until the late 1980s, Chinese technology import laws were both complex and bureaucratically cumbersome. However, the Regulations of the PRC on the Administration of Technology Import Contracts (TICR) were promulgated in 1985, and the Detailed Rules and Regulations for their implementation followed in early 1988. As a result, the approval process for technology imports has been simplified and clarified. There is now a systematic approval process for the following:

1. Contracts for the assignment or licensing of industrial property rights
2. Contracts for the licensing of proprietary technology
3. Technical service contracts
4. Contracts for cooperative production or design
5. Contracts for the importation of complete sets of equipment or production lines

The Coordinating Committee on Multilateral Export Controls (COCOM) historically banned the export of advanced technologies with actual or potential military applications to communist countries, including the PRC (Wemple, 1992). Even shipments of higher-end computers required special clearance. However, partly as a result of international lobbying by the Beijing government, foreign attitudes on the issue of transferring high technology to China have changed. The World Forum (which succeeded COCOM) has also extended a General License for technology trade to Hong Kong, which reverted to Chinese sovereignty in July 1997. Meanwhile, the U.S. government has decoupled most-favored-nation trade status from human rights issues and has ended curbs on many U.S. high-technology exports to the PRC. China is also likely to join the World Trade Organization in the near future.

These changes support the efforts to accelerate technology acquisition and further experiment with market-oriented practices in the PRC, as advocated by paramount leader Deng Xiaoping in 1992 (Jiang, 1992). As a result of the National Science and Technology Development Program (NSTDP; enacted in 1992), which has both ambitious goals and detailed prescriptions for achieving them, significant resources have been committed to rebuilding and upgrading the technological infrastructure in China. Investments averaging some U.S.$25 billion per year have improved transportation and telecommunications across much of the country. Facsimile services and electronic data communications have become common in all but the most remote parts of China, and electronic data interchange has been introduced to the coastal provinces (Burn, 1995; Qin, 1992; Zheng, 1994). This forms a solid foundation for the development of higher-technology industries, which represent a second modernization stage in

TABLE 8.1 Stages of Development in the People's Republic of China

Time Period	Initial Stage 1979-1992	Second Stage Since 1992
Foreign participants	Mostly overseas Chinese	Global business community
Major areas of development	Coastal provinces that neighbor Hong Kong and Taiwan	Outward from the Yangtze River delta
Focal point	Special economic zones	Major urban areas
Nature of business	Low technology	Higher technology
Success factors	Efficiency Staff training Personnel management Incremental change	Quality Organizational learning Technology management Substantial change

the PRC. Table 8.1 uses the conceptual framework developed in Martinsons (1988) to contrast the two stages.

Although some of the recent technology policies in China have been ill advised or poorly implemented, the country has become progressively more attractive to foreign business interests (Chen, 1993; Martinsons & Tseng, 1995). Those considering technology transfer must be prepared to tolerate considerable ambiguity, due to the lack of definitive rules or concrete government priorities to augment national technology policies and principles. However, technology infusion into many areas of the Chinese economy would capitalize on unrealized potential and produce handsome investment returns. For example, higher value-added products could leverage existing energy-generating and port-handling capacities.

Technology transfer can involve the licensing or sale of intellectual property rights, the provision of technical services, or the sharing of commercially useful knowledge. China favors the acquisition of technical know-how, to upgrade domestic production capabilities, over the import of actual production hardware, such as machinery and equipment (Wolff, 1989). With the first approach, recipients gain knowledge, are able to reduce their dependency on imports, and rapidly become more competitive (Stewart, 1988).

FORMING THE RELATIONSHIP

Foreigners are able to contribute to, and financially benefit from, economic and technological development in the PRC in a number of different ways. The potential forms of technology transfer include the licenses covering patents or other know-how, coproduction, cooperative agreements, and counter-trade, as well as wholly owned operations. However, the predominant transfer vehicle has been the contribution of technology to either a contractual or an equity joint venture (Chen, 1993; De Keijzer, 1992; Wang, 1993). Consequently, the focus of this chapter is on the use of joint ventures as a vehicle for transferring technology to China.

Joint ventures represent a viable response in the face of rapid market changes, industrial consolidation, and reduced heterogeneity across national and regional markets (Lyons, 1991; Teagarden & Von Glinow, 1990). The Chinese authorities perceive joint ventures to be an effective means of technology transfer. As a result, the PRC is likely to encourage their development until its modernization enables total self-reliance, that is, the ability to manufacture the good or provide the service without any external assistance.

A joint venture *child* pools and leverages the resources of its *parents* and enables them to share the risks and rewards. Such partnerships have typically operated in a bounded environment, with restrictions on product lines, market areas, or operational life-span (Killing, 1983). They represent a middle road between self-sufficiency and business merger (Davidson, 1987). A joint venture provides a comparatively better solution than other governance structures for opportunism, small numbers, and uncertainty in the face of bounded rationality (Beamish, 1988). The foreign investor commonly takes an equity position that ensures significant control. A minority interest can be precarious, unless the venture critically relies on the products or technical expertise of the foreign parent. This condition will be satisfied if the local parent has little knowledge of international business or modern manufacturing methods.

A joint venture requires substantial amounts of human, financial, and physi-cal resources. In the PRC, the foreign partner commonly provides much of the technical and managerial know-how, the capital, and potential access to the international market. The acquisition of technology is often cited by the local side as *the* principal reason for a joint venture. The Chinese partner typically contributes land and buildings, access to appropriate employees, and local market knowledge. The Chinese partner knows where to source raw materials, how to find customers, and can act as liaison with the authorities. High-level government contacts are invaluable when official support is needed for critical actions. Such a partnership can also help to harmonize a technology transfer program with implicit Chinese government policies.

International joint ventures have a mixed track record (Beamish, 1988; Rosser, 1990). In China, a distinctive combination of economic, political, and

TABLE 8.2 Critical Success Factors for the Transfer of Technology Into a Joint
Venture

1. Select a suitable partner.

A foreign investor should invest the time to find a Chinese party that can be an effective partner
in the technology transfer process. Complementary attributes can be the basis for business
synergy. Established relationships of the local partner can be instrumental in overcoming
bureaucratic hurdles.

2. Bridge cultural differences.

A foreign investor should be knowledgeable about Chinese cultural values and management
systems. Overseas Chinese or Westerners who truly are "old China hands" can act as a bridge
between the partners and help to overcome government bureaucracy. Unfortunately, there is a
scarcity of such individuals.

3. Develop a relationship before signing the contract.

The two partners should discuss their respective goals and objectives for the prospective joint
venture. The scope and nature of the business should be clearly specified and a comprehensive
feasibility study conducted. The contributions and responsibilities of the partners should be
clarified before the formal contract is negotiated. Nothing should be assumed or taken for
granted.

4. Facilitate the technology transfer.

A structured and systematic approach to the transfer of relevant process and/or product
technologies must be jointly planned and implemented by the partners. The foreign partner
should be prepared to provide training that facilitates the effective use of the technology.
Boundary spanners and personnel in major suppliers as well as employees in the focal venture
may need to be trained.

5. Institutionalize quality.

A quality management system, perhaps based on the ISO 9000 standards, should be
institutionalized within the venture as well as backwards along its supply chain in order to
support the technology transfer process.

cultural factors combine to present a formidable challenge to foreign participants
(Martinsons & Tseng, 1995; Newman, 1992). Many Sino-foreign ventures have
experienced major setbacks or disappointing results (Aiello, 1991). This is
despite, or perhaps because of the fact that many of them are essentially "a
Chinese state enterprise with foreign senior management and imported technology" (Shenkar, 1990). Nevertheless, joint ventures can accelerate the corporate
learning curve and provide an effective foundation for business development in
an emerging market. They have become an integral part of China's unique
environment (Newman, 1992) and the object of considerable investigation. The
factors that are commonly critical to their success are presented in Table 8.2.

Between 1979 and 1995, about 25,000 such Sino-foreign contracts were
signed, and about one third of these have commenced operations (MOFTEC,

1995). Such foreign participation has parallelled the evolution of the overall PRC economy in the past decade, with impressive overall growth being the result of periodic surges and occasional retrenchment. Sino-foreign ventures account for some 30% of the PRC's total trade value, and they have recently contributed between U.S.$60 and $80 billion per year to the economy (MOFTEC, 1995).

The Chinese say that "one hand cannot clap." This certainly applies to a Sino-foreign joint venture. Compatibility between the value systems, management approaches, and corporate cultures of the partners will be a critical factor in determining cooperative success ("Getting Hitched," 1993). Growing numbers of Chinese have been exposed to international practices, and government interference is becoming less of a problem. Those seeking a local partner are also able to choose among an increasingly sophisticated and experienced pool of enterprises.

This latter trend can be a mixed blessing for technology transfer. Most of the better connected and more established firms are already participating in one or more joint ventures. Meanwhile, managers and employees in unprofitable state enterprises may welcome the injection of capital and technology, but fear the introduction of international productivity and accountability standards. Finding an appropriate partner among a crowd of eager candidates with dubious credentials has replaced the government-arranged partnerships of the past. Relatively few domestic firms have the sophistication and business acumen to partner a higher-technology venture successfully. The prospective partner need not come from one's own industry, especially when advanced technologies and management techniques will be used.

Partner Selection and Negotiations

It is important to ascertain whether the prospective Chinese partner has the authority to negotiate and sign a contract, and to ensure that the government approves of the project. The legal status of the Chinese entity can be determined by reviewing its business license and articles of association. A potential domestic partner should be able to demonstrate that the project is both feasible and acceptable to the relevant government authorities. It should be able to produce a feasibility study report and a project authorization certificate. The former should address the following: financial and sales forecasts, site selection, and infrastructure facilities, as well as the supply of workers and raw materials.

The formation process for such an alliance usually includes two distinct phases (Lorange, Roos, & Bronn, 1992). An initial analysis considers the

TABLE 8.3 Conflicting Objectives in a Joint Venture

	Foreign Partner	*Local Partner*
Planning	Retain business flexibility	Maintain congruency between the venture and the state economic plan
Contracts	Unambiguous, detailed, and enforceable	Ambiguous, brief, and adaptable
Negotiations	Sequential, issue by issue	Holistic and heuristic
Staffing	Maximize productivity; fewest people per given output level	Employ maximum number of local people
Technology	Match technical sophistication to the organization and its environment	Gain access to the most advanced technology as quickly as possible
Profits	Maximize in the long term; repatriate over time	Reinvest for future modernization; maintain foreign exchange reserves
Inputs	Minimize unpredictability and poor quality of supplies	Promote domestic sourcing
Process	Stress high quality	Stress high quantity
Outputs	Access and develop domestic market	Export to generate foreign currency
Control	Reduce political and economic controls on decision making	Accept technology and capital but preclude foreign authority infringement on sovereignty and ideology

prospective match in broad terms on various dimensions. Conflicting objectives may be expected, as shown in Table 8.3.

A subsequent phase sees a more intensive and focused analysis accompanied by some soul-searching questions about long-term compatibility. This process has been problematic for many foreign investors. The PRC's relatively primitive and dynamic business environment during the 1980s was less than ideal for technology transfer, even when joint ventures were employed. Shan (1991) identified the following common complaints:

a. determining the respective value of each partner's actual contribution,
b. reconciling divergent goals to establish the specific basis for win-win cooperation,
c. fairly accounting for exposure to uncertainties, and
d. structuring the technology management and control framework.

Chinese negotiators can easily frustrate foreign business people who are not used to their tactics. Potential technology suppliers are often asked a seemingly endless stream of questions or requested to make repeated presentations and

TABLE 8.4 Key Stumbling Blocks in Joint Venture Negotiations

Financial investment and share of equity
Valuation of in-kind contributions
Nature and division of corporate governance
Decision-making responsibilities
Product pricing
Salary and benefits of expatriate managers and professionals
Focus and extent of staff training and development
Nature of and extent of access to the transferred technology
Sources of and required quality for supplies
Contract arbitration and dispute resolution mechanisms

---

even to provide tours of existing plants that use the focal technology. Protracted discussions will test whether the partners are committed to the relationship that is to be sealed by a contract, and not merely obliged to the written agreement. Chinese managers in our group of informants confirmed that they relied on personal integrity far more than any piece of paper. Nevertheless, a foreign partner's insistence on writing down as much possible can help to reduce the frequency and severity of disputes once the venture is in operation.

An increasingly comprehensive and uniform joint venture code and the ability to draw on a growing body of empirically derived knowledge are making it progressively easier to conclude business negotiations successfully in the PRC. Among our sample of joint ventures, such discussions lasted an average of nearly 3 years. Hard bargaining and the maintenance of a tough but fair stance are critical. Common stumbling blocks in joint venture negotiations are listed in Table 8.4.

Frontline Chinese negotiators often serve more as information conduits than as decision makers. The real authorities with respect to pricing, payment terms, and transfer process specifics are typically behind the scenes. Even then, the potential recipient's lack of technological expertise can become evident. Novel or unfamiliar concepts may have to be translated and clarified for the Chinese negotiating team. Consistent and high-quality interpretation is both scarce and critical.

A unique set of technical standards in the PRC may also require designs and specifications to be disclosed and translated by local engineers. The foreign partner may have difficulties collecting such data for purchased components from its suppliers and documenting internal expertise. Thus, it is prudent for suppliers to stipulate that documentation will be provided "as readily available."

TABLE 8.5 Contents of a Typical Joint Venture Agreement

Nature, scale, and scope of venture (including project and industry details)

Partner contributions and conditions for cooperation

Terms of operation

Market information related to customers, suppliers, and competitors

Technology needs and transfer/licensing arrangements

Estimates of workforce size, composition, compensation, and training

Environmental impact assessment

Land, site, utility, and infrastructure requirements

Demands for the supply of leading-edge technologies also may have to be resisted, because infrastructural shortcomings will preclude many potential recipients from effectively assimilating them (De Bruijn & Jia, 1993; Tsang, 1994). Licensing the technology to local suppliers should be seriously considered for many of these situations.

Joint Venture and Technology Transfer Agreements

The tangible result of successful negotiations is a joint venture agreement. Typical contents of this document are shown in Table 8.5. Stewart (1988) describes technology transfer as "a costly and difficult business, and made even more difficult if the ultimate aim is to export the high-tech products" (p. 170). Ubiquitous standard-form joint venture contracts lack the specificity or flexibility to cover the nature of most technology transfer relationships.

As a result, higher-technology ventures commonly augment the standard-form contract with a technical cooperation contract. This latter contract typically goes beyond the specifics of hardware to be transplanted or provided. The transfer process for the technology, the operating conditions at the recipient site, the nature and means of compensation, and the duration of the agreement are typically stipulated (Hendryx, 1986; Tsang, 1994). Typical contents appear in Table 8.6.

Both of these documents are likely to include capital and personnel considerations, and be complicated by cultural and social differences. The prospective partner and, perhaps more important, the relevant authorities, must be convinced that the foreign technology satisfies three conditions. It must be advanced, suitable for the Chinese situation, and offer significant economic benefits. The Chinese authorities will also want to ensure that there is a planned process for

TABLE 8.6 Contents of a Typical Technology Transfer Contract

Content, scope, and description of the technology to be transferred, including a list of relevant patents and trademarks

The amount, form, and method of remuneration to the supplier

The standards, time periods, and measures for acceptance testing of the technology

The undertaking of risks and liabilities, and the method for computing compensatory damages for contract breaches

The respective obligations related to confidentiality and the post-contract ownership of the technology

The dispute settlement mechanism

---

the localization of materials and management. Before finalizing these contracts, it is also advisable to get written guarantees for key inputs (like electricity) and rulings on the legal and tax consequences of all foreseeable transactions.

The common forms of compensation for a transferred technology include royalties, profits, and fees. A mixture of these forms can be used to diversify financial risk. Government guidelines appear to restrict the value of even the most advanced technology to less than 50% of the foreign partner's overall contribution to the venture. The Chinese will typically attempt to include countertrade provisions in the partnership agreement: The technology supplier is asked to buy back goods made by the joint venture in order to ease the foreign exchange burden of the local partner. In considering this option, it should be recognized that sales of products and services to the subsidiary can be a major profit source.

Two issues are at the heart of many technology-transfer contracts: (a) Who may use the technology? *and* (b) When can they use it? The protection of proprietary knowledge remains complex and requires customized contractual solutions rather than general prescriptions (Tsang, 1994; Wolff, 1989). Significantly, current Chinese laws allow the recipient to use freely both process and product technologies after the contracted term, unless the agreement explicitly includes the scope and period of confidentiality.

Quite a few foreign partners report that their technology has been illegally duplicated outside of the venture before the end of the contracted period. Such activities may be carried out by the local partner or by *enterprising* employees. According to the TICR, in cases of unauthorized disclosure, the only recourse for the technology supplier is against the contracted recipient, that is, the venture partner. Supplier concerns about unauthorized sales or outright thefts of technology together with local expectations that technical assistance will be provided until "specified performance levels have been met" can easily sour a business partnership (Simon, 1988). Chinese legislation does enable dispute resolution clauses to be included in business contracts. However, cultural norms favor compromise or arbitration rather than litigation.

It is prudent to reach an agreement on confidentiality and the valuation of the technological contribution even *before* the formal contract negotiations begin. Confidential information should be defined as broadly and clearly as possible. The technology recipient should explicitly agree not to disclose or duplicate such information for an extended period unless written authorization has been obtained from the supplier. Disclosures to employees should be made on a need-to-know basis. Wolff (1989) recommends that "each employee to whom such information is disclosed should be required to sign an individual confidentiality agreement" (p. 470). Provisions in the subsequent technology transfer contract may be used to make the local partner liable for confidentiality breaches by employees in the venture.

DEVELOPING THE RELATIONSHIP

Communication channels within China, both between enterprises and state authorities as well as across government departments, are weak and inefficient. Information has commonly lacked timeliness or reliability and frequently both value elements were absent. Misunderstandings of technical aspects and outdated telecommunication facilities contribute to these inefficient flows (see Zheng, 1994). Many foreign partners still use Overseas Chinese (often from Hong Kong or Singapore) or "old China hands" as information intermediaries. They can gather data about technology, production, marketing, and personnel prior to the formal negotiations.

Gibson and Smilor (1991) found that technology transfer processes can be accelerated by fostering interactive communications and personal motivation while surmounting technological equivocality and cultural distances. All four factors can be salient for transferring technology to the PRC. During much of the past half century, managers of Chinese enterprises were expected to implement state-defined plans and meet production quotas. Sourcing and sales were beyond their responsibility.

Modern management is still commonly perceived to be "a body of quantitative techniques, not as a way of thinking and acting" in the PRC (Borganjan &

Vanhonacker, 1992, p. 12). Although Chinese managers perform broadly the same tasks and activities as their Western counterparts, concepts such as marketing, performance measurement, quality control, production planning, and financial and accounting systems can be novel to many of them (Chow, 1992). This poses problems when implementing a management system to facilitate technology transfer and meet world-class industrial requirements.

Learning by doing is a necessary supplement to technical documentation and preliminary training for effective technology transfer. This increases the need to define precisely and limit clearly the scope of technology guarantees in any contracts. In order to achieve contract-stipulated objectives, venture employees will have to become thoroughly familiar with the basic technology, accept technical assistance, and use appropriate production resources (such as raw materials and equipment) when applying the technology. The venture contract duration should allow the recipient to master the imported technology.

The probability of successful technology transfer increases if the partners have complementary strengths. However, a strong local parent will have entrenched processes and behaviors. Some of these may be inherited by the joint venture. In one case, it was difficult to implement a new management style. Many of the employees and supervisors had been transferred from the local parent. They resisted change and reverted to old practices whenever they experienced difficulties with the new approach. One manager noted that "older workers like older methods." As a result, several of the pioneering ventures now recruit and hire primarily fresh graduates, whose lack of practical knowledge and work experience is more than offset by a willingness to accept new work methods.

The tradition of collective decision making can also constrain the scope and speed of organizational changes. Sustained but incremental transformations have been effective. With dynamic technology and fluid markets, the appropriate pace and nature of changes will vary, but it commonly follows four steps. Design experts will learn about the local environment, analyze the particular situation, craft a suitable system (often by adapting one from another site), and finally implement it.

Both greenfield plants and existing factories have been used. Leaseholds of up to 70 years are now being granted in some areas, and ventures are increasingly constructing their own factories. A custom-built plant using modern, imported technology often justifies the delay in commencing production. Others have used factories that were prebuilt by local authorities. The use of existing facilities can involve the following:

- taking over an entire plant and its local workers (who may be difficult to retrain)

- taking part of the existing plant and select staff from among the existing workers (which has the potential of causing rifts between those chosen and those not chosen)
- occupying a plant that has been abandoned by a state enterprise or not brought into operation by a previous venture

SUSTAINING THE RELATIONSHIP

Although it is not easy to develop a good relationship between two firms from very different business cultures, it is even harder to sustain it. Trust can be built up only over time. In addition to the legal contract, the partners are bound by a psychological contract. On every contentious issue, it is necessary to balance self-interest with the need to maintain an effective working relationship.

Both "face saving" and *guanxi* are an integral part of Chinese culture. *Guanxi* is used to denote both the special kind of relationship in which long-term mutual benefit is more important than short-term individual gain, and the intricate and pervasive personal networks that are at the essence of Chinese business. These relationships can bring cheap and reliable supplies, tax concessions, rapid government approvals, and assistance to overcome seemingly insurmountable obstacles.

Strategic Focus

The issue of introducing new technology and products often strains the partnership. One foreign parent had a wide product line and wanted to expand the scope of the joint venture in order to seize new business opportunities. However, the local partner was reluctant to change, because of its own limited expertise. In another case, the foreign partner explicitly restricted its venture to a single product. This narrow scope precludes long-range planning and new product development. Success is based on cost-effective labor, the ability to make incremental design changes, and the growing domestic market. Additional ventures were set up for other products, but each had a unique focus and specific government incentives.

Most foreign partners fear that they will not be fairly compensated for sharing their product and process know-how. Although the PRC government has progressively strengthened its intellectual property regulations, its patent-protection laws still offer limited recourse if proprietary knowledge is stolen. As a result, technology transfer is sometimes severely restricted until the terms of the initial contract have been completely fulfilled. Relatively few ventures have been able to duplicate their foreign parent's complete product line by receiving liberal technology transfer. Usually this happens only after a considerable amount of business trust has been established between the partners.

Those seeking short-term profits and protection of their own international markets will have no desire to share the fruits of their overseas research and development. However, a foreign parent may be able to profit from sales and services to its China offspring. Market development is also likely to require the continued infusion of technology in a long-term joint venture (Martinsons, 1993). Nevertheless, some foreign managers admit that new technology, such as advanced product designs or more sophisticated manufacturing processes, must be incorporated on a selective basis. This is often used as a "carrot" to maintain or renew the commitment of their Chinese partner.

Quality Operations

The economic traditions in the PRC have done little to cultivate quality (Lockett, 1988). The state has traditionally purchased all output and provided "iron rice bowl" employment guarantees. Customer satisfaction, after-sales service, and product warranties were alien concepts in a centrally planned, quota-driven production system (Martinsons & Valdemars, 1992). Many employees still view their work in terms of completing tasks rather than satisfying customer requirements. Government authorities recognize the need to improve product quality, but are leery of the social upheaval that a rapid change could bring.

Internal quality and worker safety are often undervalued by the Chinese partner. Housekeeping in joint venture plants is not a trivial matter. The Chinese can compulsively hoard both raw materials and spare parts because it has traditionally been difficult to obtain both supplies and equipment. Meanwhile, higher-technology production requires a clean operating environment. This is a decidedly alien concept to most employees, who must keep their work areas cleaner than their own living quarters.

Some ventures have set up rigid procedures to maintain process quality. Large fines are imposed for smoking in the plant, and cleanliness is an important basis for performance appraisal. Others have hired a special workforce *just* to keep the workplace clean. This was counterproductive; workers no longer perceived housekeeping as *their* responsibility. A combination of frequent communication with and substantial incentives for the workers is now commonly used to help assure quality in higher-technology ventures.

Financial Matters

In many of the joint venture agreements that have been implemented since the late 1980s, the Chinese partner has experienced difficulties contributing its share of capital on schedule. Shortages of foreign exchange have been reported to be one of the two most common problems across the PRC ("Sweet on Shanghai," 1993). High inflation, negative real rates of bank interest, and easy credit facilities have combined to create a triangular debt problem. With customers frequently defaulting on their accounts payable or delaying their payments, the local partner is frequently squeezed for working capital. Although the government injected funds to reduce the triangular debt problem in 1991, a subsequent austerity package led to a resurgence of this problem.

Chinese enterprise managers may also find it difficult to resist the lure of speculative investments in local property and stock markets. The foreign parent should carefully examine the accounting records of the prospective partner and, if possible, conduct a credit analysis of its major customers. For many local enterprises, money on a balance sheet differs greatly from money in the bank. In the past, unauthorized loans and the falling value of the local currency, the *renminbi,* complicated financial assessment. The renminbi's limited convertibility was also a vexatious issue (McKenzie, 1990). However, the unification of internal exchange rates at the beginning of 1994 and the recent stability of the renminbi are both significant steps toward the full convertibility of the mainland Chinese currency.

The use of financial indicators and budget forecasts to guide decision making has also been problematic. Traditional Chinese recording and accounting systems do not produce cash flow or cost accounting statements. Introducing a system that presents financial information to meet reporting and managerial needs typically requires enormous time and effort. The Chinese will worry that performance information from cost accounting will be used as the basis for firing selected workers.

RELATIONSHIPS WITH
MANAGERS AND EMPLOYEES

Successful technology transfer is contingent on effective human resource management. Unfortunately, the area has been a common source of problems for Sino-foreign projects. These have ranged from inabilities to find appropriately skilled workers to difficulties in terminating poor performers.

Even after years of collaboration, the partners may continue to favor different solutions to personnel problems. This simply reflects contrasting business cultures, past experiences, and ideological backgrounds.

There are significant differences between the Chinese and Western management systems (Martinsons, 1991; Martinsons & Hempel, 1995). Business in the PRC has also been argued to be "a cultural as well as an economic transaction" (DeKeijzer, 1986). Communication problems between individuals with different cultural and linguistic backgrounds are inevitable. They will occur on the shop-floor and in the boardroom. Informal dialogue is difficult when using interpreters. Subtle meanings may be missed or misunderstood, leading to problems being overblown.

Frequent and explicit communications can minimize ambiguity and inform decision making. A good understanding of the Chinese business culture is extremely valuable. However, the local partner must also be open to new ideas, even if some break with tradition. It is helpful to use international business practices and to ensure that senior staff are not only technical experts, but can also positively influence junior employees. They can also help to initiate interdepartmental communications and teamwork on multidisciplinary projects.

Partners frequently propose radically different numbers of employees for the venture. The Chinese parent will seek to employ as many local people as possible, and will underestimate labor costs. This is often based on the need to maintain good relations with the government. In negotiations involving one of the authors, the Chinese partner proposed to hire six times the number of staff needed in similar operations elsewhere in Asia.

Motivation and Compensation

Regardless of the appropriate number, people will be the key to the success of the venture. Despite the shortages of capable managers and professionals, adequate numbers of unskilled and semiskilled workers are available almost everywhere in China. However, the industriousness of the Overseas Chinese (Ko, 1995; Mackie, 1992; Redding, 1990) remains to be emulated in the PRC. One manager asked, "Why can't they do it here?" and then answered himself, "I think it's a question of the motivating force." Problems such as low productivity, low quality output, and high rates of absenteeism are widespread and difficult to resolve. They even persist in some of the most mature joint ventures.

Traditional Chinese employment contracts have emphasized punishments rather than rewards and there has been little incentive to initiate changes (Lockett, 1988). However, the reforms are removing many of the constraints on good business practices. With the disappearance of the "iron rice bowl" concept, which guaranteed lifetime employment regardless of performance, increasing numbers of workers are now motivated by the desire to retain their job. The Temporary Regulations have enabled joint ventures to introduce specific labor contracts, which can be renewed after an initial term.

Many employees have been explicitly told to work to the best of their ability and not to worry about making mistakes. However, getting staff to make suggestions or to discuss their problems is an ongoing challenge. In some ventures, management only ensures that the overall business plan is followed. Punishments are rare, and efforts focus on finding the underlying causes of mistakes and working to correct them. Others have comprehensive disciplinary codes, with punishments based on the severity of the transgression.

Despite the egalitarian tradition in the PRC, employees in many ventures are now compensated based on individual contribution. The wages of the best ones may be four to five times those of new recruits. Explicit incentives may include higher salaries and productivity bonuses. Many employees also view the joint venture as a gateway to the privileges that traditionally were reserved for the Party elite. These include overseas travel, business or technical training, and access to foreign currency. Such privileges, together with nonpay incentives, can be powerful motivating forces.

State enterprises in China typically pay meager salaries, but also provide housing and a pension as well as medical insurance and free schooling to workers and their dependents. The comparatively young age of joint venture staff reduces the burden of retirement and health care benefits. Direct compensation is also not usually a major source of dispute between joint venture partners. In fact, the foreign parent is probably more willing to pay higher salaries (by local standards) for quality workers. However, many ventures will not hire those who need *company housing*. Others provide accommodation allowances based on length of service, job level, and performance.

Employee reviews and an emerging labor market have created some flexibility to deal with poor performers. Meanwhile, workers can compete for promotion and coveted assignments. Even the authority to hire workers may now be accompanied by the unpleasant (and often frequent) task of criticizing, penalizing, and dismissing staff. Advertising and local sponsorship may be used to recruit job applicants, while formal selection procedures can include interviews, examinations, and psychological tests. These practices give joint ventures a distinct edge over state enterprises, where administrative allocation and internal recruitment remain prevalent (Child & Markoczy, 1993).

Many university graduates in China are eager to learn modern business practices and so consider joint venture employment to be an excellent career opportunity. Nevertheless, staff training and ongoing technical assistance are essential to the success of most joint ventures. Often this is done by bringing corporate trainers and technical experts to the PRC. However, with the transfer of new technologies, key employees may be sent overseas to experience successful operations firsthand. The foreign parent must resist the temptation to clone its home operations. The timing of on-site visits by foreign technical experts and trips by Chinese employees to foreign operations should be carefully planned. A steady flow of information to workers is also important. Employee anxieties will be raised if it is unclear why someone is visiting their plant, or why they are being sent abroad. The best workers may be given appropriate technical or management training after a period of corporate service. With suitable compensation packages and appropriate staff development, they become progressively more productive and dependable. They can inform expatriates about the local environment, provide access to vital contacts, and become competent managers using a combination of Chinese and Western practices.

Foreign Managers

Until sufficient numbers of local managers are developed, technology transfer ventures must rely on expatriate expertise. Unfortunately, international executives are reluctant to work in the PRC. Most of them consider even cities like Shanghai and Beijing to be *hardship* postings. Schooling for children and the cultural adjustment of the spouse are major concerns. Expatriate performance and job satisfaction levels are difficult to predict. Some can overcome considerable adversities to achieve spectacular results quickly.

The performance of others has been mediocre at best. Many among this latter group erroneously believed that they could apply a purely Western management style. They failed to account adequately for cultural differences and employee unfamiliarity with market-based production, incentive-based employment, and international accounting practices. Their subordinates then came to resent their salaries and benefits. Although there is a growing insistence that local and foreign managers with equivalent levels of responsibility receive the same salary, the total compensation package of a single expatriate may still equal that of a hundred local workers. Some ventures pay their expatriates through an off-payroll agreement or have their foreign parent pick up part of the cost.

The senior foreign manager in the venture must have strong business and political skills. The former satisfy local demands while the latter protect the interests of the foreign partner (Aiello, 1991). Many successful ventures have brought in ethnic Chinese managers who speak Mandarin, are perceived to be suitably seasoned by their subordinates, and have a knack for solving difficult problems. They understand local perspectives have and built up connections with government officials. With the rapid growth of joint ventures, the demand for such culture spanners now exceeds the supply. As a result, increasing numbers of local people, many with an overseas education, are receiving junior management appointments in these enterprises. As they gain experience and can be assigned greater responsibilities, the Shanghai ventures are reducing their reliance on expatriate managers.

EXTERNAL RELATIONSHIPS

Good relationships between the partners and the people who work for their joint venture are a necessary but insufficient condition for effective technology transfer. They must be supplemented by relationships with external parties, including suppliers and customers.

Suppliers

The PRC does not have a competitive marketplace for most components. The limited choice of domestic suppliers can make it difficult to get many critical raw materials. A key to success has been the early identification of all input material needs, so that supplier alliances can be developed and problems resolved before operations commence (Zhao, 1991). Some ventures import their essential production components. Contingency plans that include stockpiles of foreign-produced goods can be costly and time-consuming, but may be the only way to prevent a production bottleneck.

Others practice *virtual* vertical integration. They visit potential local suppliers to inspect the working conditions and equipment before signing any contract. Financial support and quality training may subsequently be provided to selected suppliers of essential raw materials. The costs of poor quality, in terms of reworks, repairs, and clean-ups; finding alternative sources; and losing goodwill may be communicated. At least two ventures sent their methods engineer and quality control specialist out to the supplier for at least a week. They provided technical assistance for the design and operation of assembly and production processes. This can reduce the problems with poor-quality products and the time required for inspecting incoming supplies. Nevertheless, most ventures still examine all delivered merchandise and order unsatisfactory shipments to be returned to the supplier.

A quality certificate may be issued when the supplier meets certain conditions. The supplier may subsequently use it to stimulate third-party sales in China or to begin to export. Some ventures have developed strong alliances with their domestic suppliers. These relationships are expected to pay off as just-in-time production becomes viable in China. The ISO 9000 standards have been a useful foundation for a comprehensive quality management system. *Guanxi* can also be helpful for procuring certain raw materials. In some cases, even monetary incentives are not sufficient to assure quality and quantity; production technology and management control must usually accompany this cash infusion. Some suppliers will initially produce acceptable components but find it difficult to maintain their quality with adequate quantities on a timely basis. They may sever links with firms that complain too much. The greatest difficulties frequently arise with the simplest components.

Customers

The problems of quality, which are typified by the question of whether the product should be acceptable to the foreign parent or need only satisfy the standards of the local market extend to export marketing. The local partner may want to generate foreign sales, but may not realize that these require a good product, attractive packaging, and delivery flexibility *in addition* to competitive pricing. Low productivity and poor quality often preclude such an approach. In some ventures, unexpectedly high operating costs have drained money that was earmarked for overseas marketing.

Local partners are often more interested in maximizing sales, rather than worrying about dissatisfied customers or lost export opportunities due to shoddy quality. They may also wish to control the price; their sense of social responsibility requires that it not be *too* high. Foreign partners will favor price increases at least in line with domestic inflation, to reflect rises in key input costs. Thus, the authority for setting both domestic and international prices is an important aspect of a joint venture contract. In many successful ventures, the foreign partner retained exclusive authority for export pricing and also ensured considerable influence on domestic prices.

Concerns may also be expressed about the possibility of domestic competition if the price is too high. Most foreign partners will view such competition as healthy for their industry and customers. They are more interested in developing the domestic market. With 1.2 billion people in China, market saturation is unlikely in the near future. The local partner may have to be convinced that reduced imports of a specific commodity have the same effect as generating exports; hard currency saved is no different than that earned abroad. The ability to repatriate venture profits since 1986 has created one more issue that must be considered.

Until the late 1980s, joint ventures were limited to export-oriented activities. As these restrictions were relaxed, some of the Shanghai ventures tried to develop local markets for their products. This has not been easy, despite international levels of quality and lower prices than their imported counterparts. Although the foreign partner can initiate market research, market segmentation, and specific promotion, it is also critical to understand local preferences and traditional selling customs.

Many local consumers and even industrial buyers continue to prefer foreign goods even when the choice appears irrational. For example, the new Shanghai Metro underground bought its escalators from the European parent firm rather than its joint venture. Foreign travel perquisites for the purchaser as well as misperceptions about the levels of technology and quality in the venture appeared to be factors in this decision.

The development of customer loyalty can be a very slow, difficult, and often frustrating process in the PRC. Nevertheless, many joint ventures have successfully penetrated the domestic market and quite a few have leveraged their first-mover advantage to establish a firm foothold. For example, a pharmaceutical venture now sells 90% of its output in China, with the majority being direct sales to Shanghai-area hospitals. Chinese consumer behavior makes this a tremendous advantage for future business development (Yau, 1993).

SUMMARY AND IMPLICATIONS

It may be said that although anything is possible, nothing is easy when doing business in China. Thousands of joint ventures have been set up to facilitate the mutually beneficial transfer of technology. Among them, only a few have been formally declared failures or abandoned. Many others, however, have been scaled back or are still losing money. Although the size and complexity of the PRC make it difficult to generalize, partner relations and issues directly related to the technology transfer process have often created serious problems.

Technology management has become an increasingly important facet of a competitive venture (De Bruijn & Jia, 1993; Tsang, 1994). As highlighted in this chapter, success requires overcoming significant political, financial, and operational hurdles. A wide array of human resource management issues must also be addressed. Extensive preparation, plenty of hard work, and the ongoing commitment of both partners are essential to deal with the unique business environment in China. Good communications between them and their employees are critical to surmount inevitable obstacles and achieve success. Nothing should be taken for granted. Commitments of any kind should be written down.

Vagueness or deferred discussion of contentious issues will inevitably lead to mistrust and major disputes. It is important that both the technology transfer process and the resulting operations in the joint venture begin as smoothly as possible within the dynamic PRC environment. Most technology-based ventures experience considerable degrees of frustration during both their set-up and early development. Nevertheless, the difficult groundwork in being there first and "eventually getting things right" commonly brings healthy financial rewards.

The partners must be patient and be dedicated to both technology transfer and business success. This dedication should be demonstrated at the beginning of their collaboration, with ample time devoted to formal negotiations and informal communications. As one manager told us, "If you want to benefit from the tremendous opportunities here, you must show your commitment." The Chinese are anxious to receive foreign technology and capital, but they are determined to avoid *spiritual pollution* by restricting the import of foreign ideologies.

The Bottom Line

There are many reasons to be optimistic about the business prospects in China. Supplies, sales, and distribution are increasingly governed by market forces. Although government interference and macroeconomic instability continue to be concerns, economic decision making has been progressively decentralized. As a result, foreign firms offering the promise of technology transfer are increasingly coveted in China and relatively free to find the best joint venture deal.

A thorough understanding of the business environment and a dedicated effort to form, develop, and sustain relationships are critical to the success of a technology transfer effort. It is hoped that the empirically derived lessons contained in this chapter will enable potential participants to develop realistic expectations as they seek to benefit from the second stage of the modernization drive in China and that they will provide useful knowledge for those who are managing the technology transfer process.

REFERENCES

Aiello, P. (1991). Building a joint venture in China: The case of Chrysler and the Beijing Jeep Corporation. *Journal of General Management, 17*(2), 47-64.

Beamish, P. W. (1988). *Multinational joint ventures in developing countries.* London: Routledge & Kegan Paul.

Borganjan, J., & Vanhonacker, W. R. (1992). Modernizing China's managers. *China Business Review, 19*(5), 12-15.

Bulletin of Ministry of Foreign Trade and Economic Cooperation (MOFTEC). (1995). [Various published reports from the Ministry of Foreign Trade and Economic Cooperation of the People's Republic of China and its predecessor, the Ministry of Foreign Economic Relations and Trade.]

Burn, J. M. (1995). The new cultural revolution: The impact of EDI on Asia. *Journal of Global Information Management, 3*(4), 16-23.

Chen, J. (1993). The environment for foreign direct investment and the characteristics of joint ventures in China. *Development Policy Review, 11,* 167-183.

Child, J., & Markoczy, L. (1993). Host-country managerial behaviour and learning in Chinese and Hungarian joint ventures. *Journal of Management Studies, 30*(4), 611-631.

China to speed up technical upgrading. (1995, May 29). *Beijing Review, 38,* 7.

Chow, I. H.-S. (1992). Chinese managerial work. *Journal of General Management, 17*(4), 53-67.

Clifford, M. (1993). Companies: Brains for hire. *Far Eastern Economic Review, 156*(38), 76-77.

Davidson, W. H. (1987). Creating and managing joint ventures in China. *California Management Review, 29*(4), 77-94.

De Bruijn, E. J., & Jia, X.-F. (1993). Transferring technology to China by means of joint ventures. *Research & Technology Management, 36*(1), 17-22.

De Keijzer, A. J. (1986). *China business handbook.* Weston, CT: Asia Business Communications.

De Keijzer, A. J. (1992). *China: Business strategies for the '90s.* Berkeley, CA: Pacific View Press.

Deng, S.-P. (1990). Status and problems of high-tech industries in China (in Chinese). *Shuliang Jingji Jishu Jingji Yangiu, 11,* 22-29.

Getting hitched. (1993, December 13). *Business China,* pp. 11-12.

Gibson, D. V., & Smilor, R. W. (1991). Key variables in technology transfer: A field study-based empirical analysis. *Journal of Engineering and Technology Management, 8*(3/4), 287-312.

Hendryx, S. R., (1986). Implementation of a technology transfer joint venture in the People's Republic of China: A management perspective. *Columbia Journal of World Business, 21*(1), 57-66.

Hu, G.-S. (1990). Scientific and technological exchanges with China: A management perspective. *International Journal of Technology Management, 5*(2), 241-243.

Hui, S.-M., & McKown, H. B. (1993). Working out the bugs. *China Business Review, 20*(5), 21-24.

Jiang, W.-B., Wang, Z.-B., & Sun, H.-F. (1993). Manufacturing technology in China. *Journal of Manufacturing Systems, 12*(3), 204-208.

Jiang, Z.-M. (1992). Accelerating reform and opening up. *Beijing Review, 35*(43), 9-32.

Killing, J. P. (1983). *Strategies for joint venture success.* New York: Praeger.

Ko, A. C. K. (1995). Towards an understanding of overseas Chinese management. *Journal of Management Systems, 7*(1), 13-28.

Kraar, L. (1993). Now comes the hard part for China. *Fortune* (Asian ed.), *128*(2), 86-92.

Lockett, M. (1988). Culture and the problems of Chinese management. *Organization Studies, 9*(4), 475-496.

Lorange, P., Roos, J., & Bronn, P. S. (1992). Building successful strategic alliances. *Long Range Planning, 25*(6), 10-17.

Lyons, M. P. (1990). Joint ventures as strategic choice—A literature review. *Long Range Planning, 24*(4), 130-144.

Mackie, J. A. C. (1992). Overseas Chinese entrepreneurship. *Asian-Pacific Economic Literature, 6*(1), 41-64.

Martinsons, M. G. (1988). Towards a tenable technology strategy. *Journal of Technology Management, 15,* 131-140.

Martinsons, M. G. (1991). Management philosophy and IT application: The East-West divide. *Journal of Technology Management, 18,* 207-218.

Martinsons, M. G. (1993). Strategic innovation: A lifeboat for planning in turbulent waters. *Management Decision, 31*(8), 4-11.

Martinsons, M. G., & Hempel, P. S. (1995). Chinese management systems: Historical and cross-cultural perspectives. *Journal of Management Systems, 7*(1), 1-11.

Martinsons, M. G., & Tseng, C.-S. (1995). Successful joint ventures in the heart of the dragon. *Long Range Planning, 28*(5), 45-58.

Martinsons, M. G., & Valdemars, K. (1992). Technology and innovation mismanagement in the Soviet enterprise. *International Journal of Technology Management, 7*(4/5), 359-369.

McKenzie, P. D. (1990). Foreign exchange and joint ventures with China: Short-term strategies and long-term prospects. *Canadian Business Law Journal, 17*(1), 114-149.

Newman, W. H. (1992). Focused joint ventures in transforming economies. *Academy of Management Executive, 6*(1), 67-75.

Qin, S. (1992). High-tech industrialization in China. *Asian Survey, 32*(12), 1125-1136.

Ratchford, J. T. (1994). Exercise the China option. *Research-Technology Management, 37*(2), 9-11.

Redding, S. G. (1990). *The spirit of Chinese capitalism.* New York: De Gruyter.

Rosser, M.-V. (1990). East-west joint ventures in the USSR and China: A comparative study. *International Journal of Social Economics, 17*(12), 22-33.

Shan, W.-J. (1991). Environmental risks and joint venture sharing arrangements. *Journal of International Business Studies, 22*(4), 555-578.

Shenkar, O. (1990). International joint ventures' problems in China: Risks and remedies. *Long Range Planning, 23*(3), 82-90.

Simon, D. F. (1988). Corporate strategy and the changing role of technology transfer: Implications for the People's Republic of China. *Mid-Atlantic Journal of Business, 25*(2/3), 35-48

Stewart, S. (1988). The transfer of high technology to China: Problems and options. *International Journal of Technology Management, 3*(1/2), 167-179.

Sweet on Shanghai. (1993, November 29). *Business China,* p. 7.

Teagarden, M. B., & Von Glinow, M. A. (1990). Sino-foreign strategic alliance types and related operating characteristics. *International Studies of Management and Organization, 20*(1/2), 99-108.

Techno-China. (1993, December 13). *Business China,* pp. 4-5.

Tsang, E. W. K. (1994). Strategies for transferring technology to China. *Long Range Planning, 27*(3), 98-107.

Wan, W.-W., & Deng, S.-L. (1995). A comparative analysis of the relationship between national economy and science-technology. *International Journal of Management, 12,* 445-453.

Wang, X. (1993). Salient features of foreign investment in southern China. *Asian Technology Review, 3*(6), 145-159.

Wemple, E. C. (1992). An export controls clash. *China Business Review, 19*(3), 30-35.

Wingrove, N. (1995). China sees tripling of R&D spending as key to 21st century economic power. *Research-Technology Management, 38*(6), 2-3.

Wolff, A. (1989). Technology transfer to the People's Republic of China. *International Journal of Technology Management, 4*(4/5), 449-476.

Woodward, D. G., & and Liu, B. C. F. (1993). Investing in China: Guidelines for success. *Long Range Planning, 26*(3), 83-93.

Xia, G.-P. (1995). Business process re-engineering—A case study. *Computers & Industrial Engineering, 29,* 367-369.

Yau, O. H. M. (1993). *Consumer behaviour in China: Customer satisfaction and cultural values,* London: Routledge & Kegan Paul.

Yin, Z.-S. (1990). *The transfer of foreign technology and the development of indigenous technological capability in China.* Unpublished doctoral dissertation, New York University.

Zhang, Y. (1992, March 9). China expands import of technology. *Beijing Review, 35,* p. 40.

Zhao, H.-X. (1995). Technology imports and their impacts on the enhancement of China's indigenous technological capability. *Journal of Development Studies, 31,* 585-602.

Zhao, L.-M. (1991). *The role of the institutional network in the effectiveness of technology transfer: the case of the U.S.-China joint venture.* Unpublished doctoral dissertation, Case Western University, Detroit.

Zheng, C. (1994). Open the digital door. *Telecommunications Policy, 18*(3), 236-242.

chapter 9

Adaptive Strategies of the Large Hongs in an Era of Political Change

IRENE HAU SIU CHOW
LANE KELLEY

On July 1, 1997, Hong Kong lost its status as a British colony and became part of the People's Republic of China (PRC). An interesting question for corporate strategists is the adaptation process of its business organizations, both China's and Hong Kong's, as Hong Kong moves from one of the most laissez faire developed economies of the world to unification with one of the most dominant socialist, communist economies, the People's Republic of China. How do businesses adapt in this unusual unification?

The history of this political relationship was initiated over 150 years ago because of trade tensions; with the British attempting to open China to the world when the Chinese rulers "considered their vast empire to be self-sufficient, containing all they would ever need, so foreign trade was conducted merely as a favour to the 'barbarians' who came to pay tribute to the celestial court" (Davis, 1990). The exports were in great demand by the British trading companies for the European markets. To avoid shipping silver to purchase the Chinese goods, the East India Company smuggled opium into China, which resulted in military actions by the United Kingdom to spread its control over the area during the Opium War of 1839 to 1842. Hong Kong Island was ceded "in perpetuity" to the United Kingdom by China in the 1842 Treaty of Nanking, and Kowloon was ceded in the Convention of Peking in 1860 at the end of the second Anglo-Chinese War. In 1898, the United Kingdom "leased" the New Territories from China for 99 years, supposedly to be able to provide a military defense against colonial powers. From the beginning, the relationship between the two countries was not a win-win relationship, but one of tension. The PRC government regards these treaties as "unequal treaties" and has always insisted that the entire territory must be returned to China upon the expiration of the 99-year lease in 1997. That has now happened.

THE JOINT DECLARATION

The United Kingdom and the PRC signed the Joint Declaration on the future of Hong Kong stipulating that the PRC would not interfere in Hong Kong in the run up to 1997, that Hong Kong would function as an autonomous Special Administrative Region (SAR), and guaranteeing the continuation of Hong Kong's unique social, economic, legal, and other systems for 50 years after 1997. Now that China has assumed sovereignty of Hong Kong, it intends to run Hong Kong on a "one country, two systems" basis. The main provisions of the Sino-British agreement are listed below:

- On July 1, 1997, Hong Kong would become a Special Administrative Region (SAR) of the People's Republic of China, with a high degree of autonomy, except in the fields of foreign policy and defence.
- The Hong Kong SAR would levy its own taxes and keep the money collected.
- The legal system would remain the same and a court of final appeal would be established in Hong Kong.
- A government composed of local people would be appointed by the chief executive, who must be approved by the PRC government after emerging from a process of election or consultation.
- Hong Kong would maintain its position as an international financial center, with its own currency, foreign exchange, and gold and securities markets.
- The Hong Kong SAR would be able to continue to participate separately in international organizations like the GATT under the name of "Hong Kong, China."
- Hong Kong would be able to issue its own travel documents, with free entry and exit.

- Government employees, including expatriates, would keep their jobs (except for some top posts), and those who are retired would continue to receive their pensions.
- Hong Kong's existing educational system would be preserved.

The first year is completed and the provisions have been met.

HONG KONG'S DYNAMIC ECONOMY

Hong Kong, with an area of 400 square miles and a population of 6.2 million (3.1 million in the labor force, less than 3.5% unemployment), was a British Colony that adopted a very laissez faire economy, perhaps the most laissez faire of the developed economies. In its approach to managing the economy, the British Hong Kong Government was determined to keep intervention at a minimum level to encourage flexibility. With capital, machinery, and entrepreneurial skills from China in the early 1950s, Hong Kong established its manufacturing base in textile and garment industries and further diversified into plastic and consumer electronics industries. Hong Kong's exports boomed in the 1960s with an average annual growth rate of 15%. It successfully transformed from a trade entrepôt after World War II to become a leading exporter of light manufacturing goods in the 1950s and 1960s and a regional financial center in the 1970s. During the 1970s, exports began to drop because of growing protectionism in developed countries and increasing competition from South Korea, Taiwan, and Singapore. In the decade of the 1970s, Hong Kong further diversified into financial services. Today, Hong Kong is one of the major international banking and financial centers in the world. Eighty-five of the world's top 100 banks are present in the territory. Exports grew at 13% a year from 1974 to 1983. The economic growth in Hong Kong, in real terms, was an average annual rate of 9.5% for the period from 1961 to 1973, 8.9% for the period between 1974 and 1983, and 7.8% for the period from 1985 to 1990. Hong Kong outperformed the Organization for Economic Co-operation and Development (OECD) countries and grew more than twice as fast as the world economy. However, after this substantial growth, the growth of its GDP slowed down to 5% in the early 1990s. Hong Kong established itself as a service center focusing on a diverse range of industries such as banking, transport, insurance, retail trade, and personal services. The service sector contributes over 80% of the GDP and employs about 80% of the labor force. In 1995, the GDP per capita was U.S. $23,360, surpassing that of the United Kingdom, Canada, and Australia, and was ranked second only to Japan in Asia.

CHANGING POLITICAL SYSTEM

Hong Kong was under British rule for over a century. Power was concentrated in the hands of the Governor appointed by England; a nominated Executive Council offered advice to him on important policy decisions, an appointed Legislative Council passed laws, and the bureaucracy administered the laws. Starting in 1982, elected members were added to the eighteen District Boards; in 1985 indirect elections of representatives on the Legislative Council were initiated. There was endless debate over the pace and direction of further political reforms in the run-up to 1997.

The Governor appointed by Britain in 1992 brought in more political disturbance. His political reforms gave the Hong Kong people more democracy than previously agreed. China openly attacked the political reforms and the stock market reacted like a roller-coaster ride. China explicitly expressed its intention to set up its own legislature to replace the one formed under the blueprint of the political reform proposal. In response, China appointed a group of wealthy and influential people as Hong Kong Advisors. A Preparatory Committee was set up in 1993 to oversee the transition of the territory. China and Britain were miles apart on political issues. Some large infrastructure projects, such as the airport and Container Terminal No. 9, were put on hold as a result of the political struggle.

RISING IMPORTANCE OF TRADE WITH CHINA

China is the world's fourth largest economy, behind the United States, Japan, and Germany. Real GNP has grown at a rate of 9% annually since the historic 1978 economic reforms. After the signing of the Sino-British agreement in September 1984 on the future of Hong Kong, trade between Hong Kong and China increased enormously. During the 1980s, Hong Kong and China built a very strong economic interdependence. China is the principal source of Hong Kong's imports. About three quarters of China's foreign direct investment in equity joint ventures came from Hong Kong and Macao. About 80% of

China's exports are either sold on or shipped from Hong Kong's container terminals.

China's open-door policy began in 1978, creating an abundance of business opportunities. Hong Kong re-assumed its role as an entrepôt for China, handling a large proportion of its exports and imports. With bilateral trade growing at an average rate of 30% per year between 1980 and 1992, China became the territory's largest trading partner, overtaking the position previously occupied by the United States. It now accounts for more than one third of Hong Kong's total trade flows, compared with 15% with the United States and 11% with Japan. The position of Hong Kong as a gateway to a rapidly developing China helped to stimulate business. China also gave new impetus to Hong Kong manufacturers by encouraging joint ventures and out-processing activities in South China. It is estimated that about three million workers are working for Hong Kong manufacturing companies along the border of Guangdong Province. Total value of the two-way trade between Hong Kong and China amounted to U.S. $127.3 billion in 1995.

THE HONG KONG STOCK MARKET
AND RED CHIP SHARES

The Hang Seng Index outperformed other financial markets in the world in 1993. With the influx of foreign capital, the Hang Seng Index rose from 5,512 to 11,888, a 115% increase. The Hang Seng Index, however, experienced wild fluctuations leading up to the conversion because of investors' fears of interference from the PRC. The Hong Kong stock market capitalization stood at $346.3 billion at the end of January 1996, the sixth largest market in the world, following New York, Tokyo, London, France, and Frankfurt. After the financial crisis in Asia, the Hong Kong stock market capitalization stood at $402 billion, the fifth largest market in the world, following New York, Tokyo, London, and Frankfurt ("World Stocks," 1998). Many of the state enterprises from the PRC took advantage of the new opportunities to list on the Hong Kong Stock Exchange.

The shares listed on the Shenzhen and Shanghai Stock Exchanges are divided into A shares, for China's investors, and B shares, restricted to investors from outside the mainland. B share issuers are formerly state-run enterprises. B shares display many flaws, like lack of transparency, slack accounting reporting and regulatory rules, and relatively high transaction costs. Shares of PRC firms (referred to as H shares) were introduced in the Hong Kong Stock Exchange in July 1993 in accordance with Hong Kong rules. Since then, 17 large state-owned enterprises in China have listed their H shares on the stock exchange in Hong Kong, raising a total of over U.S. $2.6 billion capital by the end of 1995. These companies, with the exception of Tsingtao Brewery, are in heavy industries, with generally good track records, comparatively good management, and growth potential. The H shares offer better choices than the B shares in terms of quality, transparency, and growth potential forecast in the prospectus. According to Morgan Stanley Asia's H-share Index, H shares have collectively outperformed the Hang Seng Index by more than 30%. Tsingtao Brewery was estimated to have been oversubscribed by more than 100 times at the issue price of $2.80 ("H Shares Brighten," 1993). Red chip shares doubled between July 26 and December 7, 1993. Shanghai Petrochemical was among the best performers. Despite the fact that the level of their disclosure meets the Hong Kong Stock Exchange's listing requirements, these red chip companies do not specifically deal with China's regular reform business environment. The main concerns regarding red chips by possible stockholders include changes in credit control policy, use of share issue proceeds, foreign exchange currency, changes in tax rates, treatment of value-added tax, and capital commitments. In 1995, the market reacted violently and dumped H shares, fearing further hidden problems among these mainland companies. Because of the tightening up on the macro-economic policy, state-owned enterprises were financially under pressure, as revealed in their financial statements. As a result, the Hang Seng China Enterprises Index for H shares, which had lagged behind the Hang Seng Index for the previous 12 months, plunged to a new low in November 1995, but they had been accepted in the market—commercial firms becoming capitalist.

THE TRADING HONGS

Jardine, Matheson & Co., Ltd., Hutchison Whampoa, Ltd., Wheelock and Company, Ltd., and Swire Pacific, Ltd., are the four old British *hongs* (trading conglomerates). They have dominated and controlled the economy of Hong Kong in this century. The significant impact of these hongs is reflected in Richard Hughes's (1976) comment in his book, *Borrowed Place, Borrowed Time:* "Hong Kong is ruled by Jardine Matheson, the Stewards of The Royal Hongkong Jockey Club, the Hongkong & Shanghai Bank, and the governor, in that order of descending importance." These hongs controlled every single aspect of the Hong Kong economy and played an important role in developing Hong Kong into a major trading, manufacturing, and financial center. In 1988, 14 hongs earned 75.4% of the total earnings of the 33 companies in the Hang Seng Index.

In the next section, the adaptive process of some large hongs—old English hongs, Chinese hongs, and now the new PRC hongs—will be discussed.

ADAPTIVE STRATEGIES OF THE OLD AND NEW HONGS

Jardine, Matheson & Co.

Jardine, Matheson & Co. is the oldest British hong. It was named after its founders, William Jardine and James Matheson, two well-known and experienced Far East traders from Scotland. The company was incorporated in 1832 in Canton and started its trading activities in China. In 1841, the company moved its headquarters to Hong Kong. Today its business base is mainly in the Asia-Pacific region, but it also has significant interests in the United Kingdom, Continental Europe, and the United States. Its activities cover import/export, shipping, railways, insurance, manufacturing, real estate, financing, and more. The group has operations in 30 territories and employs more than 140,000 people. Its intensive international diversification into Hawaii, South Africa, Saudi Arabia, Australia, and the United Kingdom helped it in internationalizing its business. Jardine Pacific's activities include (a) trading and distribution—primarily alcohol and luxury consumer goods; (b) construction—Gammon, jointly owned by Jardine Pacific and the United Kingdom's Trafalgar House; (c) fast food—franchises for Pizza Hut; (d) motor vehicles—Jardine International Motor Holdings, sole distributor of Mercedes Benz; and (e) information technology. In addition to its existing businesses, Jardine has further diversified into transportation, hotels, and tourism.

Compared with other British hongs, Jardine is less aggressive and more conservative in expanding its China business, partly rationalized by its massive losses through asset seizure in Shanghai in 1949. Jardine has used a defensive strategy, whereas others rushed to capture China's huge potential. Jardine's trading activities in China ended in heavy loss when the communists took over China in 1949. During the 1980s, the group embarked on a strategy to try to reduce its exposure in Hong Kong. In 1984, Jardine was the first to move its corporate headquarters from Hong Kong to Bermuda, before the Sino-British Joint Declaration was signed. Re-domiciling to Bermuda gave its assets protection against communist incursion post-1997. Jardine's strategies included selling noncore business assets and diversifying into overseas markets. Hong Kong Land sold major chunks of its Hong Kong property portfolio. Its emphasis was on a liquid-type firm. In September 1992, Jardine's primary share listing was transferred to the London Stock Exchange. The group's focus is now overseas, de-emphasizing China.

The Jardine group had a difficult time and nearly went bankrupt through a disastrous combination of heavy debt and high interest rates in the early 1980s. The company's trouble was caused by a crisis of confidence, the plunging of the Hong Kong dollar, uncertainty about China's intentions, and the collapse of the property market. The company survived and narrowly avoided bankruptcy in 1983-1984. As managing director Keswick pointed out, "It took 150 years to make your reputation and you can lose it in a day." The Jardine empire was reorganized. At the top is Jardine Matheson Holdings, which joins Jardine Strategic. Beneath this, split into many branches, are the numerous hotel, trading, food, insurance, and other subsidiaries. The new Jardine is simpler and leaner. It took 8 years to turn the company around and make it an economic power again. Today, the multinational conglomerate represents 10% of the capitalization of the Hong Kong Stock Exchange.

The impact of Jardine's strategic move was immense. Chinese authorities in Beijing attacked the Jardine Matheson group in December 1992 for its open support of Governor Cris Patten's political reform proposal. The attack caused the group's stock value to drop by HK$4.4 billion (4.2%) in one day. Jardine was the target of attack because of its involvement in the opium trade in China and the unequal treaties of Nanking in the 1800s. Jardine was seen as a symbol of colonial commerce and rule because it had maintained close links with the inner circle of the British government and represented the British corporate interest in Hong Kong. Its poor relationship with China caused an underperformance of Jardine's stock in the past few years. Jardine announced its decision to delist from the Hong Kong Stock Exchange at the end of 1994.

In recent years, Hong Kong and China accounted for 68% of its profits by geographical breakdown. In 1993, Jardine's top management visited China, aiming at a change in strategic direction. The group was actively pursuing new business opportunities in China. Jardine operated 30 small to medium-sized joint ventures in China. Jardine International Motor Holdings sold 300 Mercedes in China in 1992. The U.K.-based Robert Fleming, one of the oldest China funds, has offices in Beijing, Shanghai, and Guangzhou. Its retail chains include 7-11 franchises, Dairy Farm, and supermarket outlets in China.

Jardine tried to distance itself from its most profitable base and diversify its business and go international in order to reduce its political risks after 1997. Because of past decisions and actions, it is now difficult for Jardine to deal with the PRC. Hutchison Whampoa and CITIC Pacific are more apt to emerge as potential replacements for Jardine and to acquire the same magnitude of economic and political influence of other hongs, such as Swire.

Swire Pacific Ltd.

Swire Pacific Ltd. was set up by John Samuel Swire in 1880. Its original name was Taikoo Dockyard and Engineering Company of Hong Kong Ltd. It changed to the present name in 1974. Its original dockyard site was developed into a major residential and commercial estate. Today its business lines include Cathay Pacific Airway, a British-owned flag carrier for Hong Kong. Aviation accounts for 56% of the group's profit and 65% of the group's turnover. Other business activities include property, offshore oil, shipping services, Swire Bottlers Ltd., Coca-Cola Swire Beverage Ltd., trading, and insurance.

Swire's China strategy focuses on developing firm alliances in the PRC. It entered a number of substantial strategic alliances with China International Trust and Investment Corporation (CITIC), the PRC's investment arm. The cross-shareholding between Swire and CITIC began when CITIC injected $1 billion in exchange for a Cathay Pacific shareholding in 1987. Swire and Cathay jointly owned Dragonair (over 70%), a Hong Kong airline with flights into China. Dragonair's performance was better than Cathay Pacific's, results due to notable increases in capacity in China, particularly in Beijing and Shanghai. Swire Pacific sold one third of its shareholding in Swire Aviation to CITIC Pacific, giving the mainland investment vehicle exposure to Hong Kong Air Cargo Terminals (HACTL). The deal strengthened its ties with CITIC Pacific and added further support to HACTL's bid for the air cargo franchise at the new airport in Chek Lap Kok. In June 1996, a strategic move further integrated the parties (Swire and CITIC). CITIC Pacific increased its stake in Cathay Pacific Airways from 10% to 25%. Simultaneously, CITIC sold 17.6% of the Hong Kong Dragon Airlines (Dragonair) to the China National Aviation Corporation (CNAC). Politically, the arrangements were seen as significant in ending the growing uncertainty over the future of Hong Kong's British dominated aviation industry. The deal removed the political uncertainty that had been hanging over Cathay. Swire sold control of Cathay Pacific Airways, but this seemed to be the price of political accommodation with the 1997 handover. The move allowed

CNAC to control a large stake of Dragonair and to have its own international airline operating out of the territory. Swire's policy is seen as making a gradual and pragmatic withdrawal.

The Swire group was careful in formulating a China strategy. It formed cozy relationships with China and its state enterprises. The cross-shareholding further tightened its bonds to China, reducing the risks attached to the handover of Hong Kong's sovereignty to China in 1997 (Smith, 1993, p. 1). Swire Pacific joined with Peninsular & Oriental Steam Navigation Co. (P & O) to take equal shares (25% each) in a $615 million China joint venture to take half of the Shekou Container Terminal (Hewett, 1993, p. 20). Swire Pacific and Coca-Cola Bottling set up joint ventures in China and Taiwan to bottle Coca-Cola in Nanjing and Hangzhou; produce ice cream, soft drinks, and snack food in Guanghou; and produce aluminum beverage cans in Foshan. Cathay Pacific has operated a computerized accounting and reservations system in Guanghou. Another joint venture was formed for Hong Kong Aircraft Engineering (HAECO), building an aircraft maintenance facility in Xiamen. Swire Pacific's parent company— John Swire and Sons Ltd., based in London—reopened an office in Shanghai. The company has pursued partnership with Chinese interests (closer to the central power) in part to avoid being viewed as thoroughly colonial, thus reducing the risk attached to the handover of Hong Kong's sovereignty to China.

The relationships strengthen Swire's grip on existing business in Hong Kong by tightening the interlocking alliances. A financial analyst pointed out that "if Swire has confidence in Hong Kong's future, setting up a close relationship with China's investment arm is a smart move." It concentrates its business activities with the Hong Kong-China-Taiwan triangle. In a marked contrast to rival hongs, such as Jardine, the Swire group mapped out a clear strategy toward China: the pursuit of strategic alliances with PRC organizations. It appears that it carried this out gradually, with a high degree of caution and with strategic allies in mind. The big difference between Jardine and Swire is that the Swire group is seen to be making a commitment to China. At an extremely politically sensitive time, Swire simply played the game more aggressively than Jardine.

The Hong Kong and
Shanghai Banking Corporation (HSBC)

The Hong Kong and Shanghai Banking Corporation (HSBC) was founded in Shanghai in 1865 and was incorporated in Hong Kong in 1866. Branches were set up simultaneously in Hong Kong and Shanghai to finance the development of trade between China and the United States and Europe. Between the 1940s and the 1990s, the HSBC developed from a regional bank to a global bank. The bank, together with its subsidiaries and associated companies, provides a comprehensive range of commercial and investment banking, insurance, and other financial and related services through a global network of more than 3,000 offices in 66 countries in Asia, Europe, the Middle East, Australia, and America.

HSBC plays the role of a quasi-central bank in Hong Kong and serves as banker to the Hong Kong Government. It runs the clearing house in Hong Kong and issues more than 80% of Hong Kong's currency. It is a prominent member of the Hong Kong Association of Banks (HKAB), which acts as a medium of regulation for changes in the deposit interest rate of licensed banks. The special relationship with the government and special power in the Hong Kong banking industry give HSBC some competitive advantages. HSBC dominates consumer and business lending and controls approximately 55% of the total deposits in Hong Kong.

Hongkong Bank launched an aggressive acquisition campaign to become a global bank. HSBC made a first step in its global ambitions in the 1980s when it racked up billions in losses on a takeover of the Buffalo, New York-based Marine Midland Bank Inc. and loans to Canadian real estate developer Olympia & York Development Ltd. The group troubleshot its failing overseas subsidiaries and turned them around. Knowing about China's intention for the future of Hong Kong, it accelerated its overseas acquisition and diversification. In December 1990, the Hongkong Bank reorganized the group under a new holding company, HSBC Holdings plc. In 1991, HSBC Holdings plc was incorporated in England. Hongkong Bank is the principal subsidiary of the new group, with dual primary listings on the stock exchanges of London and Hong Kong. In 1993, HSBC Holdings successfully took over Midland Bank, the fourth largest bank in Britain, and gained a major European presence. The transaction created a bank holding company with assets of HK$1.9 trillion and 3,200 branches and offices throughout the world. Now Hongkong Bank owns Hang Seng Bank, New York Marine Midland, Marine Midland of Canada, British Bank of the Middle East, Cyprus Bank, and Hong Kong Bank of Australia. With its global network in Asia, Europe, and North America, HSBC takes advantage of time zone changes and transactions are processed 24 hours a day.

HSBC's overseas operations were not as successful as its performance in the Asia Pacific region. The Asia Pacific region comprises 37% of the group's total assets but contributes more than half of the group's profit. Top management perception is that China offers potential for financial development. Hongkong Bank is trying to establish its preeminence in China. It has 13 offices scattered throughout many major ports on the China coast. Growth through acquisition has been one of the major reasons for success in the globalization of the Hongkong Bank.

New Chinese Hongs

In the traditional hongs described previously, top management positions are held primarily by British/Anglo-Saxons. The new dominant organizations in Hong Kong are headed by Chinese Taipans. They are very entrepreneurial and deeply involved in the economic development of China. The prominent new hongs are: Li Ka-shing's Cheung Kong (Holdings), Hutchison Whampoa, Peter Woo's Wharf Holdings, Gordon Wu's Hopewell, and Cheng Yu-Tung's New World Development.

Li Ka-shing, nicknamed Superman, represents the new generation of Chinese Taipans, coming from a rice field in Chiu Chow (China) and ending up as Hong Kong's richest man. His firm, Cheung Kong (Holdings) Limited, also the parent company of Hutchison Whampoa, was incorporated in 1971 as a property owner and developer. In 1979, Li Ka-shing acquired a 22.8% share (subsequently increased to 40.8%) of the old British hong, Hutchison Whampoa. The Cheung Kong group formed a joint venture with China Resources (Holdings) Co. Ltd. to develop a site in Tin Shui Wai into a mass residential estate. In 1992, sales of properties accounted for 86% of its turnover and 60% of the profits. It has been active in forming relationships with PRC firms. It actively participated as minority interests in consortiums led by PRC interests to take over controlling interests in listed companies such as Tung Wing Steel Holdings Ltd. and International Tak Cheung Holdings Ltd. It also teamed up with a "China hong," CITIC Pacific Ltd., to make an $8.8 billion takeover bid for Mirama Hotel and Investment Co. Ltd. Hotel operations include Hong Kong Hilton and the Bali Hyatt.

Cheung Kong is keen to explore investment opportunities in property. In one development with Fuzhou City, the group holds 64.3% interest. It is also involved in power plant projects in China with Hopewell. A consortium composed of Kumagai Gumi (HK) Limited (30%), three banks from China (35%), Ringo Trading Ltd. (20%), and the group (10%), signed an agreement to develop land in Hainan. Mr. K.-S. Li, a trusted advisor to Beijing, won the multibillion dollar Yantian port project in Shenzhen.

In June 1996, Cheung Kong announced intentions to spin off and streamline its infrastructure business. Cheung Kong Infrastructure Holdings's portfolio includes local cement, concrete, and quarry operations, together with 19 mainland projects (e.g., power plants, toll roads, and bridges). Its market value is estimated at $17 billion and it forecasts a profit of more than $70 million.

Mr. Peter Woo, the son-in-law of the late shipping magnate, Sir Y. K. Pao, is the new Taipan of Wheelock and Company Limited, which was incorporated in 1918 in Shanghai as The Loan and Investment Company Limited to engage in security investment and the advancement of loans. In 1946, the company transferred its center of operation to Hong Kong. In 1980, the company acquired 30% (subsequently increased to 45%) in Wharf (Holdings) Limited. Under Wheelock Pacific are investment, retailing (Lane Crawford), distribution, trading, security, computer service, and travel. The Wheelock Properties (China) operations include Hong Kong Development, with plenty of land banked in Hong Kong and China. In 1993, property-related business contributed 79% of the pretax profit. The group signed a joint venture deal with Guangzhou Fangcum District Urban Construction Development Corp. to develop two sites in Guangzhou. It intends to commit about 10% of its balance sheet to China development. It also develops partnerships to advance selective projects that would help economic development in China.

Gordon Wu is a different type of entrepreneur with a vision of constructing the largest and most significant infrastructure for the development of China. His company, Hopewell, was incorporated in 1972. Its principal activities are building construction, project investment, and hotel operations. Huge construction and infrastructure projects are being undertaken in China, such as hotel operations, power plants, and superhighways. In 1983, the company entered a 50% joint venture to redevelop the Shenzhen Railway Terminal and the Customers and Frontier Inspection Building on the Hong Kong-China border. Other joint venture projects in China include 20% of China Hotel Complex, power plant stations, bridges, a superhighway connecting Guangzhou-Shenhen-Zhuhai, and property investment and development. The company's infrastructure business also diversified geographically into the Philippines and Bangkok.

Another China player is New World Development, which was incorporated in 1970. The company's chief executive, Cheng Yu-tung, was named Hong Kong's Executive of the Year in 1993. The group's principal activities are well diversified into hotel operations, investment, and development of property. Hotel operation (The New World Hotel, Ramada International Hotels and Resorts) has been one of its major business activities. In 1982, it participated in the property development of eight station sites along the Mass Transit Railway Corporation's Island Line. Seventy-one percent of the group's profits were derived from property sales, and 34% from rental income.

Jointly owned by the group (46.2%) and the U.S.-based Sea-Land Orient Terminal Limited (53.8%), it operated Berth 3 of the Kwai Chung Container Terminal. It also entered a consortium comprising Jardine Pacific, HK Ltd., Sea-Land Orient Terminals, Sun Hung Kai Properties, Sinotrans, and Hanjin to negotiate for the development of the $10 billion Container Terminal No. 9.

The group has been active in seeking out opportunities in the infrastructure development in Southern China. Since 1988, the company has been involved in a number of infrastructure constructions, as well as power plants, highway projects, and huge land developments in various regions in China. Between 20% and 25% of the group's net asset value is designated for investment in the PRC with a primary focus on infrastructure and property development projects. The group entered into a joint venture contract with Guangzhou Freeway Company in 1990 to design and construct Section No. 2 highway. The group is entitled to 40% of the profits for a concession period of 33 years. It also formed joint ventures with municipal and provincial governments to construct Shenhen-Huizhou Expressway and Guangzhou Zuhai Expressway. The Guangzhou Electricity Power Station is a 50-50 joint venture between the group and municipal governments to build two 300MW coal-field electricity power plants. The joint ventures are fully supported by municipal government authorities. Through joint ventures with these PRC partners, and with minimal capital investments for land costs, the group has succeeded in establishing a strong presence in China.

Another new hong, originating in Communist China but operated in the laissez faire economy of Hong Kong, is China International Trust and Investment Corporation (CITIC), headed by the red capitalist, Yung Chi-kin. CITIC, the PRC's national MNC, was set up in 1979 under the State Council in the PRC to negotiate and implement foreign investment and technology and to introduce foreign enterprises that wish to engage in joint ventures to prospective Chinese partners. It has operations in North America, Europe, and Asia, most prominently in Hong Kong. CITIC Pacific Ltd. in Hong Kong was incorporated in 1985 under the name Tylfull Co., Ltd. CITIC has a significant Hong Kong presence, with major investments in more than 500 Hong Kong enterprises. It builds extensive strategic alliances with local hongs, including Cheung Kong (Holdings), Swire Pacific, and Wharf (Holdings). Today, its business portfolio and operations include investment holdings, airline operations, trading and distribution, warehouses, property investment, telecommunications, and power generation. Its strategic stakes penetrate into every single activity in Hong Kong.

CITIC's investment in Hong Kong is estimated to be $16.6 billion through various affiliates. In August 1992, it became a constituent stock in calculating the Hang Seng Stock Index. CITIC's market capitalization was $28,220M, with

P/E ratio of 17.8, turnover of 8,384M. It is Hong Kong's number one Red Chip stock. According to a Sunday Money Survey of 15 leading brokerages, CITIC was ranked first in all five categories: best quality, transparency and management, value for long-term investment, financial strength, and regard for minority shareholders (Wong, 1993).

CONCLUDING REMARKS

The next century will probably be designated as the Pacific century. China is recognized as a major participant in international business and an emerging economic power. China's vigorous economic growth has contributed to the momentum of Hong Kong's economy. Hong Kong will benefit from the economic growth in Southern China. In the future, a significant proportion of strategic investment and revenues are going to be in Asia; more specifically, China. Yet China still has a lot to learn about the rules of the game in the international market. There is an increasing interdependent relationship between Hong Kong and China. Trade between Hong Kong and China is already more than U.S. $127 billion per year. Post-1997, Hong Kong and Southern China are clearly integrated economically. The 1997 handover offers both opportunities and threats. Hong Kong companies have long been at the forefront of an adaptable trading center linking East and West. According to a survey conducted by Mckinsey and Co., leading multinational companies are moving aggressively into China to build up market share to pre-empt entry by their big rivals. These multinational firms went through an initial learning process and are moving into the second stage of involvement in China, focusing on establishing relationships with authorities (Chen, 1994). Finding and cultivating good local partners remains vital for success.

Alliance and global diversification are commonly used strategies in managing political risk. Alliances have become an integral part of contemporary strategic thinking and provide the means to learn the Chinese way of doing business. Maintaining good relationships and cultivating a tie with China's elite are good strategies to ensure future positions in the post-1997 era. The big hongs are forming strategic alliances with Chinese partners as a means of stepping into the China market, as well as allowing them to face the outcomes of the 1997 handover with confidence through the support of their Chinese business allies. On the other hand, the Chinese partners have gained from these large trading houses by acquiring expertise for entering the international market. A synergy has been created between economic interests in Hong Kong and the PRC. Both parties will benefit from the alliance by fully utilizing the skills and expertise provided by these hongs.

So far, these large trading hongs have had little difficulty adapting their business strategies, much less so than the political institutions.

POSTSCRIPT

In the latter part of 1997, an economic crisis hit Asia. Starting in Thailand and Indonesia, it spilled over into the neighboring economies, given their strong interdependencies and interrelationships. Of course, Japan had been mired in a recession since 1990 and the crisis seemingly didn't impact on it as much as others. The Indonesian currency devalued by nearly 85% compared to the U.S. dollar. The Thai baht fell by 64% from July to November. The South Korean currency devalued by nearly 50% to the dollar.

How did the Hongs adapt? There had already been some repercussions from the July 1 conversion. Cathay Pacific, the Hong Kong airline, gave way to a PRC government agency that threatened to bring a new airline into the local scene. Cathay sold them a considerable amount of stock at a very favorable price to avoid the additional competition. Jimmy Lai, the founder of Giordano, resigned after his stores' leases in China were cancelled. He had referred to a prominent Chinese politician as a "turtle's egg."

Hopewell, the aggressive construction company, had its $25 billion contract with the Thai government to build Bangkok's mass transit rail system canceled.

The Chinese-listed firms on the Hong Kong stock market that had outperformed the local stocks lost approximately 30% of their value along with the rest of the market—from over 1,600 in July-August to less than 900. But since they had recently issued their first shares on the market, they are quite liquid-heavy in cash—and in an advantageous position to acquire local firms and assets.

Hong Kong's and China's economies are expected to continue their strong growth. A leading, if not *the* leading, Asian business magazine, *The Far East Economic Review,* reports the following economic growth rates (1997, Special Issue, p. 144):

China	1997	9.0%
	1998	9.0%

Hong Kong	1997	5.5%
	1998	4.0%
Japan	1997	1.9%
	1998	1.9%
Malaysia	1997	7.5%-7.0%
	1998	4%-5%
South Korea	1997	6.0%
	1998	2.5%
Taiwan	1997	6.7%
	1998	6.7%

In short, China and Hong Kong are forecast to have two of the highest growth rates in Asia. Their currencies are still safe, protected by large international reserves; China, over $125 billion. The Hong Kong government's estimate of its surplus for the fiscal year, $31.7 billion, has been recalculated to be over $55 billion. Tourism to Hong Kong has dropped off—by more than 30%—and Cathay Pacific is reducing its number of flights and employees, but a 4% economic growth rate is still envied by other economies at their level of development.

After the handover, a Chinese political leader was asked about the reevaluation possibilities for the Hong Kong dollar. His response was indicative of the PRC-Hong Kong relationship as of this time—interdependent economically but relatively autonomous politically, or, as they are fond of saying, "one country-two systems."

REFERENCES

Chen, K. (1994, February 16). Giants in China build-up. *South China Morning Post,* Business Post p. 1.

Davis, K. (1990). *Hong Kong to 1994: A question of confidence* (Special Report, Great Britain No. 20-22). London: The Economist Intelligence Unit.

H shares brighten to outshine index. (1993, October 27). *South China Morning Post,* Business Post p. 4.

Hewett, G. (1993, November 23). Firm alliances form Swire's China tactics. *South China Morning Post,* p. 20.

Hughes, R. (1976). *Borrowed place, borrowed time: Hong Kong and its faces.* London: A. Deutsh.

Smith, C. S. (1993, December 2). Swire Pacific stakes future on cozy ties with China. *Asian Wall Street Journal,* p. 1.

Wong, K. (1993, July 25). CITIC tops all five categories in survey. *China Business Review,* p. 1.

World stocks. (1998, February 20). *Asia Week,* p. 60.

chapter 10

The Dominance of Greater China Multinationals' Investment in China

Economic, Cultural, and Institutional Perspectives

YADONG LUO

As the 1990s have progressed, China's emergence as an economic giant has become increasingly apparent. If China continues at the present rate of growth, the World Bank expects that it will become the world's largest economy by the early 21st century. This is largely due to the fact that China presently enjoys the second greatest amount of foreign direct investment (FDI) in the world, surpassed only by the United States. The dominance of foreign investment from the Chinese community, namely Hong Kong (including Macao), Taiwan, and Singapore, in mainland China has not only spurred integration between the Chinese economy and the international business community but has also served to intensify the substantial impact of the greater China area on global trade and investment flow.

Since 1979, when China officially opened its doors to foreign investment, and up through the end of 1995, Chinese authorities approved the establishment of over 258,444 foreign-invested enterprises, involving $400.63 billion in foreign capital. Of those approved ventures, about 120,000, representing $137.80

TABLE 10.1 Statistics of Foreign Direct Investment in China: From 1979 Through 1995 (U.S. $1,000,000)

Year	Total Foreign Investment		Direct Foreign Investment		Other Foreign Investment*
	Number of Contracts	Value (billion $)	Number of Contracts	Value (billion $)	Value (billion $)
Approved investment					
1979-1982	922	6,999	922	6,010	989
1983	470	1,917	470	1,732	185
1984	1,856	2,875	1,856	2,651	224
1985	3,073	6,333	3,073	5,932	401
1986	1,498	3,330	1,498	2,834	496
1987	2,233	4,319	2,233	3,709	610
1988	5,945	6,191	5,945	5,297	894
1989	5,779	6,294	5,779	5,600	694
1990	7,273	6,987	7,273	6,596	391
1991	12,978	12,422	12,978	11,977	445
1992	48,764	58,736	48,764	58,124	612
1993	83,037	111,966	83,037	111,435	531
1994	47,490	81,971	47,490	81,406	565
1995	37,126	90,288	37,126	89,738	550
1979-1995	258,444	400,628	258,444	393,041	7,587
Realized investment					
1979-1982		1,767		1,166	601
1983		916		636	280
1984		1,419		1,258	161
1985		1,959		1,661	298
1986		2,244		1,874	370
1987		2,647		2,314	333
1988		3,739		3,194	545
1989		3,773		3,392	381
1990		3,755		3,487	268
1991		4,666		4,366	300
1992		11,291		11,007	284
1993		27,769		27,514	255
1994		34,122		33,787	335
1995		37,736		37,379	357
1979-1995		137,803		133,035	4,768

SOURCE: Data for 1979-1992: from *China Statistical Yearbook* (1993), English Edition, China State Statistical Bureau, 1993, p. 587. Data for 1993: from *The Bulletin of the Ministry of Foreign Trade and Economic Cooperation of the People's Republic of China,* Issue No. 2, 1994 (Serial No. 20), p. 10. Data for 1994: from the above *Bulletin,* Issue No. 1, 1995 (Serial No. 25), p. 13. Data for 1995: from *Foreign Investment in China,* China FIEs Association, *96*(4), Serial No. 41.
NOTE: * Other foreign investments include the value of equipment or materials supplied by foreign businesses in transactions of (a) international leasing, (b) compensation trade, and (c) processing and assembling.

TABLE 10.2 Foreign Direct Investment in China From Ten Major Countries or Regions in 1994 (Unit: U.S.$10,000)

		Actual FDI		Contractual FDI	
Rank	*Country or Region*	*Value*	*Percentage of Nation's Total*	*Value*	*Percentage of Nation's Total*
1. Hong Kong & Macao		2,017,481	59.75	4,869,252	56.81
2. Taiwan		339,104	10.04	539,488	6.53
3. United States		249,080	7.38	601,018	7.27
4. Japan		207,529	6.15	444,029	5.37
5. Singapore		117,961	3.49	377,796	4.57
6. South Korea		72,283	2.14	180,626	2.18
7. Britain		68,884	2.04	274,838	3.32
8. Germany		25,899	0.77	123,314	1.49
9. Canada		21,605	0.64	89,033	1.08
10. Italy		20,616	0.61	22,533	
Top Ten Total		3,140,442	93.01	7,521,927	90.97
Chinese community investment		2,474,546	73.28	5,786,536	69.99
Nation's Total		3,376,650	100.00	8,267,977	100.00

SOURCE: *The Bulletin of the Ministry of Foreign Trade and Economic Cooperation* (MOFTEC) *of the People's Republic of China,* Issue No. 2, 1995 (Serial No. 26), April 25, 1995.

billion in investment, commenced operation (see Table 10.1). By 1996, the industrial output and import/export volume of foreign ventures reached 13% and 39.10%, respectively, of the nation's total, employing about 16 million Chinese in 1995 (*Foreign Investment in China,* 1996). Among the FDI modes of entry, the international equity joint venture remains dominant, accounting for 52% of total FDI value in 1994 (*Bulletin of the Ministry of Foreign Trade and Economic Cooperation* [MOFTEC], 1995).

Foreign direct investment in China originates from two primary sources: Chinese community investors and Western multinationals. Although more than 40 countries from all over the world have directly invested in China ("New Patterns," 1995), as shown in Table 10.2, almost three quarters (73.29%) of the total FDI in the country has come from the Chinese community: Hong Kong and Macao (59.75%), Taiwan (10.04%) and Singapore (3.49%), comprising approximately four times the amount undertaken by Western multinationals.

Given the paucity of research in this area, the aim of this study is to illuminate the underlying rationale and to suggest viable reasons why Chinese community investors have come to dominate foreign direct investment in mainland China. For Western multinationals contemplating investment in China, today's fastest growing global economy, a look into the insights and investment rationale of their major rivals is helpful for making strategic investment decisions. Comparing the nature and distinctiveness of their own competencies with those of competitors in the host country will also enable Western multinationals to properly formulate and implement corporate-level strategies (e.g., industry selection and project-type selection) as well as business-level strategies (e.g., marketing, production, R&D, advertising). I will also explore the underlying factors contributing to the dominance of FDI established in the mainland by Chinese community investors, using economic, cultural, and institutional perspectives.

ECONOMIC PERSPECTIVES

Competence Complementarity

A fundamental driving force of cross-border cooperation lies in economic self-interest, in the exploitation of market potential or complementary resources, abilities, and skills (Hamel, 1991). Although Chinese community investors may not have competitive advantages in advanced technologies, which constitute a scarce competence necessary to the modernization of China's economy, they can greatly assist the mainland in commercializing Chinese scientists' research and inventions. A major strength of the Chinese technological system is the vast number of highly trained scientists performing quality basic and applied research. According to government data, by 1990 China had 400,000 employees working in 15,000 nongovernmental scientific research institutions, as well as unspecified thousands working in over 5,000 state-owned R&D institutions and over 1,000 tertiary educational institutions (*China Statistical Yearbook,* 1990). Unfortunately, the country's strength in basic research does not extend to the successful commercialization of research results. In the past, China's scientific and technological system was not known for introducing innovative products, particularly those combining multiple technologies, to global markets. As a result, China must learn to access expertise in commercialization; it is in these parts of the innovation process that Taiwan, Singapore, and Hong Kong can play an important role.

In recent years, Taiwan has emerged as a capable competitor among world leaders in the production and design of quality consumer electronics, computers, memory chips, and microprocessors. Expertise in these areas, while initially acquired through technology transfer, was followed by a sustained effort to enhance the ability to modify, develop, and produce domestically. Taiwan has also cultivated extensive technological linkages with other major leaders, particularly the United States, so as to continue having a source of technology to transfer. In particular, it is the Taiwanese who have studied abroad and worked in prominent firms, and have returned to bring with them a wealth of professional expertise in technical areas, business, and contacts. Hence, Taiwan has gained sound development and design capabilities through its own domestic efforts as well as the newfound knowledge brought back by its returning professionals. In addition, through its exporting success, the island has accumulated substantial foreign exchange reserves while facilitating an increase in wages and other factor costs. As a result, Taiwan appears to have become relatively strong in terms of development and design capabilities, capital, and linkages to the world's technical and business communities.

Hong Kong is renowned in the world as a commercial and financial center. Since its founding as a trade entrepôt over a century ago, the naturally resource-poor territory relied upon its trading and sales know-how to survive. In doing so, it wisely capitalized on its strategic location, ample harbor, and supportive government policies to become a worldwide commercial port. Postwar industrialization, the transition to a service and financial center, and subsequent maturation of Hong Kong's domestic market further developed its financial networks, infrastructure, and capabilities. Today, despite political uncertainty, Hong Kong serves the region's executives in the areas of finance, telecommunications, transport, and shipment. In addition, its businesses continue to buy, sell, and market goods in all parts of the world, serving the needs of the emerging Chinese market in particular. As China's economic reforms deepen, Hong Kong once again serves as an important entry point for many international firms seeking to do business with China.

Singapore is another resource-poor country; however, a strategic location along international shipping and air routes, combined with well-trained and resourceful manpower, sound management skills, and a supportive external environment, led to dynamic economic growth and a robust economy. The positive impact resulted in an apparently superior Singapore-MNC (multinational corporation) partnership, providing an international gateway for the products manufactured by FDI projects established in China. Moreover, while Singapore is in need of raw materials and a source of inexpensive products and offshore manufacturing, China needs manufactured products, machinery, advanced technical expertise, and management skills. Thus, Singapore finds itself in the enviable position of being able to offer strategic alliances to international companies seeking a base from which to launch and manage investment projects in China. In addition, investors originating in Singapore can also tap into the Southeast Asian market, of increasing importance as China pursues global market diversification in an effort to reduce its dependence on the markets of the United States and Japan. Moreover, Singapore, a country of 2.7 million people, has foreign exchange reserves exceeding $34 billion. As one of the largest financial centers in the Asia and Pacific region, Singapore investors are able to provide abundant capital resources for upcoming investment projects to be established in China.

The preceding section suggests that the three Chinese economies have different capabilities related to innovation, and that they could benefit by pooling their complementary capabilities and manufacturing their products in mainland China's investment sites, through either a technology-push or a market-pull process. In a market-pull process, starting from the downstream-market end, Hong Kong and Taiwanese firms, after identifying a particular market need, would design a product demanded by the market, raise the necessary capital, and produce it on the mainland. The finished goods would be shipped through the port of Hong Kong into international markets. China's researchers would provide technical input into product design and production. In a technology-push process, the thousands of researchers in China would discover ideas for numerous potential products and processes. Taiwan's experts would utilize their Western educations and experience to guide the development and design processes, transforming the most promising findings from China's research into products capable of meeting market needs. With relatively low labor and production costs, China's business enterprises would then take the product specifications and produce technology-based, market-oriented goods in a cost-competitive manner. These products would then be marketed, distributed, and sold, to a large degree, by the business communities of Hong Kong and Singapore. The entire process would be fueled by capital from Hong Kong's numerous financial institutions and technological expertise from Taiwan.

Market Demand Similarity and Industry Life Cycle Distinction

Apart from market opportunities that are commonly available to all international investors, the dominance of Chinese community investment on the mainland is also attributable to the similarities in demand conditions, consumer utility functions, and consumer social and cultural backgrounds between the host and home markets. The rationale behind this location pattern is consistent with Linder's model in international economics that posits that the more similar the demand preferences for manufactured goods in two countries, the more intensive is the potential trade and investment manufactured between them (Linder, 1961). It is apparent that Chinese community investors are unlikely to possess the sort of firm-specific advantages on which the power of Western multinationals is based, namely the monopoly of technical knowledge, to engage in large-scale production. Similarly, the lack of sufficient market power makes it difficult to sell differentiated, branded goods worldwide (Lall, 1984). Chinese community investors make direct investment in China by committing and contributing their unique distinctive competencies, including technologies appropriate to the local environment such as factor costs, input characteristics, demand level, and consumption sophistication.

The industrial life cycle hypothesis in the FDI literature suggests that the vigor of FDI is contingent on the differential of the industrial or product life cycle phase between home and host countries (Vernon, 1979). It is evident that industrial products and production processes from Taiwan, Hong Kong, and Singapore are being passed on in recent years to the next generation of territory—the mainland. The result is an increasing extent of intraregional foreign direct investment in the country. The division of labor in industrial production is both horizontal and vertical, resulting in increased volume of intraregional trade, increasing importance of FDI in technology transfer, and the transmission of industrial production from the layer of countries at one stage to those next in line. Although these greater China countries are adopting an export-oriented strategy, the degree of complementarity is in fact greater than the extent of competition. Members of this community now specialize in production processes according to their changing comparative advantages. Foreign direct investment has served to facilitate the development of specialization within the region.

Geographic Affinity and Production Factor Usage

It is apparent that geographic affinity represents an important factor contributing to the phenomenal growth of FDI initiated by Chinese community investors over the past years. Hong Kong and Macao are adjacent to Shenzhen and Zhuhai, both among the first four Special Economic Zones opened in 1979. Similarly, Taiwan is just opposite Xiamen, another Special Economic Zone located in Fujian province. Although Singapore is not as close to China as Hong Kong and Taiwan, it enjoys strong geographic advantages, not only due to its proximity to the mainland but also to its international air and sea routes, which straddle the time zones of Asia and Europe. It is at the heart of the economically dynamic Asia-Pacific region. For Chinese community investors, these geographic advantages reduce transportation costs and turnaround time for mainland production, obviously crucial in vertically integrated manufacturing.

The opening of China coincided with the emergence of severe labor shortages in Hong Kong, Singapore, and Taiwan and the need for restructuring within these three economies. There has been a large-scale movement of export-oriented, labor-intensive industry from Chinese community territories, particularly Hong Kong, to such mainland coastal areas as Guangdong, Fujian, Jiangsu, and Zhejiang. In addition, although international investors from Hong Kong, Taiwan, Singapore, and Macao are the major source of FDI in China, in a broad sense they are moving relatively labor-intensive activities into China in an attempt to escape rising labor costs and space constraints at home. Many Chinese community investors, particularly those from Hong Kong and Taiwan, have been operating in the same labor-intensive industries such as textiles, garments, electronics, electrical goods, metals, plastics, and toys—most have mature technologies that make up most of their prior exports. As the tightening labor market has raised wage costs in their home territories and economic expansion has made factory sites more and more expensive, moving production to China, where wage levels are fundamentally lower, becomes immensely attractive.

Chinese community businesses investing in capital-intensive or technology-intensive industries could also attain the benefits of cost minimization in the Chinese manufacturing sites. In addition to the labor cost concern, investors can acquire raw materials, semicompleted products, parts of machinery, components of equipment, and even patents at a price considerably lower than in the home market. As a result, lower direct costs of manufacturing as a result of shifting production sites to the mainland helps enhance international competitiveness (Lecraw, 1984).

CULTURAL PERSPECTIVE

Ethnic Ties

In addition to economic concerns, China's ability to attract Chinese community investors resides in ethnic ties. This can be seen from the fact that the incentives offered by the Chinese government are quite comparable to those offered by neighboring economies such as Indonesia and Malaysia, but international investors from the greater China area have undertaken much more outward investment in China than in Indonesia or Malaysia.

Contacts between China and the rest of Southeast Asia have a very long history, dating back to before the Han Dynasty (third century B.C.). There are at least 20 million ethnic Chinese living in three Indochinese states, six ASEAN (Association of Southeast Asian Nations) states, and Myanmar. However, the only state in Southeast Asia in which the Chinese are statistically dominant is Singapore. Since Stamford Raffles of the British East India Company established the colony as a free-trading port, Chinese, Indians, British, Arabs, and others have gone to Singapore in increasingly large numbers to take advantage of the economic opportunities there. By 1836, the Chinese numbered 13,700 and had overtaken the indigenous Malays, who at the time numbered only 12,500. The Chinese became the majority in 1849, making up about 53% of the total population. Today, 78% of the population is Chinese, numbering about 2.2 million, all having language, cultural, and family ties with China. Historically and culturally, Taiwan and Hong Kong have been an integral part of the mainland, and there are no obvious cultural differences existing between them and their ancestral land.

Ethnic ties have been a major influence on Chinese community-funded foreign direct investment in mainland China. There is striking evidence supporting this point: Since 1985, when the Pearl River Delta (in Guangdong), the Minnan Delta (in Fujian), and Hainan Island were designated as the three largest open regions able to offer investment incentives similar to those of the 14 open coastal cities and the four Special Economic Zones, the pattern of investment has appeared in a manner consistent with ethnic tie distributions. Specifically, investors from Hong Kong and Macao, most of them from Guangdong and Cantonese-speaking, have been focusing their investments on the Pearl River Delta. During the period from 1979 to 1993, the Pearl River Delta received one third of cumulative utilized FDI in China, and Hong Kong accounted for more than 80% of this flow. Guangdong was thus the destination of more than 40% of Hong Kong's FDI in the mainland (Sung, 1995). Similarly, their counterparts from Taiwan, most of them originating from Fujian and speaking the Minnan dialect, have been more actively engaging in the Minnan Delta. At the same time, Singapore investment projects are heavily located in Guandong, Fujian, and Hainan Island; this characteristic conforms with the ethnic feature in Singapore, where 94% of Singapore Chinese came from Guangdong, Fujian, and Hainan

Island (Kong, 1995). It is clear that ethnic relations have played an important role in spurring the Chinese community investment in the mainland and distributing the pattern of location of investment in the country.

One economic rationale behind the ethnic effect lies in the consideration of information and learning cost. Indeed, the cost of acquiring reliable information about foreign markets is large, and it is likely to seem particularly burdensome for the smaller international firms in developing countries. If someone trusted by the manager resides in the potential market, the cost of acquiring credible information is likely to be much lower than if the home office must send its personnel abroad to study opportunities. In most cases the initiatives for Chinese community businesses come from relatives or business associates in mainland China. With knowledge of the local market and access to a distribution system, these associates seek out foreign investors whom they know and trust. The role of ethnic ties also manifests itself in the partners chosen for the equity or contractual joint ventures in China. Many mainland-Chinese community partnerships are built between the same ethnically related parties.

Guanxi Networking

Another important cultural factor fostering Chinese community investment on the mainland has to do with *guanxi,* a concept that is somewhat related to ethnic ties. Its importance in the success of the Chinese community is commonly highlighted in the Chinese management literature. The Chinese word *guanxi* refers to the concept of drawing on connections or networks in order to secure favors in personal or business relations. For more than 2,000 years, Chinese culture has stressed the importance of social order. As early as the sixth century B.C., Confucius codified the individual, family, and societal ties that defined a person's proper role and position in his or her environment. Throughout China's long history of political upheavals, natural disasters, and economic scarcity, these well-defined relationships have often helped keep social chaos at bay. Traditional Chinese society is built around clan-like networks, with close family members constituting its core. Loyalty to the in-group is paralleled by a deep distrust of nonmembers. It must be understood that the concept of "family" extends largely beyond its strictly biological meaning. It can be pictured as a set of concentric circles of contacts, typically stretching from close family, to slightly distant, to more distant, and eventually embracing people who are not blood relatives but who are connected to someone in one's family or relatives, such as classmates, people from the same region, friends, friend's friends, and so on.

As Kao (1993) pointed out, the greater Chinese community encompasses an array of political and economic systems bound together by a shared tradition, not by geography. For many generations, emigrant Chinese entrepreneurs have been operating comfortably in a network of *guanxi*, laying the foundations for stronger links among businesses across national borders. Not based in any one country or continent, this community is primarily a network of entrepreneurial relationships consisting of many individual enterprises that nonetheless share a common Chinese culture. This network is an interconnected yet potentially open system and, in many aspects, provides a new market mechanism for conducting global business (Hwang, 1987). As a result, when Chinese-based economies such as Taiwan, Singapore, and Hong Kong have astonishingly large capital surpluses, financial resources will be deployed for new venture activities in these private and informal capital markets of Chinese family and clan associations without the intervention of commercial banks or government investment agencies. For instance, business links between Taiwan and mainland China were forged not through official channels but through *guanxi* networks or gray-market mechanisms. These peculiar advantages could contribute a variety of commercial privileges and a great deal of business potentials for the firm.

Networking of *guanxi* extends much farther than mere ethnic ties. In recent years many Chinese community investors have begun to locate FDI projects in regions other than Guangdong, Fujian, and Hainan. For instance, Hong Kong, Taiwan, and Singapore were all among the top five sources of FDI launched in Jiangsu province ("FDI in Jiangsu Province," 1996). It has been observed that the majority of local partners of joint ventures formed by Chinese community investors are their *guanxi hu*, or the organization in which the management has *guanxi* connections with the foreign investor. These local *guanxi hu* are usually local partners in previous business dealings such as import and export businesses, compensation trade, processing and assembly, international leasing, technology transfer, and other international business activities.

INSTITUTIONAL PERSPECTIVE

Home Government Roles

In an attempt to overcome the domestic constraints of limited resources and markets and to exploit the new opportunities available from the rapidly growing and liberalizing economies, particularly that of mainland China, various government agencies in Singapore, such as the Economic Development Board and the Trade Development Board, have provided enormous assistance and preferential treatment to the internationalization of business activities. While education is important anywhere, it was much more decisive in Singapore, where the only value-added asset was people and the government placed particular stress on not only imparting knowledge but inculcating proper attitudes and behavior. To accomplish this task, Singapore's government implemented programs to train workers and managers, for example, through the government-run Skills Development Fund. Local firms venturing abroad were also able to utilize the resources and expertise of state agencies and government-linked companies. Further encouragement was provided by two Sino-Singapore bilateral treaties: the 1985 Investment Protection Treaty and the 1986 Avoidance of Double Taxation Treaty in which the dividends paid out of profits from Singaporean investment in China became subject to only 7% withholding tax by the Chinese government, instead of the usual 10% applied to foreign investors. In addition, the Singapore government's efforts to promote the country as an investment gateway included such incentives as a reduced income tax on corporate profits (10% compared to 32%) for companies setting up regional headquarters in Singapore. By 1996, more than 20 world-class multinational firms had taken advantage of this opportunity, including Brown & Root, Data General, Molex, Foxboro, Phillips, Union Carbide, Sony, Deutsche Bank, Polysar, and Chloride Eastern. Many of these companies direct their investment in China from their Singapore offices.

The Hong Kong government has long kept intervention in inward and outward FDI flow at a minimum. In order to foster the healthy development of outward FDI to the mainland, government agencies such as the Trade Development Department in Hong Kong have assisted this flow in a very positive way. Under the guidance of government agencies, a number of investment funds specializing in China have been established, and these have invested in industry and B shares in the mainland. In 1992, the Hong Kong government helped the public listing of selected Chinese state-owned manufacturers on the Hong Kong Stock exchange (H shares and Red Chips). Apart from buying H shares and Red Chips, Hong Kong investors are also encouraged to purchase flats on the mainland. As a result of these developments, Hong Kong's already high share of China's contracted foreign investment rose from 61% in 1991 to 69% in 1992.

Relative to those of Singapore and Hong Kong, the Taiwanese government did not play a significantly positive role in facilitating outward FDI to the mainland, largely because of the absence of official ties across the strait.

Nevertheless, the fast-growing FDI on the mainland is indeed positively associated with the liberalization policy of Taiwan. Since 1987, the Taiwanese government has gradually liberalized import controls on the mainland products, including those manufactured in Taiwan-invested enterprises in China. As a result, the number of items that can be indirectly imported increased from 29 items in July 1987 to 1,654 items at the end of 1993 (Sung, 1995). Also in July 1987, Taiwan eased its foreign exchange controls and in November 1987 gave its citizens permission to visit relatives in mainland China. Furthermore, the quasi-governmental association whose primary function was to coordinate, assist, and promote bilateral exchanges across the strait was formed a few years ago. These policies are quite conducive to Taiwanese investment in the mainland.

Host Government Policies

The positive impact of the Chinese government's policies on the growth of FDI coming from greater China areas can be seen from two aspects. First, China's open-door policy and economic reforms have undergone a process of orderly expansion and gradual deepening. This character of the national policy greatly encourages the development of FDI undertaken by Chinese community investors. In 1979, special policies and flexible measures were adopted in Guangdong and Fujian provinces, and four Special Economic Zones were set up. Guangdong operates three such zones: the Shenzhen and Zhuhai, each only a half-hour train ride from Hong Kong and Macao, respectively, and the Shantou Special Economic Zone. Shantou has close links with populations of overseas Chinese, including a community in Singapore that originated in Shantou. Fujian operates the Xiamen Special Economic Zone, separated from Taiwan by a narrow strait. Since 1984, 14 port cities, Hainan Island, the deltas of the Pearl and Yangtze rivers, and the triangular area covering Xiamen, Zhangzhou, and Quangzhou in southern Fujian province have been turned into economic open zones that enjoy preferential policies in taxation, tariffs, financing, and the like. This locational pattern of openness can greatly assist Chinese community investors because of the advantages provided in geographical affinity and ethnic ties. As noted above, while most Taiwanese investors are ethnically connected with Fujianese and geographically close to Fujian province, the ancestors of Hong Kong investors were from Guangdong province, and these investors have geographical benefits in Guangdong province. This location pattern is also highly beneficial to Singapore businesses because they have been ethnically more closely associated with Hainan Island and the Pearl and Yangtze deltas.

On the other hand, the Chinese central government and local authorities have enacted a number of laws seeking to encourage FDI undertaken by the Chinese community investors. For instance, a 1988 State Council decree favors Taiwanese over other foreign investment in taxation and import controls. Also, the Law of Protection on Investments From Taiwan was issued by the State Council and approved by the National People's Congress at the beginning of 1994. According to this law, Taiwanese investment on the mainland is treated preferentially in terms of faster approval, better support services, and more concessions in tax and import controls. The governments of China and Singapore have established a periodic joint checkup system on the development of Singaporean business in China, and the Chinese government and its local agencies help find solutions to the problems Singapore investors encounter. In the Ministry of Foreign Trade and Economic Cooperation (MOFTEC), the department of Hong Kong and Macao business administration, formed in the early 1980s, has assisted greatly in fostering the healthy growth of direct investment made by Hong Kong firms. In addition, local governments such as Guangdong often provide favored treatment to Hong Kong investors.

Reverse Investment

From the very beginning of the reform period, China established overseas firms for outward investment. Subsequently—and interestingly—the overseas firms, notably those firms located in Hong Kong, Macao, and Singapore, returned to the home market to initiate more and more reverse investment, which is officially counted as FDI. Furthermore, various sources indicate that such reverse investment may account for a considerable part of the total FDI inflow in China. For instance, in the first 9 months of 1993, reverse investment launched by four China-invested companies operating in Hong Kong—the Bank of China Group, the China Resource Group, the China Travel Service Group, and the China Overseas Group—amounted to U.S.$1.5 billion, approximately 14% of China's total utilized investment inflow during the same period (Cao, 1994). In another report, a Hong Kong research institution estimated that by the end of 1991 a Chinese-invested company—the Guangdong Enterprises Group—made a total of HK$4 billion of direct investment in Guangdong province, accounting for 13% of the total FDI inflow in that province at that time. In general, China's overseas firms possess a double advantage due to their close relationships with higher People's Republic of China (PRC) authorities and their current identification as "foreign investors," providing them with a relatively strong strategic position for conducting business in China. Their intermediary role in connecting mainland China and the international markets appears to be increasing.

CONCLUDING REMARKS

The dominance of Chinese community investors in FDI established in China can be traced to both internal and external reasons. From an internal perspective, their complementary competence, geographic affinity, ethnic ties, and similar business cultures constitute critical contributions in fostering the dominance. From an external perspective, host and home government policy, market demand similarity, and different industry life cycles, as well as reverse investment, are also important factors promoting the dominance. Looking toward the future, these activities will not only promote awareness of Chinese customs and traditions among the overseas Chinese, but also bring economic benefits to both China and their home territories at large. The trend of increased networking will promote bonds as well as economic opportunities among them.

Although China plans to abolish favors to Chinese community investors as part of a reform package designed to help it gain entry to the World Trade Organization, the dominance of Chinese community-funded FDI is expected to continue due in large part to cultural, geographical, and other advantages. Indeed, the values, customs, traditions, religions, human relationships, and behaviors of a community do not change easily. China resumed sovereignty over Hong Kong in July 1997. The Sino-British Agreement specifies that Hong Kong will remain a separate customs territory and provides that China continue to treat Hong Kong investment on the mainland as "foreign" direct investment. Although there are very real political differences dividing the mainland and Taiwan, which may result in high political risk for investments, it is quite likely that Taiwan-funded FDI will keep increasing because neither the mainland nor the Taiwan government is trying to reverse the tendency toward liberalization of business development. In summary, economic forces point to a continuation of rapid economic integration within the greater China area. This hinges, however, on whether China can preserve law and order in the post-Deng era. If China does manage to maintain stability, and it does continue its pragmatic policy of reform, then it is safe to assume that Chinese community investors will continue to move to the mainland and that the community will continue to prosper at the present pace.

REFERENCES

Bulletin of the Ministry of Foreign Trade and Economic Cooperation (MOFTEC). (1995). People's Republic of China. Issue No. 2 (Serial No. 26).

Cao, H. (1994). China capital plays important role in the development of China-Hong Kong economic cooperation and trade. *Economic Reporter, 49,* 2351-2352. (in Chinese)

China statistical yearbook. (1993). Beijing: State Statistical Bureau.

China statistical yearbook. (1995). Beijing: State Statistical Bureau.

FDI in Jiangsu province. (1996, January 20). *People's Daily.*

Foreign investment in China. (1996). China Foreign Invested Enterprises Association, 96(4), Serial No. 41, p. 20.

Hamel, G. (1991). Competition for competence and inter-partner learning within international strategic alliances. *Strategic Management Journal, 12*(Special issue), 83-104.

Hwang, E. R. (1987). Face and favor: The Chinese power game. *American Journal of Sociology, 92*(4), 35-41.

Kao, J. (1993, March-April). The worldwide web of Chinese business. *Harvard Business Review,* pp. 24-36.

Kong, C. (1995). The Chinese in Singapore: From colonial times to the present. In L. Suryadinata (Ed.), *Southeast Asian Chinese: The socio-cultural dimension.* Singapore: Times Academic Press.

Lall, S. (1984). *The new multinationals: The spread of third-world multinationals.* New York: John Wiley.

Lecraw, D. J. (1984). Bargaining power, ownership and profitability of subsidiaries of transnational corporations in developing countries. *Journal of International Business Studies, 15*(1), 27-43.

Linder, S. B. (1961). *An essay on trade and transformation.* New York: John Wiley.

New patterns of FDI in China. (1995, February 9). *People's Daily.*

Sung, Y. (1995). Subregional economic integration: Hong Kong, Taiwan, South China and beyond. In E. K. Y. Chen & P. Drysdale (Eds.), *Corporate links and foreign direct investment in Asia and the Pacific.* New York: Harper Educational.

Vernon, R. (1979). The product cycle hypothesis in a new international environment. *OBES,* pp. 255-267.

PART **III**

*Emerging Finance,
Taxation, Accounting,
and Human Resource Issues*

chapter 11

China's Emerging
Capital Markets

FRANCIS A. LEES

China's transition to a more market-based economy is generating parallel changes in its financial system. These changes are not dissimilar to those taking place in other socialist or former communist nations. For example, the former communist countries in Eastern Europe are experiencing financial system changes in ways closely resembling those taking place in China.

Former communist countries have experienced similar patterns of change in the evolution of their respective financial systems, from one based on communism to one based on a more market-capitalist model. Clearly each of these countries has exhibited its own unique type of evolution. Nevertheless, several common threads are evident.

Four common starting points in this evolutionary process are identified in Table 11.1, namely a monobanking system, a limited use of money, banks following a policy loan format, and an absence of financial market instruments. The evolution in former communist countries has been similar in these four areas. With respect to the monobanking system under communism, these countries have allowed the organization of numerous banks of diversified operating styles as well as nonbank financial institutions. This evolution has generated serious transition problems, including banks with a high percentage of nonperforming loans, bank insolvencies, an unclear separation between central and

TABLE 11.1   Changes in the Financial System: Evolution From Communist to Market Capitalist Orientation

Before Transition	During Transition	Transition Problems
1. Monobanking	Diversified banks and financial institutions.	Bank insolvencies, nonperforming loans, faulty credit evaluation and screening, unclear separation of central and commercial banking. Commercial banks unfamiliar with need to compete with other institutions.
2. Limited use of money	Increasing monetization.	Inflation, related problems of instability in economic activity.
3. Banks follow policy lending approach	Fund allocation based more on credit worthiness evaluations.	Banks operating on dual basis, exit from policy loans, learning how to evaluate credit effectively for proper funds allocation.
4. Absence of financial market instruments	Introduction of capital market and money market instruments.	Public unfamiliar with new instruments. Wide swings in acceptability of new instruments. High capital market volatility and even financial crises. Difficult for bank to apply broad, indirect market-based credit restraints.

commercial banking, and a faulty credit evaluation and credit allocation process. As described below, China shares in these problems.

Second, the use of money generally has increased, with the ratio of money to GDP rising, in some cases very rapidly. Lack of experience with a highly monetized business system has led to problems of business and financial planning, and unstable economic activity. Often the lack of control over money growth has generated inflation.[1]

Third, the former pattern in which banks allocated credit based on government policy, or policy-based lending, has proven difficult to change. There are several reasons for this. Government leaders often resist change, fearful of unknown consequences waiting around the corner. Also, state enterprises need more credit to remain afloat. There may be insufficient alternate sources of credit funds, given the underdeveloped financial markets. China faces serious problems in these areas currently, and prospectively in the next decade.

Finally, there is an absence of financial market instruments. Under the communist system, bank deposits constituted virtually the only financial instrument. Introduction of financial instruments generally requires strong government policy support and a developed legal infrastructure. China has been slow to provide a strong legal infrastructure. As described below, the Chinese government's own financing need has served as a strong incentive for the introduction and development of several new financial market instruments.

FINANCIAL REFORM, 1978-1996

China embarked on gradual economic and financial reform in 1978. Since that time, China's economy and financial system have become more modernized and open to the rest of the world. The reform process itself has affected all economic sectors, with a dramatic change in 1992. In that year, the Communist Party officially recognized the possible compatibility between a market system and socialist ideals.

The adoption of a "socialist market economy" concept implies the following: Market mechanisms govern economic-financial interactions, with the public sector retaining ownership of important sectors of production. Following this, a comprehensive reform strategy is to be followed into the next century, with financial sector reform playing a key role.

Achievements

Financial sector development requires progress in three areas: institutions, instruments, and markets. Early reforms saw financial institution changes with the establishment of a two-tier banking system. The People's Bank of China (PBOC) was divested of its commercial banking activities and in 1984 became China's central bank. Credit policy continued to be subject to a national credit plan with credit quotas and direct bank finance of enterprises.[2]

Central banking received an impetus in 1995 with the new central bank law. This gave the central bank the legal foundation to operate within a market environment, guided by the State Council. The PBOC has introduced reserve requirements and loan facilities to commercial banks to reinforce its policy actions. In 1994, direct central bank lending to the government was discontinued in preparation for increased government reliance on open market finance. This signaled a phasing-out of the national credit plan.

Early in the reform years, four state-owned banks, the Agricultural Bank of China (ABC), the People's Bank of China (PBOC), the Industrial and Commercial Bank of China (ICBC), and the Bank of China (BOC), were established to improve allocation of funds to specific sectors. In 1984, new banks were allowed to operate along with the specialized banks. In the later 1980s, nonbank financial institutions emerged, creating a more competitive and complex system.

In 1994, China established three policy lending banks, which channel credit to finance investment in infrastructure and other areas. The 1995 enactment of China's new commercial bank law has encouraged market-based management and operation of financial institutions.

Financial instruments have developed quickly for the capital market, but not for the money market. Banks tend to lack the skills to develop new products. Nevertheless, huge infrastructure needs will have to be met as much by bank financing as by the securities markets. Local interbank centers are emerging, but have not grown to serve as links between regional markets.

Absence of nationally organized money markets is related to hesitant liberalization of interest rates, limited payment and settlement facilities, and inefficient administration of banks. Lack of national interbank and money markets hampers the transition to indirect monetary policy instruments. Authorities regulate liquidity by adjusting reserve requirements and utilizing the PBOC's lending facilities for banks, while maintaining relatively stable interest rates.

One of the most striking features of China's reform process has been the development of capital markets. After decades of inactivity, the authorities resumed issue of government securities in 1981. Soon after, the authorities permitted issue of other types of bonds, including enterprise bonds and enterprise shares. Beginning in 1988, secondary markets in bonds and stocks were permitted, and this has stimulated capital market development.

Institution building has tended to lead market development and liberalization. A 1986-1988 effort to liberalize interest rates was temporarily halted in the midst of an inflationary surge. Again, in the 1990s, banks and other institutions were granted freedom to vary lending rates. Foreign exchange market development has made advances, especially since 1986 when swap centers were introduced. Turnover grew steadily. In 1994, the exchange rates between swap centers were unified, and a single national foreign exchange market was created.

Evolutionary Approach

Financial reform in China has been pragmatic, gradual, and realistic. This can be explained by the size and diversity of China's vast regions, and by the decentralization of decision making that began to take place early in the reform period. Selectivity in reforms is one aspect of the experimental approach taken to financial reform. This selective approach is evidenced by creation of a limited number of Special Economic Zones (SEZs), and by limiting national stock market status to two cities: Shanghai and Shenzhen.

Given that in 1978 the financial sector was almost nonexistent, financial development started from a low level. Therefore, China's record of financial sector development has been impressive. Future success will need to emphasize liberalization of interest rates and the exchange rate system. A successful financial liberalization will require related reforms in state-owned banks, bank supervision, and accounting practices. Reforms in these areas will facilitate development of a more indirect monetary policy and the instruments that it utilizes.

In 1995, the authorities initiated measures for a nationally integrated inter-bank market and gradual liberalization of interest rates. Initiated in 1996, interest rate liberalization permits the authorities to nibble away at the massive problem of impaired credit in the state enterprises.

Lessons From Reforms

China's experience with financial market reforms provides several important lessons. First, the government waited too long before enacting legislation supporting financial market development. It was not until 1995, 17 years after China's opening, that appropriate central bank laws were put in place. Further, legislation covering negotiable instruments remains to be addressed. Commercial bank legislation also waited until 1995. This has resulted in state-owned banks remaining dependent on the government and government policy.

Second, the banking system has not developed in a manner that promotes efficient payment and fund allocation mechanisms. High savings are not fully effective in driving economic growth, due to the weak channels and lack of incentives for interregional mobilization of capital.

Third, financial liberalization has proceeded too slowly. This is evident from the government's using a regressive banking sector to maintain tight control over many aspects of business and economic decision making. This leads to market distortions and to unexpected policy shifts as the government finds savings flows and investment decisions not working in accord with policy directives.

Finally, interest rates have failed to assume the flexible role they play in advanced capitalist countries. For example, the government continues to manipulate the interest paid on government securities, to satisfy investors who face only limited alternative outlets for investible funds.

SECURITIES MARKETS

During the decade of the 1980s, China experimented with authorizing the issuance of capital market securities. As noted in the previous section, capital market development requires institutions, markets, and instruments. I describe and evaluate China's efforts to introduce bond and equity instruments, and to facilitate the development of trading markets for these securities. China first experimented with bond issuance, and shortly after took steps to organize trading of equity securities.

China's securities markets include a wide range of financial instruments. These range from government bonds (treasury bonds), to municipal government bonds, to bonds issued by state-owned banks and by large industrial enterprises. Stock issuance is permitted, but is largely restricted to selected state enterprises and some private firms.

Bond Issuance

The government has floated debt instruments since 1981. These were intended to finance budget requirements and were purchased by state and collective enterprises and local governments. Initially, sales were involuntary, with quotas assigned to enterprises based on profits or liquidity. Progressively, the government has sought to make these bonds more attractive investments by raising interest rates paid and by shortening bond maturities.[3]

Beginning in the 1990s, changes were introduced in the methods utilized to sell government bonds. Until 1991, these bonds were sold only through special committees that arranged for mandatory purchase. In 1991, selected issues of bonds were placed via an underwriting procedure. Following this, secondary market trading developed. This was furthered by making bonds negotiable, and by permitting that they be used as collateral for financing.

As early as 1989, special indexed bonds were issued. These were set at a 3-year maturity, with a coupon interest rate 1% over inflation. Other types of bond issues appeared at this time, including construction bonds and special state bonds.

During the 1980s, the government recognized the need to allow the large, specialized banks to finance their needs outside of government budgeted funds. In 1985, therefore, these banks and other institutions began to issue financial bonds to individuals. This was part of a broader task of assigning these institutions the role of mobilizing capital on a broad basis. Proceeds of bond issues were used to finance high-technology or large infrastructure projects. Two years later, large state-owned companies issued enterprise bonds. Shortly after this, construction bonds were issued by enterprises to finance the building of manufacturing or transport facilities.

By 1990, a variety of bond instruments had been issued. At that time, one third of bond issues outstanding were government bonds, one fifth were financial bonds, one fifth were corporate bonds, and one sixteenth construction bonds. At this time the major holders of government or treasury bonds were households, accounting for almost half. Enterprises held another 30%, and other investors (including financial institutions) held the remaining share of treasury bonds.

Fixed Income Instruments

The fixed income market centers on sovereign instruments. Private sector issuance is almost nonexistent. There are no major private corporations in existence. Debt issuance is limited to the central government, municipal governments, state enterprises, and financial institutions. Maturities extend to 7 years. At times in the past, 10-year maturities have been used.

The money market remains underdeveloped compared with the capital market. Instruments include interbank deposits, certificates of deposit, bills of exchange, and commercial paper. The government issues treasury bills.

Central government securities include treasury bonds, fiscal bonds, and special purpose bonds. Between 1981 and 1991, treasury bonds were sold on an allocated basis, with the central government setting the coupon, price, maturity, and size of issue. After 1991, the government elected to use more market-like processes. An underwriting syndicate came into use, consisting of banks and trust and investment companies. The authorities have indicated a desire to shift fully to a voluntary process with a primary dealer/auction system.

Treasury bonds are issued in physical form, through the PBOC branch network. Secondary trading has been permitted since 1988, with trust and investment companies and securities firms participating as brokers or dealers. The growth in this market can be appreciated when one considers that in 1994 China floated RMB 77 billion (U.S.$8.8 billion) of treasury bonds in two tranches.[4]

Fiscal bonds are fixed income instruments, used for financing budget shortfalls. With maturities of 5 to 7 years, these are held by state financial institutions that act as captive investors. A third type of security issued by the central government is the special purpose bond. These are fixed coupon, 5- to 7-year instruments. They carry market-related yields, and some have been indexed to inflation to protect investors. These finance special projects and are allocated exclusively to state enterprises.

Capital investment bonds are issued by specialized banks (e.g., People's Construction Bank of China [PCBC]) and trust and investment companies. These bonds have the implicit support of the central government. These are floated to fund long-term capital investment projects. Investors are primarily state enterprises and provincial authorities.

Financial bonds are issued by state-owned financial institutions, including the Agricultural Bank of China, the Industrial and Commercial Bank of China, and the People's Construction Bank of China. These institutions float bonds for general purposes, to cover loan losses, and to fund specific credits to enterprises. These carry short to intermediate maturities, and pay fixed coupons. Secondary trading remains at a modest level.

Corporate or enterprise bonds are relatively new, introduced in 1992. These are issued by state corporations, pay competitive fixed interest coupons, with maturities of 1 to 7 years. Several issues have been denominated in U.S. dollars.

International Bond Issues

China is a major participant in the international capital markets. Borrowing from commercial banks and bond placements has resulted in external indebtedness that approached $100 billion in 1995. Despite this large external debt, the debt service ratio is lower than that of countries such as Indonesia and India.

As a member of the International Monetary Fund and the World Bank, China has become qualified for commercial borrowing through syndicated bank loans and sale of capital market securities. China's first international bond issue was a private placement of Yen 10 billion by the China International Trust and Investment Company (CITIC) in 1982. By the end of the 1980s, China had issued approximately $5 billion of bonds on the international markets. In this period Tokyo was the most important market, but other markets were increasingly utilized, including Hong Kong, Singapore, and London. Over the period from 1993 to 1995, China's placements of International Bonds averaged $2.6 billion yearly (Table 11.2).

During the 1990s, China's specialized banks began to issue bonds more widely in New York and other markets. The first U.S. (Yankee) bond issue took place in 1993 when CITIC sold a 10-year bond in New York. Later that year, Moody's upgraded China's sovereign debt to A3. Until 1993, China's activities in the international bond markets were carried out exclusively by the so-called Ten Windows, consisting of selected banks and financial institutions. In 1994, the government sold a record $1 billion, 10-year Eurobond, and shortly after that the Bank of China announced a $500 million Yankee bond issue.

TABLE 11.2 Issue of International Bonds by Chinese Borrowers

Year	Amount (millions of U.S. dollars)
1993	2,852
1994	3,652
1995	1,433
1996	806

SOURCE: International Monetary Fund, *International Capital Markets,* September 1996, p. 93.

In 1995, state-owned bank borrowers suffered reversals as leading rating agencies downgraded their bonds, related in part to the Beijing government's requiring they stand on their own feet as borrowing entities. Four of China's biggest banks were downgraded from A3 to Baa1 (Bank of China, Bank of Communications, People's Construction Bank of China, and Industrial and Commercial Bank of China). China's sovereign rating was reaffirmed A3.[5] Ratings of leading Chinese bond issuers in the Japanese Yen sector are indicated in Table 11.3.

Trading and Settlement

Trading of fixed income securities in China is primarily on a physical basis. This operates through a network of brokers. Each trading exchange has its own procedures for settlement. Most use physical settlement. Beginning in 1994, the issuance of scripless instruments (treasury bonds) has enabled settlement through parallel book entry, with debits and credits to relevant cash and securities accounts of buyer and seller, or their respective brokers.

TABLE 11.3 Bond Ratings of Selected Japanese Yen Issues, 1994-1995

Borrower	Date of Issue	Moody's	S&P	Japan
			Rating Agency	
Agricultural Bank of China	2/95	Baa1	—	AA–
Bank of China	5/94	—	BBB	AA
China International Trust and Investment Corp. (CITIC)	7/95	A3	BBB	A+
People's Bank of China	11/95	A3	BBB+	—

SOURCE: International Monetary Fund, *International Capital Markets,* September 1996, p. 99.

Trading has been speeded by an automated screen trading network, referred to as STAQS (screen traded automated quote system). Most traders settle 2 days after trade date.

Issue of Equity Securities

Relative to bond issuance, issue of equity securities in China remains somewhat limited. The number of enterprises issuing stocks and the amount of funds raised remains modest. A major limiting factor is state ownership. Based on data in the September 1996 IMF study *International Capital Markets,* in 1995 new equity issues totaled $804 million. This compares with new equity issues of $10.5 billion in India, $9.2 billion in Indonesia, $7.3 billion in Korea, $4.5 billion in Malaysia, and $3.1 billion in Thailand.

From 1984 onward, selected enterprises were given authority to reorganize as joint stock companies and to issue securities. The primary motive of the government of the People's Republic of China in allowing issue and sale of securities was not to create an efficient capital market, but to finance government activities.

Two National Markets

In 1990, a national stock market was opened in Shanghai. Understandably, this raised ideological issues concerning ownership, profit making, and the balance between socialist and capitalist principles and institutional behavior. When the Shanghai Stock Exchange was opened, there were already many regional exchanges listing local companies. Rules for market operations were issued at the local government level. As trading in these regional markets grew, Chinese authorities found it difficult to monitor and control share issuance and trading. The opening of the Shanghai Stock Exchange in 1990 and the Shenzhen Stock Exchange in 1991 provided national trading markets, subject to central government regulation and administration, where national economic objectives and considerations would be the basis for development.

As nonprofit organizations, these two national exchanges are governed by a board of directors and use a membership system. Only full members can trade on these exchanges. Institutions related to the securities business can become members. Two classes of stocks are traded: The A shares are for Chinese nationals only; B shares are offered for foreign investor purchase only.

The number of companies listed on the two national stock exchanges increased rapidly, from only 70 in 1992, to approximately 200 in 1994. The ratio of company A share issues to B share issues is 4:1 on the Shenzhen exchange, and 6:1 on the Shanghai exchange.

Since A shares and B shares are not substitutable, there is a segmented stock market. Also, there are limits on the amount of any single B share issue a foreign investor can hold (5%). Owners of both classes of shares have the same rights, except that dividends for B shares are in foreign currency. To trade, foreign investors must contact authorized brokers. Market turnover and volatility of B shares tends to be lower than for A shares. Also, price-earnings ratios for B shares tend to be lower. In 1996, the performance of B shares was poor. The hard currency B share index in Shanghai fell to record closing lows in the period October-November 1996. This was related to record selling by foreign investors, disillusioned by poor corporate performance and repeated claims by Beijing reaffirming its ban on domestic investors trading B shares.[6]

In December 1996, a senior official of the PBOC announced China's plans for 1997 to open the domestic A share market to a limited number of foreign fund management companies. It was further explained that this did not signal a merger of the A share market with the B share market. At the time there was strong speculation that Beijing was considering opening up the A share market to foreign investment. The Shanghai stock market, whose A shares had advanced in value by more than 80% during the first 11 months of the year, rose almost 10% in one day of trading (December 3, 1996). On the same day, B shares rose 11.6% on expectations that Beijing might introduce measures to liberalize the market. A week later, B shares leaped in value by over 12% in a single day of trading as local investors poured funds into the market. Brokers attributed this rise to renewed confidence among the Chinese that they could buy B shares without being punished. Officially, domestic buying of foreign currency de-nominated shares is banned. A Jardine Fleming analyst attributed the surge in B shares to local investors taking advantage of the price difference between A and B shares. The 50% to 80% discount of B shares relative to A shares should disappear when and if Chinese stock market regulators move to merge the two markets. Thousands of new B share trading accounts were opened in Shanghai during the first 2 weeks of December 1996.[7]

Offshore Equities

China's stock markets were transformed in 1992 with the issue of B shares (hard currency issues) reserved for foreign investors. Given the difficulties of gaining access to the equity markets, some Chinese enterprises made use of unauthorized or backdoor listings on the Hong Kong Stock Exchange. These

TABLE 11.4 International Equity Issues by Chinese Enterprises

Year	Amount (millions of U.S. dollars)
1993	837
1994	320
1995	1,206
1996	687

SOURCE: International Monetary Fund, *International Capital Markets,* September 1996, p. 101.

takeovers of quoted Hong Kong companies by Chinese enterprises made possible subsequent financing through rights issues with the controlled overseas entity. Subsequently, the Hong Kong authorities tightened up on these practices. However, the ground was prepared for listing mainland Chinese enterprises in the Hong Kong stock market. In June 1993, a Memorandum of Regulatory Cooperation between the Hong Kong and Chinese authorities paved the way for these listings. Soon after, selected Chinese enterprises prepared to issue H shares in Hong Kong.

Two types of equity securities issued by Chinese enterprises include H shares issued in Hong Kong and N shares issued in New York. In 1992, the first preliminary announcement was made of an H share issue, and within 2 years, 12 different issues were listed on the Hong Kong Stock Exchange. The H shares are listed under Chinese law, but listed on the Hong Kong exchange subject to local listing and disclosure rules. Hong Kong also has Red Chip stocks, which are Hong Kong companies controlled by Chinese companies. This so-called backdoor listing permits Chinese companies to avoid going through a bureaucratic process in China to accomplish this listing. CITIC Pacific is an example of a Red Chip.

Chinese companies have listed so-called N shares on the New York Stock Exchange. These include some of the largest Chinese enterprises (Shanghai Petrochemical), electric utility firms (Shandong Huaneng), automotive and parts firms (Brilliance China Automotive and China Tire), and motorcycles (EK-Chor). The volume of international equity issues by Chinese enterprises can be found in Table 11.4.

Different Chinese enterprises have made use of capital markets in China, Hong Kong, and New York, widening their sources of equity capital. Different companies have satisfied more and less demanding financial accounting and disclosure requirements in these various markets. In this way a small number of Chinese companies have satisfied the most demanding disclosure requirements in New York, while others have been able to satisfy the demanding requirements of the Hong Kong Stock Exchange. Enterprises listing B shares in Shanghai and Shenzhen have been required to provide greater disclosure than those listing only A shares. In this way, different Chinese companies are modernizing their financial disclosure and reporting systems to the level required in the capital market (at home or overseas) whose standards they can comply with.

Regulatory Framework

China faces special circumstances in developing its securities markets. First, the economic opening after 1978 followed decades of a closed system. Second, a transition toward competitive markets and capitalism is a gradual process. Third, there was a total absence of securities market activities for decades. Finally, China's enormous needs for infrastructure financing means that numerous sources of capital must be found.

Because China is a large nation, many government units and levels of administration must be utilized to provide a comprehensive regulatory framework for its financial markets. In China, the State Planning Commission is responsible for planning in broad areas. This sets the stage for financing these related activity areas. The Ministry of Finance deals with public finance and government loans. The PBOC supervises and examines financial institutions and banks. Local governments are responsible for monitoring and oversight of stock exchanges in their respective cities.

New Issues and Securities Trading

The years 1990 and 1991 were important because two cities initiated centers for national securities trading during this period. In 1990, government leaders took steps to develop Shanghai as a financial center for investor activity. In that year, Shanghai's municipal government issued regulations for the issuance and trading of bond and equity securities.

The Shanghai branch of the PBOC has regulatory authority over securities activities in Shanghai. The Shanghai Securities Regulations, issued by the municipal government, impose registration and disclosure requirements for securities issue.

In 1992, two bodies were established: the State Council Securities Commission and the China Securities Supervision and Control Commission. The Securities Commission exercises control at the macro level.

Membership in the securities exchange is limited to securities dealers. Members are prohibited from trading listed stocks off the exchange. Securities issuance requires submission of detailed information concerning capital structure, financial status, purpose of funds raised, classes of stock, size of issue, pricing, and underwriting agreements.

In the case of trading equities, nonmembers are not allowed to trade on the exchanges. Trading is limited to spot transactions. Issuers of shares submit interim and year-end financial statements in the middle and end of each fiscal year. Insider trading and manipulation are prohibited.

Foreign joint ventures and wholly foreign owned enterprises have not been permitted to issue equity shares. PBOC officials indicate that in the future, foreign investor enterprises will be allowed to organize local subsidiaries to issue shares. Also, they will be able to organize as stock companies that issue securities locally.

NEW COMPANY LAW

In 1993, the national government approved a new Company Law. This is an important step in the direction of developing a modern financial system. The new law, which took effect July 1, 1994, provides for establishment of two types of companies, limited liability companies and joint stock companies. Limited liability companies can have between 2 and 50 shareholders, including foreign investors.

Joint stock companies can issue shares sold through stock exchanges. These are likely to have a widespread ownership. Establishment of joint stock companies requires approval of authorities designated by the State Council or provincial-local governments. According to Torbert (1994), the new Company Law may have an influence on passive portfolio investment in China.[8] As increasing numbers of state enterprises avail themselves of the new law and convert to joint stock companies and list shares on China's securities exchanges, foreign investors will have greater opportunity for securities investment in China.

OBSTACLES TO SECURITIES
MARKET DEVELOPMENT

Development of China's securities markets requires that China overcome a number of obstacles. A fundamental problem is the lack of legal and accounting infrastructure. China adopted a company law only in 1994. For the first time, the rights and obligations of shareholders, directors, and management became partly codified. Absence of an adequate bankruptcy law tends to undermine creditor confidence.

This problem becomes highlighted when PRC-based enterprises attempt to list shares or sell bonds on the international capital markets. A general handicap is that Chinese law is limited to a small number of written codes. Prior to listing mainland company shares in Hong Kong, it was necessary to ensure that Chinese directors and managers would be subject to the same legal constraints as similarly placed officers of Hong Kong companies. This was accomplished with great effort by drafting the articles of association of companies listing in Hong Kong to include the needed legal principles present in Hong Kong law.

A second obstacle is the lack of institutional investors. In the past the socialist system in China provided cradle-to-grave security, and there was little perceived need for pension funds. By 1996 it could be said that China possessed a substantial bank and financial institution system. This included six specialized banks; other commercial banks with national or regional branch networks; and numerous nonbank institutions such as trust and investment companies, financing cooperatives (urban and rural), insurance, leasing, and foreign owned institutions. Nevertheless, comparisons with other countries suggest that China is in a very early stage of financial development. It may take many years for China to grow the many types of financial institutions to the point that they can make contributions to the capital mobilization process.

A third obstacle is that the central bank plays a dual role, as both a bank regulator and a supervisor of financial market practices. This can easily create conflicts. Tight credit policies may save banks and the economy from an inflationary bubble, but may also inject instability into the capital market.

Finally, we should note that China's securities markets have been perceived to contain high risk. There is no national securities law equivalent to the 1933 and 1934 Securities Acts in the United States governing issuance of stocks and bonds, to give investors protection against abuses. Most listed companies remain under strict state control. Companies continue to be operated in many cases as political fiefs, not commercial entities.[9] China operates with interim regulations and with local rules concerning the issue or trading in the national markets, but Chinese investors do not have the level of investor protection available in Western countries.

Aside from securities market-related risk, there are significant political risks for the capital market investor. These relate to the current post-Deng period and continued uncertainty regarding China's commitment to replacing socialist practices with more capitalist methods, the growing urban labor force and related dislocations and difficult working conditions, the unsettled status of Taiwan, and the increased tension between China and its neighbors concerning offshore waters and the resources (petroleum) under these waters.

HONG KONG AND CHINA

Hong Kong Before 1997

With the return of Hong Kong to the sovereignty of the PRC in July 1997, the two economies and financial systems have moved toward a more integrated status. Some questions arise concerning the role of Hong Kong as a financial center within the larger PRC, as well as its potential contributions to servicing the finance needs of China and the region into the future.

Hong Kong has operated as one of the largest international banking and financing centers. Opportunities for onshore and offshore business have brought a high concentration of banks and an expansion in international banking and financial markets. The presence of foreign banks has been instrumental to the development of Hong Kong as an international banking center and international financial center. Parallel, the opening of China has attracted an influx of foreign banks to the PRC. Still, the PRC banking system is caught in structural problems, for example, administrative directives for loans, lack of a proper legal framework for banks until 1995, and lack of full convertibility of the domestic currency.[10]

Up to the present, many PRC state enterprises raised foreign capital in the Hong Kong banking market. Also, many foreign banks established branch offices in Hong Kong as a means of participating in the growing Chinese market. Given the increased economic integration between Hong Kong and the PRC, the government of China is committed to preserving the role of Hong Kong as an international financial center beyond 1997.

China's capital-hungry companies have been quick to use Hong Kong's capital market. In August 1996, Shanghai Petrochemical, China's largest petrochemicals enterprise, announced it was raising HK$1.04 billion through a share placement. Table 11.5 describes five share offerings in Hong Kong by Chinese state enterprises. These Red Chip share issues were made between January and August 1996, a period when the Hong Kong Red Chip Index gained more than 30% in value, while the Hang Seng Index gained only 10%.

TABLE 11.5 Red Chip Fund-Raising Activities in Hong Kong

Company	Date	Fund-Raising	Intended Use
Guangnan Holdings	25/6/96	Placing of 33 mill. new shares to raise HK $146 mill.	To fund supermarket chain expansion
Guangnan Holdings	28/6/96	Placing of 37 mill. new shares to parent company	To purchase two food processing companies
China Overseas Land	18/7/96	Placing of 390 mill. new shares to raise HK $780 mill.	To fund the acquisition of infrastructure project and construction material manufacturers
China Travel	14/8/96	Placing of 379 mill. new shares to raise HK $790 mill.	To fund acquisition of a power plant and hotel
Guandong Investment	20/8/96	Placing of 80 mill. new shares to raise HK $418 mill.	

SOURCE: *Financial Times* and ING Barings.

Regional Financial Center

Hong Kong's role as a leading international financial center is based on several factors. First, minimal regulation and taxation, and a free economy orientation have kept competition high and funding costs low. Second, there has existed a large critical mass of banks and other financial institutions, making growth a self-sustaining process. Third, given the strong business ties with proximity to China, the banking sector has benefited from the PRC's economic growth. Fourth, free movement of capital gives Hong Kong a strategic role in regional and international fund mobilization. Finally, Hong Kong's location and time zone position enables it to provide good communications and transport, as well as expertise in banking and finance.

Hong Kong has been a dominant mobilizer of international banking credits. In 1995, Hong Kong accounted for approximately 45% of the net loans to selected countries provided by BIS-Reporting Banks (Table 11.6). Between 1990 and 1995, these bank credits to and through Hong Kong increased from $69 billion to $219 billion.

International banking credits tend to be denominated in U.S. dollars. As these dollar credits become booked on the balance sheets of Hong Kong banks, they may be on-loaned as Hong Kong-dollar loans, or other currency of denomination

TABLE 11.6 Net External Assets of BIS-Reporting Banks in Selected Countries (Amounts in millions of U.S. dollars)

Borrower	1990	1995
Hong Kong	69	219
Singapore	44	117
Mexico	4	6
China	−21	−7
Indonesia	2	13
Korea	14	44
Malaysia	−4	3
Thailand	5	68
Australia	16	17
New Zealand	4	6

SOURCE: International Monetary Fund, *International Capital Markets,* September 1996, p. 30.

loans. This requires a foreign exchange swap transaction if the banks are to avoid exchange rate exposure.

Hong Kong has become one of the world's leading foreign exchange trading centers. This can be observed in Table 11.7, which indicates the estimated percentage share of world foreign exchange market turnover taking place in key trading centers. Hong Kong is slightly behind Singapore, ranking fifth in world foreign exchange trading in 1995. Both Singapore and Hong Kong are narrowing the lead enjoyed by Japan.

Hong Kong's role could become more important, especially in cases where foreign investors and bankers are not favorably disposed to specific projects in China. For example, when the United States, the World Bank, and other lenders

TABLE 11.7 Foreign Exchange Market Turnover (as percentage of total)

Market	1989	1992	1995
United Kingdom	26	27	30
United States	16	16	16
Japan	15	11	10
Singapore	8	7	7
Hong Kong	7	6	6
Switzerland	8	6	5

SOURCE: International Monetary Fund, *International Capital Markets,* September 1996, p. 31.

decided not to participate in financing the Three Gorges Dam project, the Beijing government turned to issuance of domestic bonds and to the Hong Kong market to attract foreign investor participants.

The transition to a Special Administrative Region within the PRC in 1997 has not increased political risks of conducting business in Hong Kong, at least so far.

BEYOND 1997

A 1995 empirical survey of foreign banks in Hong Kong reinforced our understanding of its special role and the areas of concern beyond 1997. The survey indicates that foreign banks operate in Hong Kong with multiple objectives, the three most important being trade finance, syndicated loans, and offshore banking activities. Potentially harmful factors in Hong Kong perceived by foreign banks include political uncertainty, high costs, and potential competitive challenge from other financial centers. Many other financial centers in Asia are still somewhat behind Hong Kong.

Since 1980, Hong Kong has become increasingly integrated into the economy of China. The PRC and Hong Kong are each others' largest trading partner and direct investor. Foreign banks with offices in Hong Kong regard the negative factors in the PRC as very important. The potential for political upheaval deters many foreign banks from going to the PRC with operating offices. Foreign banking regulations are not comprehensive or well defined. Outside the Special Economic Zones (SEZs), their activities are severely restricted. The branch of the PRC's Central Bank (PBOC) in the region determines the interest rates that can be charged by foreign bank branches on foreign currency loans and deposits.

While foreign banks are able to derive only limited advantages in the PRC, the Bank of China (BOC) group in Hong Kong and other banks from the PRC capitalize on the funding opportunities in Hong Kong. Also, they have expanded branch operations in Hong Kong. Hong Kong has grown rapidly as an offshore banking center for the PRC. In the period between 1979 and 1993, liabilities of Hong Kong banks to banks in the PRC increased by over 35% yearly. Total claims on banks in the PRC increased at an annual rate of 25%. Since 1993 this high growth has continued.

Hong Kong is now China's offshore banking center, transferring banking technology and skills. In the future, Hong Kong is likely to increase in importance as a market for equity securities issued by PRC enterprises. All of this is increasing the capital allocating efficiency of the PRC. The operational validity of Hong Kong as an international financial center is based on the presence of foreign banks and investment houses. Will business opportunities continue to exist for foreign banks in Hong Kong? We can expect that enterprises and governmental units in the PRC will wish to continue to borrow and issue securities in Hong Kong and other international financial markets. Hong Kong remains a natural choice for foreign banks beyond 1997, assuming that the PRC's economic growth rate continues at a high level and that political stability is preserved.

How stable will conditions be for Hong Kong to continue its prosperity as a financial center beyond 1997? There is no doubt that the PRC places high importance on the future role of Hong Kong as an international financial center. Several factors support this:

1. China has made large investments in Hong Kong, including manufacturing, finance, and banking.
2. The Hong Kong currency is convertible and will give the PRC government favorable indirect access to foreign capital.
3. The PRC wants to succeed in its "one country, two systems" policy. This is especially important in connection with the future status of Taiwan.

A number of problems may manifest in the future regarding the status of Hong Kong. These include the following:

1. A widening gap in income level between Hong Kong and the PRC may generate social discontent and changing policy.
2. Banks based in China may insist on more favorable treatment as compared with banks in Hong Kong. This may lead to legislative or other negative administrative measures.
3. The instincts of the Beijing regime tend toward authoritarian rule. A light touch may not be within the experience or capability of the Chinese leadership.

NOTES

1. These trends are outlined in Lees and Liaw (1996, chap. 1).
2. A more detailed analysis of this development is in Mehran and Quintyn (1996).

3. Chapter 4 of Xia, Mei, Jian, and Grub (1992) focuses on the emergence of financial instruments and resumption of bond issuance.

4. Banks (1994) provides a complete and technical description of China's fixed income instruments.

5. A detailed account of this downgrading can be found in Lees (1997).

6. Roell (1996) provides an interesting commentary concerning the government position on this matter.

7. The financial press gives a detailed account of events in the Chinese equities markets for the December 1996 period. Ridding (1996) examines the A share side, and Walter (1996) looks at the B share component.

8. Torbert (1994) provides a detailed description of the new law and analyzes its implications.

9. Walter and Roell (1996) provide a vivid picture of the conditions of financing facing enterprises in China.

10. For a detailed account of the role of Hong Kong as an international financing banking center, see Leung (1996).

REFERENCES

Banks, E. (1994). *The emerging fixed income markets in Asia.* Chicago: Probus.

International Monetary Fund. (1994, November). *Economic reform in China: A new phase* (Occasional Paper 114). Washington, DC: Author.

International Monetary Fund. (1996, September). *International capital markets: Developments prospects, and key policy issues.* Washington, DC: Author.

Lees, F. A. (1997). *China superpower: Requisites for high growth.* London: Macmillan.

Lees, F. A., & Liaw, K. T. (1996). Economic environment and reform. In F. A. Lees & K. T. Liaw, *Foreign participation in China's banking and securities markets.* Westport, CT: Quorum.

Leung, M. K. (1996, Summer). Hong Kong as an international banking center after 1997. *China Information: A Quarterly Journal on Contemporary China Studies, 11,* 34-48.

Mehran, H., & Quintyn, M. (1996). Financial sector reforms in China. *Finance and Development, 33*(March), 18-21.

Ridding, J. (1996, December 4). China to open up A-shares to foreigners. *Financial Times* [London], p. 21.

Roell, S. (1996, November 12). Shanghai B-shares hit low. *Financial Times* [London], p. 17.

Stephens, P. (1996, September 18). A present of democracy. *Financial Times* [London], p. 15.

Torbert, P. M. (1994, May-June). Broadening the scope of investment. *The China Business Review* [Washington, D.C.], pp. 4-8.

Walter, T. (1996, December 11). Local buying buoys Shanghai B-share prices. *Financial Times* [London], p. 22.

Walter, T., & Roell, S. (1996, November 12). China's markets divide deepens. *Financial Times* [London], p. 8.

Xia, M., Jian, J. H., & Grub, P. (1992). *The re-emerging securities market in China.* Westport, CT: Quorum.

chapter 12

China's Emerging Foreign Exchange System

K. THOMAS LIAW

China's foreign exchange system is unique (Bowles & White, 1994; Dipchand, Zhang, & Ma, 1994; Lees & Liaw, 1996; Roell, 1995; Yi, 1993). First, management of this system is carried out through comprehensive controls. For example, visitors received Foreign Exchange Certificates (FECs) when cashing travelers checks. The FEC[1] was denominated in the same way as the renminbi and officially had the same value. In practice, it was worth more because only FECs could be used to buy imported goods.

A second unique feature is that a strong retail orientation dominates the market. This is in contrast to mostly wholesale foreign exchange trading in developed countries. Small-scale transactions dominate due to the fractured state of swap centers, which did not encourage intermarket trading, and in part due to the limited size of investments by foreign enterprises.

Another unique feature is that the reform of China's foreign exchange and trading system has been carried out in an environment in which a complicated balance of political forces has shaped foreign exchange reforms. The political forces include the central government in Beijing, the Communist Party, the provinces to which decentralized authority has devolved, the various ministries responsible for particular industrial sectors, and external forces including international organizations such as the International Monetary Fund (IMF) and the World Trade Organization (WTO). China has taken steps to reform its foreign exchange system.[2] Major reforms were introduced in 1994 and in 1996 (*Euro-money*, 1996; House & Lehner, 1996; Lees & Liaw, 1996; Stevenson-Yang, 1996). These reforms are aimed at renminbi convertibility. The full convertibility for its current account was accomplished by the beginning of 1997. Renminbi convertibility under the capital account is still years away. Nevertheless, it can be expected that Beijing will take steps to move gradually toward convertibility of its capital account if the current reforms for the current account remain under control and if political stability is maintained.

The chapter is organized as follows. The next section describes the exchange control system in China. The modifications of the system are covered in the following section, after which foreign exchange swap markets are described. The 1994 reforms are then discussed, and the new 1996 rules are examined in the subsequent section. The last section provides a perspective concerning the future development of the foreign exchange system.

A CENTRALIZED FOREIGN EXCHANGE SYSTEM

China follows a policy of centralized control and a unified foreign exchange system. Authorities responsible for implementing this policy include the State Administration for Exchange Control (SAEC) and its branches in major cities. The Bank of China (BOC) is the nation's specialized foreign exchange bank. It operates branches overseas and participates in international financial markets and loan syndication.

In the past, the BOC handled all dealings in foreign exchange. It was responsible for allocating the country's foreign exchange reserves, arranging foreign loans, setting exchange rates for renminbi, issuing letters of credit, and carrying out all financial transactions with foreign firms and individuals. With the economic reforms that began in 1979 and the rapid expansion in foreign investment by joint ventures, offshore loans, and trading relationships, the task of administering this increasingly complex area of foreign exchange activity became more difficult.

By the mid-1980s, foreign exchange and government reserves were controlled by the SAEC under the People's Bank of China (PBOC), the central bank. Foreign exchange allocations to banks, ministries, and enterprises required approval by the SAEC. The BOC lost its monopoly on foreign exchange transactions in 1984 when a number of other specialized banks[3] and financial institutions were permitted to deal in foreign exchange. The BOC remained the principal foreign exchange bank, and has organized correspondent relations with foreign banks and set up overseas branches. The BOC also provides loans for production and commercial transactions related to exports, and conducts research on international monetary trends.

China has taken steps to introduce free convertibility gradually as it prepares for membership in the World Trade Organization (WTO). Until 1993, a dual exchange rate system was in operation, consisting of the official rate offered at state banks set by the SAEC and the PBOC, and the swap rate, which is adjusted daily and separately at various swap centers across China. The swap rate applicable in these swap centers has no direct relation to the swap rate applicable in London and other market-oriented foreign exchange centers where interest rates play a determining role. In 1995, there were about 110 swap centers active in different cities in China. Enterprises with excess hard currency swap for renminbi.

Foreign nationals visiting China use foreign exchange certificates (FECs). These were first issued in 1980 to strengthen foreign exchange control, prevent foreign currency from circulating in China, and to safeguard the status of the renminbi. FECs are exchanged for foreign currencies at the BOC. Officially, one FEC is valued at one renminbi. In actuality, the FEC is worth more on the black market.

Foreign investment enterprises open renminbi deposit accounts and foreign currency deposit accounts in China with the BOC or other banks that are approved for this purpose. All foreign currency transactions are carried out through these accounts. An enterprise may borrow foreign currency from banks or enterprises outside China, but such borrowing must be reported to the SAEC.

A foreign joint venture may not pay dividends unless profits are available. Prior to any dividend payment, part of the profits must be set aside for worker bonuses and benefits, an enterprise expansion fund, and a reserve fund. A joint venture must generate sufficient foreign currency from operations to cover dividends. An alternative is to purchase the required foreign currency from a swap center. At times, swap center exchange rates were significantly higher than the official exchange rates. A final requirement for remitting a dividend abroad is that the joint venture must file an application with the SAEC.

Chinese enterprises and foreign investment enterprises that wish to invest outside China must obtain approval from the SAEC with regard to the foreign exchange aspects of the investment, and submit an application to the relevant government agencies. Examination and approval procedures are complicated. The investing enterprise must have its own foreign currency resources for the intended investment, and must set up a profit guaranty fund to be deposited in a special account in an authorized bank. Profits obtained from the foreign investment must be remitted to China within 6 months after year-end.

MODIFICATION OF THE CENTRALIZED SYSTEM

Before the 1979 reforms, foreign trade was an insignificant part of the overall economic activity. China had abstained from foreign borrowing. Management of the foreign exchange system was a relatively uncomplicated affair. Due to the limited contacts and small volume of international transactions, foreign exchange shortage was minimal. The foreign exchange budget was balanced primarily by keeping exports and imports in balance.

With China's market opening, the Beijing government wanted to ensure that foreign exchange inflows would grow rapidly enough each year to permit the realization of ambitious industrial development programs. Since the opening of China, there have been dramatic changes in the scale and scope of managing the foreign exchange system, enactment of numerous laws and provisions to implement a comprehensive exchange control system, and rapid expansion of the overall foreign exchange budget of the People's Republic of China (PRC).

Foreign Investments

Foreign direct investment has played a key role in China's economic opening and its industrial development. Shortly after the December 1978 communiqué initiating the opening, senior Communist Party leaders announced China would welcome foreign investment. In 1979, the joint venture law and creation of the first Special Economic Zones (SEZs) were approved. Initially, only four zones were established. It was expected that most industries in the SEZs would process imported materials and components for export. In this regard, these zones were to be "engines creating foreign exchange." Initially, most of the foreign investment in the SEZs was from overseas Chinese businesses.

The four SEZs and the provinces in which they were located, Guangdong and Fujian, gained the flexibility to provide tax concessions to foreign investors, financial subsidies from Beijing, and the ability to enter into attractive foreign exchange revenue contracts. Since 1980, Guangdong and Fujian have been able to retain most of the taxes and industrial profits generated by the enterprises. Fiscal incentives provided strong motivation to shape economic development in a pragmatic manner that assured high profit and growing enterprise revenues.

A key aspect was the foreign exchange retention arrangements, which were very generous. The SEZs and Guangdong and Fujian could retain virtually all hard currency earned from trade. By the year 1984, officials from other provinces coveted the benefits enjoyed in the four SEZs and Guangdong and Fujian. However, they could not attract foreign investors without being granted discretion over taxation and investment contracts similar to that in the original SEZs. Pressure from other provinces resulted in the State Council in 1984 extending the freedom given to the original SEZs to 14 coastal cities and Hainan. In 1985, the State Council extended these freedoms to the Pearl River and Yangtze River deltas, and to the Min River area. In 1988, the open policy was extended to the entire coastal zone. By 1992, almost 2,000 industrial development zones had been set up, many of them located in inland areas.

Trade Issues

Before 1979, strict centralized trade controls operated as strong disincentives. The ministry responsible for foreign trade operated a small number of foreign trade corporations, and through them enforced mandated export and import programs with prices set at levels that were not related to competitive world prices. All foreign exchange revenues were controlled by the ministry. Business enterprises were not offered incentives to participate in foreign trade. State enterprises lost money by importing foods and other goods at world market prices, and selling these at low government subsidized prices.

Beginning in 1979, the government had several objectives as it undertook foreign trade reform: (a) Increase exports to provide foreign exchange, (b) expand imports of advanced technology machinery and equipment, and (c) reduce the government's losses from subsidized trade. The course adopted was moderate decentralization of authority and control over foreign trade, from the Ministry of Foreign Trade and Economic Cooperation (MOFTEC) to provinces and industrial ministries. Authority to conduct trade was not given to individual firms. In this way, China could better retain centralized bureaucratic control over foreign exchange. Also, this enabled government officials to control the distribution of rewards generated by an expanding foreign trade sector.

One key part of the new trade and exchange control regime was a system of foreign exchange retention. As an incentive, local enterprises and governments could retain a share of foreign exchange export earnings. In part, this aimed at offsetting the dampening effect on export profits from the overvalued Chinese currency. Foreign exchange retention rights ultimately provided highly valuable import rights. This was related to the growing need for imports of equipment and consumer goods, resulting from years of economic isolation and a pent-up demand for these imports. Local and provincial officials controlling trade and the ability to gain foreign exchange and foreign exchange retention benefits became extremely powerful, both politically and financially.

The 1986 provisions for encouragement of foreign investment granted the right to foreign joint ventures to sell in the domestic market and to convert local currency earnings into foreign exchange. Authority to interpret the guidelines, to establish whether a joint venture qualified for this preferential treatment, was delegated to local and provincial authorities. Further, decentralization of trade authority gave local authorities the ability to issue import and export licenses. Since the central government treasury subsidized domestic currency losses from exporting, local authorities had strong incentives to export more, regardless of the subsidy losses incurred. In some years these losses cost the government an amount equivalent to 2% of China's GNP (Shirk, 1994). The purpose was to promote high export growth, which increased hard currency earnings, providing a means for importing a greater quantity of scarce commodities.

The Beijing government attempted to retain partial control over its decentralizing foreign exchange system by regulating exchange rates. Frequent exchange rate adjustments were used as a means of influencing the relative profitability of export and import activities.[4] Also, a dual exchange rate was created in 1981. At that time the internal settlement rate was set at 2.80 yuan per U.S. dollar, compared with the official rate of 1.53 yuan per dollar. The lower exchange rate was a strong disincentive to imports.

In 1987-1988, the central government responded to the problems of persistent financial losses in foreign trade and weak export performance. The reform taken was referred to as foreign trade contracting. It set three targets each province must meet. These included foreign exchange earnings amounts, foreign exchange amounts remitted to the central government, and the amount of local currency made available to subsidize losses on export sales. By 1991, subsidies for export losses were eliminated. Foreign exchange retention rates were adjusted periodically to influence the attractiveness of export transactions.

Foreign Exchange Performance

Since the economic opening, China's exports have grown rapidly. China's high export growth strategy is an important part of an overall strategy to expand its access to foreign exchange resources. Each year, exports provide a dominant component of China's foreign exchange earnings. Foreign exchange reserves increased from $2 billion in 1979 to $30 billion in 1990, to more than $80 billion in the second quarter of 1996 (*International Financial Statistics,* September 1996), and to $140 billion in early 1998.

DEVALUATION AND LOCAL SWAP MARKETS

Over the period from 1979 to 1996, China transformed itself from a closed economy to a major trading nation. This was achieved by administrative arrangements that focus on management of the overall foreign exchange position. Selected groups in China were rewarded with opportunities to participate in limited openings and rapid increases in particular types of trade-cum-investment activity.

China is poised to move ahead. This requires adopting greater exchange convertibility and market access, which are norms of the world system under the IMF and WTO. In China, local and central government officials want to retain access to international business. Ministries with industrial responsibility depend on government protection from strong international competition. Some key economic groups, including the machinery and electronics industries, have expressed preference for reforms so they can compete globally. Groups that require modern equipment and consumer goods and the requisite foreign exchange will also espouse a more liberal foreign exchange regime.

Devaluation Between 1979 and 1994

The foreign exchange system in China has been modified many times to achieve better export performance. Soon after the economic opening, the export inhibiting effects of an overvalued renminbi became apparent. To offset this, administrative allocation of foreign exchange was adopted as a means of subsidizing exporters. Under the foreign exchange retention system, numerous problems appeared, including upward pressure on prices of goods purchased for export and the need to operate export activities at a loss to generate foreign exchange. Given the financial losses associated with export subsidy, the Ministry of Finance advocated renminbi devaluation and limits on renminbi expenditures by enterprises aimed at generating foreign exchange from exports.

Between 1979 and 1994, the Chinese government gradually devalued the renminbi.[5] The trend reversed in 1995. This is evident from the exchange rate data; the exchange rates were 1.5, 1.5, 1.7, 1.9, 2.0, 2.8, 3.2, 3.7, 3.7, 3.7, 4.7, 5.2, 5.4, 5.8, 5.8, 8.7, 8.3, and 8.3 in each year from 1979 to 1996, respectively

(International Financial Statistics, various years), and the rate remains at 8.3 yuan per U.S. dollar in 1997 and 1998. China also created an officially sanctioned swap market for foreign exchange. Between 1981 and 1984 dual rates existed, aimed at encouraging growth in trade volumes. Nevertheless, losses in this period were substantial. The State Council eliminated the dual rates in 1985, but they reappeared in the form of swap center rates, which vary from the official rate of exchange.

In 1986 the government devalued the renminbi, and further devaluation took place in 1989 and 1990. By 1994 the official exchange rate was 8.7 yuan to $1. The devaluation was aimed at compensating for the relatively high inflation and to achieve a better balance of exports and imports.

Impetus for reform of the foreign exchange system came largely from outside China. These demands called for more rapid market opening and convertibility of the renminbi. Foreign investors wanted greater freedom to sell their products in the domestic market and to have the right to repatriate profits in hard currency. Reforms also called for elimination of dual rates. Under the dual rate system, foreign companies were penalized. Their investment was valued at the higher official rate, but local profits were converted into dollars at the lower swap market rate.

The Swap Centers

Beginning in 1985, the Chinese government experimented with a parallel foreign exchange market. This took the form of opening local swap centers where foreign exchange could be traded. The swap markets were referred to as Foreign Exchange Adjustment Centers. These centers were established by the SAEC. In 1986, this agency and the swap centers operating under its jurisdiction were placed under the administration of the PBOC. The swap markets were organized by province and managed according to the local needs in each region. By 1995, more than 110 swap centers were operating. Currency prices differed somewhat from one center to another. Local officials discouraged transactions between swap centers located in different regions of the country.

Access to these swap centers varies. When the Shanghai center was established, participation was limited to foreign investment enterprises. By contrast, the Shenzhen center allowed both Chinese and foreign enterprises to participate. Foreign investment enterprises experienced differences in their access to swap centers from one city to another. Before entering the swap market, enterprises must receive approval from local government authorities. Swap markets are dominated by small traders, due in part to the tendency of foreign investors to operate on a small scale to limit risk, and due to the administrative obstacles to entry and the lack of integration of swap markets. As late as 1993 it was difficult to find a swap market transaction of $100,000 or more.

The renminbi valuation faced downward pressure in the swap markets due to a perennial scarcity of hard currency, the national policy of restricting outward expenditures by individuals visiting Hong Kong, and the speculative rumors concerning the future status of China and the renminbi currency in world markets (WTO membership). An informal market trading renminbi against Hong Kong dollars developed in Hong Kong. This proved to be a safety valve for traders concerned about the value of the yuan. Early in 1993, the renminbi was trading in Hong Kong at 12 yuan to the dollar. The swap market rates in China tend to follow the Hong Kong market rates. In the second half of 1993, the swap market value of the renminbi rose to 8.7 yuan to the dollar. By 1995, the exchange rate declined to 8.3 yuan per dollar, and it remains at that level.

The Dual Exchange System

Between 1986 and 1993, China maintained a dual exchange system consisting of an official rate adjusted periodically, and a depreciated, market-determined rate set in the Foreign Exchange Adjustment Centers (swap markets). Under this system, domestic enterprises and foreign corporations were required to surrender export receipts at the official rate. They received retention quotas as a proportion of their export earnings. The retention quotas entitled the holder to purchase foreign exchange at the official exchange rate. These could be traded in the swap market. Foreign-owned enterprises were allowed to retain all their foreign exchange and to transact in foreign exchange in the swap market.

In 1991, a uniform retention scheme was adopted. Through the retention quota, domestic exporters were reimbursed for exports at swap market rates for 70% to 80% of their export earnings. Under this scheme the state had the right, which it exercised, to purchase up to 30% of the retention quota at the swap market rate.

Domestic enterprises were also required to sell the foreign exchange from exports to domestic banks. Individuals were required to repatriate foreign exchange earned from working abroad, but could retain such earnings in foreign currency accounts kept at the designated banks. Foreign exchange remitted from abroad to Chinese residents also could be held in foreign currency accounts with domestic banks.

Foreign exchange remitted or brought into China by foreigners could be converted at the official exchange rate into FECs. FECs could be used in domestic transactions. Upon leaving the country, foreigners were permitted to reconvert up to 50% of the original FECs at the official exchange rate. After-tax profits of joint ventures could be remitted through their foreign exchange accounts. Foreign employees of joint ventures could remit salaries and other income earned in China after payment of taxes and deduction of living expenses.

The SAEC had the main responsibility for monitoring China's external borrowing. All such borrowing had to be registered with the SAEC. Loans from international financial organizations and foreign governments required clearance from the State Planning Commission and approval of the State Council. Medium-term and long-term commercial borrowing, including bond issues, required prior approval by the SAEC. Foreign direct investments were subject to MOFTEC approval, with the exception that many provincial and local governments had approval authority within specified limits.

By 1993, China had made much progress in liberalizing the exchange and trade system. Mandatory planning of trade was reduced, and approximately 80% of foreign exchange transactions were taking place at an exchange rate determined in a relatively open market. Despite these improvements, the exchange and trade system contained major distortions and restrictions.

THE 1994 REFORMS

By late 1993 China was preparing to introduce major reforms in its foreign exchange regime, merging the swap market and official rates and moving toward limited renminbi convertibility. In December 1993, the government announced its intention to unify the exchange rates, cancel the foreign exchange retention system, and ultimately eliminate the foreign exchange certificates. The exchange rates were unified at the swap rate of 8.7 yuan to the dollar on January 1, 1994.

In March 1994, the PBOC indicated that the swap centers would remain open for foreign enterprises to trade foreign exchange. Convertibility is limited to trade-related activities. It was anticipated at that time that it would take 6 years (until the year 2000) to move to conversion of currency from nontrade current account.[6] Capital account convertibility is not expected in the near future. This is because of the huge domestic demand for capital. The 1994 reforms retain administrative control of access to foreign exchange markets. An exporting enterprise requires a valid certificate to be able to convert renminbi for foreign exchange.

The Exchange System in 1994

Domestic enterprises are required to sell their foreign exchange receipts to designated financial institutions. In the case of foreign-owned enterprises, foreign nationals, foreign direct investment, and foreign borrowing and issue of stocks and bonds abroad, foreign exchange receipts may be held in foreign currency accounts. FECs were gradually withdrawn from circulation at the official rate prevailing at year-end 1993. The renminbi was made the only legal tender in China, effective January 1, 1994; foreign exchange must be converted into renminbi to meet local expenditure needs.[7]

The PRC abolished the requirement that approval be obtained from the SAEC for purchase of foreign exchange for trade and related transactions. Foreign exchange for trade transactions may be purchased from designated financial institutions by the importer upon presentation of valid invoices or commercial bills. In the case of imports subject to licensing or quotas, presentation of the relevant documentation is required. To pay for trade-related services, foreign exchange may be purchased upon presentation of contracts or payment notices.

A unified exchange rate is determined in an interbank market. Effective April 1994, the China Foreign Exchange Trading System (CFETS) became operational. This consists of the Shanghai center, linked to a nationally integrated electronic system for exchange trading. This system accounts for the bulk of foreign exchange transactions. This national market eliminates the fragmentation of foreign exchange market operations that prevailed in the past. To trade in this new system, a financial institution must become a member of CFETS. Only designated local banks and their branches are allowed to buy and sell foreign exchange among themselves on their own accounts. Other financial institutions, including foreign banks, may sell foreign exchange or trade among themselves on behalf of customers.

Trading Rules

The CFETS was established to coordinate renminbi transactions nationwide. Operating in Shanghai, the CFETS consists of an interbank trading market as well as a swap market to which foreign enterprises have access. The Center sets the daily exchange rate with reference to the weighted average of the previous day's transaction rates. The Center is linked to all of China's swap centers. Initially, the CFETS traded both U.S. and Hong Kong dollars.

Domestic enterprises generally must convert foreign exchange earnings into renminbi for deposit into a local account at a bank authorized to settle foreign exchange transactions. When the enterprise needs foreign currency it may buy foreign exchange directly from the bank, provided it has the necessary documentation and approval.

The new unified exchange arrangement operates as a managed float. At commencement of daily trading, the PBOC announces a reference rate based on the average buying and selling rates of the previous day's close. Movement of the renminbi against the U.S. dollar is limited to 0.3% on either side of the reference rate. The PBOC intervenes in the interbank market to keep the exchange rate within this limit.

Rules for Foreign Enterprises

Unlike domestic enterprises, foreign enterprises are not compelled to convert foreign exchange revenues into renminbi. Instead, they conduct their exchange transactions through the local swap centers, where they can exchange currency with other foreign enterprises. Foreign enterprises have the right to retain all their foreign exchange in designated banks. They must use the swap centers to balance their foreign exchange needs. Foreign enterprises are required to obtain approval from the SAEC for exchange transactions in the swap centers.

Since the economic reforms after 1978, foreign-owned enterprises have been required to operate according to a system of self-sufficiency in foreign exchange. Foreign enterprises are required to balance their foreign exchange revenues and expenditures. The complex legal framework governing foreign enterprises in this respect includes the Foreign Investment Law of 1979 and implementing regulations, the exchange control regulations of 1980, the implementing rules and regulations, and the investment contracts establishing foreign-owned enterprises.[8]

In general, a foreign-owned enterprise is expected to generate foreign exchange revenue, through exports, to cover its foreign exchange expenditure (profit remittance, imports, expatriate salaries). A foreign enterprise must submit a foreign exchange budget each year and provide reports of revenue and expenditure. Approval of the budget is the basis for approving applications to purchase foreign exchange during the ensuing year.

The PRC has modified operation of the balancing requirement over time, as conditions and policy requirements altered. In 1986, the balancing requirement was broadened to include the entire foreign enterprise sector. Foreign enterprises with a shortage of foreign exchange were allowed to purchase foreign exchange from other foreign enterprises with a surplus through the swap centers, subject to SAEC approval. Rapid growth in the swap centers and participation of domestic enterprises enabled the swap centers to become the principal means for foreign enterprises to meet their foreign exchange needs. One problem was that the swap centers were locally based, and trading among the swap centers was not integrated.

With the introduction of reforms in the exchange system in January 1994, foreign enterprises continue to be allowed to retain all their foreign exchange in local banks and to trade foreign exchange in the swap centers. With the issuance of rules in April 1994, a foreign enterprise wishing to open a foreign exchange account must apply to the SAEC to obtain a foreign exchange registration certificate. Also, each transaction in the swap centers requires approval from the SAEC. The foreign exchange system in effect has two segments: an interbank market for domestic enterprises, and the swap centers for foreign enterprises. Foreign exchange trading for foreign enterprises in the swap centers is electronically linked to the CFETS and is fully integrated with trading in the interbank market. The interbank foreign exchange rate is established in this integrated trading. All transactions in the swap centers that are not linked to the CFETS take place at that rate.

The SAEC administers the rules detailing the opening of foreign exchange accounts by foreign-owned enterprises. Prior to the 1994 reform, a foreign enterprise could establish a foreign exchange account after receiving a business license from the State Administration of Industry and Commerce (SAIC). According to the rules put into effect in 1994, a foreign enterprise must apply to the SAEC to obtain a Foreign Exchange Registration Certificate (FERC). After obtaining an FERC, the enterprise may open a foreign exchange account. The administrative rules for obtaining an FERC are quite detailed. These rules include the requirement that the foreign enterprise must submit an opinion from the SAEC concerning the enterprise's ability to balance its foreign exchange requirements.

Different types of foreign exchange accounts are available, depending on the defined use of that account. When the enterprise opens a foreign exchange account in an authorized bank, the bank will fill in on the FERC the parameters of receipt and payment permitted. The bank must examine each payment into or from the account to determine its agreement with the intended use of the account. This information must be reported to the SAEC monthly.

THE 1996 INITIATIVES TO
MOVE TOWARD CONVERTIBILITY

In February 1996, China published a new set of foreign exchange regulations to go into effect on April 1. There were three main reasons for reform. First, major changes had taken place in the foreign exchange control system. Second, many changes had occurred in the foreign exchange operational mechanism, which broke the monopoly position of the BOC in foreign exchange and introduced a competitive mechanism. Third, the content of foreign exchange control had gone far beyond the scope specified in the 1980 Regulations. A new system was required to meet the objective economic needs in the new environment. Again, in June 1996, China announced additional steps to deregulate the foreign exchange market. The June 1996 initiatives were aimed at renminbi convertibility under current account.

The April Reforms

There are seven chapters in the April 1996 reforms ("PRC Regulations," 1996, pp. 20-24). Chapter One states the policy objectives of improving the management of the exchange system, maintaining an equilibrium in balance of payments, and promoting sound economic growth. Circulation of foreign currencies is not permitted, and foreign currency is not allowed to be quoted for settlement in PRC. Chapter Two outlines foreign exchange control for current account transactions. Chapter Three sets forth provisions of foreign exchange control for capital account transactions. The activities in foreign exchange business permitted for designated financial institutions are listed in Chapter Four, from Article 26 to Article 31. Policies on the renminbi exchange rate and the foreign exchange market are contained in Chapter Five, from which it is clear that the exchange rate for renminbi is a managed floating exchange rate. Legal consequences for failure to comply with the new regulations and ancillary provisions are documented in Chapters Six and Seven. The new regulations became effective on April 1, 1996. The 1980 Regulations, issued on December 18, 1980, and related rules were repealed at the same time.

The basis for adopting new regulations was the limited convertibility of the renminbi under current accounts. There are basically no restrictions on revenues and expenditures involving trade-related transactions; however, strict control measures have been adopted for foreign income and expenditures under capital accounts. Any relaxation in foreign exchange control under capital accounts is believed to lead to fluctuation in capital flows, thereby adversely affecting stable economic development.

These regulations are applicable to foreign exchange income and expenditures, and related business transactions. The regulations bear no applicability to free trade zones, including both border trade and reciprocal trade between residents in border areas.

Profits, dividends, and bonuses accruing to foreign investors in foreign-funded companies need not be examined and approved by the SAEC. Individuals in need of foreign exchange for private purposes when leaving China can purchase foreign exchange within established quotas at designated banks. Those wanting more than set quotas may apply to the SAEC, and may purchase foreign exchange at designated foreign exchange banks by presenting a certificate of approval.

The June 1996 Deregulation

On June 20, 1996, China announced that it would take a series of additional steps to make renminbi more easily convertible. The first step, which went into effect July 1, 1996, allows foreign companies to trade foreign currency at all designated banks, a privilege Chinese firms have had since April 1994. The move is significant because it assures foreign companies that they can send profits back home. The changes will speed up the move toward full convertibility of yuan. China's central bank governor Dai Xianglong indicated that China would make its currency fully convertible for the current account by the end of 1996, 4 years ahead of the target date set by Vice Premier Zhu Rongji (*Euromoney,* 1996; House & Lehner, 1996). This was accomplished. One of the safeguards against a possible sharp fall in the renminbi is China's huge foreign exchange reserve, more than $140 billion in early 1998. China has created indirect and market-based policy instruments as well. A national renminbi interbank market was established in early 1996. The PBOC also started open market operations through buying and selling Treasury issues. This will help in developing flexible interest rates and reducing intervention.

China has not set a target date for achieving convertibility in its capital accounts. Capital account transactions, including direct and equity investments, still require government approval. China will also raise the ceiling on the amount of foreign currency that can be exchanged by individuals. In addition, restrictions on the amount of foreign exchange used by companies for nontrade purposes will be lifted. All these new initiatives will allow China to meet convertibility conditions set by the IMF.

The move toward convertibility began in 1994 when China eliminated the dual exchange system. In April 1996, China began an experiment to allow foreign banks in Shanghai, Shenzhen, Dalian, and Jiangsu to handle sales of currencies for yuan. Part of the experiment allowed foreign-funded companies to buy exchange at authorized banks. The June announcement extended this experiment nationwide.

The deregulation will increase foreign investor confidence. Foreign companies also retain a right to keep foreign currency earnings in bank accounts. This also moves China closer to qualifying for membership in the WTO. As a result of the June 1996 deregulation, the swap centers may wither away, though foreign-funded companies can still use them as well as banks for foreign exchange transactions. Foreign companies will move away from swap centers because of a lack of liquidity and differential commissions.

The deregulation announced on June 20, 1996 may not drastically change the way foreign companies do business in China. It does mark a significant milestone in China's financial reforms. However, as Beijing deregulates on one front, it is imposing new rules on others. For one, the operating accounts of foreign-funded companies may no longer swell with foreign exchange, they must sell everything in excess of a state-set limit. Also, since March 1996, China has imposed annual hard currency audits on foreign companies. Those who pass the audit receive a "white card" that grants the right to a hard currency account. Finally, China has made rules allowing it to force foreign companies to transact currency through a single authorized bank.

Overall, China's progress is significant. It is meeting IMF guidelines for current account convertibility. Looking forward, it can be expected that China will also gradually move toward convertibility in its capital account if the current deregulation remains under control and if there is no political instability.

CONCLUSIONS

This chapter documents the historical development of China's emerging foreign exchange market. The centralized control task was carried out by the SAEC and the BOC. The gradual relaxation of foreign exchange control, both the rationale and new policies at each stage, is examined. Until 1996, all activities in the foreign exchange market were regulated mainly by The Provisional Regulation of the People's Republic of China on Exchange Control issued by the State Council on December 18, 1980.

Major reforms or deregulation initiatives were introduced in 1996. Central to the 1996 reforms is renminbi convertibility under current account. However, convertibility for capital account transactions is still years away. Further moves toward capital account convertibility will depend on the smooth transition of the current deregulation and on political stability. China's new premier, Zhu Rongji, recently announced that China will undertake continuous foreign exchange systems reform, will not devalue renminbi, and will help protect the stability of the Hong Kong dollar upon the request of the Hong Kong government, whatever the cost. Nevertheless, it is expected that the recent financial crisis in Asia will make the central government more circumspect toward the convertibility of capital accounts.

NOTES

1. As discussed under "The 1994 Reforms," the FECs were withdrawn from circulation at year-end 1993.

2. See Lees and Liaw (1996) for a more detailed discussion on the historical development of the foreign exchange system.

3. These include the Agricultural Bank, People's Construction Bank, China Industrial and Commercial Bank, and China International Trust and Investment Companies.

4. As noted in the next section, there had been a series of devaluations since 1979. The exception was in 1995 and 1996, when the exchange rate was 8.3, where it remains.

5. The exchange rate here is expressed in number of yuan per U.S. dollar.

6. The current account has been convertible since December 1996.

7. In southern Guangdong, the use of Hong Kong dollars is pervasive.

8. See Lees and Liaw (1996, chap. 4) and Wong (in press) for a detailed discussion of securities regulations and practices in China.

REFERENCES

Bowles, P., & White, G. (1994). *The political economy of China's financial reforms.* Boulder, CO: Westview.

Dipchand, C. R., Zhang, Y., & Ma, M. (1994). *The Chinese financial system*. Westport, CT: Greenwood.

Euromoney. (1996). *Euromoney guide to emerging markets currencies*. London: Author.

House, K. E., & Lehner, U. C. (1996, June 20). China to loosen controls on currency. *Wall Street Journal*, p. A12.

International financial statistics. (various issues). International Monetary Fund.

Lees, F. A., & Liaw, K. T. (1996). *Foreign participation in China's banking and securities markets*. Westport, CT: Quorum.

PRC regulations on exchange control. (1996, May 13-19). *Beijing Review*, pp. 20-24.

Roell, S. (1995, October). Foreign exchange with Chinese characteristics. *Euromoney*, pp. 54-57.

Shirk, S. L. (1994). *How China opened its door*. Washington, DC: Brookings Institution.

Stevenson-Yang, A. (1996, March-April). Easing up on foreign exchange. *China Business Review*, p. 4.

Wong, K. M. (in press). Securities regulations in China and their corporate finance implications on state enterprise reform. *Fordham Law Review*.

Yi, G. (1993). *Money, banking, and financial markets in China*. Boulder, CO: Westview.

chapter 13

China's Emerging Taxation System

HOWARD GENSLER

The Chinese have undertaken one of the greatest economic reforms in history. They have methodically and consistently pursued a market conversion with courage and commitment. Although the road has not always been smooth, they have demonstrated remarkable resilience and an admirable capacity to learn and improve. A central pillar to a decentralized economy is a rational, compulsory, and universal system of public finance. The Chinese have developed a comprehensive modern system of taxation that ensures that everyone will make a contribution to the public good. Income, sales, products, services, land, imports, and exports are taxed. While it may be possible to avoid an income tax or a sales tax, the probabilities are remote—and becoming smaller every year—and alternative systems exist to collect a contribution for the community chest. This chapter briefly discusses the relationship between decentralization and taxation, overviews the basic Chinese tax system, highlights the tax factors for foreigners, and then hypothesizes on the general direction in which the tax system can be expected to evolve. It is hoped that this chapter will aid businesses in knowing what the lay of the land looks like today, and what may lie just over the horizon.

TAXATION AND DECENTRALIZATION

The 1979 economic reform of the People's Republic of China (PRC) undertook the conversion of a centralized command economy to a decentralized market economy. The immediate implication of such a conversion is a system of taxation. Where the economy is one large conglomerate with all profits consumed by the central authorities, no tax system is needed. However, if each individual productive entity is to operate independently, set its own prices, purchase its own materials, hire its own labor, invest in its own capital, and market its own goods, it must retain its own revenues, but the public sector must be supported. Welfare, defense, roads, education, public health, the criminal justice system, and a host of other public sector activities must be funded. Hence, once a centralized economy converts to a market system, a tax system must be developed.

The Chinese have undertaken the development of a socialist market economy. The ownership and management of the means of production is a separate issue from the price-setting mechanism. Whether a system is capitalist, communist, socialist, or fascist depends on who owns and manages resources. In capitalism, ownership and management are private. In socialism, ownership and management are public. In fascism, ownership is private but management is public. In Hitler's Germany, private companies were ordered by the state to perform, produce, and operate pursuant to the state's goals and plans. In communism, ownership is public but management is private. The Native Americans held land in common, but each could hunt privately. The Israeli kibbutz and the Russian mir are additional examples of communes in practice. The price-setting mechanism varies from a command system where prices are fixed by the government, to a market mechanism where price is set under perfect competition. The United States had a command price mechanism in World War II and again under Richard Nixon's brief wage- and price-control regime. The way prices are set is a separate issue from the way property is controlled.

The Chinese have created a number of large state enterprises. They have privatized a great many productive entities. In the near future, with the aid of a new bankruptcy law, the Chinese economy will be restructured. A few large dominant state enterprises will produce a large portion of the gross national product (GNP). A vast number of small, medium, and even large private firms will generate a majority of the output. Prices will be set relatively competitively by the market. The Chinese will still have a distinctly Chinese socialist economy represented by several dominant state enterprises in key industries, but the entire economy will be decentralized with prices set by the market. Under this economic organization, all enterprises, including state enterprises, will need to make a contribution to the government, in the form of taxation, to support public projects.

OVERVIEW OF THE CHINESE TAX SYSTEM

The Chinese taxation system is a multifaceted system similar to well-developed public finance systems in the West. There are three major categories of taxes: income; sales; and excise, including real property taxes. The employment of taxes in China is the same as in the West: to raise revenue, to compensate for externalities, and to influence behavior. There are three main income tax schemes: the Individual Income Tax (IIT), the (Domestic) Enterprise Income Tax (EIT), and the Foreign Investment Enterprise and Foreign Enterprise Income Tax (FEIT). There are three main sales taxes: the Value-Added Tax (VAT), the Business Tax (BT), and the Land Appreciation Tax (LAT). There are four main excise taxes: the Consumption Tax (CT), the Resource Tax (RT), the Stamp Tax (ST), and Customs Duties (CD). There are numerous minor taxes that are generally excise-type taxes.

The legislation covering these taxes comes in the form of laws (L), Tentative Regulations (TR), Detailed Regulations (DR), Supplemental Regulations (SR), notices, and rulings. Laws are passed by the People's Congress. Tentative Regulations are generally passed by the State Council. Detailed Regulations are usually passed by the Ministry of Finance. Notices are usually issued by the State Taxation Administration, alone or with the Ministry of Finance. Rulings are usually issued by the State Tax Administration. Not all tax areas are covered by laws. Often a Tentative Regulation will be the highest authority on the subject. Detailed Regulations provide specific details to the general Laws and Tentative Regulations. Supplemental Regulations add subject areas to Tentative Regulations or Laws. For instance, the Value-Added Tax Tentative Regulation (VATTR) is the highest authority in that area of tax law. The VAT Detailed Regulations (VATDR) explained many aspects of the VATTR in greater specificity. The Supplemental Regulation for the VAT Accounting Guidelines added rules on accounting procedures for the VAT at the same level of generality (and authority) as the VATTR. Notices respond to a specific issue, and rulings answer a specific question submitted from a provincial tax agency. This organization of authority is very similar to the United States' use of the Tax Code (Laws), the Treasury

Regulations (Detailed Regulations), and the Revenue Rulings (Rulings and Notices). A private letter ruling system has not yet been developed.

The three income tax systems cover individuals, domestic enterprises, and foreign enterprises. Domestic enterprises are treated differently from foreign enterprises. Special incentives are provided to foreign companies to locate or invest in China. It is important to understand the Chinese concept of an "enterprise." The Chinese tax "enterprises," not corporations. Separate legal status is not required to invoke a second level of taxation. An "enterprise" is a business with eight or more employees. The enterprise is taxed. The profits are then paid to the owner. The profits are then taxed as dividends, profits, or other business income. There is no (U.S. style) "Subchapter S" pass-through-type relief. Business income is subject to two levels of taxation. The "eight employee" definition permits some tax planning, but is certainly limited. The Chinese provided for different enterprise income tax systems depending on the ownership and management structure of the enterprise. Two foreign enterprise tax systems were consolidated into one system in 1991. Five different domestic enterprise tax systems were consolidated into one system for 1994.

There are several sales taxes in China. Unlike traditional sales tax systems, the Chinese tax goods, services, and real estate. They generally employ the incremental European value-added tax approach. The scope of this scheme is unusually broad. In some ways, the taxes can be viewed as supplemental income taxes (rather than alternative income taxes as in the U.S. alternative minimum income tax). These taxes are often referred to as turnover taxes. This term is appropriate because it reflects when the tax is imposed as opposed to the amount subject to tax. The entire sales amount is generally not taxed.

There are several excise taxes in China. The main ones are the Consumption Tax, Resource Tax, Stamp Tax, and Customs Duty. However, there is a tax on vehicles and several taxes on real estate to consider, among other lesser taxes. In the next section, each of the principal taxes is reviewed.

Individual Income Tax

The Chinese consolidated a domestic (citizen) and foreign (resident) individual income tax system into a single unified individual income tax system effective January 1, 1994 (IITL sec. 1). This tax law is very simple but provides a basic foundation. The scope of the tax is comprehensive (IITL sec. 2). Unlike the English approach, where only defined items are subject to tax, the Chinese adopted the American approach where only defined items are excluded from tax. Accordingly, it is a true income tax where all income is within its scope (gross income), defined deductions are permitted, and a tax rate applies to the adjusted or taxable income amount (IITL secs. 6 and 3; IITDR secs. 8-11).

The first main issue concerns the scope of gross income. Residents are taxed on worldwide income (again, like the Americans and unlike the English) (IITL sec. 1). Nonresidents are taxed only on China-sourced income (IITL sec. 1). A visitor who is present in China less than 90 days in a tax year and whose salary is paid from an employer outside of China is not taxed on salary accrued while present in China (IITDR sec. 7). A resident is one with long-term contacts. Family, property, friends, business, residence, physical presence, and other social and business ties are factors employed to determine residency (IITDR sec. 2). One is not considered a resident if one is absent for more than 30 continuous days in a tax year or for more than 90 days total in a tax year (IITDR sec. 3). Even if one is deemed a resident, one can apply to be taxed on only China-sourced income for the first 5 years (IITDR sec. 6).

The second main issue concerns the period and categorical approach to income. Different types of income are subject to different exemptions and tax rates. The calculation period depends upon the type of income. Wages and salaries are allowed an 800 RMB (renminbi) monthly exemption and are taxed on a progressive scale from 5% to 45%. Business income is permitted no exemption, is calculated annually, and is taxed progressively from 5% to 35%. Independent contractor income, rent, and royalties are taxed on each installment payment and are allowed a 20% or 800 RMB exemption per installment. Real estate gains are net of expenses. Other income is taxed at 20%. If a single payment exceeds 20,000 RMB, the marginal tax rate increases 50% (e.g., from 20% to 30%). If a single payment exceeds 50,000 RMB, the marginal tax rate doubles (e.g., from 20% to 40%) (IITL secs. 3, 6, and 9; IITDR secs. 8-11, 17-22, and 26-28).

Deductions receive scant attention in the individual income tax law. There is a basic deduction of 800 RMB per month. While this amount seems small, it effectively exempts the vast majority of the citizenry from income tax obligations. In 1993, the year the new Income Tax Law was passed, only nine cities had average household incomes in excess of the exempt amount. Urban incomes exceeded rural incomes. Accordingly, most urban dwellers were exempt from income tax levies, and the vast majority of rural residents had incomes below the threshold amount.

Foreigners are allowed a higher cost of living exemption of an additional 3,200 RMB per month (IITDR sec. 28). The cost of acquiring property and the selling costs are deductible (IITDR sec. 19). Charitable donations up to 30% of adjusted gross income (gross income less business deductions and the base [personal] exemption) are allowed (IITDR sec. 26). Interestingly, there is no provision for depreciation in the individual income tax law. This fairly substantial oversight provides enormous tax sheltering possibilities. However, there is no loss carry-over provision. Given the lack of a depreciation system, this can have potentially devastating tax consequences. A large expenditure may be written off in one year since there is no requirement to spread the deduction out over time. However, if there is insufficient income to cover the expense, the excess deduction would be lost since there is no loss carry-forward provision.

Some income is exempt from taxation. Generally, these items constitute interest on government bonds or a welfare payment (IITDR secs. 12-16). Some individuals may be exempt from taxation. Generally, these are sympathetic characters such as victims of disaster, widows of revolutionary martyrs, handicapped persons, and the aged (IITL sec. 5).

Income tax is subject to withholding. Interestingly, the government has provided for a 2% service fee for withholding income taxes. The employer or other payer of the income is required to withhold income taxes and submit them to the government. There are penalties for not withholding. However, if the payer complies, the government will pay the withholder 2% of the taxes withheld. The payer must submit all of the taxes. The government will send the withholder a check at a later date (IITL secs. 8 and 11; IITDR sec. 42).

Domestic Enterprise Income Tax

All domestic, independently accountable, income-earning enterprises in China are subject to the enterprise income tax (EIT), whether private or state-owned (EITTR secs. 1 and 2; EITDR secs. 3 and 4). Enterprises are taxable on worldwide income (EITTR sec. 1). There is a depreciation system. Assets that have a useful life in excess of 2 years and that cost more than 2,000 RMB are to be depreciated (EITDR secs. 26 and 29-35). Moreover, there is a 5-year loss carry-forward provision (EITDR sec. 28). Certain items are nondepreciable as in the West, such as land and intangibles (EITDR sec. 31). Accrual accounting must be used (EITDR sec. 54). Inventory may be accounted under LIFO, FIFO, the weighted average method, or the moving average method (EITDR sec. 35). The tax rate is a flat 33% (EITTR sec. 3).

Foreign Enterprise Income Tax

The Foreign Investment Enterprise and Foreign Enterprise Income Tax (FEIT) system represented an advancement in that it consolidated two tax systems into one. Moreover, it served as a model for the domestic consolidated system that was passed 2 years later. The FEIT taxes income sourced in China for foreign enterprises and also for foreign investment enterprises whose headquarters are outside of China (FEITL secs. 1 and 2). If a foreign investment enterprise has its headquarters in China, worldwide income will be taxed (FEITL sec. 3). The tax rate is a flat 33% as in the EIT (FEITL sec. 5). The FEIT provides for depreciation, loss carry-forwards, and accrual accounting as in the EIT (FEITDR secs. 30-51; FEITL sec. 11; FEITDR sec. 11). The main difference between the EIT and the FEIT is the vast system of tax havens provided for foreign enterprises, which is discussed in greater detail below. Basically, certain types of enterprises established in certain zones qualify for a tax holiday (usually 2 years), a tax reduction (usually 50% for the next 3 years), and a permanent low rate (usually 15% or 24%; FEITL secs. 6-10).

Land Appreciation Tax

Real estate gains are taxed under the income taxes and the Business Tax (IITL sec. 2; EITTR sec. 5; FEITDR sec. 2; BTTR sec. 1). In addition, these gains are taxed under the Land Appreciation Tax (LAT) as well (LATTR sec. 2). Because the net gains are taxed, this tax is similar in practice to an income tax; however, it is supplemental. The LAT does not replace income taxation of real estate gains. There is a three- or four-level tax treatment of gains from real estate. With respect to the LAT, the allowable deductions are quite generous. All associated expenses are deductible: acquisition cost, repairs, improvement, finance (including interest payments), taxes (Business Tax, Stamp Tax, Urban Maintenance and Construction Tax, and the Education Surcharge), selling expenses, environmental mitigation expenses, and other costs (LATTR sec. 6; LATDR sec. 7). Only the net gain is subject to LAT (LATTR sec. 4). The tax rates range from 30% to 60% (LATTR sec. 7).

There are limited exemptions available: (a) residential property developers who earn less than 20%, (b) property owners who cooperate with a public condemnation or eminent domain proceeding, and (c) employees who have been transferred after occupying the residence for at least 5 years (LATTR sec. 8; LATDR secs. 11 and 12). This concludes the income taxes in the PRC. Next the sales type taxes are examined.

Value-Added Tax

The Value-Added Tax (VAT) is a tax on goods (VATTR sec. 1). The tax rates range from 0% to 17% (VATTR secs. 2 and 16). The tax is on the incremental value of the good added (VATTR sec. 8). The 0% tax rate applies to exports (VATTR sec. 2). It permits one to recover the taxes paid on input items where the finished goods are exported (VATTR sec. 25). The 10% rate applies to duty-free agricultural products (VATTR sec. 8). The 13% rate applies to grains, vegetable oil, tap water, central heat, air conditioning, gas, books, periodicals, fertilizers, and farm products (VATTR sec. 2). The 17% rate applies to all other goods (VATTR sec. 2). Some goods are exempt: contraceptives, used books, agricultural products sold by the producer, imported equipment, handicap aids, and used articles (VATTR sec. 16).

VAT is applied to the total sales price, including all charges of any nature whatsoever (VATTR sec. 6). Packaging, delivery, quality, handling, financing, other taxes, and any other conceivable charge is included in the price (VATDR sec. 12). Invoices are provided on sale (VATTR sec. 8). Invoice control is central for obtaining a deduction on the price paid for inputs (VATTR sec. 9). Where a bulk purchase is made and a portion of the purchase does not go into the finished good, an apportionment must be made (VATDR secs. 20 and 23).

VAT must be paid to the local tax office where the company's headquarters are located (VATTR sec. 22). If a company sells goods in more than one tax district, the company must obtain an out-of-district license and pay taxes to its "home" district (VATTR sec. 22). If a license is not obtained, the company must pay 6% on total sales within each district to each district (no input VAT deduction) and pay the normal VAT on total China sales to the home district without receiving any credit for VAT paid to the other districts (Supplemental Regulation on Some Special VAT Issues, sec. 4).

The new VAT system became effective January 1, 1994 (VATTR sec. 29). Foreign companies that were established prior to the new VAT can obtain a refund of excess taxes paid under the new system over the old turnover tax system for a limited period (Resolution on the VAT, Cons. Tax, and Bus. Tax on Foreign Enterprises, sec. 2. Hereinafter "Resolution").

Small businesses may avoid the onerous accounting requirements of the VAT system and pay a flat 6% on total sales (VATTR secs. 11 and 12). They receive no credit for VAT paid on inputs, and they may not provide an invoice on their goods to buyers that the buyers may use for input VAT deduction purposes (VATTR sec. 13). While the lesser tax rate and simpler accounting are attractive opportunities, in practice such small businesses find that many regular VAT businesses do not want to buy from them because of their inability to obtain a corresponding VAT deduction.

Business Tax

The Business Tax was part of the January 1, 1994 tax reform. The Business Tax is a sales tax on services (BTTR sec. 1). The rates are generally low, and the tax is generally applied to the entire service income (BTTR secs. 2, 4, and appendix). A few industries may pay tax on their share of the total revenues (BTTR sec. 5). Sales of intangibles and sales and gifts of real estate are also subject to the Business Tax (BTTR sec. 1).

Unlike the VAT, some tax rates for certain items are set at the local level within a range established by the central government (BTTR sec. 2). Transportation, construction, communications, culture, and sports pay 3%. Finance, insurance, services, and sales pay 5%. The entertainment industry is taxed at between 5% and 20% (BTTR appendix).

Transportation, tourism, contractors, arbitragers, finance, and entertainers may pay tax on their share of the revenue (not just their profit) (BTTR sec. 5). For instance, suppose a bank lends money at 10% that is obtained at 8%. The bank would pay tax on only 2%. Or suppose a general contractor won a 1 million RMB contract but owed subcontractors 600,000 RMB. The general contractor would pay tax on 400,000 RMB. The general contractor would not be allowed to deduct his own expenses for labor and material.

Some sales may involve goods subject to VAT and services subject to Business Tax. Careful records must be maintained or the highest applicable tax rate (potentially 20% under Business Tax or 17% under VAT) will apply to the entire transaction (BTTR sec. 3).

Charitable, social, agricultural support, medical, cultural, and educational services generally are exempt from the Business Tax (BTTR sec. 6). Sales below 800 RMB per month are exempt (BTTR sec. 8; BTDR sec. 27). However, if sales exceed 800 RMB, the entire amount is subject to Business Tax (BTDR sec. 27). Excess Business Tax under the new system over the old system may be refunded for foreign enterprises as was the VAT (Resolution sec. 2).

Generally, the Business Tax rates are low: 3% or 5%. In effect, the Business Tax operates as an alternative minimum income tax. The income tax system is fairly rudimentary and may be avoided without too much effort. The Business Tax with its relatively complete lack of deductions prevents anyone from completely avoiding a tax burden.

Consumption Tax

Consumption Tax is generally considered to be part of the turnover tax scheme. While it is a tax on the total sales price of an item, it is a targeted tax on a few items and is not of general application. Accordingly, it is more accurately described as an excise tax. Consumption tax is levied on tobacco, alcohol, cosmetics, jewelry, fireworks, gasoline, tires, motorcycles, and cars (CTTR sec. 2 and appendix). These items are generally the subject of "sin taxes."

The consumption of these goods is harmful to society, imposes burdens on society, or is considered immoral. Cars and other motor vehicles produce pollution and wear out the roads. They, accordingly, are subject to an additional tax. Alcohol and tobacco impose health costs on society and are taxed to compensate society for medical expenses and other losses. Cosmetics and jewelry are not generally approved of in the modern Chinese state, particularly cosmetics. They are also luxury items, making them ideal revenue raisers (taxes can be imposed without major impacts on production). The tax rates range from 3% to 45% (CTTR appendix). Some items are taxed by volume: Wine is taxed at 240 RMB per ton. Gasoline is taxed at 0.2 RMB per liter (CTTR appendix). Exports are exempt (CTTR sec. 11). This is consistent with the sin tax view of the levies. If the goods are consumed abroad, no domestic harm is done.

Resource Tax

The Resource Tax is also generally considered to be part of the turnover tax system. It is also a targeted tax and is accordingly more like an excise tax than a general sales tax. The Resource Tax applies to the extraction of crude oil, natural gas, coal, salt, ferrous metal ore, nonferrous metal ore, and other nonmetal ore (RTTR sec. 2 and appendix). The rates range from 0.3 RMB per ton to 60 RMB per ton (RTTR appendix). There are no commercially significant exemptions from the Resource Tax (RTTR sec. 7). It is interesting that there are no export exemptions for this tax. This tax is imposed on nonrenewable resources. Accordingly, the tax is a severance tax compensating the state for the acquisition of an asset. The fact that the resource is exported is therefore irrelevant. The policy behind the tax explains the difference in treatment.

Stamp Tax

The Stamp Tax (ST) dates to 1988 and applies to a wide range of documents that are "concluded or received" in the PRC (STTR sec. 1). These documents include real estate sales contracts, leases, bailments, loans, insurance, contracts, licenses, and books of accounts (STTR sec. 2). Stamp Tax applies to both the buyer's copy and the seller's copy, but not to record copies (STTR sec. 8). Tax rates range from 0.0005% to 0.1%, depending on the type of document (STTR sec. 3 and appendix). Failure to affix stamps to a subject document may result in a fine of up to 20 times the amount due (STTR sec. 13). In addition, the documents may be confiscated. Also, the document may not be admitted to a court. Consequently, a suit to enforce a right under the document cannot be commenced without first paying the Stamp Tax (Neumann, 1996).

Urban and Village Maintenance and Development Tax

The Urban and Villages Maintenance and Development Tax (UVMDT) is a local tax ranging from 0.4% to 0.6% of total sales revenues. Agriculture and social welfare organizations are exempt from the tax (Lam, 1996d).

Customs Duties

Customs duties apply to very few exports but to a great number of imports. Export duties apply to silk, animal bone, metallic ore, and metallic articles. The duty varies from 10% to 100%. On the other hand, there are more than 6,000 import duties. The tariff rate ranges from 0 to 20% for basic necessities, 10% to 50% for necessities, 50% to 100% for common goods, and 100% to 180% for luxuries. In order to comply with the World Trade Organization, China reduced the overall average duty from 35% to 23% on April 1, 1996. There are substantial limited exemptions for foreign companies constructing projects in China and a general exemption for assembly plants in approved areas where the assembled parts are promptly exported (Lam, 1996a).

Real Estate Taxes

There are several taxes on real estate. These taxes are similar to property taxes and special assessments. The Urban Real Estate Tax dates back to 1951 and was retained in 1994. For foreigners, the tax is 1.2% of the original property value per year or 18% of the rental income. For Chinese citizens and organizations, the tax is either 1.2% of the original property value per year or 12% of the rental income. In 1973, local residents were exempted from the Urban Real Estate Tax and charged under the Real Estate Tax. The tax ranged from 1% to 5% of the market value of the property (Lam, 1996c).

The Farmland Use Tax applies to any domestic business that uses farmland for a nonagricultural purpose. The tax rates are set locally (Li, 1996c).

The Land Use Tax was published in 1994 but has not yet been implemented. This pending law replaces the Urban and Towns Land Use Tax of 1988. The tax is on the user of land. Rates range from 0.3 RMB per square meter to 30 RMB per square meter depending on the population of the town (Lam, 1996b).

Vehicle and Vessel Use Tax

Motorcycles, cars, bicycles, carts, and boats are taxed an annual amount ranging from 1 RMB per ton to 2,000 RMB per vehicle, depending on the type of vehicle. There are several exemptions, but most of them apply to the government only (Lam, 1996e).

Miscellaneous Taxes

There are a large number of taxes in the PRC. The following list certainly is not exhaustive. Such a list may not be possible to construct. However, the taxes enumerated here may give a sense of the depth of taxation in China.

The Regulatory Tax on the Direction of Fixed Assets Investment applies to projects and industries that the government prefers to shift investment away from. The tax rates range up to 30%. Luxurious personal residences are a prime target of this tax (Li, 1996d).

The Securities Transaction Tax has been proposed but has not yet been enacted (Li, 1996e).

The Slaughter Tax amounts to 4% of the value of swine, sheep, or cattle when slaughtered (Li, 1996f).

The Banquet Tax applies to a dinner in excess of some base amount set between 200 RMB and 500 RMB. The tax is 15% to 20% of the amount in excess of the base exemption. Foreigners are exempt from the tax (Li, 1996b).

The Agriculture Tax ranges from 13% to 19%. It is imposed on basic cash crops such as sugar, cotton, hemp, tobacco, and potatoes. The average annual estimated yield is taxed, not the actual yield. The tax may be paid in cash or in kind. Foreign enterprises are exempt (Li, 1996a).

TAXATION ISSUES FOR FOREIGNERS

There are several specific provisions in the Chinese tax law for foreigners and foreign enterprises. The large number of generous tax exemptions and tax reductions for qualified enterprises make the PRC a significant tax haven. In addition, the harsh worldwide scope of the income tax is mitigated by a reasonably devised foreign income tax credit. The sales taxes are exempt for exports. These concessions will be reviewed in this section.

TABLE 13.1 XYZ Corporation (in RMB)

	U.S.	Canada	PRC
Gross revenues	9,000,000	5,000,000	3,000,000
Taxable income under local rules	3,000,000	4,000,000	1,000,000
Tax paid to foreign government	600,000	2,000,000	to be determined
Taxable income under PRC rules	2,000,000	3,000,000	1,000,000

Foreign Income Tax Credit

Individuals and enterprises subject to worldwide income taxation by the PRC may claim a tax credit for income taxes paid to a foreign government (IITL sec. 7; IITDR secs. 30, 31, and 32; EITTR sec. 40; FEITDR sec. 84). The amount of the credit may not exceed the amount of tax that would have been paid to the PRC. Excess tax paid may be carried forward for 5 years. The formula for calculating the credit is

$$C = T \ (F/W),$$

where: C = Maximum Foreign Income Tax Credit, T = Total Income Tax on Worldwide Income under PRC Tax Rules, F = Foreign Income from a Specific Country under PRC Tax Rules, and W = Worldwide Income under PRC Tax Rules.

For example, suppose XYZ Corp. has the information shown in Table 13.1. Suppose the tax on 6,000,000 is 2,000,000. The tax credit for the United States is computed as follows:

$$C = 2,000,000 \times (2,000,000/6,000,000) = 666,667.$$

Since XYZ Corp. paid 600,000 to the United States, it can claim a credit here of 600,000, and will have to pay an additional 66,667 to the PRC.

The tax credit for Canada is computed as follows:

$$C = 2,000,000 \times (3,000,000/6,000,000) = 1,000,000.$$

Since XYZ Corp. paid 2,000,000 to Canadian income taxes, it can claim the full 1,000,000 tax credit. However, the excess taxes paid to Canada can be used to offset other PRC income tax liability. The excess tax paid can be carried forward for 5 years to shelter future income earned only from Canada. It cannot be used to shelter PRC income or other non-Canadian foreign income.

The tax due on the Chinese income is:

$$2,000,000 \times (1,000,000/6,000,000) = 333,333.$$

Accordingly, XYZ Corp. pays 600,000 to the United States, 2,000,000 to Canada, and 400,000 to the PRC. In addition, it has an excess credit of 66,667 to apply against Canadian income for 5 years.

Tax Treaties

The PRC has executed 42 bilateral tax treaties. These treaties generally provide for relief from double taxation. Residents of a tax treaty nation may be present in China up to 183 days and not be subject to income tax. The United States, the United Kingdom, Canada, Australia, New Zealand, Singapore, India, Germany, Japan, and Russia have all signed tax treaties with the PRC (Chippindale & VanderWolk, 1996).

Tax Havens

There are seven general types of tax concession districts in China. An enterprise must comply with various requirements, such as type of business activity, and must also be located within the district. There are national concessions as well.

National Tax Concessions

The enterprise income tax is 33%. The national portion is 30%, and the local portion is 3% (FEITL sec. 5). As a practical matter, the local governments tend to offer the same tax concessions as the national government. A 2-year tax holiday and a 3-year 50% reduction of the national enterprise income tax is given to enterprises that are engaged in production and have an operating term of at least 10 years (FEITL sec. 8; FEITDR sec. 75). Unlike corporations in the West, which are perpetual, enterprises must declare an approved operating period. This is fundamentally a formality. The period can be extended. As a practical matter, a corporation that "commits" to 10 years could dissolve after 2 or 5 years. In fact, this strategy is often employed, to the consternation of the tax authorities.

An enterprise that exports at least 70% of its production also qualifies for a 50% reduction of the national income tax (FEITL sec. 8; FEITDR sec. 75).

An enterprise that is certified to be a technologically advanced enterprise may qualify for an additional 3-year 50% tax reduction (FEITL sec. 8; FEITDR sec. 75).

Foreign investors are exempt from individual income tax on dividends from foreign investment enterprises. If a foreign investor reinvests a dividend for at least 5 years, 40% of the enterprise income tax paid on such dividend will be refunded. If the reinvestment is made in an export-oriented or technologically advanced enterprise, 100% of the enterprise income tax paid will be refunded (FEITL sec. 10; FEITDR sec. 80).

If a foreign enterprise purchases materials in China on which VAT has been levied and then exports such materials, 9% of the 17% VAT may be refunded (Notice 92). The tax burden for foreign businesses is heavily dependent upon the locations in which they invest and operate. This is detailed below.

Special Economic Zones. A foreign investment enterprise (FIE) operating in a designated Special Economic Zone (SEZ) and engaged in production and business operations qualifies for a 15% income tax rate. Service enterprises in an SEZ qualify for a 1-year exemption and a 2-year 50% reduction of income tax (FEITL sec. 8; FEITDR sec. 75). Income derived from an SEZ by a foreign company is subject to only a 10% withholding tax (FEITDR sec. 75). Goods produced in an SEZ (20% or more value added) are exempt from export duties. Some products in some SEZs qualify for a VAT exemption (Capener & Childs, 1996).

Economic and Technological Development Zone. FIEs engaged in production qualify for a 15% income tax in an Economic and Technological Development Zone (ETDZ) (FEITL sec. 8; FEITDR sec. 75). The reduced 10% withholding tax on interest and dividends applies to ETDZ-based income for foreign investors (Capener & Childs, 1996).

Open Coastal Cities. A production FIE in an Open Coastal City (OCC) qualifies for a 24% national income tax rate. If the FIE is also an export-oriented firm, the national income tax rate is reduced to 12%. Technology-intensive FIEs qualify for a 15% tax rate (FEITL sec. 8; FEITDR sec. 75). Local governments may reduce or exempt the local income tax in their own discretion. The withholding tax for foreign investors is again reduced to 10% (Capener & Childs, 1996).

Open Coastal Economic Areas. Production FIEs in an Open Coastal Economic Area (OCEA) qualify for a 24% national income tax rate. Technology-intensive FIEs qualify for a 15% rate (FEITL sec. 8; FEITDR sec. 75). The provincial government may exempt local income taxes on a case-by-case basis. The withholding tax rate is reduced to 10% for foreign investors (Capener & Childs, 1996).

High and New Technology Industrial Development Zones. FIEs certified as technology-intensive firms located within a High and New Technology Industrial Development Zone (HNTIDZ) qualify for a 15% national income tax rate (FEITL sec. 8; FEITDR sec. 75). To qualify as a technology-intensive firm, 30% of the employees must be technical personnel with university degrees and 3% of gross revenues must be spent on research activities (Capener & Childs, 1996).

Border Open Cities. Any FIE located in a Border Open City (BOC), upon approval of the local tax agency qualifies for a 24% income tax rate (FEITL sec. 8; FEITDR sec. 75). Some BOCs may lower the rate to 14%, give a 5-year exemption, and provide a 5-year 50% reduction for production FIEs (Capener & Childs, 1996).

State Tourism and Vacation Areas. FIEs in a State Tourism and Vacation Area (STVA) qualify for a 24% income tax rate (FEITL sec. 8; FEITDR sec. 75).

Bonded Zones. Bonded Zones are exempt from customs duties. Goods imported into a Bonded Zone pay no import duties. Goods exported from a Bonded Zone pay no export duties (Capener, 1996). Companies are therefore able to import parts and materials, assemble them, and re-export them without customs duties. However, goods passing in and out of a Bonded Zone to China are subject to import and export duties. In effect, a Bonded Zone pushes the customs duty border back to its border with China.

Local Tax Relief. In addition, local governments are often empowered to grant exemptions from local taxes such as local enterprise income tax, Real Estate Tax, Vehicle and Vessel Use Tax, and Land Use Tax (Capener & Childs, 1996).

Tax Relief for Exports. The Value-Added Tax and the Consumption Tax are exempt or refundable for exports. Although the system is designed to provide for a full refund of Value-Added Taxes for exports, the PRC has modified the policy for FIEs, allowing a refund of only 9% rather than 17%. Several notices have been issued where some tax policy has changed or been clarified such that an item of taxation is disavowed. Taxes already paid under the void tax generally are retained rather than refunded. If a taxpayer failed to pay the tax in the past, no tax will be sought, but if the taxpayer paid the tax, no refund will be given (Kan & Yip, 1996; Shum, 1996). Though this approach seems peculiar from a Western perspective, it is an expedient approach often resorted to in the PRC. The 9% VAT refund for FIEs is the result of a transitional period where no refunds, though allowed under the law, were forthcoming as a matter of practice. The best approach is to consider the entire policy to be very generous and to be grateful for any relief or refund awarded under any circumstance.

TAXATION TRENDS

If one word had to be chosen to describe the PRC tax system, my choice would be "progress." The Chinese have maintained simple, short, and direct tax laws. There are numerous examples of complex, convoluted systems, but these approaches (thankfully) have been uniformly rejected.

The Chinese have made remarkable progress in a very short period of time. They have carefully and methodically struggled with the enormous conversion process from a centralized command economy to a decentralized market economy. As the private sector has developed, and as the Chinese have become more comfortable with the operation of a market economy, they have modified, liberalized, and rationalized their tax system. The rapidity of their response to a changing environment is nothing short of exceptional.

The Chinese have consolidated multiple individual, enterprise, and foreign enterprise income tax systems into one tax system for each. Disparate turnover tax systems for foreigners and residents have also been unified. This unification movement is a healthy development in the tax law.

I would predict that the foreign enterprise income tax system and the enterprise income tax system will be merged together in 10 to 20 years. The Chinese will soon realize that the generous tax breaks provided foreign companies are not required. China has a vast and incredibly cheap labor force. Capital seeks cheap labor, which is why China is the number one beneficiary of foreign investment. The main difference between the two enterprise income tax systems is the tax concessions for foreigners. Once the Chinese realize that these tax breaks can be phased out without seriously impeding the in-flow of capital, they will phase them out. In my opinion, the days of the tax incentives are numbered, and the foreign enterprise income tax system will soon look like (or rather be merged with) the domestic enterprise income tax system.

I also predict that the individual income tax system will soon abandon its categorical approach to income. Income will be income, whether from salaries, profits, or royalties. Also, the monthly reporting system will be abandoned for an annual reporting system with monthly or quarterly withholding requirements. A depreciation system should soon be provided as well.

Among all of the tax preferences, I believe that the export incentives in the VAT system and the Bonded Zone system for Customs duties will survive the longest. The Chinese are intent on industrializing, and employment and exporting will remain high on the national agenda for generations to come.

CONCLUSION

The PRC tax system is relatively simple. The deductions are often generous. The tax incentives for foreigners are certainly generous. The tax rates are not unreasonable. The Business Tax rates are low as a rule, and allow for taxation of net revenues rather than gross revenues where a hardship would result. The VAT rates are fairly high, but there is substantial relief for foreigners. The income tax system has numerous opportunities for relief. Even the Customs Duties can be avoided nicely. Overall, the tax system has been made quite friendly for foreign investors and foreign companies. Anyone doing business in China would be well advised to consult a tax attorney before setting up an office, in order to take maximum advantage of the many tax incentives available.

Appendix 1: China Tax Resources

For an updated service of English translations of Chinese tax laws, regulations, notices, and rulings from the recent wave of reform in late 1993 to the present: *China Tax Reporter,* edited by Howard Gensler. Jiliang Yang, Chief Translator. FT Law & Tax, an imprint of Pearson Professional (Hong Kong) Ltd., Asian House Suite 1808, 1 Hennessy Road,

Wan Chai, Hong Kong. Phone: (852) 2863-2600. Fax: (852) 252-6646.

For an updated service of commentary on Chinese Taxation: *China Taxation,* by Jefferson VanderWolk. FT Law & Tax, an imprint of Pearson Professional (Hong Kong) Ltd., Asian House Suite 1808, 1 Hennessy Road, Wan Chai, Hong Kong. Phone: (852) 2863-2600. Fax: (852) 252-6646.

For a bound volume of descriptive articles of the components of the Chinese Tax System: *China Tax & Accounting Manual,* edited by Howard Gensler. Asia Law & Practice Publishing Ltd., an imprint of Euromoney (Jersey) Ltd. I/F Chinachem Hollywood Centre, 1-13 Hollywood Road, Central, Hong Kong. (1996). ISBN 962 7708 82 8.

For a bound volume of Chinese tax and business laws with commentary: *Guide to China's Tax and Business Laws,* edited by Howard Gensler. Translations by Jiliang Yang. FT Law & Tax, an imprint of Pearson Professional (Hong Kong) Ltd., Asian House Suite 1808, 1 Hennessy Road, Wan Chai, Hong Kong. Phone: (852) 2863-2600. Fax: (852) 252-6646. (1995). ISBN 962 661 001 8.

Appendix 2: Authorities

IITL: Individual Income Tax Law (Oct. 31, 1993).

IITDR: Individual Income Tax Detailed Regulation (Jan. 28, 1994).

EITTR: (Domestic) Enterprise Income Tax Temporary Regulation (Dec. 13, 1993).

EITDR: (Domestic) Enterprise Income Tax Detailed Regulation (Feb. 4, 1994).

FEITL: Foreign Investment Enterprise and Foreign Enterprise Income Tax Law (April 9, 1991).

FEITDR: Foreign Investment Enterprise and Foreign Enterprise Income Tax Detailed Regulation (June 30, 1991).

VATTR: Value-Added Tax Temporary Regulation (Dec. 13, 1993).

VATDR: Value-Added Tax Detailed Regulation (Dec. 25, 1993).

Supplemental Regulation on Some Special VAT Issues (Dec. 28, 1993).

BTTR: Business Tax Temporary Regulation (Dec. 13, 1993).

BTDR: Business Tax Detailed Regulation (Dec. 25, 1993).

CTTR: Consumption Tax Temporary Regulation (Dec. 13, 1993).

CTDR: Consumption Tax Detailed Regulation (Dec. 25, 1993).

RTTR: Resource Tax Temporary Regulation (Dec. 13, 1993).

Resolution: Resolution of the Standing Committee of the National People's Congress on the Application of the Tentative Regulations on the Value-Added Tax, the Consumption Tax, the Business Tax, and Other Taxes on Enterprises with Foreign Investment and Foreign Enterprises (Dec. 29, 1993).

LATTR: Land Appreciation Tax Temporary Regulation (Nov. 26, 1993).

LATDR: Land Appreciation Tax Detailed Regulation (Jan. 27, 1995).

STTR: Stamp Tax Temporary Regulation (Aug. 6, 1988).

STDR: Stamp Tax Detailed Regulation (Sept. 29, 1988).

CL: Customs Law (July 1, 1987).

IETR: Import and Export Tariff Regulation (Mar. 18, 1992).

Notice 92: Ministry of Finance and State Tax Administration Notice, Caishuizi 92 (Nov. 23, 1995).

REFERENCES

Capener, C. R., & Childs, M. G. (1996). Special investment areas and concessions. In H. J. Gensler (Ed)., *China tax and accounting manual*. Hong Kong: Asia Law & Practice.

Chippindale, E., & VanderWolk, J. (1996). Tax treaties. In H. J. Gensler (Ed)., *China tax and accounting manual*. Hong Kong: Asia Law & Practice.

Kan, S., & Yip, G. (1996). Consumption tax. In H. J. Gensler (Ed)., *China tax and accounting manual*. Hong Kong: Asia Law & Practice.

Lam, I. (1996a). Customs duties. In H. J. Gensler (Ed)., *China tax and accounting manual*. Hong Kong: Asia Law & Practice.

Lam, I. (1996b). Land use tax. In H. J. Gensler (Ed)., *China tax and accounting manual*. Hong Kong: Asia Law & Practice.

Lam, I. (1996c). Real estate tax. In H. J. Gensler (Ed)., *China tax and accounting manual*. Hong Kong: Asia Law & Practice.

Lam, I. (1996d). Urban and village maintenance and development tax. In H. J. Gensler (Ed)., *China tax and accounting manual*. Hong Kong: Asia Law & Practice.

Lam, I. (1996e). Vehicle and vessel tax. In H. J. Gensler (Ed)., *China tax and accounting manual*. Hong Kong: Asia Law & Practice.

Li, J. (1996a). Agricultural tax. In H. J. Gensler (Ed)., *China tax and accounting manual*. Hong Kong: Asia Law & Practice.

Li, J. (1996b). Banquet tax. In H. J. Gensler (Ed)., *China tax and accounting manual*. Hong Kong: Asia Law & Practice.

Li, J. (1996c). Farmland use tax. In H. J. Gensler (Ed)., *China tax and accounting manual*. Hong Kong: Asia Law & Practice.

Li, J. (1996d). Regulatory tax on the direction of fixed assets investment. In H. J. Gensler (Ed)., *China tax and accounting manual*. Hong Kong: Asia Law & Practice.

Li, J. (1996e). Securities transaction tax. In H. J. Gensler (Ed)., *China tax and accounting manual*. Hong Kong: Asia Law & Practice.

Li, J. (1996f). Slaughter tax. In H. J. Gensler (Ed)., *China tax and accounting manual*. Hong Kong: Asia Law & Practice.

Neumann, P. A. (1996). Stamp duty. In H. J. Gensler (Ed)., *China tax and accounting manual*. Hong Kong: Asia Law & Practice.

Shum, E. (1996). Value added tax. In H. J. Gensler (Ed)., *China tax and accounting manual*. Hong Kong: Asia Law & Practice.

chapter 14

The Development of
Accounting in China

SHOUHUA ZHOU
DAVID C. YANG

China's economic reforms and open-door policy have a far-reaching influence on the Chinese accounting system. Following establishment of the Enterprise Accounting Standards on July 1, 1993, the Chinese accounting system is being modified to be more compatible with international accounting standards. It is predicted that in the near future the Chinese accounting system will be compatible with international accounting systems and will have a great bearing on the development of international accounting. This chapter analyzes the past, present, and future development of the accounting system in China to give readers an understanding of both China and its accounting system.

In the early period of the People's Republic of China (China, hereafter), the Chinese accounting system corresponded to the planned economy. China learned accounting theories and methods mainly from the former Soviet Union and gradually developed its distinctive accounting system under the planned economy. After China adopted its open-door policy, however, and especially after China developed its unique socialist market economy, the accounting theories and methods learned from the former Soviet Union lost their value. Therefore, China is now establishing an accounting measurement and reporting system that is based on the Enterprise Accounting Standards. Since the economic reforms and the establishment of a socialist market economy, the accounting system in

China has progressively improved. It is predicted that by the year 2000, China will develop an accounting system with not only the strengths absorbed from other countries but also with distinct features. The development of an accounting system in China can be described in the following three stages: (a) the accounting system under the planned economy, (b) the contemporary accounting system in China, and (c) the future development of an accounting system in China.

THE ACCOUNTING SYSTEM UNDER
THE PLANNED ECONOMY

The political and economic policies of a country determine its accounting system. As mentioned above, under the planned economy, China learned from the former Soviet Union and established an accounting system according to the principle of "Centralized Leadership and Divisional Management." This accounting system was to adapt to the needs of various businesses and common ownership. The main features of this system were as follows:

Following the principle of "Centralized Leadership," the accounting system emphasized standardization. The main focus was that the Ministry of Finance regulated the standardization of the accounting systems of business enterprises. Accounting policies, accounting management methods, expense and expenditure standards, and accounting reports had to follow the regulations set by various industry ministries. Enterprises did not have the right to make any changes. This resulted in too much governmental intervention, too many constraints, and enterprises having no autonomy.

The accounting system was established based on different economic units and the structure of ownership. Before the accounting reforms of 1993, China's accounting system, even though it had been established and approved by the Ministry of Finance (or established by the economic units and then reported to the Ministry of Finance for approval or filing), changed according to the structure of ownership and economic units. This was because there were no uniform accounting principles. In other words, different departments and enterprises with different ownership structures had their own accounting policies, accounting methods, and reporting methods. This led to a lack of consistency and comparability. A typical example was that accounting clerks in the merchandising industries did not understand accounting reports prepared by accounting

TABLE 14.1 The Balance Sheet

Capital Expenditure	Capital Origins
Fixed fund	Fixed fund assets
Current fund	Current fund origins

clerks in the manufacturing industries. Worse yet, different industries had different departments and their accounting systems were different. Therefore, accounting clerks in equipment manufacturing companies, which were classified as mechanical industries, did not understand accounting reports prepared by electronics manufacturing companies, which were classified as light manufacturing industries.

Diverse bookkeeping methods were used in China. Before the accounting reforms of July 1, 1993, bookkeeping in China consisted of increase/decrease,1 cash-based, and debit/credit methods. Bookkeeping theories differed for the various bookkeeping methods. The differences were fundamental, and they severely affected the function of accounting as a business language.

Accounting reports were prepared for the planned economy. Before the accounting reforms, accounting reports were prepared mainly for reporting to the upper-level division. The accounting reports did not consider the needs of the investors (including the debtors and owners). Balance sheets were the main focus of accounting reports, which also included profit and loss statements, product costing budgets, and capital management reports. The balance sheets prepared in China during that period were different from those prepared in the West. The content and basic format is shown in Table 14.1: Capital expenditure (i.e., assets) equaled capital origins (i.e., the rights of debtors and owners). There was a balanced relationship between the expenditure of fixed assets and the origins of fixed assets, the expenditure of liquid assets and the origins of liquid assets, and the account of capital expenditure and capital origins. This kind of accounting and reporting system could therefore not effectively reflect the financial conditions, operation results, and the flow of capital of business enterprises.

The traditional accounting system in China over-relied on the regulations of national finance and taxation. Under the planned economy, business enterprises in China did not enjoy any autonomy. The financial activities of raising capital, using capital, and distributing capital were regulated by the national economic units. The accounting system was under the control of national finance and taxation, and was a part of the national finance. As a result, national finance and taxation determined the financial activities of business enterprises. Also, the regulation of the financial problems directly determined the accounting system of business enterprises.

THE CONTEMPORARY ACCOUNTING SYSTEM IN CHINA

Since the establishment and development of the socialist market economy, the accounting system in China has undergone a dramatic change, starting from July 1, 1993. The main features of this change follow.

Using International Accounting Standards

Compared to the old accounting system, the Enterprise Accounting Standards include the following breakthroughs:

1. Use of realization, conservatism, matching, and materiality principles that are recognized internationally
2. Regulation of bookkeeping methods to use the internationally recognized debit/credit method
3. Use of a new accounting equation: Assets = Liability + Owner's Equity
4. Simplification of the accounting and reporting process

Coexistence of the Accounting System and Accounting Standards

Even though the Chinese government announces the accounting standards for business enterprises, China also announces the accounting standards corresponding to various industries. Accounting standards determine various accounting industries' accounting systems. Accounting standards provide the foundation for a uniform accounting system. The industry accounting system is designed and established according to the requirements of the Enterprise Accounting Standards and to meet the characteristics of various businesses. This new accounting system provides comparability; it is different from the old accounting system, which was determined by the type of business. The Enterprise Accounting Standards issued by the Ministry of Finance were approved by the Congress of China. The Ministry of Finance has the authority to promulgate the accounting systems to be used by industries.

The Rapid Development of Public Accounting

Because of the need for economic reform, the profession of certified public accountant was established in China as early as 1980. Since the economic reforms and the establishment of the socialist market economy, the number of certified public accountants has increased rapidly. By March 1997, China had 120,000 certified public accountants. In order to regulate the conduct of certified public accountants, China announced first its "Rules of Certified Public Accountants in the People's Republic of China" and then the first series of "Principles of Independent Public Certified Accountants in the People's Republic of China." The newly announced "Principles of Independent Certified Public Accountants in the People's Republic of China" and the Enterprise Accounting Standards serve as a foundation for the development of an international accounting system in China.

THE FUTURE DEVELOPMENT OF CHINA'S ACCOUNTING SYSTEM

In order to fulfill the needs its future economic development, China's accounting system will follow the trend discussed below.

Standardization of Accounting and Management System

According to the "Rule of Accounting in the People's Republic of China," the Ministry of Finance will continue to regulate the accounting system in China. The Ministry of Finance will accomplish this mainly through the announcement of standards. Meanwhile, the Ministry of Finance will tighten the regulations regarding the structure of the financial accounting systems of business enterprises and will help establish an accounting system that will correspond to contemporary businesses. In order to reach this goal, the Ministry of Finance will require that large and medium-sized state-owned business enterprises have a comptroller (e.g., a Vice President of Finance) to direct financial accounting activities in the enterprise. Within the enterprise, the comptroller will play the role of financial commander and establish a responsible accounting system.

Separation of Finance and Accounting

In the past, China was under a planned economy. Enterprises had no autonomy, and their financing depended on the government. Enterprises could not and did not need to raise capital from external sources, nor could enterprises participate in investment activities. The capital management and financial policies of enterprises were under the control of governmental departments. Although enterprises had increased their autonomy in the early period of establishing the socialist market economy, their concept of financial management was still vague. The concepts of time having a value and of risk/return factors in financial management were new to enterprises. Therefore, financial management still depended on accounting. With better market structure and environments, however, the financial management of enterprises will undergo a tremendous change. Presently in China, the slogan, "Management of enterprises should focus on financial management," responds to this need. It is expected that the financial management of business enterprises in China will be separated from accounting, and that this will become a key concept for business operations.

Maturity of the Accounting Information System

To enable lawful, reliable, accurate, and complete accounting information, enterprises must follow the Enterprise Accounting Standards and provide standardized financial information. To reach this goal, the Ministry of Finance will finish working on the fundamental accounting standards and issue technical accounting standards soon. Besides the business accounting principles, the Ministry of Finance also pays particular attention to the accounting principles of constructing business units to enhance the pace of auditing reforms.

Accordingly, it is predicted that China will eventually dismiss the industry accounting system and use technical accounting standards to regulate the accounting work of business enterprises while following Enterprise Accounting Standards. Enterprises will establish their own accounting policies and will design accounting systems with their own unique features.

Progress of Public Accounting

The Chinese government pointed out clearly at the end of 1996 that the accounting reports of all foreign-invested enterprises, limited liability companies, and listed companies have to be audited by certified public accountants. Similarly, the accounting reports of large and medium-sized state-owned enterprises have to be audited by certified public accountants. Before the year 2000, all enterprises will have to follow the auditing principles of certified public accountants. In accordance with the principle, "Regulated by law, supervised by government, guided by market, self-disciplined by industry," China is intensifying its enactment of public accounting principles. While enacting its first series of independent certified public accountant principles, China is planning to establish and enact its second series of independent certified accountant principles. Hence, the accounting profession will develop rapidly in the future.

Education and Selection of Accountants

To meet the needs of a socialist market economy, the Ministry of Finance has held nationwide certified public accountant examinations in the past few years. The examination attracts about 2 million candidates annually. In order to improve the skills of accountants in China, particularly of the poor quality of accountants in medium-sized and small enterprises, the Ministry of Finance proposes that 80% of the accountants working at the level of state-owned enterprises, privately owned enterprises, and collectively owned provincial enterprises or above will have to be high school educated, and 40% of the accountants working at the other economic units will have to be high school educated. In the continuous improvement of accountants' skills and qualifications, on-the-job training and various professional examinations to educate and select accountants are provided.

As China plans for the 21st century, it is undertaking accounting reforms that should be of interest in other parts of the world.

NOTE

1. The increase/decrease method uses the increase (+) and decrease (–) signs to record the assets and rights as in a double journal entry method. It is used by accounting clerks in China and had been widely used in the retailing industry before the enactment of the Enterprise Accounting Standards. For example, a business enterprise borrows $20,000 from a bank. The journal entry to record this transaction is:

Increase (+): Bank Deposits $20,000
Increase (+): Bank Loans $20,000

chapter 15

The Development of Accounting Information Systems in China

Problems and Prospects

JINGXIN WANG

DAVID C. YANG

The use of computers in China started relatively late. There were only a few enterprises that used computers for accounting data processing in the 1970s. Computer applications in China developed rapidly in the 1980s (Coll, 1988; Guo & Sun, 1987; Maier, 1988), and at an even faster pace in the 1990s (Chen & Yang, 1995), and there has been an upsurge in computer applications in accounting. This chapter reviews the current development of accounting information systems in China and discusses the unique problems and prospects of the issue.

BACKGROUND

There are two reasons for this upsurge in computer applications in accounting in China. The first relates to the influence of the worldwide application of computers in data processing. Technological developments have led to a rapid increase in the access to information, which has resulted in an "Information Explosion." This presents challenges to China's resource allocation and

323

timeliness to advance in this technological revolution. After the Third Plenary of the Eleventh Party Congress, China adopted its open-door policy in 1978. Through its "Inviting In" and "Sending Out" method, China imported new technology in information processing and computers to achieve wide applications for computers.

The second reason relates to the development of a commodity (or market) economy in China during the past years, which has brought more autonomy to Chinese enterprises. Marketing has been expanded and socialist competition has appeared. Therefore, enterprises have started to make demands for the control and application of economic information. This has led to the need to change the existing archaic data-processing technology. Computer applications to economic data processing have thus become inevitable. In the meantime, due to the reformation of the Chinese economic management system, enterprises have been decentralized. The ministry of each industry has undergone changes in the structure of its power and responsibilities. They have shifted their management orientation from a horizontal management style to a vertical management style. Direct control has shifted to indirect control. Thus, the demand for economic information has changed in form and content. The manual method of information and data processing is incapable of meeting the demand under the new situation and so the use of advanced information processing tools such as computers has become highly desirable.

CURRENT DEVELOPMENT

To be able to meet the demands of the current situation, the State Council has established an Electronics Vitalization Leading Group. In every province, municipality, and autonomous region there are newly established branch offices in charge of the organization and administration of the production and application of computers. In the past few years, the Leading Group has done much in developing the production and application of computers in various areas.

In 1986, China drafted its Seventh Five-Year Plan based on its experience in carrying out the Sixth Five-Year Plan. The Seventh Five-Year Plan stipulated that during this period, China would set up 11 large information systems, the operations of which would affect China's policies and economy. In the meantime, the Seventh Five-Year Plan provided several preferred policies in locating funds for computer applications, importing technologies, and encouraging production. These policies have created favorable conditions for further development of the production and applications of computers.

Under the leadership and impetus given by the central government and local governments, several provinces, municipalities, and major accounting departments have gradually set up Accounting Computerization Leading Groups. These groups have launched "Appraise Through Comparison" campaigns and organized seminars and conducted "Exchanges of Experiences." Many enterprises have started purchasing equipment, training technical personnel, and conducting the analysis and design of accounting information systems. In accounting circles, computer application is experiencing a tremendous surge.

In the current surge of computer applications in accounting, there appear to be several new features. They are mainly as follows.

Improvement of the Systematic Function of Accounting Software

If computers were used for accounting purposes in the past, the accounting information system was independent by itself. Today, an accounting information system is a subsystem of the corporate administration or the management information system. Therefore, internal system coordination and integrity need to be taken into consideration. Good connections between each of the subsystems need to be properly arranged to improve automation of the whole data-processing system.

Improvement of the Scientific Function of Accounting Software

Most accounting software is being developed in accordance with "Software Engineering" requirements. The development has been step by step, according to the stage of the software life cycle. Modular and structural designing have been adopted in developing the software, and logical designing has been separated from physical designing. A top-down approach or modular approach has been used.

Improvement of the Practicality of Accounting Software

In developing software, most enterprises also pay attention to its safety, confidentiality, accuracy, reliability, efficiency, and maintainability. Therefore, when the software is put into use, most accounting staff feel secure and are willing to accept the system. After they have worked with computers for a while, they partly or totally quit manual methods and begin to apply computers to their accounting data processing.

Improvement of Efficiency
of Accounting Information Flow

Some enterprises use PC floppy disks to upload accounting information to mainframes for producing accounting summary reports. The time spent on preparing and summarizing accounting reports is shortened and the accounting information is thus more timely.

Accounting Personnel
Become Computer Literate

Some staff have prior experience in accounting. With practice, they acquired computer application technology and thus are able to take responsibility for operating and maintaining the accounting information systems. Others, however, have prior experience in the area of computer software engineering. With practice, they are able to analyze and design accounting information systems and to work out favorable results. As a result, the application of computers in accounting has been solidified and developed and a sound foundation for a rapid development of accounting software has been laid.

CURRENT PROBLEMS AND PROSPECTS

The development of computer applications in accounting has also raised some questions. The main ones are discussed below.

Standard Accounting
Computerization Principle Needed

An urgent need is felt for the formulation of a standard accounting computerization principle.

There is a set of national accounting rules and regulations that accounting staff are required to follow strictly. At present, each enterprise has its own system design and procedure design. In order to ensure both strict compliance with and conformity to the rules and regulations, standard accounting computerization principles and requirements are needed. Some of the considerations include the following.

a. *Legality:* The computerization method and the data-processing procedures must follow the relevant state rules and regulations.

b. *Scientific:* System design must have clear objectives, a rational structure, and be highly scientific. Any subversive accident should be avoided.

c. *Safety:* The system must have sufficient safety measures to ensure the security of the accounting data.

d. *Reliability:* The system must have the necessary internal control functions and examination measures to ensure the accuracy of the accounting data.

e. *Maintainability:* The system must be suitable for the ever-changing accounting environment. It must allow easy adjustment and modification.

f. *Testability and Veracity:* The system must be able to preserve a good audit trail, must be easy to test and verify, and must be convenient for auditing.

g. *Documentation:* The system must be able to keep complete documentation to assist examination and understandability of the system design.

h. *Additional Requirements:* The system must have a complete administrative setup to keep track of the system's design, modification, and storage, including file conversion, data storage, and auditing of the data. An administrative system is also necessary for the operators' work requirements to ensure smooth operation. Furthermore, detailed standards should be set up in the system for input, output, coding, documentation, and data-processing procedures.

Standardization and Uniformity of Accounting Software

Individual enterprises are developing their own accounting software. Being self-designed and self-applied, software development is duplicated, which results in a waste of labor power and money. Besides, it becomes difficult to improve the software technology. Many people have suggested the possibility of developing standard, compatible accounting software. Once it is developed, it can be used by all enterprises and will avoid the duplication of labor.

One argument against standard accounting software is that to design an accounting information system, the particular functions of each enterprise should be taken into close consideration. Any software designed without knowledge of the particular field can hardly be applicable. Enterprises in China differ in thousands of ways; therefore, it is fairly difficult to develop standard and compatible accounting software. However, the following solutions could be applied.

Select a reasonable range of enterprises that the software can be applied to. Standardized accounting software cannot possibly be applied to all enterprises and departments. Even to develop standardized software for enterprises within the same industry can be very difficult. Generally speaking, enterprises in the fields of administration, production technology, production organization, and the like represent a good selective range. For instance, cotton spinning, wool spinning, and knitting departments within the textile industry; and glass, brick-making, and cement departments within the construction and materials industry can be good ranges. Accounting software aiming at the functions of these ranges can be compatible and used by many enterprises in these industries.

Find similarities among industries and develop standard and compatible function modules. Because each enterprise differs from the others, it is difficult to develop a standard accounting information system. However, it is possible to determine the parts that enterprises have in common and to develop standard and compatible function modules. There are many similarities among the different enterprises due to the similarities in computer data processing technology. There is also a similarity in the general character of accounting systems, administration, production technologies, and production organizations. For example, a standard function module can be developed and put in use in different enterprises for generating accounting reports, settling accounts, and calculating salaries and depreciation.

Enterprises that have the same objective conditions but use different calculation methods should be made uniform through standardization. These enterprises should develop standard function modules to realize uniformity. Owing to historical or academic reasons, there are enterprises that have the same objective conditions although they use different calculation methods. An example of this is in account settlement where some use the debit and credit method, some use the increase and decrease method, and others use the receipt and payment method. In such situations, similar enterprises can be made uniform by following China's Enterprise Accounting Standards.

For enterprises with similar functions but completely different objective conditions, several selective modules can be developed for selective uses under different situations. Modular and structural designing should be followed as a principle. An accounting information system will be divided into many function modules. Any of these systems that can be standardized should use the standard modules. Several different function modules can be developed for selective uses under systems that have completely different objective situations because data processing cannot be forced to be uniform.

Allow some self-definition of data and calculation methods. In designing the standard software, keep some items for self-definition. Let the enterprises define these items for themselves when they begin to use the system. For instance, room should be left for certain words and phrases in documents and records, lists, items in accounting descriptions and reports, calculation formulas, and the like, to allow enterprises to make their self-definitions according to their particular needs. The system can be put into use after the self-definition.

Some dual development may be unavoidable. If the above methods are not applicable to the enterprises, then necessary adjustment and modification should be made to the standard software before it is put into use to ensure its proper application to the particular enterprise. However, because the above methods are first tried in the enterprise, this dual development generally will not be a big job.

Electronic Data Processing Auditing Systems

With the development of accounting computerization, it is necessary to establish China's electronic data processing (EDP) auditing system.

There have been a great number of changes in accounting data processing with the computerization of accounting, mainly the storage of accounting data on tapes and disks; input and output of accounting data through hardware; the centralization and automation of accounting data processing; and the sequential internal control of accounting data processing. Therefore, auditing is facing some new problems and requirements. The traditional methods of auditing are no longer applicable. An EDP auditing system is required to ensure the reliability of a computerized accounting data processing system. China is learning from the experiences of other countries. At the same time that accounting information systems are being developed, China is also developing computer auditing standards and procedures.

Accounting Reform

With the development of accounting computerization, accounting reform is needed in the existing accounting system. This reform should maintain the uniformity of the socialist accounting and conformity of the accounting data specification.

The state has set up certain uniform accounting rules and regulations. Most of these were set up for manual accounting operations. Some regulations will not apply to the requirements of computer data processing. For example, some required accounting reports are excessively wide, which is unsuitable for computer printouts, and some accounting series numbers need to be modified for storage. All of these need proper adjustment, modification, and supplementation based on the functions and requirements of computer accounting data processing to enable the application of the computer in accounting.

Technical Problems in Accounting
Data Processing by Computers

Besides the above problems, there are several technical problems in accounting data processing by computers.

Efficiency and Accuracy of the Original Data Input. Because accounting data processing requires input of Chinese characters, the input efficiency is very low; input speed cannot match that of the actual computer operation. Another concern is how to ensure the accuracy of the input data, and how to avoid mixing the inputs of debits and credits.

Efficiency of the Output. Because the output of accounting records requires printouts in Chinese and in rows and columns, the speed of output is very slow. Some have suggested printing out on paper that is preprinted with rows and columns so that only the numerical numbers need to be printed in the rows and columns. This can eliminate excessive running of the printer. Some enterprises are planning to try this method.

Structure of Accounting Information Systems. At present, the structure of the accounting information system is basically the manual analog processing procedure. There has been very little adjustment to the manual analog processing procedure while switching to the computerized method. This makes it easier to gain acceptance by the accounting staff and approval from administrative departments. Once computers are put into use, however, some of these procedures will prove to be unreasonable. Therefore, structure reform is believed necessary.

Coding Technology. Because the data volume of an accounting information system is large and its contents are complicated, coding of accounting items, materials, fixed assets, staff, product supplies and distributors, and so on, should help to prevent mistakes and make data processing easier. However, the coding technology has yet to be studied and developed.

CONCLUSION

Economic reform in China has been going on for almost 20 years. The computerization of accounting is more difficult in China than in the United States, partly due to the economic reform. With the development of computerized accounting in China, it is hoped that the above-mentioned problems will gradually be solved and that China's accounting computerization will constantly improve to suit the construction of the modern Chinese economy.

REFERENCES

Chen, J., & Yang, D. (1995). The development of the computerization of accounting in China. In J. Blake & S. Gao (Eds.), *Perspectives on accounting and finance in China* (pp. 229-235). London: Routledge & Kegan Paul.

Coll, J. H. (1988, Spring). Computers in China: Where the Chinese are; Where they want to be. *The Journal of Applied Business Research,* pp. 17-25.

Guo, P., & Sun, Q. (1987). General review of computer technology and application in China. *Computers in Industry,* pp. 113-117.

Maier, J. H. (1988, November). China's OSI: Blossoming of the first flower? *Data Communications.*

16

Major Emerging Issues in Human Resource Management

CHERRIE JIUHUA ZHU

It is two decades since China instituted its economic reforms in late 1978. The continuing massive economic growth rates due to the reforms have exacerbated the shortage of skilled personnel at all levels (Stening & Ngan, 1997). Training and development of human resources have thus become one of the major emerging issues in human resource management (HRM) in China. The focus of this chapter is on exploring the training and development of employees in China's industrial sector by utilizing data and analysis based on a literature review and a survey I conducted in China between 1994 and 1995. The chapter begins by examining training and development practices before and after the reforms in the industrial sector. This will identify the traditional training and development system under a planned economy, and will highlight the impact of economic reforms upon the old system and changes in this system since the reforms. Survey data related to training and development in China's enterprises are then discussed and analyzed. The discussion and analysis will lead to the implications of current training and development practices in China for business and management, especially for international investors. Finally, this chapter

AUTHOR'S NOTE: This chapter is based on the paper, "Human Resource Development in the Transition of Economic Systems in China," *Asia Pacific Journal of Human Resources,* Vol. 35, No. 2 (in press). Reprinted with permission from *Asia Pacific Journal of Human Resources.*

briefly examines the function of China's trade unions in HRM under current transitions as another emerging issue.

TRAINING AND DEVELOPMENT PRACTICES

The People's Republic of China (PRC) is the world's most populous nation and has the largest workforce in its industrial sector compared with other countries. However, this abundant labor force has not been utilized effectively owing to many factors, including China's highly centralized economic planning system from 1949 to the late 1970s, its low education levels, and its inadequate attention to the development of professional and managerial skills. Combined, these factors have seriously constrained China's economic development. However, this situation has started to reverse since the economic reforms. These reforms brought unprecedented changes to many areas of management, such as deregulation of the employment system by replacing the labor allocation system and opening the labor market; introduction of motivation and competition mechanisms; and reduction of lifetime employment, guaranteed wages, and social welfare. In addition, a nationwide vocational education and training network was reestablished in an enhanced format, with the intention of bolstering the government's new focus upon employment training. These reforms have had great impact upon China's HRM, especially upon employees' training and development.

Laaksonen (1988) points out that "the educational level of a nation and its overall educational system have a great impact upon management and especially its possibilities to manage the enterprises effectively and profitably" (p. 70). The educational system under China's planned economy was certificate-oriented, while the training system for employees was centrally planned and usually uniform nationwide. These systems have undergone radical changes since 1978. This section first examines the training and development system in a highly centralized economy, and then reviews the impact of economic reforms on such a system, and finally highlights the changes that have occurred since the reforms.

Training and Development System
Under a Planned Economy

From the founding of the PRC in 1949, a centralized economic planning and regulatory structure was adopted on the basis of the Soviet experience (Child,

1990; Hare, 1983). Under this planned economy, the traditional education system "enrolled all students according to state quotas and then all graduates would be assigned by the state" (Laaksonen, 1988, p. 249). Meanwhile, at the enterprise level, there was "a consistently high degree of state involvement in the provision and regulation of manpower training resources" (Nyaw, 1995, p. 202).

The education system was made to focus on general secondary school education rather than vocational and technical education, even though less than 10% of secondary school leavers could enter tertiary institutions (Lu & Chen, 1990; Yue, 1985). Both Holton (1990) and Zhao (1994) point out that the emphasis on general education and on obtaining high school certificates deprived many junior and senior high school graduates of employment opportunities because they lacked the vocational and technical skills necessary for employment. Meanwhile, the higher education system closely followed the Soviet model, taking a narrow approach to course design and placing emphasis on traditional abstract theories rather than practical or vocational training. As a result, many graduates were narrowly trained and lacked the ability to solve practical problems at work.

As for the employee training system, it was generally classified into two parts, one for blue-collar workers and one for cadres, that is, white-collar employees such as managers and engineers. The training program for workers was planned by the Department of Training under the Ministry of Labor. The jurisdiction over cadre education and training rested mainly with the Department of Training of the Ministry of Personnel and the State Education Commission.

Training for blue-collar workers was primarily in the form of apprenticeships and technical school education (Guan, 1990; Zhao, 1994). The number of apprentices and technical school students was decided by the state, with enterprises, or technical schools, having no discretion on filling their quotas as they needed. Apprentices were usually offered lifetime employment upon starting training, and technical school students were assigned employment by the state after completing 2 to 3 years of study. Apprenticeship training generally supplied enterprises with junior-level skilled workers after 1 to 3 years of on-the-job training, while technical schools normally trained middle-level skilled workers (Guan, 1990). However, highly centralized planning made it difficult to match each enterprise's training and production needs, and training was mainly provided for new workers rather than for the further career development of existing employees. This impeded the advancement of the overall educational level of the workforce (Yu & Xin, 1994).

The training for cadres, especially managers who were also Party members, was mainly offered by schools run by the Communist Party of China (CPC) at central, provincial, and municipal levels (Su & Zhu, 1992). Training priority was usually given to political studies, such as the theories of Marxism, Leninism, Mao Zedong Thought, and the Party's policies and documents (Lin, 1989; Zhao, 1986). Laaksonen (1988) asserts that the bottlenecks in Chinese economic development are caused especially by the lack of experts in various fields. This is a sound assertion given that the government under Mao's regime tried to avoid emphasizing the importance of expertise. A politically pure, all-round person was preferred to a nonpolitical technical expert in the cadre selection, because cadres, under a planned economy, "were expected to be careful implementors of state-defined plans for their particular enterprises. Their jobs focused on meeting set production goals and maintaining the engineering techniques necessary to ensure fulfilment of those quotas" (Borgonjon & Vanhonacker, 1992, p. 12). The politically oriented training for cadres inevitably caused a great shortage of qualified managers in China's industry, and this became a serious problem in the reforms.

During the Cultural Revolution (1966-1976), all of China's training systems collapsed and school education virtually ceased. Consequently, a generation of the Chinese labor force was deprived of a proper education, while the older generation's knowledge and skills withered and decayed as intellectuals were scorned and many were sent to undertake manual work for "reeducation" (Nelson & Reeder, 1985).

Impact of the Economic Reform on the Training and Development System

When economic reforms began in the late 1970s, China's workforce was inadequately educated and trained. In 1980, a survey covering 20 million industrial employees in 26 provinces and cities was conducted and found that 8.2% of employees surveyed were literate or semiliterate; 32% had less than 9 years of education; 40.8% had completed year 9; 15.9% had finished year 12; and only 3.1% had tertiary education (Yu & Xin, 1994). The technical level of workers was also quite low as indicated by a sample population survey (Yu & Xin, 1994). In 1982, the state conducted the Third National Sample Census, in which 10% of the population was surveyed. According to this survey's results, 71% of all Chinese technical workers were below technical level grade three (average skilled worker); 23% were between grades four and six (middle skilled level); and only 2% were in grades seven and eight (senior level). This low level of skills naturally impedes development in industrialization and improvement in labor productivity (Yue, 1985).

TABLE 16.1 Chinese Cadre's Age and Education Received in 1983 (N = 18.5 million and percentage was based on this number)

Age	Percentage of Total Cadres	Tertiary Education (%)	Year 12 (%)	Year 9 (%)	Below Year 9 (%)
More than 50	19.1	n/a	n/a	n/a	n/a
41-50	33.5	20	34	34	12
31-40	23.7	22	47	24	7
Less than 30	23.7	20	64	15	1.4

SOURCE: Zhao, 1986, p. 130.

While the educational and technical levels of workers were very low, many of the managerial staff also lacked adequate technical training for their positions (Chan, 1990). According to Zhao (1986), in 1983 the state investigated the education level of different age groups of its 18.5 million cadres in 29 provinces and major cities. Table 16.1 shows that 33.5% of these Chinese cadres were aged between 41 and 50, and 46% of them had completed only 9 years or less of education. It can be seen that cadres under the age of 30 received more education (64% of them finished year 12). It is worth noting that education for people under the age of 30 was disrupted by the Cultural Revolution, which "left one entire young generation without adequate education and training" (Laaksonen, 1988, p. 228).

The economic reforms have provoked dramatic changes in the work environment of most Chinese enterprises. In particular, the industrial reforms have greatly freed enterprises from restrictions of the state administration. The individual enterprise has become a relatively autonomous production unit responsible for its own profits and losses, capable of transformation and growth, and of acting as a legal entity with clearly defined rights and duties (Riskin, 1987; Sha, 1987). China adopted a "Director Responsibility System" in 1984 and then replaced it with a "Contract Management Responsibility System" in 1986 (Child, 1994; Wang, 1990). Both systems requested the director or manager to assume full responsibility for the enterprise. These increased decision-making powers have changed the manager's role from that of "merely an administrator responsible for carrying out government orders to a manufacturer and marketer of goods with full powers to decide on management matters and full responsibility for the enterprise's performance" (Sha, 1987, p. 699). Borgonjon and Vanhonacker (1992) note that the performance of Chinese managers no longer depends "as much on political or technical aptitude as on the ability to pinpoint market opportunities, to solicit financing, and increasingly, to match competition from foreign enterprises" (p. 12). These managers now need a totally new set of skills to be successful under the pressure of increased autonomy, competition, and uncertainty.

The lack of adequately trained management was identified by the government as a major problem in achieving modernization and implementing industrial reforms (Child, 1994; Warner, 1993). Laaksonen (1988) noted that the Chinese government was determined to improve managers' quality by offering both training opportunities and examination assessment. In 1979, the China Enterprise Management Association was set up by the State Economic Commission to coordinate management education by establishing training courses with domestic and foreign education institutions. These training courses have enabled Chinese managers to learn modern management concepts and methods. In 1984, China first offered national examination for directors and senior managers to test their basic understanding of economics and general knowledge of business management. The state emphasized that those who failed these tests should not be allowed to remain at their posts (Laaksonen, 1988). This obviously created pressure on managers to undertake further training to update their technical and managerial skills so as to prevent loss of positions.

The reforms have called not only for an urgent training and upgrading of managerial staff, but also of blue-collar workers. Lu and Chen (1990) stressed that many young workers were unable to work in advanced production lines imported from foreign countries owing to their technical incompetence. Similarly, international joint ventures often complained of the shortage of skilled workers (Holton, 1990; Tretiak & Holzmann, 1993). Child (1994) claims that "the effective use of high technology equipment, often imported or copied from abroad, remains a serious problem in Chinese industry" (p. 173). This workforce deficiency was recognized by the government, and in China's Sixth Five-Year Plan (1981-1985), the government stated that "vocational training of incumbent cadres, managerial personnel, and laborers on the payroll was considered one of [the] fundamental tasks of the nation" (*The Sixth Five-Year Plan,* 1984, p. 22).

The government's emphasis on labor market reforms, together with a series of changes in employment, also placed pressure on individual employees to seek further training and education. Changes such as the abolition of the "iron rice bowl," the requirement for double certificates (education certificate and vocational qualification certificate) for employment, and increased competition for jobs in the open labor market made technical competence and educational qualification prerequisites for obtaining better employment. These changes are now discussed in optional detail.

Training and Development Since the Reforms

The reforms in employee training and development started with emphasis being given to improving the quality of China's human resources, such as a 9-year education being compulsory for every young person, the development in vocational education and management training, and the increase in education investment from 5% of the national total financial expenditure in 1949 to between 18% and 20% in 1990 (Pan & Yang, 1991).

In early 1981, the State Council issued "The Decision Concerning Strengthening the Task of Worker Education" (hereafter called the Decision), which stated that

> worker education is the important route to developing the nation's human resources and strengthening their intellectual capabilities. It is a dependable safeguard to help sustain the continuous growth of the nation's economy and is closely related to the success at constructing the country to become a modern one. (as quoted in Nyaw, 1995, p. 202)

The Decision also stipulated that achievement in employee education and training would be a major criterion for assessing managers' performance and an enterprise's operation (Yu & Xin, 1994). Between 1981 and 1985, over 30 million young workers attended junior-middle-school level (to between years 7 and 9) education courses and junior-skilled-level technical training programs to compensate for what they missed during the 10-year chaos (1966-1976) (Guan, 1990).

In May 1981, the state reintroduced apprenticeship programs and emphasized that "apprentice training will be one of the major and effective methods for newly employed workers" (Guan, 1990, p. 34). However, this system, which offered training after employment, was debated and challenged in early 1989 at a seminar conducted by the Ministry of Labor. Guan (1990) noted that one of the proposals supported by seminar participants was introduction of preemployment traineeships rather than postemployment apprenticeships. This meant that enterprises would recruit trainees and supply them with a living allowance during their training, and at the end of training an examination to test both knowledge and skills would be given. The trainee could be offered a job, contingent upon the successful completion of the preemployment training program. This practice sought to break the iron rice bowl for apprentices by linking training directly to employment and thus improving the quality of training. This proposal was implemented experimentally in some areas in the early 1990s and, because of its success, it was formally written into China's Labor Law in 1994. This legitimation will be explained in a later section.

In 1990, the Ministry of Labor promulgated "The Regulations for Worker's Technical Grade Examination" (hereafter called the Regulations), which defined examination content, including political and technical aspects. Examination results would decide the worker's technical grade and also be related to job arrangement and total remuneration as required by the Regulations. This official call for the linkage between training, examination, job arrangement, and compensation encouraged employees to grasp technical skills (Guan, 1990; Zhao, 1994). This examination system was widely implemented, but has been replaced gradually since the mid-1990s by the vocational qualification verification system.

In 1993, the Resolution adopted at the Third Plenary of The Fourteenth Congress of the CPC specified that "the state should stipulate the qualification requirement and employment criteria for different occupations and adopt the practice of double certificates, i.e. education certificate and vocational qualification certificate" (China Vocational Qualification Development and Verification [CVQDV], 1994, p. 8). This was the first time since 1949 that vocational training was given the same priority as liberal education. The government's recognition that the German model of a dual education system was appropriate for China was the result of learning from foreign countries' experience in vocational education since the reforms (Guan, 1990). The double certificate practice aims to achieve an outcome similar to Germany's dual training system, where young people attain vocational knowledge and skills. This practice is now implemented in middle-level vocational education institutions, such as technical and vocational schools. It is also introduced to the workforce training system as a replacement for the old worker technical grade examination. This enables workers to take the training course of their choice and to be more flexible in job selection. The double certificate practice will soon extend to the private sector to enable self-employed people and the rural labor force to increase their technical competence (CVQDV, 1994). The adoption of double certificates indicates that a reform is under way to maintain balance between theoretical knowledge and practical skills, so as to supply the labor market with technically competent graduates rather than school leavers lacking vocational skills.

The preemployment training and the vocational training and education were legitimized in the *Labor Law of the People's Republic of China* (hereafter called the Law) effective in January 1995. According to the Law, "laborers to be engaged in technical work must receive pre-job training before taking up their posts" (Article 68). The Law also proclaims that the state shall determine occupational classification, set up professional skill standards for the occupations classified, and practice a system of vocational qualification certificates (Article 69). In addition, the government shall authorize organizations in charge of the examination and verification of the professional skills of laborers.

The government's emphasis on employee training and development has witnessed a rapid growth in vocational education and training. According to relevant reports (*China Labour Daily,* August 8, 1996, p. 1; Guan, 1990; Li, 1994), the number of technical schools increased to 4,521 with 1.98 million students at the end of 1995, compared to 334 technical schools with 0.12 million students in 1966. The employment training centers established by large enterprises or local government since the reform increased to more than 2,700 across the country at the end of 1995, and 1.22 million people received training in 1995. As the traditional labor allocation system is replaced by an open labor market, vocationally trained graduates have to compete for jobs in the market. This competition, in turn, has placed pressure on vocational schools and individual students. Schools have to offer courses according to market demands to attract more students. Students have to grasp knowledge and skills in order to be technically competent and competitive.

Management Education Since the Reforms

While training for vocational and professional skills has been emphasized, further training for adults, especially cadres or managers, has been carried out with equal vigor. Since the 1980s, many institutions for adults' further education have been established, such as Worker-Staff College, TV University, and Management Training College (Lu & An, 1991; Zhao, 1995). These institutions enroll part-time and full-time students and usually offer only a 2-year college associate diploma (nondegree, called *Da-Zhuan* in Chinese). Among China's labor administration and managerial staff, 35% had obtained a *Da-Zhuan* diploma in 1990 in contrast to 14% in 1982 (Zhao, 1995, p. 273). Meanwhile, a nationwide program of management training has been introduced by the State Economic Commission (SEC). The SEC collaborated with institutions from the United States, the United Kingdom, Germany, Canada, Japan, and the European Economic Community (EEC) to run management training courses, including the MBA program. In the late 1980s, more than 15 universities in China formally set up MBA courses under the coordination of the State Education Commission (Child, 1994). Wang (1990) reported that "during the period 1979-1985, more than 8 million managers and supervisors passed some sort of management training courses" (p. 204). The Ministry of Personnel, the authority controlling all cadres, has also conducted various training programs for managers. For instance, since 1992 the Ministry of Personnel organized senior managers from enterprises to attend "human resource management training programs" in Singapore (Lu, Chang, Zhang, Yu, & Liu, 1994). Child (1994) notes "the scale of China's management education and training effort is impressive and is a clear manifestation of the regime's determination to modernise the economy" (p. 174).

TRAINING AND DEVELOPMENT IN
CHINA'S INDUSTRIAL ENTERPRISES

During 1994 and 1995, I went to China to conduct research work, including a survey, on HRM practices in the industrial sector. This section details and analyzes relevant results to illustrate the current situation and practice of employee training and development in China's industrial enterprises. The survey questionnaire builds on the work of Von Glinow on best international human resource management practices (Von Glinow, 1993). Shenkar (1994) argues that the validity of questionnaires designed in the West for non-Western societies such as China is open to question, especially when translation is required. To minimize such problems, I, with bilingual skills and over three decades of personal experience in China, checked the translated questionnaire and made some alterations to reflect local idioms and differences in written Chinese (a simplified set of characters as commonly used in the PRC was adopted). This helped the Chinese respondents to understand the questions better, and made the survey more suitable to the Chinese context.

In the survey, 850 questionnaires were distributed to managerial and nonmanagerial employees in enterprises covering four major ownership categories: state-owned enterprises, collectively owned enterprises, privately owned enterprises, and international joint ventures. After distributing questionnaire forms, I conducted seminars at each enterprise to explain the purpose and importance of the survey and to answer respondents' questions. The most typical concern of respondents was that of disclosure of their views. This fear could be understood, considering the frequent political purges that people have suffered since the PRC was founded. To reduce such fear and avoid any possible uncertainty, it was stressed again that all answers were strictly confidential and anonymous, and I collected them personally.

A total of 440 usable questionnaires were returned by respondents. The questionnaire included a wide range of topics regarding human resource man-

TABLE 16.2 Highest Education Level Completed (%)

Education Level	All Respondents (N = 424)	Respondents at Managerial Level (N = 302)
High school certificate or less	26.7	18.9
Some university education*	42.9	45.4
Bachelor's degree	27.1	31.8
Some post-graduate education	0.7	1.0
Post-graduate degree	2.6	3.0

NOTE: * Two-year college associate diploma (nondegree, called *Da-Zhuan* in Chinese).

agement practices, such as staffing, performance appraisal, training, and development. Survey questions relevant to this chapter covered three aspects: (a) type of training programs offered; (b) the extent to which training is being and ought to be used (classified into "Is Now" and "Should Be" questions); and (c) perceived effectiveness of training and development in terms of employee job satisfaction and organizational operation.

Of 440 respondents, 71% (313 respondents) were at management level (managers and supervisors) and the rest (127 respondents) were nonmanagerial (workers and technicians). More than two thirds of respondents (68%) were male, and 69% were aged 30 to 49. Educational backgrounds indicate that 73.3% of all respondents had attained tertiary level qualifications (see Table 16.2). This is because the survey was conducted mainly in three major well-developed and industrialized cities—Shanghai, Tianjing, and Nanjing. The educational level in these cities is much higher than in other areas. It is worth noting, however, that a significant number of respondents had received a 2-year college associate diploma (42.9% of total respondents and 45.4% of those at managerial level), a consequence of the government's promotion of further education since the reform as previously discussed.

The response rate was quite high at 52%, but the data have two major limitations. First, some HRM practices were not in existence, and employees were not aware of such management practices, so they simply left some questions unanswered. For example, in some enterprises performance appraisal was conducted solely by managers without informing employees (Zhu & Dowling, 1997). Second, as the comparison of results from "Is Now" (current practices) and "Should Be" (ideal practices in the future) questions was subjected to paired-sample *t* tests, any incomplete answer, that is, one answered only

"Is Now" or "Should Be," was excluded from processing. Some respondents had no idea on how training and development should be practiced in the future, and thus only answered "Is Now" questions (on average, 340 respondents answered "Is Now" questions whereas only 284 answered "Should Be" questions). As a result, sample size varies from 270 to 424 for different items because of missing data.

Response options were based on a 5-point, Likert-type scale ranging from 1 = "Not at all" to 5 = "To a very great extent." For the question of perceived effectiveness of training and development, this chapter groups results of 1 and 2 into a "low" category; the results of 3 are "medium," and 4 and 5 have been grouped into a "high" category.

Survey results related to training and development are analyzed and discussed in terms of three aspects. The first is types of training programs offered, including on-the-job and off-the-job training, induction and orientation for new employees, occupational skills, technical and profession skills, and management development programs. The second is the purpose of training and development, classified into four groups: to remove performance deficiencies, to update technical knowledge and skills, to increase the adaptability of the workforce, and to increase employee commitment (Schuler, Dowling, Smart, & Huber, 1992). The final aspect is the perceived effectiveness of training and development in terms of (a) increasing employee performance, (b) increasing job satisfaction, and (c) the overall effectiveness of the organization.

Types of Training Programs Offered

Table 16.3 indicates that state-owned enterprises (SOEs) offer more training programs than the other three types of enterprises. This reflects a high degree of state involvement in training and development and the level of state control over SOEs. State ownership still dominates industry, such that SOEs usually had "a consistent set of personnel practices" such as training and development (Zhao, 1994, p. 7). International joint ventures (IJVs), mostly formed with SOEs, offered more off-the-job training (40% compared to 27% in collectively owned enterprises and 17% in privately owned enterprises), technical and professional skills training (72% compared to 59% and 53%, respectively, for collectively and privately owned enterprises), and management development programs (47% compared to 44% and 29%, respectively). This could be attributed to the influence of both the state and foreign companies. Dalton and Austen (1995)

TABLE 16.3 Types of Training Programs Offered in Chinese Enterprises With
Different Types of Ownership

Training Offered	SOEs (N = 176) %	COEs (N = 72) %	POEs (N = 18) %	IJVs (N = 77) %	General (N = 343) %
On-the-job training	92	83	78	68	84
Off-the-job training	58	27	17	40	45
Induction/Orientation	69	46	75	73	65
Occupational skills	85	70	71	63	76
Technical/ professional skills	81	59	53	72	73
Management development	77	44	29	47	62

find that most foreign companies have recognized that "training for local employees is critical to successful operations. Good training and development can make up the shortfall in skills, while also providing a company with a considerable competitive edge in the market" (p. 60). Furthermore, as more employees prefer to work in the nonpublic sector such as international joint ventures (IJVs), it is easier for IJVs to recruit preskilled workers who might have been trained in state-owned enterprises. This explains why those ventures offer less basic technical training such as on-the-job training (68% in IJVs and 92% in SOEs) and occupational skills training (63% in IJVs and 85% in SOEs). It should be noted that privately owned enterprises (POEs) offered many fewer training programs for employees, and this may be attributed to their informal management practices and profit-focused short-term strategy. Yuan (1992) points out that profit-maximizing has become the major purpose for many POEs, which usually offer a higher salary to employees but pay little attention to employee training and career development. Thus employees working in POEs may lack further training opportunities.

The Purpose of Training and Development

The major purposes of training and development are classified into four groups as defined by Schuler et al. (1992, p. 329); namely, to remove performance deficiencies, to update technical knowledge and skills, to increase the adaptability of the workforce, and to increase employee commitment. Ten survey questions were composed to determine the extent to which training is

TABLE 16.4 The Extent to Which Training Is Used for the Purposes of Removing
Performance Deficiencies and Updating Technical Knowledge and
Skills

Variable		Number of Pairs	Means	S.D.	t Test
When first	(Is now)	283	3.65	.711	11.30*
started work	(Should be)		4.14	.576	
To remedy poor	(Is now)	285	3.52	.781	12.16*
performance	(Should be)		4.10	.695	
To improve	(Is now)	283	3.72	.733	11.64*
technical ability	(Should be)		4.23	.615	
To prepare for	(Is now)	277	3.32	.905	12.56*
future job	(Should be)		4.04	.751	

* $p < .0005$.

being used currently ("Is Now") and should be used in the future ("Should Be")
to serve these four major purposes.

Paired-sample t tests were used to assess differences between existing and
preferred practices. The test results reported in Tables 16.4, 16.5, and 16.6 had
two major indications. First, by examining the means of "Is Now" and "Should
Be" answers, it can be seen that the current training and development practice
patterns are different from the perceived patterns in the future. Second, the
differences identified between current and future practices are statistically
significant ($p < .0005$). The details of these results are discussed below.

Table 16.4 indicates that training is currently used for removing performance
deficiencies and updating technical skills in the medium to high range (means
of "Is Now" questions range from 3.32 to 3.72). Comparing data in Tables 16.4,
16.5, and 16.6, it can be noticed that training is most frequently used for
employees when they first start work (3.65) and to improve employees' technical
ability (3.72). However, a higher proportion of respondents expected that
training should continue to serve these two purposes (means of "Should Be" are
4.14 and 4.23, for the first and third questions, respectively, in Table 16.4).
Statistically, such differences were significant, that is, t^1 (df) = 11.30 (281), $p <$
.0005 and t^3 (df) = 11.64 (282), $p < .0005$ (t^1 and t^3 refer to the t values of the
first and third questions, respectively, in Table 16.4). This indicates that these
two purposes would be a predominant feature of training in the future. The
remaining data in Table 16.4 also indicate that there is a clear trend toward
increasing the use of training for remedying poor performance and preparing

TABLE 16.5 The Extent to Which Training Is Used for the Purpose of Increasing Workforce Adaptability

Variable		Number of Pairs	Means	S.D.	t Test
To build teamwork	(Is now)	270	3.09	.911	12.32*
	(Should be)		3.75	.764	
To improve interpersonal abilities	(Is now)	276	2.88	.891	12.34*
	(Should be)		3.54	.824	
To have multiskills	(Is now)	276	3.29	.901	12.96*
	(Should be)		4.03	.721	

* $p < .0005$.

employees for future employment from a current moderate to large extent (e.g., means increase from current 3.52 and 3.32 to 4.10 and 4.04, respectively, in the future). These findings are consistent with the government's emphasis on vocational training and technical education. They also reflect the fact that training is focused more on job-related skills and improvement of labor productivity because enterprises now have to face competition in the market, rather than depend on the state regardless of their performance.

The data in Table 16.5 indicate that except for helping employees to be multiskilled (the mean of "Is Now" was 3.29), training is used at a relatively low level for increasing workforce adaptability. Currently, the means of "Is Now" for building teamwork and improving interpersonal abilities were only 3.09 and 2.88, respectively, while the means of "Should Be" for these two items were 3.75 and 3.54, respectively. This indicates a moderate increase in the future. In contrast, multiskilling is now receiving more attention than it did under a planned economy. Holton (1990) notes that "since the great majority of employees in the state-owned enterprises spend their entire working lives in the unit to which they are initially assigned, there is no perceived need to train people broadly" (p. 124). Many Chinese managers believed that the way to improve labor productivity was to teach everyone to do one task well (Nelson & Reeder, 1985). This situation has not been improved since the economic reforms, when scientific management techniques such as specialization and the division of labor became popular in Chinese industries (Chan & Senser, 1997; Riskin, 1987; Zhao, 1995). However, an increasing pressure on enterprises reallocating redundant employees has called for cross-skilling and multiskilling training. Enterprises, especially state-owned, have been required by the state to find jobs for those retrenched employees rather than sending them home. Liu (1994) reported

TABLE 16.6 The Extent to Which Training Is Used for the Purpose of Increasing Employee Commitment

Variable		Number of Pairs	Means	S.D.	t Test
To help understand	(Is now)	274	3.20	.842	12.31*
business	(Should be)		3.86	.755	
To teach employees	(Is now)	277	3.15	.850	14.39*
about values	(Should be		3.88	.723	
To provide reward	(Is now)	272	2.76	.932	12.06*
	(Should be)		3.51	.953	

* $p < .0005$.

that by mid-1994 more than 200,000 retrenched employees in China had received cross-work training offered by their organizations, and 80% of them had obtained new jobs. This case provides strong support for the development of multiskilling in China.

Multiskilling, together with other technical training rather than behavioral training, remains standard practice in China's manufacturing sector (Von Glinow & Teagarden, 1990). Although Wang (1990) argued that management training in China had started to include some short courses of organizational psychology, the survey results show only a low to moderate usage of training for behavioral training such as team building and interpersonal ability. Laaksonen (1988) notes that there is a great power distance between top and middle management in China, as "Chinese top management holds nearly all the strings of decision-making in its hands, and allows very little power to lower levels" (p. 316). This traditional bureaucratic structure in Chinese management, plus inadequate behavioral training, can make the adoption of teamwork difficult for most Chinese enterprises (Dalton & Austen, 1995).

Dalton and Austen (1995) claim that employee commitment to the company can be increased in Chinese enterprises by teaching employees certain values, such as equality between top management and workers, and by introducing an approachable management style that looks after the individual. Geringer and Frayne (1990) also believe that training can be used to encourage people to think and behave in ways consistent with the company's cultures, objectives, and interests. However, the data in Table 16.6 indicate that training is currently used at a moderate level to help employees understand their company's business and value systems (means of 3.20 and 3.15, respectively). Nevertheless, far more respondents believed that training should be used in the future to increase employ-

TABLE 16.7   Results of Perceived Effectiveness of Training and Development Practices (%)

Response Scale	Increasing Employees' Performance (N = 385)	Increasing Job Satisfaction (N = 373)	Overall Effectiveness of Organization (N = 387)
Low	7.5	9.9	6.0
Medium	28.1	33.0	25.8
High	64.4	57.1	68.2

ees' awareness of the company's business and cultures (means of 3.86 and 3.88, respectively).

Table 16.6 also shows that training is used at a low level for providing reward (mean = 2.76). The expected increased use for this purpose (3.51) is modest compared with other purposes. Using training merely for reward rather than for finding a match between organizational and personal needs is often because "very few enterprises have drawn up systematic programs for the training and development of their managers and employees, based on anything like an audit of future needs and personal potential" (Child, 1994, p. 174). In many organizations the decision to send an employee for training is often centralized, and is often influenced by one's connections rather than one's merits or needs (Laaksonen, 1988; Wang, 1993). Where connection-oriented favoritism rather than systematic training programs based on training needs is practiced, it is difficult to provide training as a real nonmonetary reward.

The Perceived Effectiveness of Training

The perceived effectiveness of training was addressed by three questions exploring the effectiveness of training and development as currently conducted in the enterprise. Data in Table 16.7 are skewed more toward the medium to high level. This demonstrates a very positive attitude toward current training practices. To cross examine the reliability of these data, factor analysis and Spearman's rank-order procedure were utilized to ascertain' correlations between training practices and perceived effectiveness. The results (ranging from 0.22 to 0.38, $p < 0.01$) indicated that all of the correlations departed significantly from zero, though none of them were especially impressive. However, there was a tendency for respondents to give a subjective assessment of their own enterprise.

This is especially true in China, where culturally, overt criticism and conflict are actively avoided (Weldon & Jehn, 1993). Considering the limitations of the responses, the survey results here indicate only that training and development practices have been recognized as an effective tool in individual and organizational development.

In spite of the moderate to high level of effectiveness perceived by respondents, the literature reveals many inadequacies and limitations in China's training system. In 1994, the Beijing Youth Study Association conducted a survey on young employees' feedback about their work (Lu, 1994). The survey results related to training disclose that of 1,508 respondents, 34.0% had never been offered any training opportunities; 28.9% received only one technical training course; and 20.4% attended one political education class. When the respondents were asked about their knowledge of economic management, 54% said they were totally lacking in such knowledge. The survey results indicate that further education and career development offered to employees is far from sufficient. This could be attributed in part to managers' passive attitude toward training and the lack of support from other management practices. For example, since the adoption of the "Contract Management Responsibility System" in 1984, managers with short-term contracts adopted a short-term strategy in their production, marketing, and profit making, with little emphasis on employee training. Meanwhile, training is often seen as costly and risky by many Chinese managers, because their enterprises may not receive immediate returns on training, and employees may leave the organization after training (Yu & Xin, 1994; Zhao, 1995). Furthermore, given the widespread lack of complete human resource management practices, it is difficult to achieve progress in the training and development system alone (Von Glinow & Teagarden, 1990).

IMPLICATIONS OF CURRENT EMPLOYEE TRAINING AND DEVELOPMENT

China is at a stage of dramatic transition toward a more market-oriented economy, and these changes are accelerated partially by the return of Hong Kong to the PRC, because Hong Kong is much more developed in its market economy and more experienced in developing some Western-style HRM practices. Current reforms and progress in employee training have facilitated the transition by increasing vocational training and education, emphasizing management development, and improving workforce quality. The state requirements for training have profound implications for business and management. First, enterprises need to increase their commitment and investment in employee training programs because of new legislation, market competition, and a changing workforce. Second, foreign partners in international joint ventures in China need to place more emphasis on both management and employee training and development to achieve better performance. Third, training programs need to be related to organizational strategies to be effective. Finally, training and development need to run in conjunction with other human resource management practices. These implications are discussed below.

The Need to Increase Commitment and Investment in Training and Development

The enterprises surveyed have all offered various training programs, with a focus on new recruits, and on the existing workers so as to update their technical knowledge and skills. This suggests training and development have been used as a means of implementing enterprise reform, and it indicates progress in management. However, it has been 20 years since the reforms and there is still a shortage of highly skilled workers and experts in China, as well as a scarcity of qualified managers (Benson, 1996; Child, 1994). This fact, together with challenges from areas such as legislation, market competition, a young workforce with more surplus laborers, the changing nature of jobs, and the changing economic structure, demands increasing commitment and investment in employee training programs. The major challenges are identified and discussed in the following sections.

The Legitimized Requirement for Training and Development. In 1981, the State Council of China stipulated that enterprises should set aside a minimum of 1.5% of the total wage bill as a recurrent fund for employee education and training (Lu, 1987). Following this, some local governments made their own requirements, or local rules, for employee training and development funds. For instance, in the early 1990s, the provincial government in Jiangsu specified that each enterprise should increase its investment in employee training and development from 0.5% to at least 2.5% of its total wage bill (Xu & Wang, 1994). Furthermore, the Labor Law has a special chapter on vocational training and requires that

> the employing unit shall establish a system for vocational training, raise and use funds for vocational training in accordance with the provisions of the State, and

provide laborers with vocational training in a planned way and in the light of the actual situation of the unit. (Article 68)

This is the first time since the PRC was founded that China has enshrined the requirement for employee training and development in law. In May 1996, the state issued "The Vocational Education Law" to legitimize the development of both vocational education and employment training (*China Labour Daily,* August 8, 1996, p. 1). Benson (1996) points out that the Chinese government plans to train or retrain 90% of the urban labor force and 50% of the surplus rural labor force between 1996 and 2000. Government policies and legislation have evidently pressed enterprises to place more emphasis on employee training and development.

Competing in a More Market-Oriented Economy. The economic reforms have facilitated the growth of new enterprises in the private sector, and this has placed increasing competition on state-owned enterprises. As Yabuki (1995) notes, Chinese official statistics reveal the share of the gross value of industrial production contributed by state-owned enterprises fell from 74% in 1982 to 48.1% in 1992. Meanwhile, nonpublic owned enterprises were showing remarkable growth, from a zero base in the mid 1980s to 10% of total industrial production in 1990. One of the main reasons for declining growth rates in state-owned enterprises is their unacceptably low productivity. Yabuki (1995) reveals that "the labour productivity of the non-state sector foreign-invested and individually operated enterprises is over three times that of state-owned enterprises" (p. 49). Both Riskin (1987) and Yabuki (1995) point out that such low productivity is directly related to low levels of workforce education and technical training, as well as inadequate enterprise management. With less protection from the central government, state-owned enterprises have to select the most relevant training programs to address the issue of poor productivity rather than just fulfilling training quotas assigned by the government or conducting training as a perfunctory task.

China's Young Workforce With More Surplus Laborers. Between 1962 and 1975, China's population increased by 360 million, with the majority of this population surge now part of the workforce and comprising half the national labor force (Hu & Lu, 1994; Xiao, 1995). Hu and Lu claim that by the end of 2005, China will have a young workforce. However, it will not be effectively utilized unless enterprises are willing to offer more training. In 1991, a research center of the

China Science and Technology Commission conducted a questionnaire of young employees and heads of enterprises across 10 major cities in China (Wang, 1993). According to this survey, the most unsatisfactory aspect of the young employee's working life is lack of corporate training. The results revealed that 53.9% of employees surveyed have never attended any occupational or technical training classes. When asked about their major purpose for training, employees noted their desire to improve technical skills in order to be more competent in their jobs. Meanwhile, 60.6% of the managers admitted the purpose of training was merely to enable employees to meet basic production requirements. These results indicate that young employees' willingness to be trained is often undermined by some managers' short-term approach to training. In order to be more productive and competitive, managers should invest further in training these young employees, as this will result in a more competent and, hopefully, more committed workforce.

While China has a relatively young workforce, many state-owned enterprises are facing the dilemma of reallocating rather than retrenching their increased surplus of employees as requested by the government (Zhu & Dowling, 1994). The adoption of the "responsibility system" and "scientific management" has emphasized full work loads and productivity improvement. This resulted in a rapidly increasing number of redundant laborers. In 1995, there were 15 million redundant employees in urban areas who remained on the pay roll and were waiting to be reallocated to other jobs (Shi, 1995). The Shanghai Academy of Social Sciences conducted research concerning the reemployment situation of redundant employees in 1988 and 1994 (Tao, 1994). This study finds that more retrenched employees prefer to be retrained by their organizations before reemployment. The study indicates that in 1988, 20% of the 1,841 redundant workers investigated selected retraining for new employment, and this percentage increased in 1994 to 31% (the number of workers investigated in 1994 was 950). Obviously, training helps to increase employability, and "having a workforce that is characterized by its employability is probably a necessary prerequisite for corporate survival" (Greer, 1995, p. 6).

The Changing Nature of Jobs and the Changing Economic Structure. In 1987, Johnston and Packer predicted that in the 21st century, "jobs that are currently in the middle of the skill distribution will be the least-skilled occupations of the future, and there will be very few net new jobs for the unskilled" (p. 100). Job skills become more complicated with the development of technology and advancing industrialization. Between 1979 and 1993, China's GDP (Gross

TABLE 16.8   The Composition of the Chinese Workforce in the Primary, Secondary, and Tertiary Industries: 1978, 1990, and 2000

Year	Primary Industry Number*	%	Secondary Industry Number*	%	Tertiary Industry Number*	%	Total Workforce Number*
1978	285	70.5	71	17.4	49	12.1	405
1990	346	60	126	21.9	104	18.1	576
2000	276	43.4	176	27.7	184	28.9	636

SOURCE: Yang, 1996; Yao, 1996.
NOTE: *in millions.

Domestic Product) grew at an average annual rate of 9.3% (The Statistical Yearbook of China, 1994). This boom in China's economy has facilitated foreign investment, which has brought in advanced technology and sped up changes in the nature of employment.

The changing nature of jobs is also closely related to the improvement of China's economic structure. Table 16.8 shows the composition of the Chinese workforce in the primary, secondary, and tertiary industrial sectors between 1978 and 2000. It can be seen that in 1978 only 12.1% of the total labor force was engaged in the tertiary sector, but this figure is expected to increase to 28.9% in 2000 (Yang, 1996; Yao, 1996). With more laborers moving from the primary and secondary industries to the service industries, vocational and employment training has become essential for acquiring competent employees. To catch up with these changes and to prepare for the future, enterprises have had to invest in employee training and development.

The Need to Emphasize Training of Both Labor and Management in Joint Ventures

According to the official statistics, by the end of 1995, 160 countries and regions had put a total investment of U.S.$160 billion into 259,000 projects in China, making the country the largest investment recipient among the developing countries in the world (Li, 1996). Meanwhile, these foreign invested ventures recruited nearly 9 million Chinese employees (*Economic Daily,* February 19, 1997, p. 3). However, many researchers (see Melvin, 1996, and Nyaw, 1995) have pointed out that the quality of China's labor force is significantly lower than that of other industrialized countries. For example, the percentage of senior technical workers in the workforce is over 40% in Japan and Germany, but only

1% in China. This shortage of skilled workers is partly attributed to passive or narrowly defined training, "in contrast to the Western HRM notion of planning for long-term staff development" as noted by Warner (1993, p. 46). Warner's comment was supported by the survey results obtained from my research, which indicated that training was focused more on the remedy of current performance deficiencies. Due to the lack of a sense of career development, employees tend to change jobs frequently, in pursuit of higher wages rather than skills development. In order to have competent employees, the foreign partners of joint ventures have to invest in employee training to make their venture successful.

With more multinational corporations (MNCs) expanding their businesses into China, it has become a key strategy for many MNCs, such as Motorola, to localize management so as to develop a large corporate presence in China (*China Business Review,* July-August 1996, p. 46; Melvin & Sylvester, 1997). While seeking to hire more Chinese nationals for executive jobs because of their communication skills, local contacts, and understanding of the domestic market (Kamis, 1996), many MNCs have noticed that Chinese managers may lack decision-making skills and individual initiatives as the consequence of traditional education and training systems. Thus it is essential to offer corporate management training programs that address not only job-specific hard skills but also management soft skills, such as problem-solving skills in the context of crisis or high-pressure situations (Melvin, 1996).

The Need to Link Training and Development to Organizational Strategies

The results of the survey I conducted during 1994 and 1995 indicate that more than 65% of the enterprises surveyed offer training courses to new recruits and the existing workforce. However, it appears that the separation of training programs from organizational strategies, a lack of systematic planning, and insufficient evaluation of training programs are still major problems in China's employee training (Huang, 1994; Zhao, 1995). For instance, it has often been found that employees' education level was increased after training, but that their technical skills and productivity remained stagnant (Zhao, 1995). It has also been noted that some enterprises offered training programs simply as required by the government or legislation, rather than out of their own perceived production needs (Yu & Xin, 1994). Such problems are primarily a legacy of the former planned economy where managers were simply the followers and implementors of the government's instructions. On the other hand, training programs offered in China's manufacturing enterprises focus primarily on the technical side.

Warner (1993), who has researched management practices in China's manufacturing enterprises, claims "training remains narrowly defined in contrast to the Western HRM notion of planning for long-term staff development" (p. 46). In order to link training and development closely to organizational strategies, enterprises need to identify their short- and long-term training needs, design training programs that address technical and behavioral issues, and have an evaluation system in place to check "if the training and development program met its objectives" (Schuler et al., 1992, p. 355).

The Need to Integrate Training and Development With Other HRM Practices

In general, training and development should be strategically related to other HRM practices, such as staffing, appraisal, and compensation, which are complementary (Harris & DeSimone, 1994; Schuler et al., 1992; Zhao, 1995). The problems identified in China's training and development, as discussed above, indicate that there is a strong need to implement more HRM practices. According to a report of the Ministry of Labor (*China Labour Daily,* June 8, 1996, p. 1), by the end of 1995, more than 60% of the state-owned enterprises' workforce, that is, 45 million employees, had their wages linked to the company's economic efficiencies and individual performance. Meanwhile, over 30 million employees' wages were based on the skills of their working positions. The reform in compensation has placed significance on the improvement of job skills through training.

An HRM model proposed by Zhao (1995, p. 74) for Chinese enterprises highlights the significance of training and development and their dependence upon other functions, such as utilizing performance appraisals to identify training needs and linking compensation to performance to enhance training achievement. This model proposed to carry out five practices: to attract potentially qualified job applicants through human resource planning and recruitment and selection; to utilize employees effectively with the help of performance appraisal and compensation; to develop employees' potential via education and training; to raise employees' initiative by adopting motivational practices; and to retain key employees by integrating and implementing HRM practices, especially training and development. The model introducing Western HRM concepts and practices is being taught in many Chinese universities' management subjects and introduced to Chinese managers in their training courses. As the government continues to push for the implementation of modern management practices, enterprises will be under more pressure to integrate training and development with other HRM practices.

THE FUNCTIONS OF CHINA'S TRADE UNIONS IN HRM UNDER TRANSITIONS

China's trade unions, fully named the All-China Federation of Trade Unions (ACFTU), used to "transmit the party line to workers, encourage production, engage in political education, and execute a range of welfare chores" (Hoffmann, 1974, p. 134). Created by the Communist Party, the trade unions are always strongly influenced by the Party and are "just another voice within the state and party apparatus" (Chan & Senser, 1997, p. 113). Generally, the trade unions were of a nonconfrontational nature before the reforms, when there was little conflict between employees and management. This was because workers were mainly employed by the state and were offered secured positions with their wages and welfare centrally controlled and adjusted.

Since the reforms, management, especially in international joint ventures and privately owned enterprises, has been granted more or even full autonomy to hire and fire employees, to determine employee compensation packages, and to abolish lifetime employment. For example, different wage systems were tried or adopted by enterprises, such as floating, structural, or "blurred" (i.e., unpredicted) wage systems (see Jackson, 1992; Nyaw, 1995). Meanwhile, a labor contract system was implemented nationwide. By the end of May 1996, 88.7% of the workforce in China was under the labor contract (*China Labour Daily*, August 8, 1996, p. 1). Consequently, labor relations in China are no longer just between employees and the state, but increasingly between workers and foreign investors or their representatives, private employers, and managers who have become legal representatives of enterprises.

It has been reported that many labor relations disputes occurred since the reforms due to unjustified dismissals, unequitable wage packages, and even physical punishment (see Chan & Senser, 1997; Zhao, 1995; Zhu & Dowling, 1994). L. Z. An (1996) argues that the trade unions should play an important role in reducing such disputes and conflicts by participating in more activities. These include the unions' participation in constituting a series of labor-related laws and regulations, such as the "Labor Protection Law" and the "Minimum Wage Law"; assisting and advising individual workers when they sign labor contracts, and supervising the implementation of the contracts; advocating the adoption of a collective contract and signing this contract on behalf of employees; being actively involved in mediation of labor disputes; and supervising the implementation of the "Labor Law" within the enterprise. Does An's argument suggest that the trade unions have or will have new functions in HRM practices under current transitions when there are more conflicts between labor relations?

Many researchers have noted that the trade unions remain a non-Party apparatus to link the Party and the workforce and to facilitate management (see Brown & Branine, 1996; Jackson, 1992; Laaksonen, 1988). Warner (1993) also claims that "there is little comparison between western collective bargaining and the Chinese model of labour management with the trade unions in a subordinate role in the enterprise" (p. 49). This is especially true now when the CPC has endeavored to strengthen its position in the state-owned enterprises. In a recently issued document (*The Notice of Further Strengthening the CPC's Role and Improving the CPC's Construction Work in the State-owned Enterprises*; see *People's Daily,* March 11, 1997, p. 1), the Central Committee of the CPC has stressed that the political leadership of the Party over the enterprises is always of great significance, and that the Party branch of an enterprise should be involved in major decision making, such as business strategies, development planning, budgeting, and hiring and firing of middle-level and senior-level managers. The CPC also emphasized in this document that all cadres of an enterprise, that is, managers and white-collar employees, including heads of trade unions, should be managed by the Party. This means that only the Party branch will have the power to recommend managers who are above the middle level and to monitor and comment on the hiring and firing decisions made by the general manager or the board of directors. The Party branch is also responsible for training, appraising, and monitoring managerial staff at all levels. Considering the increased authority of the CPC in enterprises, there is no doubt that the trade unions will only be able to follow the Party's instruction.

However, while the trade unions are still passive supporters of management in state-owned enterprises, they may gradually become active defenders of workers' interests in international joint ventures and wholly foreign-owned companies in China. Nyaw (1995) has noted that "one unique aspect of the trade unions of joint ventures in China is that they deal directly with foreign partners or their representatives with regards to labour disputes or grievance" (p. 210). Similarly, when I conducted a field study in China, I also noticed that Chinese partners of joint ventures often used the trade unions to negotiate with their foreign partners in terms of wage increase or welfare distribution.

Trade unions are not mandatory in joint ventures, but the Labor Law has legitimized laborers' right to form and participate in the trade unions. The ACFTU in May 1994 announced a campaign to organize unions in all overseas-funded enterprises, and in September 1996, the ACFTU reported that 48,000 out of 120,000 such enterprises had been unionized (Chan & Senser, 1997). Although Chan and Senser argue that the trade unions have little or no impact even when they are in place, the government has called for the establishment of trade unions in those enterprises to protect local employees from being exploited or unfairly treated by foreign investors (Zhao, 1995). Therefore, the trade unions will help the state to monitor and supervise the foreign partners of joint ventures (when foreign investors hold a majority of ownership) or foreign employers of wholly foreign-owned companies in implementing the Labor Law, especially in the area of HRM, such as employee compensation, training, and contract termination.

CONCLUSION

This chapter has examined training and development practices in China's industrial enterprises under a planned economy and the progress achieved since China's transition to a more market-oriented economy. The literature review and my primary research demonstrate that training and development have been adopted widely as a means of implementing enterprise reforms. Child (1991) claims that the training of Chinese staff may not only develop their technical competence to work with new methods and technologies, but also recognize individual worth and offer incentives, "neither of which were much encouraged in the typical Chinese enterprise" (p. 104). This suggests that the sort of training and development offered in China's enterprises is currently limited when compared with the Western HRM model or the Japanese management model (Warner, 1993). As long as the training and development system remains one of the key factors "in determining China's ability to compete in world markets" (Gregory & Wales, 1996, p. 29), the role of training and development is expected to continue to increase in the future as indicated by various surveys and researchers (e.g., Benson, 1996; Child, 1994; Warner, 1993; Zhao, 1995).

The market-oriented economic system that facilitated employee training practices since the reforms began indicates that China is striving to be readmitted as a viable member of the World Trade Organization. As such, it will soon face the more rigorous competition of the world economy. A critical factor for China will be its ability to fashion a competitive workforce. Considering the problems identified with China's workforce, the discussion in this chapter has concentrated on the need for enterprises to engage in an expanded range of training and development. Consequently, both the public and private sectors must pay more attention to the improvement of human resources for competitive reasons.

While employee training has become one of the major emerging issues in China's HRM, the chapter also briefly explored a potential new role played by the trade unions in international joint ventures and wholly foreign-owned enterprises. With an increase in labor relations disputes in those enterprises, trade unions would likely be used to protect Chinese employees' interests and to reduce such conflicts. Therefore, foreign investors should also seek cooperation with the trade unions in their management of enterprises in China.

REFERENCES

An, L. Z. (1996). Discussion on labor relations under the transition. *Laodong Jinji yu Renli Ziyuan Guanli* (Labor economy and human resource management) (Vol. 2, pp. 8-9). Beijing: China's People's University. (in Chinese)

Benson, J. (1996, June 13). The sleeping giant slumbers no more. *People Management,* pp. 22-26.

Borgonjon, J., & Vanhonacker, W. R. (1992, September-October). Modernising China's managers (Special report). *The China Business Review,* pp. 12-18.

Brown, D. H., & Branine, M. (1996). Adaptive personnel management: Evidence of an emerging heterogeneity in China's foreign trade corporations. In D. H. Brown & P. Porter (Eds.), *Management issues in China* (Vol. 1, pp. 191-213). New York: Routledge.

Chan, A. H. H. (1990). Managerial reforms in Chinese enterprises: The roadblocks that remain. In J. Child & M. Lockett (Eds.), *Advances in Chinese industrial studies.* London: JAI.

Chan, A., & Senser, R. A. (1997, March/April). China's troubled workers. *Foreign Affairs,* pp. 104-117.

Child, J. (1990). The character of Chinese enterprise management. In J. Child & M. Lockett (Eds.), *Advances in Chinese industrial studies* (pp. 137-152). London: JAI.

Child, J. (1991). A foreign perspective on the management of people in China. *The International Journal of Human Resource Management, 2*(1), 93-107.

Child, J. (1994). *Management in China during the age of reform.* Cambridge, UK: Cambridge University Press.

The China Business Review. (various; references in text).

China Labour Daily (*Zhongguo Gongren Ribao*). (various, references in text).

China Vocational Qualification Development and Verification (CVQDV). (1994). *Enhancing China's vocational qualification verification system* (Vol. 7). Beijing: Vocational Qualification Verification Centre of the Ministry of Labor. (in Chinese)

Dalton, T., & Austen, G. (1995). *Operating successfully in China: Lessons from leading Australian companies.* Melbourne: International Market Assessment.

Economic Daily (*Jingji Ribao*). (various; references in text).

Geringer, J. M., & Frayne, C. A. (1990). Human resource management and international joint venture control: A parent company perspective. *Management International Review, 30* [Special issue], 103-120.

Greer, C. R. (1995). *Strategy and human resources: A general managerial perspective.* Englewood Cliffs, NJ: Prentice Hall.

Gregory, M., & Wales, T. (1996, June 13). A glimpse of shopfloor life. *People Management,* pp. 26-29.

Guan, Y. T. (Ed.). (1990). *An introduction to vocational training.* Beijing: China's Labor Press. (in Chinese)

Hare, P. (1983). China's system of industrial economic planning. In S. Feuchtwang & A. Hussain (Eds.), *The Chinese economic reforms* (pp. 185-223). London: Croom Helm.

Harris, D. M., & DeSimone, R. L. (1994). *Human resource development.* Fort Worth, TX: Dryden.

Hoffmann, C. (1974). *The Chinese worker.* Albany: State University of New York Press.

Holton, R. H. (1990). Human resource management in the People's Republic of China. *Management International Review, 30* [Special issue], 121-136.

Hu, A. G., & Lu, H. (1994). Characteristics and issues of China's human resources. *Laodong Jinji yu Renli Ziyuan Guanli* (Labor economy and human resource management) (Vol. 3, pp. 5-10). Beijing: China's People's University. (in Chinese)

Huang, J. F. (1994). *Modern enterprise organization and human resource management.* Beijing: People's Daily Press. (in Chinese)

Jackson, S. (1992). *Chinese enterprise management: Reforms in economic perspective.* New York: Walter de Gruyter.

Johnston, W. B., & Packer, A. (1987). *Work force 2000: Work and workers for the 21st century.* Indianapolis, IN: Hudson Institute.

Kamis, T. L. (1996, July-August). Education for the PRC executive. *The China Business Review,* pp. 36-39.

Laaksonen, O. (1988). *Management in China during and after Mao in enterprises, government, and party.* Berlin: Walter de Gruyter.

Labour law of the People's Republic of China. (1994). Printed by the Ministry of Labour of the People's Republic of China.

Li, H. Y. (1994). Establishing a professional skill development system to improve workforce competence. In Z. J. Zhang (Ed.), *Study on China's labor system reform* (pp. 216-223). Beijing: China Labor Press. (in Chinese)

Li, J. G. (1996). Chinese economy before the year 2000. *China Today, 45*(6), 16-17.

Lin, D. Z. (1989). *China's contemporary personnel administration system.* Beijing: China Personnel and Labor Press. (in Chinese)

Liu, J. Q. (1994). New approach to the issue of unemployment. *Laodong Jinji yu Renli Ziyuan Guanli* (Labor economy and human resource management) (Vol. 12, pp. 25-27). Beijing: China's People's University. (in Chinese)

Lu, H., & Chen, J. (1990). *Strategic issues in human resource planning in the People's Republic of China.* Working Paper for the Asian HRD Planning Network, International Labor Organization, Asian Employment Program, New Delhi.

Lu, H. J. (Ed). (1987). *Enterprise labor management.* Beijing: China Labor Press. (in Chinese)

Lu, H. J., & An, H. Z. (Eds.). (1991). *Personnel and labor administration in contemporary enterprises.* Beijing: China Labor Press. (in Chinese)

Lu, Y. (1994). Cross-century human resource development. *Laodong Jinji yu Renli Ziyuan Guanli* (Labor economy and human resource management) (Vol. 12, pp. 66-73). Beijing: China's People's University. (in Chinese)

Lu, Z. Y., Chang, Y. S., Zhang, F. H., Yu, Q. H., & Liu, R. R. (1994). *Human resource management in Singapore.* Beijing: China Electronic Industry Press. (in Chinese)

Melvin, S. (1996, March-April). Training the troops. *The China Business Review,* pp. 22-28.

Melvin, S., & Sylvester, K. (1997, May-June). Shipping out. *The China Business Review,* pp. 30-34.

Nelson, J. A., & Reeder, J. A. (1985). Labor relations in China. *California Management Review,* 27(4), 13-32.

Nyaw, M. K. (1995). Human resource management in the People's Republic of China. In L. F. Moore & P. D. Jennings (Eds.), *Human resource management on the Pacific Rim* (pp. 185-216). Berlin: Walter de Gruyter.

Pan, J. Y., & Yang, Y. Y. (1991). Serial thinking of human resource development in China. In J. Y. Pan (Ed.), *The first resources of China* (pp. 1-13). Beijing: Machine-building Industry Press. (in Chinese)

People's Daily *(Renming Ribao).* (various, references in text).

Riskin, C. (1987). *China's political economy: The quest for development since 1949.* New York: Oxford University Press.

Sha, Y. (1987). The role of China's managing directors in the current economic reform. *International Labour Review,* 26(6), 691-701.

Schuler, R. S., Dowling, P. J., Smart, J. P., & Huber, V. L. (1992). *Human resource management in Australia.* Australia: HarperEducational.

Shenkar, O. (1994). The People's Republic of China: Raising the Bamboo Screen through international management research. *International Studies of Management and Organisation,* 24(1-2), 9-34.

The sixth five-year plan of the People's Republic of China for economic and social development (1981-1984). (1984). Beijing: Foreign Language Press.

Shi, S. H. (1995). A new system for utilising human resources. *Laodong Jinji yu Renli Ziyuan Guanli* (Labor economy and human resource management) (Vol. 9, pp. 8-10). Beijing: China's People's University. (in Chinese)

The statistical yearbook of China 1994. (1994). China: State Statistical Bureau.

Stening, B. W., & Ngan, E. F. (1997). The cultural context of human resource management in East Asia. *Asia Pacific Journal of Human Resources, 35*(2), 3-15.

Su, T. L., & Zhu, Q. F. (Eds.). (1992). *Fundamentals of personnel.* Beijing: Beijing Normal College Press. (in Chinese)

Tao, Y. (1994). Dilemma and option of surplus employees. *Laodong Jinji yu Renli Ziyuan Guanli* (Labor economy and human resource management) (Vol. 10, pp. 37-39). Beijing: China's People's University. (in Chinese)

Tretiak, L. D., & Holzmann, K. (1993). *Operating joint venture in China.* Hong Kong: The Economist Intelligence Unit.

Von Glinow, M. A. (1993). Diagnosing "best practice" in human resource management practices. *Research in Personnel and Human Resource Management* (Suppl. 3), 95-112.

Von Glinow, M. A., & Teagarden, M. B. (1990). Contextual determinants of human resource management effectiveness in international cooperative alliances: Evidence from the People's Republic of China. In A. Nedd (Ed.), *International human resource management review* (Vol. 1, pp. 75-94). Singapore: McGraw-Hill.

Wang, F. Y. (1993). Young people's working attitude and expectations in China's urban areas. *Laodong Jinji yu Renli Ziyuan Guanli* (Labor economy and human resource management) (Vol. 7, pp. 27-34). Beijing: China's People's University. (in Chinese)

Wang, Z. M. (1990). Human resource management in China: Recent trends. In R. Pieper (Ed.), *Human resource management: An international comparison* (pp. 195-210). Berlin: Walter de Gruyter.

Warner, M. (1993). Human resource management "with Chinese characteristics." *The International Journal of Human Resource Management, 4*(1), 45-65.

Weldon, E., & Jehn, K. A. (1993). Work goals and work-related beliefs among managers and professionals in the United States and the People's Republic of China. *Asia Pacific Journal of Human Resources, 31*(1), 57-70.

Xiao, Y. N. (1995). On human resource development. *Laodong Jinji yu Renli Ziyuan Guanli* (Labor economy and human resource management) (Vol. 9, pp. 10-15). Beijing: China's People's University. (in Chinese)

Xu, W. J., & Wang, X. Z. (1994). Development trend in China's employees' training. *Laodong Jinji yu Renli Ziyuan Guanli* (Labor economy and human resource management) (Vol. 8, pp. 44-46). Beijing: China's People's University. (in Chinese)

Yabuki, S. (1995). *China's new political economy: The giant awakes* (S. M. Harner, Trans.). Oxford, UK: Westview.

Yang, J. X. (1996). Study on China's tertiary industry development and its demand of labor in different locations. *Laodong Jinji yu Renli Ziyuan Guanli* (Labor economy and human resource management) (Vol. 11, pp. 15-20). Beijing: China's People's University. (in Chinese)

Yao, Y. Q. (1996). The quality of human resources: A critical driving force of China's development. *Laodong Jinji yu Renli Ziyuan Guanli* (Labor economy and human resource management) (Vol. 12, pp. 9-11). Beijing: China's People's University. (in Chinese)

Yu, L. J., & Xin, Z. X. F. (Eds.). (1994). *Introduction to enterprise labour management.* Beijing: China Labour Press.

Yuan, E. Z. (Ed.). (1992). *China's private economy: Current situation, development and evaluation.* Shanghai: Shanghai People's Press. (in Chinese)

Yue, G. Z. (1985). Employment, wages and social security in China. *International Labour Review, 124*(4), 411-422.

Zhao, L. K. (Ed). (1986). *Introduction to personnel management.* Beijing: China Labor Press. (in Chinese)

Zhao, S. M. (1994). Human resource management in China. *Asia Pacific Journal of Human Resources, 32*(2), 3-12.

Zhao, S. M. (1995). *Human resource management in China's enterprises.* Nanjing: Nanjing University Press. (in Chinese)

Zhu, C. J., & Dowling, P. J. (1994). The impact of the economic system upon human resource management practices in China. *Human Resource Planning, 17*(4), 1-21.

Zhu, C. J., & Dowling, P. J. (1997). Performance appraisal in China. In J. Selmer (Ed.), *International management in China.* London: Routledge & Kegan Paul.

Index

About the Editors

Lane Kelley is Professor of International Management at the College of Business Administration, University of Hawaii. For more than 20 years, he has been writing and researching business practices and cultures of Asian business firms. In 1996, he was a visiting scholar under the Fulbright Program at Korea University. In 1992-1993, he was a visiting professor at the Chinese University of Hong Kong. In 1990, he spent his sabbatical as a visiting fellow at the Korean think-tank, KDI. At the University of Hawaii he has served as Director of the Pacific Asian Management Institute (1986-1990), Director of Graduate Studies (1986-1990), and Department Chairman (1981-1988), and Director and Founder of the Pacific Asia Consortium for Business Education and Research. He was responsible for preparing the proposal and was the principal investigator on one of the first five CIBER-Title 6 grants. He is a past president of the Association for Business Simulation and Experiential Learning. He has worked as a consultant and executive trainer for U.S., Polynesian, and Asian firms. His text, *Human Resource Management in Action,* has been adopted in over 400 colleges and universities. He has recently published *International Business in China* (1993). His research on Asian management practices has been published in academic journals such as the *Academy of Management Journal, Journal of International Business Studies,* and *Advances in International Comparative Management.* He is a coauthor of the text *Business Strategy: An Asia Pacific Focus* (1997).

Yadong Luo is Associate Professor of International Management at the College of Business Administration, University of Hawaii. He earned his Ph.D. from Temple University. His research interests are in the area of international management, with focus on global strategy, international cooperative ventures, foreign direct investment, and Chinese management and business. He has published over 60 research articles in professional journals. Recently, his research has appeared in such refereed journals as *Journal of International Business Studies, Organization Science, Journal of Mangement Studies, Journal of International Management, Journal of World Business, Management International Review, Journal of Business Research, International Business Review, Journal of Small Business Management, The International Executive, Long Range Planning, Business Horizons, Bulletin of Economic Research, Asia-Pacific Journal of Management, International Journal of Management, Human Systems Management,* and *Group and Organization Management,* among others. He recently published *International Investment Strategies in the People's Republic of China.* His new book, *Entry and Cooperative Strategies in International Expansion,* is in press. Before he came to the United States in 1992, he taught at leading universities in China, published dozens of articles in leading journals in China, and served as a provincial official in charge of international business for 6 years.

About the Contributors

Clement Kong-Wing Chow is Associate Professor in the Department of Marketing and International Business, and the Associate Director of Hong Kong Institute of Business Studies, Faculty of Business, Lingnan College, Hong Kong. He received his Ph.D. from the University of Western Ontario. He has conducted research in a variety of areas including pricing issues, productivity and efficiency issues in Chinese industries, foreign direct investment, and small business and entrepreneurship in China. His work has appeared in professional journals including *Journal of Business Research, Journal of Global Business, Journal of Business Venturing, Small Business Economics, Journal of Small Business Management,* and *International Small Business Journal.*

Irene Hau Siu Chow is Professor of Management at the Chinese University of Hong Kong. She earned her BBA Degree from the Chinese University of Hong Kong, and an MBA and Ph.D. from Georgia State University. She was on leave visiting at the National University of Singapore in 1990-1991. In addition to her teaching duties at the University, she has also conducted executive training courses and development programs in the areas of human resource management and managerial skills. She has published widely in both local and international journals. Her research interests focus on human resource management, Chinese business, and comparative management.

Howard Gensler is Editor-in-Chief of the *China Tax Reporter* (Hong Kong: FT Law & Tax). He obtained a J.D. from University of California, Berkeley and a Ph.D. in Economics from the University of California, Irvine. He is a faculty member at the California State Bar, and a visiting lecturer at the University of California, Irvine, Department of Economics and at CSU Fullerton, Department of Management.

Chung-Ming Lau is Associate Professor and the Head of the Department of Management, Faculty of Business Administration, the Chinese University of Hong Kong. He received his Ph.D. in management from Texas A&M University. His research interests include managing strategic change, managerial cognition, organization culture, and Chinese management. He publishes in *Academy of Management Journal, International Business Review, Entrepreneurship: Theory & Practice, Asia Pacific Journal of Management, Research in Organizational Change and Development,* and *Journal of Organizational Change Management.*

Francis A. Lees is Alois J. Theis Professor of Global Finance at St. John's University. He has authored 10 books and numerous monographs and articles on international finance and business. His coauthored text, *Global Finance,* is used extensively around the world and is being translated into Russian. He has been a consultant to the U.S. Government, Royal Commission on Electric Power (Toronto), The Conference Board, and numerous organizations and institutions. He was a Fulbright Research Scholar in Brazil (1987-1988), and is cited in *Who's Who in America.*

K. Thomas Liaw is Associate Professor of Finance at St. John's University. His principal areas of teaching and research include capital markets, trading, investment banking, and risk management. He coauthored a recent book, *Foreign Participation in China's Banking and Securities Markets.* He has cochaired the annual conference on Asian Business and Economics for several years, and edited several books on emerging markets, including *Emerging Markets in Asia, Globalization of Asian Economies and Capital Markets,* and *Economic Integration and Financial Markets in Asia.* He has published journal articles in the areas of pricing deposit insurance, swaps, M&As, market risks, and emerging markets. His current projects include investment banking and pricing coupon rolls. He has been a consultant in private placements and valuation. He holds his Ph.D. from Northwestern University.

Maris G. Martinsons is Associate Professor of Business and Management at the City University of Hong Kong, Research Director of the Pacific Rim Institute for Studies of Management (PRISM), and Pacific Rim Editor for the *Journal of Applied Management Studies*. His research, teaching, and consulting focus on the strategic management of information resources, IT-enabled organizational change, and cross-cultural technology transfer.

Hang-Yue Ngo is Associate Professor at the Department of Management, the Chinese University of Hong Kong. He received his Ph.D. in sociology from the University of Chicago. His research interests include labor and employment, gender issues, and organizational studies. He publishes in various international refereed journals and contributes chapters to management books.

Mike W. Peng is Assistant Professor of Management at the Ohio State University and a Visiting Assistant Professor of International Business at The Chinese University of Hong Kong. He obtained his Ph.D. in business administration from the University of Washington. He is the author of *Behind the Success and Failure of U.S. Export Intermediaries* (1998) and *Business Strategies in Transitional Economies* (Sage, in press). His research has been published in a wide variety of academic and professional journals, such as the *Academy of Management Review, Organizational Studies, Journal of International Business Studies, Journal of Business Research,* and *The China Business Review*.

Oded Shenkar is Professor of International Management at the Faculty of Management, Tel-Aviv University, and the College of Business Administration, University of Hawaii at Manoa. He is currently the Visiting Ford Motor Company Designated Chair in Global Business Management at the Fisher College of Business, Ohio State University. Professor Shenkar's research focuses on East Asia. He has published several books, and his numerous articles have appeared in *Academy of Management Review, Academy of Management Journal, Management Science, Organization Studies,* and *Journal of International Business Studies,* among others.

Li Sun is Vice President in Charge of Mergers and Acquisitions at Guoxin Securities Company, Shenzen, China. He obtained his M.Phil. degree from the Chinese University of Hong Kong and his B.A. from the People's University of China in Beijing. He has published a number of books in China, including *Corporate Image Strategy* (China Business Press, 1996), *Family Business* (China Economic Publisher, 1996), *Corporate Buyouts, Mergers, and Property-*

Rights Transactions (China Chamber of Commerce Press, 1995), and *Strategy for Mergers and Acquisitions* (China Economic Publisher, 1994).

J. Justin Tan is Associate Professor of Management in the College of Business Administration at California State University, San Marcos. His research areas are strategic management, international business and joint venture management, and entrepreneurship. He has published more than 20 papers in academic journals such as *Strategic Management Journal, Entrepreneurship: Theory and Practice, International Business Review, Advances in International Comparative Management, Asia Pacific Journal of Management, International Journal of Management,* and *Asian Pacific Business Review,* among others. His recent research has focused on management issues in China. His most recent research project is a cross-national comparative study of Chinese entrepreneurs, sponsored by a Chiang Ching-Kuo Foundation Fellowship. He works regularly with companies in the United States and China.

Choo-Sin Tseng is Associate Professor of Business and Management and a member of the Contemporary China Research Center at the City University of Hong Kong. His research, teaching, and consulting interests focus on the internationalization of PRC firms and market entry issues in the China context.

Jingxin Wang is Professor of Accounting at the People's University, China.

Aimin Yan is Assistant Professor of Organizational Behavior at Boston University. He earned his Ph.D. from Pennsylvania State University. His current research involves negotiations, control structure, and performance of interfirm collaborative arrangements; strategic alliances; and international joint ventures. His study of U.S.-China manufacturing joint ventures won him the Barry M. Richman Award for Best Dissertation of 1994 from the International Management Division of Academy of Management. He has served as consultant in negotiations and management of joint ventures in China to both American and Chinese organizations. His scholarly work has appeared in *Journal of Applied Behavioral Science, Advances in International Comparative Management, Academy of Management Journal, Advances in Global High-Technology Management, China Business Review, Journal of Applied Management Studies, Journal of International Business Studies, Human Relations,* and a number of edited volumes. He teaches international management, organizational behavior, organizational management, and organization theory in the undergraduate, MBA, and doctoral programs at Boston University.

David C. Yang is Professor of Accounting and the Director of the School of Accountancy at the College of Business Administration, University of Hawaii at Manoa. He received his BA degree from the National Taiwan University, his MBA from the University of California, Berkeley, and Ph.D. from Columbia University. He is also the President of Chinese Accounting Professors Association—North America. He has taught at Peking University and National Taiwan University, and has consulted on accounting and financial management concerns for major firms in China and the United States.

Shouhua Zhou is Professor of Accounting and Associate Dean at the College of Management at the University of Chemical Engineering and Deputy Secretary-General of the Accounting Society of China. He has been involved in designing Chinese auditing standards and has published several books and articles in journals such as *Finance and Accounting, Accounting Research,* and *Journal of Certified Public Accountant.*

Cherrie Jiuhua Zhu is Lecturer of Human Resource Management and other management subjects at the Department of Management at Monash University, Australia. She has published and presented papers internationally in the areas of human resource management and international management. Besides teaching and research, she is also involved in consultation to business. She has taken part in business negotiations and the establishment of joint ventures, has been involved in the development of management training programs, and has also helped to form HRM policies and regulations for Australian companies' joint ventures in China.